The Founding Flies

The Founding Flies

*43 American Masters,
Their Patterns and
Influences*

MIKE VALLA

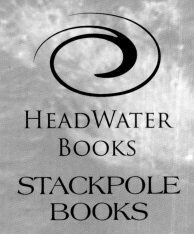

HEADWATER
BOOKS

STACKPOLE
BOOKS

To my wife, Valerie
And in memory of Walt and Winnie Dette

Published by
STACKPOLE BOOKS
5067 Ritter Road
Mechanicsburg, PA 17055
www.stackpolebooks.com

Printed in China

First edition

10 9 8 7 6 5 4 3 2 1

Photos taken by the author except where noted.

Library of Congress Cataloging-in-Publication Data

Valla, Mike.
    The founding flies : 43 American masters, their patterns and influences /
Mike Valla. — First edition.
        pages   cm
    Includes bibliographical references and index.
    ISBN 978-0-8117-0833-3 (hardcover) — ISBN 0-8117-0833-0 (hardcover)
    1. Fly tyers—United States.   2. Fly tying—United States—History.   3. Flies,
Artificial—United States—History.   I. Title.
SH451.V337   2013
799.12'4—dc23
                                                    2012047300

CONTENTS

ACKNOWLEDGMENTS

As would be expected with a book of this scope, many individuals stepped forward and offered assistance, support, and enthusiasm to ensure a work that all could be proud of. They provided resources, information, and best of all, access to their private fly collections so that I could photograph examples of the work of America's fly-tying masters who made our sport what it is today.

Special thanks to our fine fly-fishing museums: American Museum of Fly Fishing, Catskill Fly Fishing Center and Museum, Pennsylvania Fly Fishing Museum Association, and the Rangeley Outdoor Sporting Heritage Museum. I am also grateful to David Johnson, of Visalia, California, who helped me acquire information not only concerning Buz Buszek, but also on many of the West Coast fly-tying greats who long since passed away. And loving thanks to my wife, Valerie, who endured yet another project.

Thanks go as well to Tim Abbott, Rick Ackel, John Bailey, Tom Baltz, Keith Barton, Don Bastian, Jack Berryman, John Bonasera, Dave Brandt, John Capowski, Mary Dette Clark, Brett Damm, Chris Del Plato, Tom Deschaine, Pat Dorsey, Robert Dotson, Cal Dunbar, Debbie Elmer, Herb Eriksson, Christine Fong, Joe Fox, Keith Fulsher, Brad Gates, Andrew Gennaro, Jerry Girard, Ralph Graves, Matt Grobert, Mike Heck, Lance Hidy, Tom Hoffmaster, Skip Hosfield, Tom Houf, Joe Humphreys, Frank Johnson, Larry Kennedy, Jim Krul, Bob Lay, Cory Layton, Bill Leary, Eric Leiser, Mark Libertone, Don Lieb, Anne Lively, Mike Martinek Jr., Rob Matarazzo, Gary Miller, Ed Ostapczuk, Don Palmer, Ted Patlen, Eric Peper, Sandy Pittendrigh, Jim Pruit, Jannifer Puyans, Jim Quimby, Dave Richey, Randy Roehl, Ted Rogowski, Lee Schechter, Mark and Jill Schwarz, John Shaner, Ed Shenk, Eric Stroup, Bob Summers, Agnes Van Put, Ed Van Put, Pat and Gary Waller, Michael Wilkerson, Joan Wulff, Gerard Zazzera, Barbara Wuebber, John Shewey, Doug Ouellette, Bert Darrow, Jim Slattery, Rick Bannerot, Bill Stuart, and Lou Kasamis.

And special thanks also to Jay Nichols and Amy Lerner at Stackpole for making this book possible.

INTRODUCTION

But to one who has time, and is anxious to become conversant with all that pertains to our gentle craft, there is no in-door occupation so absorbing and time-killing [as fly tying], and one forgets in it little annoyances or heavier cares, and almost finds at home a substitute for the pleasures of the stream.

—Thaddeus Norris, *American Angler's Book* (1864)

The history of fly tying, its remarkable evolution, and the stories behind fundamental fly patterns that emerged from the vises of our founding fly tiers are absorbing and fascinating tales. Like fly tying itself, studying those who made the craft what it is today can also serve as a substitute on those long winter nights when we cannot be on a stream casting our favorite patterns, many of which evolved from the founding flies.

What this book refers to as the "founding flies" were archetypes created many years ago, patterns that eventually evolved into the contemporary fly styles we tie on our vises today and fish on our favorite waters. Many of those earlier flies are now either moribund or completely dead, and many of the fly tiers who once crafted them have been long forgotten or are remembered less and less with the passing of each season. They've been lost in the sea of contemporary tiers who are now at the helm of our sport. It seems that so much is happening with the myriad developments in the hobby of fly tying that we have little time to be concerned with what is now long past. And that is a sad point.

This book covers 43 masters who helped make fly fishing and fly tying what they are today. My incentive in putting this work together was to help ensure that the icons who carved the way for new fly pattern development are not forgotten, nor their unique patterns lost. In it, individuals who were—and still are—passionate about the old-school tiers tell their stories about patterns crafted by classic tiers they consider heroes. One thing that became immediately apparent through the course of writing this book was the level of passion surrounding some of the classic tiers and the patterns that they created. Not everyone has forgotten these tiers or their flies.

In the course of writing this book I had the great pleasure of corresponding with fly anglers and fly tiers all over the country, those who still remember and admire their own fly-tying heros. I tried to get as close to the source as possible, seeking out individuals who were either admirers of a fly tier that I was researching, or even close friends with the person. The outpouring of help, encouragement, and advice was overwhelming. Many invited me into their homes, "private museums," and even to their favorite fishing locations so that I could gain a firsthand understanding of how the founding flies came to be.

There were trips to Wyoming, Montana, Idaho, Michigan, Wisconsin, Maine, Vermont, Pennsylvania, and of course my own stomping ground in the Catskills of New York state. The trips enabled me to cast my own line in the waters that made the founding flies so significant in our fly-fishing history—and evolution. Casting an Adams dry fly on Mayfield Pond and the Boardman River in Michigan, where Charlie Adams first fished the pattern. Seeing for the first time Maine streamer tier Carrie Stevens' cottage at Upper Dam in the Rangeley, Maine, region. Fishing a Ray Bergman pattern on the Firehole River in Yellowstone and a Don Martinez high-floating dry fly on the Madison.

Plopping a deer hair ant on Chauncy Lively's favorite, Young Woman's Creek in Pennsylvania. Such travels were almost requisite to gaining a better understanding of the waters that made our founding flies so effective.

Yet when personal visits to faraway locations may have been too difficult, there was an army of people everywhere who helped me track down important information to complete my task—crafting this book. It was my pleasure to meet many of them and shake their hands.

There was no magic formula that determined which tiers were included. Those decisions had nothing to do with the volume of new patterns a "classic" fly tier created. Len Halladay was selected for the influence of only a single pattern—the Adams. George Griffith was selected solely for the Griffith's Gnat. Others developed many patterns, like Polly Rosborough and his dozens of nymphs or Keith Fulsher and his many patterns, especially his Thunder Creek baitfish.

Sometimes selection had to do with what information was available on a tier, as sufficient details were required to craft a good chapter. I would have loved to cover Syd Glasso, a classic West Coast tier, but it proved difficult to get my hands on enough good material concerning his flies and the development of his patterns. There were also other considerations when making final selections. One fundamental criterion was the era in which the tiers made their names. This work covers the time period between the mid-1800s and late 1960s. The tiers and fly anglers presented here had already achieved recognition by then or did so during that time period. Some of those selected, such as Dave Whitlock and André Puyans, continued to create flies beyond 1969, but they had already made their marks.

In explaining how the tiers were selected for inclusion, I'd be remiss not to admit to some personal bias. Many of them were *my* heroes who sustained my interest in fly tying over many years. I have fond memories of many of the fly-tying greats, going back to my teenage years in the 1960s. Even as a 14-year-old kid, I couldn't get enough of such icons such as Joe Brooks, Helen Shaw, Keith Fulsher, Vince Marinaro, Chauncy Lively, Ed Shenk, and others, such as the "Catskill school" fly tiers. However, I was also very aware, at a young age, of West Coast greats such as Polly Rosborough and Buz Buszek. Buz was gone two years before my own tying thread first touched hook shank, but his shop was still in existence in Visalia, California.

Some readers might be disappointed that their own heroes do not appear in these pages. Although it sounds like an easy excuse, a book like this can be only so long. If you don't find one of your own heroes here, chances are that I indeed considered the individual for inclusion. And I did a lot of fretting about having to leave out some of the tiers that I also deeply admired.

CHAPTER 1

Mary Orvis Marbury
(1856–1914)

Mary Orvis Marbury. Mary was only 20 in 1876 when she supervised the team of half a dozen ladies who produced fishing flies for the Orvis establishment.

In a March 25, 1915, letter to his protégé Roy Steenrod of Liberty, New York, Catskill region fly tier Theodore Gordon wrote of Mary Orvis Marbury's now classic *Favorite Flies and Their Histories* (1955) that it was a "very heavy, handsome book (the devil in the trunk), yet I hauled it about with me for years." Marbury's work featured 32 chromolithographic color plates with 291 flies. Her book served as the standard fly-tying reference of its era. As Gordon further commented, "the amount of information is really remarkable."

Mary was the daughter of Charles F. Orvis, the founding father of the now well-known purveyor of fly-fishing goods who began making rods for Manchester, Vermont, vacationers who came to fish the neighboring Battenkill River during the 1800s. Her father encouraged participation in the thriving business, which expanded into a successful mail-order company. Flies as well as rods, reels, and other sporting commodities became increasingly in demand. Mary was only 20 in 1876 when, after receiving tying lessons from an accomplished tier, she directed and supervised the team of half a dozen ladies who produced fishing flies for the

McCloud, tied by Lee Schechter. The McCloud was created by Charles for Horace D. Dunn, a San Francisco angler who named the fly for a California river. It appears in Marbury's book.

Manchester, Vermont. Mary Orvis Marbury crafted her now classic book in this quaint village, home of the Orvis Company.

Orvis establishment. Many early American fly fishers turned to Orvis to fill their fly boxes with flies that would net bass, trout, and other fish species.

Favorite Flies and Their Histories was a compilation of notes from correspondence Charles Orvis solicited from some 200 anglers from across North America over two or three years concerning their favorite patterns. Regarding the solicited recommendations, Mary Orvis Marbury commented, "These letters are records of actual experiences, and conclusions deducted from the same. We feel, therefore, that they cannot fail to be of great assistance to any one who may wish suggestions regarding new waters." The book is a thorough encyclopedia, arranged geographically, that enabled customers to select patterns for fishing their favorite haunts. Its text provided testimony on the effectiveness of favorite flies, their origins, and theories about fly pattern design and morphology.

Many of the fly patterns recommended by those anglers returning correspondence to Orvis were of British stock, since the dependence on classic fly patterns from across the great pond had not yet significantly changed. However, although American fly-tying know-how was still in its infancy, Marbury's book showcased many patterns fresh off American vises. British "fancy" patterns, such as the colorful Alexandra with its peacock sword wings and bright red dyed waterfowl quill strip adjoining them, were featured along with the Coachman. Yet our own Royal Coachman, joined by other American salmon, trout, and bass creations, was right on their tails.

The Royal Coachman's appearance in Marbury's book, and the story surrounding its 1878 creation by New York City fly dresser John Hailey, symbolized the early birth of American fly-tying creativity—flies tied for salmon, trout, and bass were

well represented. Like the colorful Royal Coachman, many of the trout flies featured in the book's color plates were flamboyant, intricately crafted eye-catchers worthy of both an angler's curiosity and a trout's interest. Trout tempters featuring large dazzling wings, accented with colorful silks and tinsels, and brightly highlighted with dyed plumage of all sorts and varieties were also among the patterns introduced in Marbury's work.

Charles Orvis, Mary's father. Marbury's *Favorite Flies and Their Histories* was the result of correspondence Orvis solicited from anglers concerning their favorite patterns.

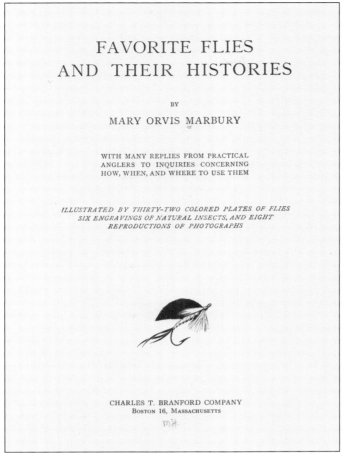

Left: Favorite Flies and Their Histories was a landmark publication, still admired as an important early reference that featured the "founding flies" of early American fly-fishing endeavors. *Right:* Marbury's work featured 32 chromolithographic color plates with 291 flies.

It is obvious that many trout flies presented in Marbury's book, in all of their showiness, were not imitative, or even suggestive, of aquatic insects, as were the fly designs with which British chalkstream anglers currently were experimenting. A fly angler would have to push the limits of his or her imagination to conclude that the Grasshopper pattern, sent to Charles Orvis by Harry Pritchard of New York and showcased in *Favorite Flies*, appeared anything like a real hopper, as did the one that Michigan's Art Winnie designed many decades later.

Labeling the pattern flamboyant would be an understatement; it looks more like a salmon fly. The now classic Parmachene Belle, invented by Henry P. Wells for fishing the Rangeley Lakes region in Maine, bears little resemblance to a living food morsel. However, Marbury quoted Wells as saying, "Unless I am deceived, these large trout take the fly not as an insect, but as some form of live bait."

Favorite Flies also included colorful, traditionally tied European salmon flies, yet one such salmon pattern, in a rare instance, arose from American hands: the Notion came from Brookline, Massachusetts, fly maker John Shields's vise. Marbury said that although the fly was originally intended as a landlocked salmon pattern, it was equally effective for Atlantic salmon, trout, and bass. As Marbury put it, the Notion "is very beautiful, the gilt and golden brown harmonizing perfectly . . . it is a fly that many anglers 'take a notion to,' and value for the good it does as well as for its beauty."

Many of the 19th-century American trout flies were indeed beautiful tidbits, works of art that typify the once popular "attractor" preference practiced and embraced by many fly fishers in that time. Orvis-tied "lake" and bass flies, presented in both Marbury's book and among those in *Fishing the Fly*, an 1883 book written by Charles Orvis and A. Nelson Cheney that predated Marbury's work, were striking examples of a fly tier's art. Such colorful patterns, commonly called "gaudy" flies, were also among the 80 bass flies eventually featured in the early Orvis company catalogs. Three of these colorful classic bass patterns are the McCloud, Imperial, and Williams.

The McCloud, a pattern featured in both *Favorite Flies* and the 1905 Orvis catalog, was created in 1979 by Charles Orvis for Horace D. Dunn, a San Francisco angler who named the fly. Dunn believed that the pattern, which is sometimes inaccurately labeled the "McLoid," would fish well on California's McCloud River. The fly's acceptance by

Dunn in California exemplifies just how far Charles Orvis and his daughter reached out across America for input concerning "favorite flies," regardless of location. Of interest in the fly's morphology is its tail, which swings up in a loop to the wing.

Like the McCloud, the Imperial and the Williams are equally colorful, intricately crafted patterns. The Williams was featured in the 1893 Chicago World's Fair, and also appeared in the 1905 Orvis catalog, where it was listed as a bass fly. The Imperial, also a bass pattern, appeared in the same catalog as well as in Charles Orvis's *Fishing the Fly*. Beyond the book's function as an important fly pattern reference, Marbury's work proved inspirational, serving as a valuable guide for other early fly tiers. The book still serves that purpose: contemporary Marbury and Orvis old-fly aficionados turn to this and other such publications in their quest to tie their own examples of early American fly-tying art.

In celebrating the rerelease of Marbury's book in 1988, *New York Times* writer Ann Barry called the work a landmark publication and said that "a fly tier and fisherman with a nostalgic bent might take pleasure in duplicating and testing the old patterns." A small but enthusiastic number of fly tiers have taken pride in replicating the patterns presented in the book. Lee Schechter from East Haddam, Connecticut, and John Bonasera from Yardley, Pennsylvania, are two talented fly tiers who have taken an interest in the old patterns that served as the foundation for American fly tying.

Lee Schechter has the "nostalgic bent" Barry spoke of. As Schechter explained: "My interest in the Marbury flies was stirred from the first moment years back when I saw the book *Favorite Flies*. The fact that these were tied for bass and other American species fascinated me. Though I'm primarily a saltwater fly fisherman, my tying horizons expanded over the years to include traditional "gaudy" wet flies of the 19th century and in particular those of Mary Orvis Marbury as I discovered the beauty and historical significance of these classic patterns. A fascinating aspect of this genre of flies that certainly influenced my attraction to the patterns, and in fact my tying style, is the gaudy nature of the flies and the colorful, robust, but flowing and symmetrical design characteristic of the patterns. The flies were tied to fish—materials were selected based on function, partly on color, and were not hard for many to obtain. I have incorporated the style of long tails, full tapered and robust bodies, full flowing collars, and larger wings into my style, whether I am tying these classic wets or other select patterns."

While the patterns of Mary Orvis Marbury are indeed works of beauty, they were tied not as presentation pieces but as fishing flies. Some modern anglers, such as John Bonasera, cast vintage patterns on their favorite waters. John described his affinity for these flies: "Of all the flies one can tie, there's a special place in my heart for blind eye, gut-leadered wet flies. By today's standards, these crude, sometimes gaudy and overly dressed flies may seem incapable of luring a fish, but if you travel far enough into the headwaters of a tiny unnamed brook or creek, they perform as well as any modern dressing. Thoughts of small streams, bamboo fly rods, and native brook trout consume my thoughts always. Dressing and studying old wet flies consume all my free time."

It is almost coincidental that all these flies were—and still are—worthy of a shadow box. Although as far as we know, not one fly featured in Marbury's book was created from her own design, *Favorite Flies and Their Histories* was a landmark publication that cataloged the myriad patterns fished by American anglers in her era. The flies are reminiscent of a time long past in the history of fly tying in America.

Parmachene Belle, tied by John Bonasera. This famous fly was created for fishing Parmachenee Lake in Maine. (The common spelling of the fly name is different from the lake.)

Notion, tied by Lee Schechter. As Marbury put it, the Notion "is very beautiful, the gilt and golden brown harmonizing perfectly . . . it is a fly that many anglers 'take a notion to,' and value for the good it does as well as for its beauty."

Imperial, tied by Lee Schechter. This bass pattern did not appear in Marbury's book, but it was in the 1905 Orvis catalog as well as in Charles Orvis's *Fishing the Fly*.

Grasshopper, tied by John Bonasera. This Grasshopper pattern, which looks more like a salmon fly, is featured in Marbury's book.

Williams, tied by Lee Schechter. The Williams was featured in the 1893 Chicago World's Fair and appeared in the 1905 Orvis catalog, where it was listed as a bass fly.

Royal Coachman, tied by John Bonasera. This early Royal Coachman, from Marbury's book, was tied with all the bells and whistles. Later versions were much simpler in style.

CHAPTER 2

Thaddeus Norris
(1811–1878)

Called the "Father of American Fly Fishing," Thaddeus Norris influenced many 19th-century fly tiers and anglers. Theodore Gordon was greatly influenced by Norris, whom he called, "Uncle Thad," and his *American Angler's Book*.
Photo from 1931 Derrydale Print

In his classic 1963 book, *The Treasury of Angling*, Larry Koller called Thaddeus Norris "the greatest American fisherman of the century." Norris was one of the earliest American fishing authors; he penned *The American Angler's Book* (1864) and later *American Fish Culture* (1868). Jerry Girard, a fly-angling artifact collector fascinated with fly-fishing history, provided interesting biographical information on Norris in a 2003 article in the *Art of Angling Journal* titled "Thaddeus Norris, Jr.: America's Greatest Fly Fisherman." Girard wrote, "Thaddeus Norris, Jr., was born in Culpeper, Virginia, near Warrington, on August 15, 1811, and at the age of 18 moved to Philadelphia to join with other relatives. The Philadelphia Norrises were a wealthy family and Thaddeus was a gentleman angler, and by virtue of his occupation, a well dressed one too . . . He gained the reputation as the *Father of American Fly-Fishing* and as a pioneer in the evolution of fly-fishing and the development of the American split bamboo rod."

Norris is probably best known for his influential *American Angler's Book*, a highly regarded work noted for the impressive scope of its subject matter. The thick volume examined everything

Common fly patterns in Norris's era and from his book (tied by John Bonasera). They were tied on snelled hooks and were of simple design, both winged and wingless primarily wet flies.

from angling tackle to fish species and breeding. Of particular interest to early fly tiers was an entire chapter devoted to "fly-making." In writings in the late 1800s and early 1900s, Theodore Gordon chimed in on Norris's book. Gordon, who tied his trout flies along Catskill waters in New York State, mentioned Norris frequently in his early *Fishing Gazette* writings. "Have you ever read Thaddeus Norris's *American Angler's Book*?" he asked his readers in his February 27, 1892, *Gazette* notes. Gordon described Norris's work as his "book of books for many years." It is no wonder that Gordon held Norris's work in such high regard. In a March 19, 1910, *Forest and Stream* article titled "Little Talks about Fly Fishing," Theodore Gordon wrote that Thaddeus Norris's book had taught him to tie trout flies, and his bait-fishing days were over.

As is true with many fly anglers, Gordon's early years involved fishing bait, in his case under the tutelage of an older man named Docky. "Fortunately a copy of Norris's *American Angler's Book* came into my possession," Gordon wrote in the same *Forest and Stream* article. "Uncle Thad's easily comprehended instructions enabled me to ties flies for myself." In March 1909, a year before the article was published, Gordon sent a letter to noted British fly angler G. E. M. Skues, in which he said, "I first learned to make flies at the age of 13 years from Norris. Body first, hackle next, and wings tied on last. This, I suppose, is the oldest method of tying flies." The "fly-making" instruction provided to Gordon through Norris's pages marked the beginning of what later became known as the Catskill school of fly tiers.

Norris was fishing Catskill waters such as the Beaverkill and Willowemoc well before Gordon made his mark as a dry-fly man on those streams. In a chapter on trout fly fishing in his *American Angler's Book*, he described fishing dry flies such as the Grannom and Jenny Spinner—two old British patterns—on the Willowemoc, patterns that proved effective when wet flies failed. Norris wrote that "a brace of trout would take them at almost every cast, and before they sank or were drawn away." He often fished both flies together with the Jenny as a dropper. The Jenny was tied with a white floss body palmered with light dun or white hackle and was labeled a "hackle" pattern.

Norris also described additional patterns that proved effective in his fishing. He divided his chosen patterns into two groups: wingless hackle/palmer flies, such as the Jenny Spinner, and winged flies, such as the Grannom. The patterns were crude and simple ties by modern standards. Norris's preferences reflected his belief that only a reasonable assortment of patterns was necessary.

Pennsylvania fly-fishing author Charles M. Wetzel, who has been referred to as the American Halford for his prolific contributions to fly-fishing entomological literature from the 1940s and '50s, offered some thoughts on Norris's preferred patterns. In an article titled "American Progress in Fly Fishing," which appeared in the June 1944 issue of *Pennsylvania Angler* magazine, Wetzel pointed out that Norris "clung to the hackle and palmer flies that had been used successfully in the past." He also noted that even 80 years after its publication, Norris's book "has been gaining popularity, and is in a way a landmark, due to its accurate portrayal of the then existing conditions, and the homely philosophy of the author."

"Uncle Thad," as Gordon called him, favored flies now mostly forgotten. His wingless group included the Dotterel, Ginger Hackle, and Grouse Hackle. Winged flies included the Alder Fly, Yellow Sally, Governor, Black Gnat, and Gray Drake. Norris held a pragmatic view concerning the best flies to tie and fish, respecting British contributions to the sport, yet recognizing that American waters require different approaches.

British influences were present in Norris's work, as would be expected. Most all of the trout flies Norris listed were common patterns that had been described before his book was published. Thomas C. Hofland's *The British Angler's Manual* (1848), Alfred Ronalds's *The Fly-Fisher's Entomology* (1839), and Francis Francis's *A Book on Angling* (1867) presented many of the same flies. These three British authors no doubt influenced Norris; he mentioned them in his book, along with many of the same pattern names. The Dotterel was described by Hofland, who called it "one of the surest flies that can be used in the north of England, where it has long been a first rate favorite." Thaddeus Norris thought enough of the fly to seek out a substitute for the dotterel feathers, which were then unavailable, winging the fly with barred feathers from partridge or snipe and tying it on a small Kirby hook. Norris described it as "killing on well-shaded waters, especially toward sunset."

However, Norris believed there was no need to clutter his American fly book with large numbers of patterns already described by British authors such as Edward Chitty and Alfred Ronalds. He also felt that a collection of half a dozen imitative patterns would suffice.

Another Norris favorite was the Coachman, tied in four shades from white to dark. Norris's Coachman fly wings varied not only in shade, but also in materials. He made no mention of the feather used for his white-winged Coachman but called for interesting feathers for the other three shades. He used "tame pigeon" for his light lead-shaded Coachman, a gull's feather for a darker version, and blue heron for the darkest of the series. Theodore Gordon mentioned Norris's four-shaded Coachman series in a May 10, 1913, *Fishing Gazette* piece titled "American Notes: Fowls, Hackles, Insects, Etc."

In his 2003 article, Jerry Girard said that Norris's work "was the first book by an American author that provided detailed instructions and illustrations for fly-tying and discussed the various furs and feathers and materials that were available." Indeed, Norris presented a thorough materials list that covered all the necessities for fly making. He also included

Early American winged wet flies, tied by Thaddeus Norris, attached to the 1860 vintage fly wallet that he owned. *Jerry Girard collection*

notes offering insights into the use of tinsels, dubbing materials, hackles, winging feathers, and tying silks.

Interestingly, Norris suggested that fly makers not be concerned about silk thread color: "If the silk is fine and strong it matters little about the color, for the only place it is visible after the fly is finished is at the fastening off of the head." More than 50 years after he offered that argument, Catskill school fly tiers like Walt and Winnie Dette and Harry and Elsie Darbee were saying the same thing. In his book written with Mac Francis titled *Catskill Flytier*, Harry Darbee said, "I've never gone in for all those silk colors when the head of the fly is supposed to be a certain color. The fly head we tie is so small that color makes no difference."

This is not to suggest that Darbee and others of his era had read Norris's views concerning tying silk. Rather, Darbee's argument reflects the simplicity of that time and the pragmatic approach taken by fly tiers. It was an era of simple materials and simple tools, and the flies that emerged from Norris's vise reflected that simplicity in their design.

Mixed in among the simple winged patterns in Norris's trout fly arsenal were wingless "hackle" palmer flies. In describing tying the palmer flies, Norris delved into a controversy still discussed among modern fly tiers: hackle barb fiber length relative to hook size and the hotly debated word *proportions*. His hackle barb length arguments were so compelling it is a wonder his words are not quoted more often: "In choosing your feathers," he said, "the length of the fibres

should be in proportion to the size of the hook, or rather the length of the shank." If the protruding hackle barbs are too short, once wound on the hook, more hook than hackle would be offered to a curious trout's eye—"like a long legged boy in a bobtail coat"—making the fly less attractive to the fish. The converse situation, where the hackle barbs extended too far below the hook bend, presented a fly likened to "a short legged boy dressed in his daddy's long coat." In this case, a trout approaching the fly would have to open its mouth very wide to engulf its perceived prey, or else that strike would be short and the fish would "go off with a few hair-like fibres between his teeth."

A small hook didn't necessarily equate to a small fly; tackle stores often sold large flies that were tied on small hooks. Norris stated that hackle length should never extend much below the bottom of the hook. He said that even winged flies should be tied with hackle not more than half the length of the hook shank, which he used as a guide rather than the hook gap as used today.

Norris's thoughts pertaining to such matters as hackle size and proportions demonstrated his willingness to look at artificial flies from the trout's perspective. He tied and sought flies that would catch fish. His tying suggestions were helpful yet often flexible. He recognized that "there are several ways of tying flies; nearly every fly maker has something peculiar in his method." A century after Norris offered his words, Catskill fly tier Art Flick write in his *Master Fly-Tying Guide*,

"There are many ways of putting together a dry fly and I would be the last to intimate that my method is superior to other ways." In closing the chapter titled "Fly Making," Norris offered these comforting words to the novice fly tier: "Do not throw away all your first attempts that appear big-headed or wild in their habiliments, for a much rougher-looking fly than you suppose will kill."

There is no doubt that Thaddeus Norris truly loved his craft. As he wrote about fly tying, "To those who have not leisure, or fish but seldom, it does not pay for the trouble and patience bestowed on learning it; such persons had better buy their flies than make them. But to one who has time, and is anxious to become conversant with all that pertains to our gentle craft, there is no in-door occupation so absorbing and time-killing, and one forgets in it little annoyances or heavier cares, and almost finds at home a substitute for the pleasures of the stream."

And there is no doubt that at least one student of his craft, Theodore Gordon, was inspired by reading those words. As Gordon wrote in an article titled "Letters from a Recluse," published April 28, 1906, in *Forest and Stream*, "If one has leisure, fly making is an absorbing occupation and there is considerable satisfaction in taking trout with the work of one's own hands."

Black Palmer "Hackle" fly, tied by Thaddeus Norris. Norris frequently fished simple patterns such as the palmers, consisting of a simple body with hackle wrapped from the hook bend to the hook eye. *Jerry Girard collection*

Dotterel, tied by John Bonasera. As with many of the patterns described by Norris, this one also came from Hofland's *British Angler's Manual* (1848). Norris didn't have access to dotterel feathers, so he substituted partridge or snipe.

Alder, tied by John Bonasera. Another pattern sketched in Norris's book and interpreted by Bonasera. Norris fished two of them together, with one as a dropper, in low water. The Alder was tied with a black mohair body, picked out at the head to simulate legs, much the same as is done with many contemporary nymphs.

Grouse Hackle, tied by John Bonasera. Norris said the fly was good on clear water.

Ginger Hackle, tied by John Bonasera. Norris said this pattern should be used as a dropper fly rather than a "stretcher," the terminal fly on the gut leader.

Red Spinner, tied by John Bonasera. This pattern, sketched in Norris's book, looks nothing like what we now commonly call a spinner. The original was tied with hog's wool dyed reddish brown and winged with starling.

Palmer, tied by John Bonasera. Norris liked peacock herl bodies on his palmer patterns but sometimes used floss. He advocated ribbing the fly body with gold thread (likened to tinsel).

CHAPTER 3

Theodore Gordon
(1854–1915)

Theodore Gordon, the "Father of Dry-Fly Fishing in America." *Catskill Fly Fishing Center and Museum collection*

Theodore Gordon was called the "American Walton" and the "Catskill Thoreau," but most fly anglers consider him the "Father of Dry-Fly Fishing in America." While he is almost always associated with his impact on American fly tying and dry-fly fishing, through his long association with Catskill region waters, Gordon first dipped his lines in Pennsylvania limestone streams as a 14-year-old boy.

Little is known about Theodore Gordon between the time when he first started dabbling for trout as a boy and his eventual move to the banks of the Neversink River in the Catskills, although many believe he was an educated man, and the quality of his writings supports that speculation. The combination of poor health and a financial disaster affecting a Georgia railroad are said to have led to his life as a relative loner on the Neversink. Gordon found solitude on the river, with its scenic charm as it flowed through the mountain valleys and its crystalline water. He described it "as limpid as air," saying, "the smallest object can be seen distinctly at a depth of many feet." Yet as author John McDonald wrote in his May 1946 *Fortune* magazine article,

The Gordon, tied by Theodore Gordon. Beyond the Quill Gordon, another dry fly bears Theodore Gordon's name: the Gordon. The Gordon dry fly, initially named the Golden Brown Spinner, is a sparkling pattern. *Bill Leary collection*

Theodore Gordon fishing with his "mystery woman." Gordon called her his best fishing chum, but her identity remains a mystery. *Catskill Fly Fishing Center and Museum collection*

titled "Fly Fishing and Trout Flies," "What moral shock drove him from a life of gay splendor at Delmonico's in New York City to a shack on a stream will never be known." American fly fishers would be ever grateful, however, as it was Gordon who helped sever the dependence on British fly design for fly fishing on American streams. And it was thanks to Gordon that the famous Catskill school of fly tiers was born.

Gordon's path to becoming an ardent and talented early fly tier began with Thaddeus Norris, and he left a legacy through his influence on Catskill tiers such as Rube Cross, Herm Christian, Roy Steenrod, Walt and Winnie Dette, Harry and Elsie Darbee, Art Flick, and Ray Smith. Gordon's inspiration was responsible for establishing the historic Catskill fly-tying lineage, which still continues today.

In Gordon's time, it was next to impossible to find anyone who was available to teach fly tying. Books were the only means Gordon had at his disposal to open up the world of fur, feathers, and hooks. In 1906, Gordon wrote in the *Fishing Gazette*, that he learned to tie "every type of artificial fly from the largest salmon fly to the smallest midge from books." "Uncle Thad" Norris's work taught Gordon to tie flies, but he also studied British fly tier H. G. McClelland's 1898 work, *The Trout Fly Dresser's Cabinet of Devices; or, How to Tie Flies for Trout and Grayling*. However, books were not the only driving forces behind Gordon's fly-tying endeavors.

In 1890, Theodore Gordon corresponded with British angler and author Frederick Halford, who sent him 48 dry flies that had proved successful on the slow-moving, placid English chalkstreams. Scrutinizing Halford's creations, Gordon realized that these floaters were ill suited for the swift-running American Catskill streams. This led Gordon to design dry flies that were better suited for his own waters. Chief among his creations was the historic Quill Gordon, his signature pattern. The Q.G., as he sometimes referred to it, has

not lost its popularity on Catskill streams such as the Beaverkill, Willowemoc, Neversink, and Schoharie, as well as on many trout waters around the globe. Many fly tiers point to the Quill Gordon as the first Catskill-style dry fly they tackled at the vise.

An article in the February 1967 issue of *Field & Stream* included Harry and Elsie Darbee's three favorite dry flies, and the Quill Gordon was among them. The Darbee fly-tying duo belonged to the Catskill school that followed Gordon. After retrieving this issue of the magazine from the school library and sneaking a look at the faint photo of the fly while sitting in an eighth-grade geology class, I was determined to tie it someday. It seemed an interesting pattern with its stripped peacock eye quill. It wasn't too long after I studied the small photo of the fly that appeared in the article that I tied the pattern for the first time.

Gordon embraced stripped peacock quills for use in dry-fly bodies. As he wrote in the July 1907 *Fishing Gazette*, "The peacock quill certainly makes a very natural-looking ribbed body for many flies, and I should be glad to have it in all colours." Gordon also said that he tied his beloved Quill Gordon in three different shades, sometimes tinging the quill with yellow. The variety of peacock fowl from which he obtained the peacock eyes used for the stripped quill did not escape his scrutiny. He liked the old English blue breed variety as opposed to the dark green birds from China or Spain. The Asiatic variety did not provide the light-colored quills he preferred.

Regardless of the peacock fowl variety, of paramount importance to all Catskill school tiers was that the stripped quill taken from the eye feather exhibit segmentation once stripped of its fuzz. While there are morphological differences in Quill Gordons tied by Gordon's closest protégés, Roy Steenrod and Herm Christian, their ties remain true to the pattern's original dressing, with its wood-duck wings, dun hackle, and segmented quill body. Rube Cross, the Dettes, the Darbees, Art Flick, and other Catskill notables such as Mahlon Davidson all embraced Gordon's trademark dry fly, the Quill Gordon, or sometimes called the Gordon Quill by tiers such as Rube Cross and the Dettes in their early tying years.

By the summer of 1906, British angling writers had begun to take notice of Gordon's fly. A letter written on August 11 of that year by R. B. Marston, editor of the London-based *Fishing Gazette*, appears in John McDonald's *The Complete Fly Fisherman* (1947): "Mr. Gordon makes a handsome trout fly. I should think few, if any, American anglers know much about our flies and fly making and dry fly fishing as he does. He sent me a fly on an eyed hook dressed by himself, called the 'Quill Gordon,' quill body, silver grey hackle, with a bunch of summer duck [wood-duck] fibers for wing—it would kill anywhere." Thus, in a reverse twist, Theodore Gordon's American creation colonized British waters. The Quill Gordon was later sold by British supply houses such as Hardy's.

Yet beyond the Quill Gordon, another dry fly bears Theodore Gordon's name. The Gordon dry fly, initially named the Golden Brown Spinner, is a sparkling pattern. Four years before Marston gave his nod to the Quill Gordon, he acknowledged the Gordon pattern in the July 1902 *Fishing Gazette*: "The flies Mr. Gordon sends would kill on any trout river . . . the 'Golden Brown Spinner' is like a small mayfly—summer duck [wood duck] wing, badger hackle, and golden body. Mr. Gordon says his friends find it kills so well they call it 'The Gordon.'"

On April 12, 1906, Theodore Gordon wrote to one of the most noted fly anglers in England, G. E. M. Skues, describing his Gordon: "I gave a dealer in N.Y. a pattern and he has sold great numbers of them for several years. It has been dressed as big as a salmon fly for use in Maine lakes. I call it the Golden Brown Spinner, but it is usually known as the Gordon. When dressing it small I make it so that it can be used wet or dry. It cocks very well even without splitting wings as any fly will do if hackled right, dry fly fashion."

Whereas the Quill Gordon has survived the intervening years since its creation, the Gordon has fallen out of favor with contemporary fly fishers and tiers. But for many years, it was a standard dry-fly pattern on Catskill streams. Elsie Darbee included it in A. J. McClane's *Standard Fishing Encyclopedia* color fly plates. Walt and Winnie Dette, another Catskill school husband-and-wife tying team, carried it in their early 1935 shop catalog.

While the Quill Gordon and the Gordon are the two dry flies most associated with Theodore Gordon, his talent was not restricted to dry flies. He was a "dry-fly man" for certain, but another of his creations was a big beast of a fly called the Bumblepuppy. Gordon's Bumblepuppy, a name that referred

Right: Theodore Gordon's favorite Beaverkill River pool. *Below:* Covered Bridge Pool, upper Beaverkill River.

to a game of whist played without regard for the rules, has received only modest attention compared with the Quill Gordon. Yet the Bumblepuppy has a much more interesting story attached to it, with all of its pattern variations and its significance in American fly pattern history.

Joseph D. Bates Jr. wrote in an October 1952 *Pennsylvania Angler* magazine article titled "Stories of Famous Streamer Flies: The Bumblepuppy" that "it is too rarely realized that Gordon deserves his place among angling immortals for giving us the streamer fly, too. He refers many times in his letters to flies dressed to imitate baitfish." Bates's words were written shortly after his book *Streamer Fly Fishing in Fresh and Salt Water* was published in 1950. In researching Gordon's little-known fly for his book, Bates visited with Gordon's protégé Roy Steenrod, who was still living and tying flies in the Catskills. Bates also corresponded with Herman Christian, whom Gordon had given some of the original Bumblepuppy flies. Steenrod and Christian were considered closest to Theodore Gordon, and much of what we know about Gordon's history and his flies—including the Bumblepuppy—is attributed to them. Both are significant figures in their own right in the history of Catskill fly tying and fishing, and they were highly influenced by Gordon.

Steenrod, the creator of the famous Hendrickson dry fly, first met Gordon in 1901. He worked in the Liberty, New York, post office, where Gordon frequently stopped in to mail flies to his customers. The two men eventually became close friends. Herm Christian, whom Gordon referred to simply as Christian, was Gordon's neighbor who learned to tie flies out of necessity, since Gordon was unable to supply the numbers of flies he needed. He essentially tied flies without a vise, using the tool only for the final tying steps. Christian was an interesting personality; he not only tied flies and fished, but also hunted, trapped, raised bees, and made maple syrup. He always maintained that Gordon refused to share his fly-tying techniques with anyone. But Steenrod claimed that Gordon did indeed teach him to tie flies—under a code of honor that the courtesy not be disclosed to others at that time.

Both Steenrod and Christian, in turn, influenced others who became Catskill fly tiers. Steenrod had interaction with Walt and Winnie Dette during their early tying years, in the late 1920s. Christian's tying skills greatly influenced individuals such as George Parker Holden, author of the books *Streamcraft* (1919) and *The Idyl of the Split-Bamboo* (1920), both considered classics.

Both Christian and Steenrod knew a lot about the history of the Bumblepuppy, a fly Joseph D. Bates Jr. called "the first tangible streamer fly ever used." Gordon's gaudy Bumblepuppy represents a significant departure from his dry-fly-centric interests. In his June 1946 "Wood, Field and Stream" column, *New York Times* outdoor writer Raymond Camp quoted fly-angling historian and author John McDonald's

thoughts on Gordon's Bumblepuppy. McDonald called Gordon a " meticulous theorist" who created the Bumblepuppy "as counterpoint to his elaborate theory of insect imitation. He tied it often throughout his career on the Neversink." McDonald featured the fly in his May 1946 *Fortune* article titled "Fly Fishing and Trout Flies." John Atherton's color illustration in the article shows but one variation of Gordon's creation; there were many.

Apparently Theodore Gordon couldn't quite decide just how the Bumblepuppy should be tied. In his article, McDonald relied on Gordon's description in the April 25, 1903, issue of the *Fishing Gazette*, where Gordon called the Bumblepuppy "great medicine," when played in cleared water, its jungle fowl eyes pulsating with each movement of the specimen. In a May 1906 article, Gordon continued to show his admiration for his strangely named fly: "My extraordinary Bumblepuppy kills because it is wonderfully alive. It is about as good for one gamefish as another, showing that as a rule it is not taken as a fly at all. It was created to take black bass in the first instance." Two years later, in the same magazine, Gordon commented that his fly was good in situations where bass were feeding on minnows. He sent samples of his fly to the *Gazette*'s editor, R. B. Marston, but said he recognized that it was "difficult to induce anglers to try new patterns" if they appear peculiar.

At the end of Gordon's 1903 article, Marston provided readers with the Bumblepuppy's dressing. This was a garish version, tied with a red silk and silver tag, red or yellow chenille butt, and white chenille body ribbed with bright silver tinsel. Its white goose quill wings, in this case shouldered with wigeon, though usually teal made for a handsome fly. Roy Steenrod and Herm Christian described other versions.

In Joseph D. Bates's October 1952 *Pennsylvania Angler* article, he quoted Roy Steenrod as saying, "The Bumblepuppy meant to Mr. Gordon any fly to which there was no name. He tied many of them. I called on Herman Christian, a fly tier friend of Gordon's, and we both are of the opinion that the fly I am sending to you was the favorite and the one of which he often spoke as having taken so many fish within the lakes of Rockland county. I know that Gordon was tying these flies as early as 1880."

Bates repeated Steenrod's comments in his 1966 book, *Streamer Fly Tying and Fishing*. One would hardly assume that the "Steenrod version" Bumblepuppy sent to Bates—and which Steenrod said was Gordon's favorite—was a variation of the fly described by John Marston. It's hard to understand why Theodore Gordon didn't attach different names to the patterns, as the materials used were so different. The Steenrod fly sported a plain chenille body, with no ribbing, a characteristic found in other Bumblepuppy versions.

The story of the Bumblepuppy is further confused by Herm Christian's comments that appeared in Bates's *Pennsylvania Angler* article and were also repeated in Bates's

Roy Steenrod, Gordon's closest friend and protégé. *Catskill Fly Fishing Center and Museum collection*

books. These tell a different story concerning Gordon's favorite version. "I am sending you a fly like Mr. Gordon made for me (with red ribbing), and one like I make (with the white chenille but no ribbing)." Christian wrote to Bates. "Mr. Gordon almost always put a stripe on the body, either of gold, silver, copper, tinsel, or some kind of wool."

Bates tried to make sense of all the Bumblepuppy variations, saying, "Thus it would seem the 'twenty kinds of Bumblepuppies' tied from time to time by Theodore Gordon were a progressive attempt by him to arrive at what he thought was the ideal pattern. Quite obviously, Theodore Gordon was far in advance of his time in developing streamers and bucktails, since his early work compares favorably with that of others done decades later."

The progression of the Bumblepuppy may have had something to do with the evolution of the fly's intent. In Gordon's earliest discussions of the fly, he spoke of it as a bass pattern, although he hinted that the fly was as "good for one game fish as another." Later, on July 29, 1906, Gordon said of trout, "I can make them run at a Bumblepuppy. They won't take it but it is great fun and I spot all their lies." These comments would lead one to believe that for trout, the fly was nothing but a teaser.

Ray Camp provided additional information in his May 22, 1946, "Wood, Field and Stream" column in the *New York Times*, where he quoted Alfred W. Miller, who wrote under the pen name Sparse Grey Hackle, concerning Gordon's use of the fly as a trout enticer. Sparse Grey Hackle mentioned a story that had appeared in the February 1936 issue of the *Anglers' Club Bulletin*, the story written by the then editor of the *Bulletin* Fred White. The article, titled "Theodore Gordon in the Pre–Dry Fly Period," told how White had met Gordon in the summer of 1895 or 1896 on Frog Brook, near DeBruce. Gordon showed White "a strange looking bunch of feathers" that he said could sometimes raise fish. A couple

years later, Gordon again met White on water, this time at the Brooklyn Fly Fishers Club on the Beaverkill. White was not fishing well, though the water held plenty of trout. Gordon explained to White that one "had to get them interested" before the trout would hit. Gordon again brought out the strange fly and told White it was called a Bumblepuppy. Once Gordon teased the trout, he switched to a smaller fly, on which he then caught them. However, Gordon's Bumblepuppy was far from just a teaser.

A few years later, Theodore Gordon began to appreciate the pattern's potential—it wasn't just a bass fly. In a 1913 letter to Roy Steenrod, Gordon sang the praises of the fly and its ability to take bass, bream, rockfish, perch, sunfish, pike, salmon, striped bass, pickerel, and big trout in the Esopus when they were feeding on minnows. On March 30, 1915, Gordon wrote in a letter to Guy Jenkins, "I must manage to send you a couple of small Bumblepuppies for big trout on the larger class of streams. At times they are very deadly, particularly on the Esopus and lower Beaverkill." In another letter to Steenrod that same year, Gordon wrote, "Would like to take mascollange [muskellunge] on stout fly tackle and an enormous Bumblepuppy fly."

The Bumblepuppy might not have taken a gargantuan muskie as Gordon hoped, but it did take a record *Field & Stream* fishing contest brown trout—a 13-pounder. The monster brown was taken by Waldemar Kesk in the lower Catskills below the mouth of the Mongaup River, in the Delaware River.

It's puzzling that the Bumblepuppy has fallen out of popularity, given the number of fish species it is able to bring to the net, including large fish such as Kesk's record Delaware River brown trout. However, the fly occasionally surfaces in discussions surrounding Theodore Gordon's imaginative flies. His Quill Gordon dry fly will always be labeled his signature pattern, yet the little-known Bumblepuppy is not likely to be forgotten as one of Gordon's most interesting patterns.

Theodore Gordon's Bumblepuppy—in its many variations—is still tied today by Catskill aficionados such as Teddy Patlen and John Bonasera. The late Chauncy K. Lively reintroduced it to readers in the March 1972 issue of *Pennsylvania Angler*.

It is unclear what inspired Lively to revisit Gordon's forgotten fly. Perhaps he came upon Sparse Grey Hackle's 1971 book, *Fishless Days, Angling Nights*, which described the fly. In his classic October 1963 *Outdoor Life* article titled "Best All-Round Trout Fly," Joe Brooks described a Bumblepuppy adaptation created by his friend Dan Bailey called the Missoulian Spook. Dan crossed Gordon's pattern with a Muddler Minnow and came up with this hybrid. (See chapter 22.)

Whether the pattern was truly, as Joseph D. Bates maintained, "the first tangible streamer pattern ever used" seems not to matter. The Bumblepuppy is a founding fly—one of the first "legitimate" streamers created, if not *the* first.

Quill Gordon, tied by Theodore Gordon. Considered Gordon's signature fly, it is still a popular dry fly fished on Catskill waters and around the globe. *Bill Leary collection*

Two dry flies tied by Theodore Gordon. The fly on the left, with its mallard flank wings, is similar to the Queen of Waters, minus the gold tinsel ribbing. The one on the right is a Whirling Blue Dun, of which there are many versions. Gordon started a "little collection" of all the pattern variations. *Bill Leary collection*

Quill Gordon, tied by Mike Valla. Contemporary versions of the Quill Gordon are different from Gordon's originals. The wings are more upright and the hackle is wrapped more uniformly.

Ginger Quill, tied by Theodore Gordon. Gordon wrote in the *Fishing Gazette* in July 6, 1907, that peacock quill "certainly makes a very natural looking ribbed body for many flies and I should be glad to have it in all colours." He used it not only for his Quill Gordon, but for other dry-fly patterns as well. *Bill Leary collection*

Light Cahill, tied by Theodore Gordon. The Light Cahill, generally attributed to William Chandler of Neversink, New York, was popular in the Catskills as far back as Theodore Gordon's time. Gordon mentioned the fly in a 1915 letter to Roy Steenrod. *Bill Leary collection*

Bumblepuppy, tied by Mike Valla. Theodore Gordon designed many variations of this original fly. Joseph D. Bates Jr. featured this version, tied by Herm Christian, in *Streamer Fly Tying and Fishing*. Bates called it the first "tangible streamer."

Bumblepuppy, tied by Mike Valla. This version was featured in John McDonald's May 1946 article on trout flies. John Atherton provided a color illustration of the Bumblepuppy in the article.

Quill Gordon, tied by Herm Christian. Christian, another Gordon protégé, fished the Neversink River with his mentor. *Catskill Fly Fishing Center and Museum collection*

Bumblepuppy, tied by Mike Valla. Chauncy K. Lively's version uses a badger hackle palmer.

Fan Wing Royal Coachman, tied by Roy Steenrod. *Catskill Fly Fishing Center and Museum collection*

Hendrickson dry fly, tied by Roy Steenrod. The Hendrickson is the signature fly of Steenrod, who was highly influenced by Theodore Gordon. *Bill Leary collection*

CHAPTER 4

Reuben Cross
(1896–1958)

Rube Cross at his tying table in 1934, tying a Fan Wing Royal Coachman. *Edwin Way Teale photo courtesy of the University of Connecticut Libraries*

The early school of Catskill fly tiers, beginning with Theodore Gordon, was an impressive group that included Herm Christian, Roy Steenrod, the Dettes, and the Darbees on the banks of the Beaverkill, Willowemoc, and Neversink, while the upper Catskills were represented by tiers such as Art Flick on the Schoharie and Ray Smith on the Esopus. One of the most talented Catskill tiers, who practiced his craft on the banks of the Neversink and at Lew Beach on the Beaverkill, before he relocated later in life to Rhode Island, was Reuben Cross.

Many consider Cross's dry flies, along with Christian's and Steenrod's to a lesser degree, the very earliest patterns representing what is known as the Catskill style. Theodore Gordon crafted dry flies that were better suited for his swift Catskill streams than the patterns created for British chalkstreams, but the Cross flies that followed epitomize Catskill dry-fly design. Cross's stiff-hackled dry flies, gems that were tied with natural fur bodies and upright wood-duck or double-slip mallard quill wings, are still considered the most beautiful ever cast on a Catskill stream. The handsome Cross-tied dry fly is archetypal of the Catskill style.

Cross Special, tied by Mike Valla. Cross said he "put a Light Cahill body on the Gordon Quill, making it a 'cross' breed." He further explained that he had no intention of having the name of the fly "hooked" to his own surname, but in short time it was very much associated with his surname.

Just how Rube Cross learned to tie such beautiful flies is often the subject of streamside discussions. It has been said that Cross learned to tie flies from Theodore Gordon, a point accepted by fly-angling author John McDonald, respectfully doubted by Roy Steenrod, and adamantly protested by Herm Christian. Both Steenrod and Christian were Gordon protégés. Steenrod was the closest to Gordon, with Christian right behind him. Cross undoubtedly was in and out of the Gordon home, but just what tying information Gordon may have revealed to him, if any, remains a mystery.

Cross explained it in Harold Hinsdill Smedley's 1944 book, *Fly Patterns and Their Origins*: "I started fly tying because I didn't have the ten cents to buy all the dry fly hooks that I wanted in 1906. There was no one in those days that would share any secrets in tying the dry fly, or any other kind. Theodore Gordon who was about 'IT' in those days, used to stay in Neversink and we were quite good friends, so I got a few of his flies and worked, trying to copy them." (According to Sparse Grey Hackle, "old timers always referred to a fly as a 'fly hook.'")

In Sparse Grey Hackle's *Fishless Days, Angling Nights* (1971), we learn that Herm Christian had a strong opinion about the theory that Cross had received direct fly-tying instruction from Gordon: "As a flytier, there is one outstanding fact about Theodore Gordon. He never taught anybody to tie; he never showed anybody anything, even me." In commenting on Christian's words, the author noted, "The foregoing positive statement was directed against a once-famous Catskill tyer, Rube Cross, who, Christian angrily said, told people he had learned to tie from Theodore Gordon." It is well accepted that Roy Steenrod received tying instructions from Gordon on the condition he not reveal the courtesy that was extended to him.

If Cross did not learn from directly from Gordon, or at least from studying Gordon's flies, it's possible he could have learned tying techniques from British fly tier H. G. McClelland's 1898 book on tying flies for trout and grayling. Others from what McDonald called the "peerless school of Sullivan County fly tiers"—Gordon, Walt Dette, Harry Darbee—cited McClelland's book as an influence on their tying. Additional early Catskill region fly-fishing authors and fly tiers who frequented Catskill streams, such as George Parker Holden and Preston Jennings, also referenced McClelland's writings. Techniques such as preparing double duck quill slip wings for dry flies are found in both McClelland's work and Rube Cross's books, which appeared in the late 1930s.

No matter how Rube Cross learned to tie, whether from books or from Gordon, the fact is that he tied a beautiful fly. Yet before writing his books, he was just as secretive about his tying methods as Theodore Gordon. In Gordon's era and Cross's early years, the art of fly tying was often kept a closely guarded secret. Early American fly tiers crafted flies for meat and potatoes, as Walt Dette used to say, and Catskill

Upper Beaverkill River, not far from Lew Beach. Cross spent his final Catskill years at Lew Beach before relocating to Rhode Island. The river's crystalline waters still flow through a magnificent valley in the Catskills.

tiers were no exception. Their livelihood was dependent, to some extent, on income from selling flies to a growing number of fly-fishing enthusiasts. Some learned Cross's techniques indirectly. Cross suspected competition when Walt Dette, of nearby Roscoe, New York, on the Beaverkill, simply wished to learn to tie for his own fishing needs. When Dette approached Cross in the late 1920s about learning to tie flies from him, he found out in a hurry that it wasn't going to happen. Instead, Dette dismantled Cross's flies to learn his tying secrets.

A decade later, Cross was finally willing to share his secrets. Once his book *Tying American Trout Lures* was published in 1936, amateur fly tiers were finally able to learn

THE **AMERICAN** MAY 1941
FLY TYER 15c

Reuben R. Cross of Lew Beach, New York   One of the Country's Foremost Fly-Tyers
Tying His Famous Cross Special

Official Publication of the North American Fly-Fisherman

Rube Cross, in the May 1941 issue of the *American Fly Tyer*.

some of Cross's tying methods. The book helped further his reputation as an accomplished fly tier, building on background information written in Edwin Way Teale's December 1934 *Outdoor Life* story titled "Reuben R. Cross: Dry Flies from a Kitchen Workshop." Cross's *Fur, Feathers and Steel* (1940) came next, followed by *The Complete Fly Tier* (1950). In *Tying American Trout Lures*, black and white photos illustrated the Rube Cross style. Dry flies including the Gordon Quill, Royal Coachman, Bivisible, and Cross Special—his signature pattern—were shown in all their delicacy and sparseness. His characteristic turle knot space, the clean bare hook shank behind the eye, was also displayed in the four dry flies in the book's opening black and white photo plate.

While existing examples of Theodore Gordon's dry flies do not always reveal the small clean space behind the hook eye that typifies Cross's floaters, Gordon acknowledged in his early writings that the "turle knot was the best." In an article Gordon wrote for the *Fishing Gazette* in September 1907, he revealed that he discovered the turle knot, named after a British angler, Maj. William Greer Turle, in one of Halford's books. A few years later, in 1913, Gordon wrote, "Most dry fly men use the turle knot but I prefer the outside figure of eight learned from Captain Frank Wemyss of Wales." Rube Cross—and the Catskill lineage that followed

his style—continued to feature the clean space behind the hook eye, whether or not they used the turle or some other tippet attachment.

The Dettes and Darbees, because of Rube Cross's influence, continued to leave the turle space in their dry flies, their style exhibited since the 1930s. Early Dette catalogs made a point of saying that each dry fly "is tied well back on the hook, leaving a free eye clear of varnish and preventing the leader from chafing the head of the fly." Use of the turle knot also keeps the fly firmly in line with the tippet, preventing up-and-down fly movement—a "stiffening" effect, as Pennsylvania limestone waters great Vince Marinaro wrote in *A Modern Dry-Fly Code* (1950).

Regardless of the functional effect of leaving the small turle space, Rube Cross described in his dry-fly-tying instructions how to create the clean area behind the hook eye. In *Tying American Trout Lures*, Cross disclosed his step-by-step method that ended with the turle space. To outline his tying technique, he chose a pattern called the Whirling Dun. (Cross used the same recipe for the Whirling Dun as found in Ray Bergman's 1945 book, *Trout*; there are several versions. In a 1914 issue of the *Fishing Gazette*, Theodore Gordon wrote, "I have seen so many Whirling Duns that I made a little collection from a number of dressers.")

Cross's tying sequence in crafting his Whirling Dun is interesting compared with the "typical" step-by-step methods for assembling dry flies. He did not use a bobbin, as characteristic of many Catskill tiers, including the Dettes, the Darbees, and Art Flick. He first ran an 18-inch-long piece of silk through some beeswax. After securing the silk at the hook bend, he attached brown hackle barbs to the hook shank. Next, he embedded a spindle of muskrat fur into a couple-inch-long section of silk, then rubbed it between his hands to create a firm body section, which he left at the hook bend for the moment. He then wound the main tying silk up the hook shank, ending ⅛ inch behind the hook eye. With the tails tied in and the fur body still hanging off the same area back at the bend, he now wound the thread section embedded with the fur dubbing up the shank, ending ⅛ inch back from the eye. Then came the wings, at this late step in the process.

It was at this point that he attached and divided the double-slip, slate-shaded dusk quill wings. In the more typical sequence, practiced today, the wings would have been attached *first*. Once the wings were attached, he wound the body fur up the hook shank and secured it, then wound the brown hackle collar, two and a half turns in back of the wings, then initially two turns in front of the wing. He created the turle knot space by using the tips of his thumbnail and index fingernail to shove the front hackle back to the wing butts as he continued to wind the hackle.

When all the hackle was wound on, it amounted to about three turns total in front of the wing. After he tied the fly off at the head, he again shoved the hackle back with his finger-nails, creating the space behind the hook eye. Rube Cross recommended a ¹⁄₁₆-inch space, but many of his dry flies exhibited a lengthy bare space behind the eye, something also found in early Dette flies, such as their Bivisibles.

Surprisingly, the entire sequence that Cross described—tails first, then wings, then body, and finally hackle—was not what Walt and Winnie Ferdon (soon to be Dette) and Harry Darbee discovered when they untied Cross's dry flies, examining his tying in reverse to learn his secrets. "That's not what the unwrapping revealed," Walt insisted one late summer evening many years ago when I sat at Walt's side at his tying bench. "When we untied those flies (back in the late 1920s), the wings were set *first*—then the tails, then the body, then the hackle." Walt used to give Cross the benefit of the doubt and said that maybe Cross changed his technique. Winnie, on the other hand, believed that Cross may have deliberately changed his technique in the description in his book to keep his true methods secret.

While Rube Cross may have held his tying methods a closely guarded secret in his early years at the vise, he was

Walt Dette, tying a Fan Wing Royal Coachman. Dette was highly influenced by the Rube Cross dry-fly style.

more willing to share his talents at the popular sportsmen's gatherings, such as the Macy's Show in New York City. By the time he published *Tying American Trout Lures* in 1936, Cross began tying at shows. Keith Fulsher, a gifted fly tier who is well known for his Thunder Creek streamers, but also ties a wide variety of fishing flies, recalls Rube Cross's instruction at such a sports show in the mid-1950s.

He recently shared the following with me: "I first met Cross in 1955 at the New York City sports show. He was tying flies at the booth of a representative for St. Croix, a Wisconsin rod maker who was located only 30 miles from my Wisconsin hometown. I was tying for the Anglers Cove, a New York City fly-fishing shop, and our booths were side by side. I got to know him quite well. I was interested in his method of tying dry flies, especially his method of tying on wood-duck wings, as I needed a lot of help in those days on drys; my specialty was streamer flies and salmon flies. He used to take me behind the scenes when he wasn't demonstrating and tie a fly for me and explain what was going on, always giving me the fly he tied in the process."

The wood-duck wings that Keith Fulsher mentioned were made from a favorite feather used in Catskill dry-fly patterns. Of the 16 effective dry-fly patterns listed in Cross's *Tying American Trout Lures*, half used lemon wood-duck flank feathers for wings. His list included a pattern called the Cross Special, Rube's signature dry fly. In *The Treasury of Angling* (1963), Larry Koller tells the story of asking Cross what was so special about the Cross Special, which he tied with "great horny hands." Cross's response: "Not a damned thing. I just have the material, it takes fish as well as the Quill Gordon or Hendrikson [*sic*], and I've got my name on it."

Before Cross gave this explanation concerning his trademark fly, he had offered Harold Smedley more details concerning the Special. Rube told Smedley that the Cross Special was a cross between the Gordon Quill and a Light Cahill. Smedley quoted Cross: "I first tied it because the two flies were the best and most popular on Catskill streams, and I thought the 'cross' should be good, and it has been as effective as any I know. All I did was put a Light Cahill body on the Gordon Quill, making it a 'cross' breed." Cross further explained he had no intention of having the name of the fly "hooked" to his own surname; however, in a short time it was. The Cross Special was indeed a good fish taker. An angler named Samuel Wait, from Schenectady, New York, wrote to Cross on July 12, 1949, praising its success on Adirondack region streams, far to the north of the Catskills. Wait wrote, "The thing that pleased us the most was that about the only dry fly the trout would take was your Cross Special."

The majority of Catskill tiers today focus their attention on Rube Cross's wood-duck winged dry flies, the Cross Special among them. Cross also tied and popularized other dry flies, such as the Quack, a fly very similar to a hair-winged Royal Coachman that was tied for Leonard C. Quackenbush, who was a member of the Beaverkill Trout Club. Yet Rube Cross was far from just a dry-fly tier, and there are plenty who still tie the streamer, bucktail, and nymph patterns that appeared in his *Complete Fly Tier.*

His Art Neu streamer, named for a fly angler who was well known at the time, a pattern that has similarities to Theodore Gordon's Bumblepuppy, with its white chenille body and scarlet wool ribbing. It proved effective for Neu on Delaware bass waters as well as for trout on the Beaverkill. Bucktails such as the Beaverkill, Jack Schwinn, and Ray Arden were also featured in Cross's pages.

The Carrot and Black was a favorite nymph, a simple orange pattern labeled the Carrot Nymph by Elsie Darbee in *A. J. McClane's Standard Fishing Encyclopedia* color fly plates. Rube Cross contributed many patterns, from dry flies to streamers, during his Catskill years, an era that witnessed burgeoning excitement in the fly-fishing world. But, as they say, this too passed.

After spending most of his life in his beloved Catskills, Cross, who was born on his father's farm near Neversink Village in 1896, relocated to Providence, Rhode Island, where he continued to tie flies until his death in 1958 at age 62. There's plenty of speculation why Cross left the Catskills for a new life in Providence. Ed Van Put's fine book, *Trout Fishing in the Catskills* (2007), reveals that in his early life, Cross had wandered outside the Catskills from time to time but always returned; he had firmly set his feet in Catskill soil by April 1925.

But changes came to the Neversink region in the late 1930s, with the construction of a great dam that created Neversink Reservoir. In response, Cross moved to Lew Beach on the upper Beaverkill. But tragedy struck there, too, and he returned from a local dance one night to find his house on fire; the flames destroyed virtually everything he owned. He had always scratched out a living, working as everything from a janitor to a taxi driver. "It is little wonder Rube developed ulcers," Harry Darbee wrote in *Catskill Flytier.*

Once in Rhode Island, where Cross worked in a munitions factory, he kept in touch with his friend Harry Darbee and continued to tie flies and attend sports shows in New York City. Cross had a good relationship with Darbee, who said his friend Rube "gave much more to fly tying and fly fishing than he ever got back in return." Although Walt and Winnie Dette did not interact with Rube Cross to the extent that Darbee did, they gave him due acknowledgment: "We have always given Rube Cross credit for our tying style. The fact that he refused to show Walt his tying methods did nothing to change our admiration for his beautiful dry flies."

Rube Cross's life as a Catskill fly tier sadly came to an end too soon. Yet he still lives with us in the memory of his dainty dry flies that served as the foundation for the Catskill fly-tying style.

Art Neu, tied by Mike Valla. Art Neu was a well-known fly angler in Cross's era. He fished the pattern for Delaware River bass, but it also performed well for Beaverkill trout. It appears to have Bumblepuppy fly influences.

Ray Arden, tied by Mike Valla.

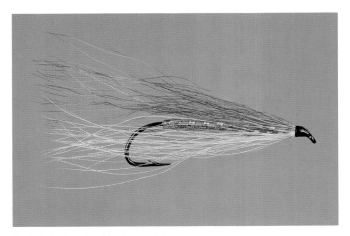

Jack Schwinn, tied by Mike Valla.

Beaverkill, tied by Mike Valla.

Wickham's Fancy, tied by Rube Cross. This is an old British pattern credited to Dr. C. Wickham of Winchester, England. Theodore Gordon called it a standard pattern. Note the double slip mallard quill wings, also of British origin, and the turle knot space behind the hook eye. *Bill Leary collection*

Wickham's Fancy, tied by Walt Dette in the late 1930s. Note the similarity to Rube Cross's Wickham's Fancy. Walt and Winnie Dette always credited Rube Cross with their dry-fly style. *Mary Dette Clark collection*

Whirling Blue Dun, tied by Rube Cross. This pattern has several variations. Cross used the Whirling Blue Dun in his books to explain his dry-fly tying procedures. *Bill Leary collection*

Quill Gordon, tied by Rube Cross. Cross changed the style of Theodore Gordon's signature pattern into what is commonly known as the Catskill-style dry fly. *Bill Leary collection*

Blue Quill Fan Wing, tied by Rube Cross. Fan-wing dry flies were very popular in Cross's era. *Bill Leary collection*

Brown Mallard, tied by Rube Cross. Cross used bronze mallard flank for the wings. *Mike Valla collection*

Gray Hackle Yellow, tied by Rube Cross. Cross often left a pronounced turle knot space on his flies. Other Catskill school fly tiers adopted the style in their dry flies. *Catskill Fly Fishing Center and Museum collection*

Light Cahill, tied by Rube Cross. The Light Cahill, a fly Theodore Gordon admired, is still a popular classic Catskill pattern. *Ted Patlen collection*

CHAPTER 5

Walt and Winnie Dette

(1907–1994; 1909–1998)

Walt and Winnie tying flies in the 1940s at their home in Roscoe, New York. *Mary Dette Clark collection*

Fan-Wing Lady Beaverkill, tied by the Dettes in the late 1930s. Fan-wings were very popular dry flies during this decade. It was not unusual for standard patterns, such as the Lady Beaverkill, to be dressed with wood-duck or mallard breast feathers to create the sail-like dry flies. *Mary Dette Clark collection*

Walt Dette's fly-tying history began in the late 1920s in an upstairs room at the Criterion, a movie house once located dead center in the village of Roscoe, in the Catskill region of New York state. The owner of the movie house at that time, Bert Cable, frequently stopped by Sipple's Drug Store, directly across the street, en route to the nearby diner. A young man named Walt Dette worked at the drugstore and frequently spoke with Cable about the idea of renting out space above the movie house for the purpose of winding guides on fishing rods. About that same time, Walt decided to stock shelves at Sipple's with fishing tackle, as it was a perfect location from which to sell the gear to anglers who traveled to the Beaverkill River and surrounding streams in search of trout and relaxation. Cable agreed to Walt's idea at a rental fee of $12 a month.

Not only was the movie house convenient to Sipple's, but it also happened to be located across the street from where a young woman named Winifred Ferdon, known as Winnie, worked at the village bank. The young Dette likely saw Winnie daily from the upstairs window at the movie house where he and his childhood friend, Harry Darbee, worked on fishing rods. That year, 1927, Walt and Winnie started dating.

Winnie's family operated a popular local hostelry called the River View Inn. The large hotel on the banks of the Beaverkill catered to both fly anglers and summer guests. Ferdon's Pool, or Ferdon's Eddy, as Winnie preferred to call it, was a stretch along its river frontage that became renowned for the birth of the Hendrickson dry fly, the famous pattern that Roy Steenrod tied for his fishing friend A. E. Hendrickson. Steenrod had been a frequent visitor at the inn for years, since when Winnie was just a young girl.

Walt, Winnie, and Harry in 1927. The three spent much time together in their early years, tying trout flies and roaming the Beaverkill. *Mary Dette Clark collection*

Other famous fly anglers came through the inn's doors too, including George M. L. La Branche. No doubt Winnie's exposure to fly anglers staying at the inn played some role in her interest in the sport. But it was Walt's tinkering around with fly tying in his rented room at the Criterion that prompted Winnie to also learn to craft trout flies. Wrapping guides on rods was of no interest to the young Winnie Ferdon, but fly tying was another matter.

At first Walt, Winnie, and Harry were simply fooling around while attempting to tie trout flies; they had no plans at that time to sell them to visiting fly fishers. Walt asked Rube Cross, the talented fly tier from the nearby Neversink River, to teach him to tie flies. The young Dette promised Cross that he simply wished to learn to tie flies for his own fishing needs and would not compete commercially with him. As Walt reported, however, Rube Cross told him to go to hell. Walt's solution was to purchase a few dozen flies from Cross, then take them apart to learn his tying methods. The trio would have to learn Cross's secrets by fly autopsy.

Perhaps Walt Dette was attracted to Cross's dry-fly style, or maybe it was the overall beauty of Cross's flies that inspired him to untie those he had purchased. Other local tiers, such as Roy Steenrod, may have been willing to assist Walt. It seems peculiar that the three did not simply approach Steenrod for assistance in learning to tie flies. He had stayed at the River View Inn many times throughout Winnie's childhood, and he was known to be a kind and helpful man during her years living at the River View Inn. Entries in her 1928 diary would lead one to assume he was more open about fly-tying methods. By that time, Theodore Gordon, whose fly-tying secrets Steenrod had promised not to disclose, had been dead for more than 15 years.

On May 19, 1928, a couple months before her marriage to Walt, Winnie wrote in her diary, "Mr. Steenrod went down to the room [at the River View Inn] tonight and tied a couple of flies. He sure is quick at it. He told us where we could get material. Says he ties about 500 dozen a year. He was awfully nice about it. I was afraid he might think we were just a bunch of crazy kids." Winnie's words suggest that she watched his tying technique. Other diary entries from that same year reveal that Walt and Winnie visited Steenrod at his home in nearby Liberty, where, she wrote, "he showed us a lot of things" and "didn't act as though he thought we were a couple of foolish kids."

All three of the "crazy kids" became gifted tiers who, through their talented hands, continued the Catskill tying legacy that had begun with Gordon. Winnie's diary tells us she tied her first trout fly on December 2, 1927, at age 18. The story describing the circumstances leading to Walt and Winnie's early endeavors selling trout flies, something they had not planned to do, is a remarkable tale. More thorough descriptions of that early history can be found in Eric Leiser's book *The Dettes: A Catskill Legend* (1992); my 2009 book,

Beaverkill River, Upper Barnhart's Pool. Walt and Winnie Dette first tied flies commercially at the River View Inn on the banks of Ferdon's Pool, a short distance upstream from Upper Barnhart's. *Photo by Valerie Valla*

Tying Catskill-Style Dry Flies; and an article titled "Winifred Ferdon Dette: Diary of a Catskill Fly Tier," in the Fall 2007 issue of the *American Fly Fisher*.

The patterns the Dettes tied and sold are still known as Catskill classics, among them Quill Gordons, Dark Cahills, Dark Hendricksons, Bivisibles, Quacks, Woodruffs, Conovers, Fan-Wings, and many others. The flies were crafted using natural furs, including muskrat and red fox, and silk bodies, sometimes ribbed with narrow flat gold tinsel, a remnant of the old British ways. They also tied British classics, such as the Wickham's Fancy, Cowdung, Blue Quill, and Queen of Waters, all tied in the style of Rube Cross.

As with Cross's patterns, wood-duck flank feathers along with double-slip duck quill wings were omnipresent in the Dettes' dry-fly lineup. They also used hackle point wings on many of their dry flies. One of their most noted drys tied with hackle point wings is the Corey Ford, a pattern Walt named for a dear friend. During the 1950s and 1960s, Corey Ford, a well-known humorist, wrote a monthly column in *Field & Stream* magazine called "The Lower Forty Hunting, Shooting and Inside Straight Club," about the adventures of a fictional group of sportsmen living in Vermont. His writings were anthologized into books, including *The Minutes of the*

Lower Forty, one of Walt's favorite books. Ford's April 1952 *True* magazine article titled "The Best-Loved Trout Stream of Them All" was another favorite of Walt's.

In that story, as well as in an earlier article that appeared in the June 1931 issue of *Vanity Fair*, Ford wrote of the fly Walt named after him: "There is only one other request I have to make. Mr. Dette, it appears, has succeeded in manufacturing a Corey Ford Fly. Now if he would only manage somehow to manufacture a Corey Ford trout, which can be guaranteed always to take this lure, my satisfaction will be complete." Ford described the version of the pattern that appeared in the earliest Dette catalog—gray body, blue-gray hackle, cream hackle point wings.

In the 1952 *True* story, Ford told of the Beaverkill and his adventures on the river during the '30s and '40s, saying, "I was born on the Beaverkill myself, in a manner of speaking. I learned to cast a dry fly over Barnhart's Pool." It's a lovely tale about the pools and the personalities who cast loops over their waters during those glorious years, such as Theodore Gordon, Roy Steenrod, Rube Cross, Ted Townsend, John Alden Knight, Bill Schaldach, Mel Rosch, John Taintor Foote, and John McDonald. And of the Dettes, Ford wrote: "Today Walt and his attractive wife Winnie have risen to the

Mary Dette Clark now occupies the tying bench where her mother, Winnie, once crafted her Quill Gordons and Red Quills.
Mary Dette Clark collection

top of their profession, fashioning some of the most perfect feathered lures produced anywhere. Perhaps I am prejudiced: Walt named a trout fly after me once—the Corey Ford fly."

The Corey Ford pattern is dressed in a couple variations, the one described by Ford being the first. By the late 1930s, another version appeared, this one with a somewhat light greenish cream fur body, light hackle point wings, and creamish hackle. The Corey Ford wasn't the only pattern that the Dettes changed and varied; their Coffin Fly is another pattern with multiple versions.

The Coffin, a pattern that Walt and Winnie's daughter, Mary Clark, loves to tie, did not always feature the characteristic upright divided zebralike teal flank wings. That version of the Coffin was developed well after the original pattern was first tied. The contemporary Dette Coffin Fly uses a completely different body and tails than those on the original pattern, first tied in 1929 by Walt Dette for his friend Ted Townsend, who codesigned the pattern. Townsend wasn't a fly tier, but the Dettes knew him well since he stayed for long periods at the River View Inn. The Coffin was created to imitate the large *Ephemerella guttulata* mayfly and has an interesting history.

The story goes that Townsend attended a funeral the day it was designed and suggested tying a fly with black hackle point wings and black tails and naming it Coffin Fly. It was hackled with medium to dark badger. By the late 1930s, the Dette Coffin Fly tails were changed to wood-duck flank fibers. The second version of the fly held on until at least

the early 1970s. The Coffin body was commonly tied with pig's wool, a material mentioned in Thaddeus Norris's *American Angler's Book* (1864). The third version of the Dette Coffin Fly, the pattern still tied by Mary, has characteristic striking teal wings, poly yarn body palmered with clipped badger hackle, and peccary tails. In a January 7, 1984, letter to R. T. Bersal of Catskill, New York, Walt mentioned the origin of the Coffin Fly and the newest version: "Ted Townsend did not tie but also was someone we knew very well, as he stayed at the hotel for weeks at a time, suggested the name. It has been modified to being called the Carpenter-Coffin as we borrowed the use of teal wing from a Pennsylvania pattern."

The Dette Coffin Fly represents one of Walt's earliest creations. He wasn't focused on inventing a large inventory of his own patterns, but even in his later years at the vise, he always exhibited creativity. Walt tweaked flies to suit the needs of fly anglers who came through the Dette shop doors. His Delaware Special and Delaware Adams dry flies provided alternatives to the popular Henryville Special, a Pennsylvania pattern created by Hiram Brobst. Walt enjoyed tying the Henryville and often had neat rows of them lined up across the rear of his tying table, fresh off his vise. But the Delaware Adams, a pattern Walt started experimenting with in the 1970s, quickly became one of the most popular patterns he ever created. It's a good floater, easily visible on water, and takes fish.

Mary Dette in the 1940s. Mary became part of the Dette fly-tying tradition after graduating from college and not long after getting married in 1953. *Mary Dette Clark collection*

Other renowned fly tiers such as Helen Shaw expressed interest in Walt's Delaware Adams. In a letter dated June 15, 1982, from Shaw to the Dettes, following a recent visit to Roscoe, she inquired about obtaining a few of the new flies. "Hermann [Shaw's husband] had fully intended to ask you to sell him a couple of flies called the 'Delaware Adams,'" she wrote, "but in the midst of all the interesting conversations, it completely slipped his mind. That's one 'Adams' with which I am not familiar, but I'd dearly love to surprise him with them."

While Walt enjoyed experimenting with new patterns, the shop bins were primarily stocked with Catskill classics, which were the patterns most often requested by mail order. The Dettes tied large numbers of Art Flick's Red Quills, Grey Fox Variants, Dun Variants, March Browns, Grey Foxes, and others. The Quack Coachman, which Rube Cross created based on a fly that Leonard C. Quackenbush from the Beaverkill Trout Club brought to him in the early 1930s, still fills the Dette fly bins today. The Dettes were also custom tiers, supplying the needs of local fly-fishing club members. One such customer was Scotty Conover, a member of the Brooklyn Fly Fishers. One of the Dettes' most effective patterns, brought to the couple in 1934 and tied exclusively for its creator, is the Conover. Scotty Conover stipulated that it be tied only for him and no other customers. But after some time had passed, he eventually said the Dettes could tie the fly for anyone. Harold Hinsdill Smedley featured the Conover in *Fly Patterns and Their Origins* (1944).

Flies such as the Coffin, Delaware Adams, and Conover, along with all the classic Catskill patterns, have many believing that the most effective Dette flies were floaters. It is true that when talk turns to the Dette flies, the topic centers largely around the duo's beautifully crafted dry flies, art forms tied in the spirit of Rube Cross. However, Walt and Winnie also created some interesting nymph patterns that still remain in demand in the shop now operated by daughter Mary Clark and her grandson Joe Fox.

Nymphs that produced well for Catskill anglers and were sought from the Dette shop included the Dickie, March Brown, Yellow Stonefly, and Isonychia.

The Dickie, a simple pattern designed by Dette family friend Ernie Maltz, is tied with peacock herl and a grizzly hackle collar. Maltz was so insistent concerning its effectiveness that he sent a letter to angling author Ray Bergman describing the pattern, which Winnie used for Atlantic salmon. Bergman included the pattern in a later version of his book *Trout*. The Dettes' Stonefly and March Brown nymphs are also effective patterns, but of all their nymphs, the Isonychia is probably the best fish producer. Its body of blended muskrat and red wool is wrapped with natural gray ostrich herl, which pulsates when the fly is fished, giving the impression of the gills found in the natural it imitates, the *Isonychia bicolor*.

The Isonychia nymph was one of the first flies Walt taught me to tie, more than 40 years ago, in my teenage years. Walt showed other fly-tying techniques to this "crazy kid" as well. These episodes in my early days of tying aren't easily forgotten; memories of the time spent with Walt at his bench those many years ago have never grown hazy. The story of my experiences while I was staying with the Dettes is covered in detail in *Tying Catskill-Style Dry Flies*, so I won't repeat it all here.

After reading Cecil Heacox's 1969 *Outdoor Life* article "The Charmed Circle of the Catskills," and William J. Schaldach's 1944 *Currents and Eddies*, I decided to take a bus alone (at age 15) from Binghamton, New York, an hour away to fish the Beaverkill River and Willowemoc Creek for a days' fishing adventure. I stopped in the Dette fly shop upon my arrival in Roscoe, New York, where I met Winnie. "Are my flies OK?" I asked her. But her attention that morning quickly turned from the quality of my trout flies to why I was alone without food or water.

She sent Walt out looking for me that evening, for fear I might miss my bus back home. He found me fishing alone on the Willowemoc and graciously offered me a bedroom at their home for a week or two. Walt phoned my mother, but mom quickly turned down the offer. I was eventually allowed to return, and from that time forward, I stayed with the Dettes on many occasions, particularly during teenage and college summers during the 1970s but also many times off and on after those years. The Dettes knew I had a burning passion to learn everything that I could about tying quality trout flies, especially in the Catskill style.

My first lesson at the vise with Walt and Winnie took place in late June or early July 1969 at the old Dette house, which now sits vacant at the end of Cottage Street in Roscoe. The flies in my box were poorly tied, yet Walt and Winnie said nothing about my tying skill that was anything less than encouraging. "Work on that figure eight around your wings on that Adams," Winnie said in a kind voice, "but you have nothing to be ashamed of, young man."

The first session offered such instruction, tempered only with suggestions, not criticisms. Walt would say something like "You're not doing anything wrong, but I do it this way, which works well for us. Try it." The session that evening did not result in one single fully tied fly. Walt concentrated on tying suggestions—how to dub a fur body, set wings, cock tails at the hook bend, master a whip-finish. The Dettes emphasized hackle and material selection not only that first evening, but throughout all the early years I spent with Walt and Winnie.

At that time, Walt was working for the city of New York at Deposit, where he was engaged with sampling the quality of water discharging from Pepacton and Cannonsville Reservoirs. During the day, when he was working, he allowed me to sit at his bench and tie—all day if I'd like. Walt encouraged

> Stone Fly Nymph   4/1/64   Hook 9672
>
> Tail - Hen Phes.
> Ribbing - Gude-Wind Rod silk Color 541 Nylon size A
> lacquered - 1strand for 12 Hook - 2 Strand for 10 Hook
> Body - Yellow Wool
> Thorax - Mixed light fox fur + Orchard Sport yarn #710
> lemon color #117 + Brown fur.
> Hump - Brown Turkey
> Legs. - Brown Partridge. Tie in Hackle before
>   fastening off hump.

Yellow Stonefly Nymph dressing card and sample fly, tied by the Dettes in 1964. The Dettes cataloged their popular patterns to ensure uniformity when selecting materials for a pattern. *Mary Dette Clark collection*

practicing with any tying material he stored in the large tin boxes that lined the shelves. Later in the evenings, we both tied together and discussed different patterns that filled the shop bins. Those early influences led to changes in my own dry flies, which took on the appearance of Dette and Cross styles. Walt died in 1994 and Winnie in 1998, but their talents live on in the hands of those who still practice their tying style.

Today Mary Dette Clark and Joe Fox (her grandson) carry on the Dette Catskill fly-tying tradition at the shop on Cottage Street, two doors down from the Dette home where I first stayed, and where Walt and Winnie moved their shop in 1972. Mary first started tying flies around 1954, when she was expecting her first child, Gary. At the tying table where her mother, Winnie, tied flies for many years, Mary contin-

ues filling orders for Coffin Flies, Red Quills, Quill Gordons, and many other Catskill patterns. The flies stand on their noses in rows along the green blotter attached to her bench. Mary's flies are identical to Walt and Winnie's, tied with the same degree of care and uniformity for which the Dette flies have always been known. Collectors are sometimes frustrated that it can be impossible for the untrained eye to tell whether flies were tied by Walt, Winnie, or Mary. And sitting at her side is Joe, in his twenties, crafting flies such as the Delaware Adams, which his great-grandfather Walt designed years before his birth. Joe has also introduced his own patterns at the shop, creations that take large trout on his favorite Catskill waters. Joe ties a fine fly, displaying the same Dette perfection.

Conover, tied by the Dettes in the late 1930s. It was first tied for Scotty Conover, a member of the Brooklyn Fly Fishers Club, in 1934. It is still a popular Catskill dry-fly pattern. *Mary Dette Clark collection*

Corey Ford, tied by the Dettes in the late 1930s. There are a couple different versions of this pattern. The most well known is tied with cream hackle point wings, dun or black hackle barb tails, muskrat fur body, and dun hackle. It's named for Corey Ford, a humorist and friend of Walt Dette. *Mary Dette Clark collection*

Woodruff, tied by the Dettes in the late 1930s. Johnny Woodruff, for whom the fly was named by Chester Mills of the well-known William Mills & Son tackle house in New York City, frequently fished the Beaverkill River and stopped by the Dette fly shop. Woodruff did well with the pattern on the Brooklyn Club water on the upper Beaverkill. *Mary Dette Clark collection*

Early-era Coffin Fly, tied by the Dettes in the late 1930s. Some Dette patterns, such as the Coffin Fly, evolved over time. *Mary Dette Clark collection*

Popular Dette nymphs, tied by the Dettes. Top, left to right: March Brown, Dickie. Bottom: Isonychia, Yellow Stonefly. The nymphs featured here were obtained from Walt and Winnie Dette's fly file, where all of their prototypes were cataloged for future reference. Walt and Winnie's great-grandson, Joe Fox, still sells these patterns in the Dette Shop in Roscoe. *Mary Dette Clark collection*

Late-era Coffin Fly, tied by Mary Dette Clark in 2008. This is the version Mary is known for. *Mike Valla collection*

Quill Gordon, tied by the Dettes in the late 1930s. A great example of an early-era Dette-tied Quill Gordon. The Dettes liked to counter-wrap their stripped peacock quill bodies with tying thread to secure the fragile material. *Mary Dette Clark collection*

Delaware Adams, tied by Walt Dette. Walt's creation quickly became known as one of his signature patterns. It floats well, is easily seen on water, and takes fish. *Mike Valla collection*

Bradley, tied by the Dettes in the late 1930s. William Bradley, an early member of the Beaverkill Trout Club, requested that the Dettes custom tie this fly. It was tied in several variations. *Mary Dette Clark collection*

Quack, tied by the Dettes in the late 1930s. Rube Cross first tied the pattern for Leonard C. Quackenbush, a member of the Beaverkill Trout Club. Walt Dette enjoyed tying the fly; one would often see rows of them, standing on their noses, lined up across the back of his tying table. *Mary Dette Clark collection*

Gordon, tied by the Dettes in the late 1930s. The Gordon dry fly, initially named the Golden Brown Spinner, is a sparkling pattern that bears its creator's name. *Mary Dette Clark collection*

Blue Quill, tied by the Dettes in the late 1930s. Blue Quill dry flies were once popular both in England and on Catskill waters. They are sometimes still tied, in small sizes, for the tiny *Paraleptophlebia* mayfly emergences on Catskill streams such as the Willowemoc Creek. *Mary Dette Clark collection*

Dark Cahill, tied by the Dettes in the late 1930s. Fifteen years before the Dettes tied the fly shown here, Theodore Gordon mentioned in a letter to Roy Steenrod that the Dark Cahill was on a list that a successful Beaverkill angler had sent him. It's still a popular pattern on Catskill waters. *Mary Dette Clark collection*

Dark Hendrickson, tied by the Dettes in the late 1930s. This is still a popular classic Catskill pattern. *Mary Dette Clark collection*

Fan-Wing Queen of Waters, tied by the Dettes in the late 1930s. Traditionally tied with mallard flank wings, this is another classic pattern tied in fan-wing form. *Mary Dette Clark collection*

Parmachene Belle, tied by Joe Fox, Mary Dette Clark's grandson, who now operates the Dette fly shop along with Mary. Joe ties a full range of pattern styles—both classic Catskill patterns and colorful flies such as this one, among many others.

Elsie and Harry Darbee at their tying bench. *Photo by Lefty Kreh, Catskill Fly Fishing Center and Museum collection*

CHAPTER 6

Harry and Elsie Darbee
(1906–1983; 1912–1980)

When the Dettes began selling trout flies in earnest, something Walt had never intended to do, it soon became apparent that they needed help to keep up with the growing demand. At first the Dettes tied their flies at the River View Inn on the Beaverkill River at Roscoe, New York, the hostelry owned by Winnie's parents. Eventually the Dettes moved out of the hotel to a home on nearby Academy Street in Roscoe village. During the Great Depression, they lost the River View Inn but continued to tie trout flies at their Academy Street home. Winnie's meticulous records show that by 1930, they had tied nearly 500 dozen flies at $3 a dozen. Large wholesale fly orders were arriving from Folsom Arms, a sporting goods company in New York City, so to help meet the demand for trout flies, Walt and Winnie asked their friend Harry Darbee, who at the time was living in New Paltz, New York, if he'd like to join their enterprise as a third partner.

Darbee responded in a letter dated May 4, 1933, that he'd like to return to Roscoe and join them. He did so but wound up staying with the Dettes only briefly. The Dettes were expecting

Rat-Faced McDougall, tied by Harry Darbee. In *Catskill Flytier*, Darbee wrote, "I suppose the flies Elsie and I are best known for are our clipped-hair patterns, in particular the Rat-Faced McDougall."
Catskill Fly Fishing Center and Museum, Fontinalis Fly Fishermen Club collection

the birth of their second child, and at the same time, the business was expanding so rapidly that it was obvious to all three that even more help was sorely needed. As Harry wrote in *Catskill Flytier*, "In order to stay at the vises we needed someone to sort materials." A well-known local fishing guide, Pop Robbins, suggested a young woman named Elsie Bivins, who lived on Academy Street across from the Dette home and growing fly-tying operation. The Dettes hired Elsie in the spring of 1934. Elsie expressed a strong desire to learn fly tying, and through Harry Darbee's instruction, she became a very skillful tier. At the same time, romance bloomed between the two, and by the winter of that year, Harry proposed to Elsie.

Harry passed on to Elsie the tying techniques he had learned from dismantling not only Rube Cross's flies, with Walt and Winnie Dette, but also flies tied by Theodore Gordon and his protégés Herm Christian and Roy Steenrod. "Untying their threads was like entering a temple of worship," he said.

Eventually, with their combined fly-tying capabilities, Harry and Elsie Darbee were ready to go out on their own. On January 11, 1935, Walt, Winnie, and Harry signed a dissolution agreement, and a new venture was started: the E. B. and H. A. Darbee fly-tying business. Elsie Darbee quickly rose to become one of the most talented fly tiers in America, in some ways surpassing Harry's skills at the vise. The two continued to tie trout and salmon flies at their shop on the banks of Willowemoc Creek for the remainder of their lives.

Thousands of well-known fly anglers and tiers came through the doors of their home shop along old Route 17 in Livingston Manor, New York. A veritable "who's who" list visited their two-story clapboard home in search of Darbee flies, tackle, and most anything else concerned with fly fishing. Among the important figures in fly-fishing history who used the Darbees' patterns, Ed Hewitt obtained large numbers of his Neversink Skaters from them, and John Atherton listed them as a source for his dry-fly and nymph patterns.

While Harry and Elsie were custom fly tiers, serving the needs of fly fishers looking for something different or supplying patterns made popular by others, they also created and tied their own gems. Their workhorse patterns were meant to capture fish, not be displayed in shadow boxes. The Darbees crafted well-tied flies, admired by many, but Harry wrote in his book, "Fussing over a fly to get lifelike effects or because you want some kind of perfect example of a tier's art has never appealed to me."

Indeed, one of Harry's favorite patterns to which he has a connection was a not-so-pretty dry fly with a not-so-pretty name: the Rat-Faced McDougall, a clipped deer hair pattern with an interesting history. As Darbee wrote, "I suppose the flies Elsie and I are best known for are our clipped-hair patterns, in particular the Rat-Faced McDougall." This pattern, created in the summer of 1939, was first tied as a spin-off of

Harry Darbee at his tying bench. *Photo Poul Jorgensen, Catskill Fly Fishing Center and Museum collection*

a clipped hair body dry fly originally called H.A. Darbee's Special Mayfly and later dubbed the Beaverkill Bastard for the peculiar mating of a deer hair bass bug with a trout fly. The Bastard was tied on a 3XL hook with a clipped deer hair body and hackle point wings.

When Harry's friend Percy Jennings suggested that the Beaverkill Bastard might prove even more productive if tied on smaller hooks, Darbee responded, "Why don't you do it?" These new flies, similar yet smaller versions of the Beaverkill Bastard, were tied with cream grizzly hackle point wings, clipped tannish gray deer hair bodies, and ginger hackle collars and tails. A young friend of Jennings's daughter gave the fly its new name. Later, at the request of a well-known Darbee customer, C. Otto von Kienbusch, the fly's wings were changed to white calf. Von Kienbusch was partially blind from glaucoma, and the white wings enabled him to more easily spot the fly on the water.

The pattern in all of its incarnations quickly caught the attention of fly-fishing and fly-tying personalities. Roderick Haig-Brown, an icon in Pacific Northwest fly-fishing circles and beyond, wrote to Harry Darbee praising the Rat-Faced McDougall, along with the Irresistible, for bringing him "many friends and considerable business." Haig-Brown took steelhead on the fly. In *The Complete Fly Tier* (1950), fellow Catskill-born fly tier Rube Cross mentioned that the Rat-Faced McDougall was Alex Rogan's favorite. Rogan was *the* premier fly tier as far back as the 1920s and was considered a champion of the Atlantic salmon fly in his era. Cross included the fly, along with the Beaverkill Bastard, in the book's black and white photo plates.

The Rat-Faced McDougall is closely related to another dry fly with a clipped deer hair body that Darbee included

Field & Stream

AMERICA'S NUMBER ONE SPORTSMAN'S MAGAZINE

383 MADISON AVENUE • NEW YORK 17, N. Y.

Please Address Reply To:
A. J. McCLANE
Fishing Editor
262 Orange Grove Road
Palm Beach, Florida

June 8, 1964

Mr. Harry Darbee
Livingston Manor, New York

Dear Harry:

In haste. Just returned from Europe. The flies
received and they look great! We are going to a
roto press on the color, so the finished plates
should be magnificent. I will send you originals
as received.

Fished the Traun in Austria. You'd feel at home.
They put *their* highway right down the best riffles.

Will write soon.

Sincerely,

A. J. McClane

AJMcC:pm

Letter from A. J. McClane to Harry Darbee concerning McClane's forthcoming *Standard Fishing Encyclopedia*, which would feature hundreds of Darbee-tied flies. *Catskill Fly Fishing Center and Museum collection*

Dave Brandt at his tying table in Oneonta, New York. Brandt frequently hung out at the Darbees' shop and took an interest in Harry's patterns, such as the Two Feather Fly.

on his "Deadly Dozen" list in *Catskill Flytier*: Joe Messinger Sr.'s still-popular Irresistible. Darbee's own clipped deer hair Coffin, another spin-off from the Beaverkill Bastard, sported a body of clipped white deer body hair and black hackle point wings, similar to the early Coffin Fly that Walt Dette developed with Ted Townsend in 1929. The flies in the Darbees' clipped deer body hair family—the Beaverkill Bastard, Rat-Faced McDougall, and Coffin—are interesting patterns still talked about and fished today. But those patterns weren't the only dry flies created by the Darbees; they are also remembered for other floaters.

Among the dry flies found in the Darbee fly bins were all the Catskill classics—flies going back to Gordon, Steenrod, and Cross. Yet Harry's hands created other dry-fly patterns not well known outside the Catskills. One of the Darbees' first originals was the Flatwater Pale Ginger, a pattern created for midsummer fishing. Tied in sizes 14 to 20, the fly was crafted entirely with ginger shade hackle—tails, wings, and palmering along a bare hook shank. In the late 1930s, Harry developed his own fly, Darbee's Green Egg Sac, also called the Shad Fly, as a caddis imitation. A simple pattern, it has since fallen out of general use on Catskill streams.

Another unique Darbee dry fly, called the Two Feather Fly, was born from Harry's idea of creating an ultralight pattern to serve his friend Terrell Moore's need for large mayfly naturals such as the *Isonychia*, or Slate Drake.

In *Catskill Flytier*, Harry explained that the Two Feather Fly was originated thanks to Moore's ongoing encouragement, a persistence that eventually led to A. J. McClane's October 1960 *Field & Stream* magazine article featuring the fly. The pattern didn't survive over the years, however. As Harry said, "It was too much of a novelty to last and gradually faded out of existence." The pattern showed some inventiveness in its style: one hackle formed the tail, body, and wings, and a second hackle was wound at the wings, as in most other dry flies.

Harry Darbee's Two Feather Fly and Rat-Faced McDougall dry flies are considered among his better-known patterns. Yet he and Elsie tied a full range of patterns, including beautiful wet flies, streamers, nymphs, and salmon flies. Perhaps the greatest influence the Darbees had on other fly tiers, especially during the 1960s, was through A. J. McClane's *Standard Fishing Encyclopedia* (1965). The beautiful color fly plates in McClane's masterpiece featured not only the Darbees' own creations, but also many flies invented by other renowned fly tiers, such as Cal Bird's Stone Flies. The Darbee plates in this work were the "go-to" fly pattern dressing references popular in that era. Both Harry and Elsie did a tremendous job for McClane—and at a modest fee.

Elsie sent an invoice dated July 22, 1964, to McClane, charging the book's publisher 60 cents each for the 45 dry flies and 40 nymphs featured in the monumental work. The Darbees charged similar relatively low prices for the stream-

Willowemoc Creek, Livingston Manor, New York. The Darbees lived near the banks of this quaint Catskill stream. *Photo by Valerie Valla*

ers and salmon flies they tied for the book. The prices were modest even in that era. The 20 salmon flies tied by Harry provided many tiers a first reference into that fly-tying style.

One salmon fly pattern that didn't appear among the 20 was one of Harry's own creations, Darbee's Spate Fly. A black and white photo of this fly appeared in Rube Cross's *Complete Fly Tier*. A letter from Darbee to Cross dated August 9, 1949, made clear Harry's enjoyment at fishing waters such as the Margaree in Cape Breton, Nova Scotia. "This is a clear, wadeable stream," he wrote, "and aside from the size of game pursued, it is much like fishing the Beaverkill." He tied the Spate Fly for that noted salmon water in 1946 and used it when the stream was in spate, high and turbid.

Darbee also fished other well-known salmon flies on the Margaree, such as the Green Highlander tied on a light wire hook in "reduced" form as a riffling pattern, but his Spate Fly drew interest from Joseph D. Bates Jr. In preparation for his forthcoming book, *Atlantic Salmon Flies and Fishing*, Bates sent Darbee a letter on October 20, 1969, requesting that he submit a sample of his Spate. "I note that you did a fly called the Spate Fly," Bates wrote. "Could you do this one and one of your deer-body floaters?"

The appearance of Darbee's Spate in Bates's book might have surprised readers, many of whom likely assumed

wrongly that Harry and Elsie were entrenched in Catskill patterns, especially the delicately tied wood-duck winged dry flies that epitomized the tying style of that region. It is true that their Catskill patterns served to inspire others who learned at their benches.

Harry and Elsie Darbee's talents at the tying vise were passed on to others who practice the craft along old Route 17, the road that runs along the Willowemoc Creek, where the Darbees practiced their craft for decades. Walking into Frank Kuttner's little fly shop on the Beaverkill Road in Livingston Manor, one is quickly reminded of the influence and inspiration he received from the Darbees. Framed photos of Harry and Elsie occupy the walls not far from his tying table. Kuttner used to watch Elsie tie flies, although her nimble fingers moved faster than Frank's eyes. A couple of years ago, when I visited with Frank at his shop, he shared remembrances of Elsie. "Elsie used to show me a thing or two and she would say how to do this or that, and this is how I do it. Then I would have to say to Elsie, 'One more time, please.'"

Others who admired the Darbees and were greatly influenced by their tying skills include Catskill-region fly-fishing historian and accomplished fly fisher Ed Van Put; Dave Brandt of Onenota, New York; and Catskill Fly Fishing Center and Museum executive director Jim Krul. Brandt was not only fond of Darbee patterns, such as the Two Feather Fly, but also admired Harry's conservation efforts in trying to stop Beaverkill River streambed destruction when construction on Route 17 was being planned in the 1960s. Krul recalls his routine trips to the Darbees', where he was always welcomed, especially by Elsie, who really liked him. The Darbee shop was always a "must stop" for anglers fishing the Willowemoc or Beaverkill, and no doubt many admirers learned a tying tip or two from Harry or Elsie Darbee.

In addition to his fly-tying influences, Harry Darbee's selective rooster breeding led to the quality genetic hackle that fly tiers everywhere depend on today. Walt Dette detested raising his own roosters, but Harry enjoyed developing his

hackle line, and his flock once reached nearly 1,000 birds. He was generous about handing out eggs to others interested in raising hackle roosters. A Minneapolis lawyer named Andy Miner received four dozen eggs from Harry in 1954. Miner, in turn, did some of his own selective breeding and also handed out eggs to many others who also had an interest in developing hackle for trout flies. Darbee hackle DNA found its way into flocks developed by breeders such as Bucky Metz, Charlie Collins, Tom Whiting, and Ted Hebert. Much more information concerning Darbee's influence on hackle breeders, as well as the famous fly-tying couple's history as Catskill fly tiers, appears in Darbee's book *Catskill Flytier* and in my *Tying Catskill-Style Dry Flies*.

Lady Beaverkill, tied by the Darbees. This pattern was once one of the most popular dry flies fished on Catskill waters. *Catskill Fly Fishing Center and Museum collection, Fontinalis Fly Fishermen Club collection*

Pink Lady, tied by Harry Darbee. This fly was one of George M. L. La Branche's favorite patterns. *Catskill Fly Fishing Center and Museum collection, Fontinalis Fly Fishermen Club collection*

Beaverkill, tied by the Darbees. Theodore Gordon wrote about the pattern in his 1906 *Fishing Gazette* story. It's based on a British fly but colonized the Catskills well before Gordon's appearance on the Beaverkill River, for which it is named. He believed it was tied to imitate sedge flies. *Catskill Fly Fishing Center and Museum, Fontinalis Fly Fishermen Club collection*

Ginger Quill, tied by the Darbees. Harry recognized that double-divided duck quill slip wings were dying out, but he said that "these wings are still excellent and durable when properly tied." The Ginger Quill was a favorite on his list of patterns with a similar wing style. *Catskill Fly Fishing Center and Museum collection, Fontinalis Fly Fishermen Club collection*

Irresistible, tied by the Darbees. Joe Messinger's Irresistible is similar to Harry's clipped deer hair body Rat-Faced McDougall. *Catskill Fly Fishing Center and Museum, Fontinalis Fly Fishermen Club collection*

Darbee's Green Egg Sac, tied by Harry Darbee. Harry created this pattern in the late 1930s but later abandoned it. However, he changed the original dressing and then called it a Shad Fly, designed for use during early caddis emergences in the Catskills, a time that coincides with Delaware River shad spawning runs. *Ted Patlen collection*

Two Feather Fly, tied by Dave Brandt. Harry said of this fly, "It was too much of a novelty to last and gradually faded out of existence."

Coffin Fly, tied by Elsie Darbee. The Darbees were well known for their clipped hair patterns such as this Coffin version. Harry wrote, "I have had some real big ones on this fly." *Mike Valla collection*

Gold-Ribbed Hare's Ear, tied by the Darbees. This was an old British pattern tied later as a dry fly in the Catskill style. Harry placed the Hare's Ear on his "Deadly Dozen" list. *Catskill Fly Fishing Center and Museum, Fontinalis Fly Fishermen Club collection*

Light Cahill, tied by the Darbees. Harry Darbee called this pattern, made popular on Catskill waters, one of "the best dry flies ever devised." Created by William Chandler on the Neversink River, it's now fished on many trout waters throughout the country. *Catskill Fly Fishing Center and Museum, Fontinalis Fly Fishermen Club collection*

Black Gnat, tied by the Darbees. The Darbees included many old British patterns in their fly bins, tied in the Catskill style. *Catskill Fly Fishing Center and Museum, Fontinalis Fly Fishermen Club collection*

Brown Bivisible, tied by the Darbees. Ed Hewitt frequently turned to the Darbees to tie supplies of his pattern for his own use. *Justin Krul collection*

Tups Indispensable, tied by the Darbees. The Tups caused much commotion in the British chalkstream region of Devon and Cornwall, and not many were privy to its secrets. Theodore Gordon fished the pattern on his Catskill waters. Few knew the dubbing mix ingredients first used by its creator, R. S. Austin. Elsie Darbee tied the pattern for inclusion in McClane's *Standard Fishing Encyclopedia*. *Catskill Fly Fishing Center and Museum, Fontinalis Fly Fishermen Club collection*

Light Hendrickson, tied by the Darbees. Harry called Roy Steenrod, who developed the Light Hendrickson, "a mighty sporting figure on the stream." The Darbees tied hundreds of this pattern for fly anglers who came to the Catskills to fish the *Ephemerella subvaria* mayfly hatch. *Mike Valla collection*

Gray Wulff, tied by the Darbees. Harry discovered the worth of fishing dry flies for Atlantic salmon during an outing on the Margaree River. After a nearly fruitless outing fishing sinking patterns, Harry finally took some fish on a Gray Wulff. *Catskill Fly Fishing Center and Museum, Fontinalis Fly Fishermen Club collection*

Salmon Fly, tied by the Darbees. Harry did not restrict his tying to classic Catskill dry flies; he also tied many salmon patterns. *Ralph Graves collection*

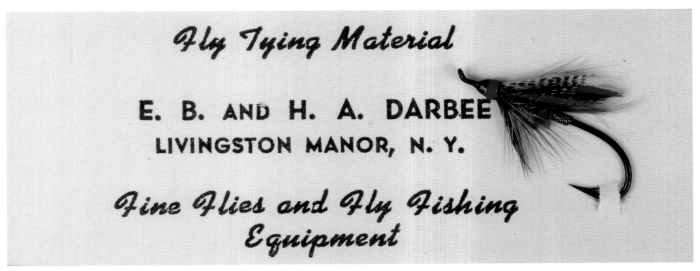

Salmon fly, tied by the Darbees. *Ted Patlen collection*

Pale Evening Dun, tied by the Darbees. This classic has fallen out of favor but once was tied in abundance by the Darbees and the Dettes. Theodore Gordon tied this vintage British pattern in 1915 for friend Guy Jenkins, who lived on the Neversink River. *Catskill Fly Fishing Center and Museum, Fontinalis Fly Fishermen Club collection*

Darbee's Spate Fly, tied by Lee Schechter. Harry Darbee originally tied this fly in the 1940s for the Margaree River in Nova Scotia when that famous salmon stream was in spate, high and turbid.

Art Flick at his tying table. *Photo by Lefty Kreh*

Many consider Art Flick's Red Quill his signature pattern. He tied it to imitate the male *Ephemerella subvaria* mayfly, a common species on his home Schoharie Creek. He used stripped Rhode Island Red hackle quill for the body. *Mike Valla collection*

CHAPTER 7

Art Flick
(1904–1985)

Art Flick was referred to as the "Sage of the mighty Schoharie Creek" and the "Laird of Westkill," the quaint little tributary that flowed outside his home in the Catskill Mountains of New York state. Even today, nearly 30 years after his passing, it's difficult to fish those waters without thinking of this Catskill region fly tier. Flick loved those streams, studying, protecting, and writing about them over the course of his life. Flick probably would have liked best to be remembered as an ardent conservationist, yet many fly anglers think of him primarily as a member of the classic Catskill school of fly tiers. However, Art Flick did much more than tie trout flies in his lifelong devotion to the sport of fly fishing and all that surrounds it.

From 1934 until 1960, before it burned to the ground a couple of years later, Flick operated the Westkill Tavern, an inn that stood just steps from

Art Flick's Schoharie Creek. Much of Flick's research concerning mayfly emergences and trout-fly selections included in his *Streamside Guide* occurred on this Catskill trout stream. *Photo by Valerie Valla*

his Schoharie. Iconic figures such as Ray Bergman, Dana Lamb, and Preston Jennings stayed at the popular inn, which catered mainly to fly anglers and hunters in search of trout and grouse. It is not surprising that Jennings frequented the Westkill Tavern, as it was Flick who contributed much of the entomological field research that appeared in *A Book of Trout Flies*, Jennings's epic work that was first published by Derrydale Press in 1935 and reprinted by Crown Publishers in 1970. There was mutual admiration between the two ardent anglers.

Jennings played an enormously important part in Art Flick's development as a fly tier. In Cecil Heacox's classic article in the May 1972 issue of *Outdoor Life*, titled "The Catskill Flytyers," Flick gave credit to Jennings for getting him started in the pastime that would occupy his life. Flick said, "The greatest compliment I ever got on my tying was the time Preston told me, 'we have now reached the point where the pupil is doing a better job than the teacher.'" Art Flick continued where Jennings left off when he published his slender, pocket-size *Streamside Guide to Naturals and Their Imitations* (1947).

Flick put his fly rod aside for three years, during the mid-1930s, to assemble the mayfly emergence tables that would form the basis of his *Streamside Guide*. Considered a classic, Flick's *Guide* described for readers the important aquatic in-

sect species, especially mayflies, that emerged from the Schoharie's riffles and pools over the course of the fishing season. Along with his basic emergence tables, Flick provided information concerning trout fly patterns that could best imitate them. The patterns that Flick popularized in his book were not fancy attractor patterns; they were basic patterns tied to imitate almost all of the important mayflies found on the Schoharie.

Although dry flies were not the only patterns Flick described in his book, he is remembered first for the floaters he presented in his book pages. Some were his own creations; others were flies developed by earlier tiers that he had tweaked or slightly changed. Flick's selection included dry flies still well known and fished today—Quill Gordon, Hendrickson, American March Brown, Grey Fox, Light Cahill, Blue-Winged Olive, Dun Variant, Cream Variant, Grey Fox Variant, and Red Quill. Flick stood by this dry fly "hot list" for his entire career and consistently trumpeted their effectiveness on his home waters. He also encouraged patrons of his Westkill Tavern to try his selections.

Flick once said that he was trying to cater exclusively to fly anglers over other kinds of guests. He realized that the best strategy to attract fly fishers was to develop a set of patterns that would consistently produce well for them. Flick theorized that if his inn guests asked for advice on what flies would perform on neighboring streams, and he could show them successful patterns that took fish, he'd make new friends. And he could also expect return visits from them, assuming they were pleased with everything else at the hotel. Such strategy indeed worked for Flick—his famous dry-fly series was a performer for all.

Beyond promoting the series on his own Catskill streams, Flick crossed state lines into Pennsylvania, where he continued to promote the patterns that worked so well for him on the Schoharie. In the May 1952 issue of *Pennylvania Angler*, Flick crafted a story titled "Dry Fly Perception," in which he described himself as "a strict advocate of matching the hatch." He folded into the article his unabashed belief that his dry-fly series would "pretty much take care of fishermen right through the season, to successfully imitate the important mayflies that appear on most of our streams."

Fly tiers and followers of Catskill history might assume that the Red Quill, a fly created to imitate the *Ephemerella subvaria* male, was Flick's favorite, since many view it as his signature pattern.

He was proud of the Red Quill, to be sure, but his favorite on-water pattern was the Grey Fox Variant.

His mentor, Preston Jennings, also promoted a fly with the same name, although Flick altered the pattern, substituting stripped hackle quill for the gold tinsel body Jennings preferred. Flick also added a third hackle shade to the mix, combining brown hackle with the ginger and grizzly that Jennings

Preston Jennings at his tying table. *Catskill Fly Fishing Center and Museum collection*

liked. The Grey Fox Variant no doubt had Pennsylvania readers scratching their heads; the pattern hardly looked anything like a large natural Green Drake mayfly, *Ephemera guttulata*. Flick would be the first to say—and he did—that the large Grey Fox Variant looked like "a bale of hay floating down," but he still stood by the pattern as a hatch matcher. However, he commented that Green Drakes were not all that important on his Schoharie, writing, "I for one would never miss them." An additional value of the Grey Fox Variant, as well as the Cream Variant and Dun Variant, was its effectiveness as a general searching pattern at times when there were no hatches on the water and fish were not feeding.

So insistent was Flick that the Variants were great performers, regardless of the season, that he once told *New York Times* outdoor writer John W. Randolph that he'd use them all summer. In Randolph's May 18, 1958, article, Flick insisted he could take trout all summer on only six flies—the Variants in various sizes. He believed that presentation was more important than pattern and challenged anyone to prove him wrong. As effective as his Variants proved for Flick in the summer, however, during the spring his fly box was undoubtedly filled with Quill Gordons, Hendricksons, and his own Red Quills.

The Red Quill is indeed Art Flick's signature pattern. Flick fully acknowledged that he borrowed the name from an old English pattern. British fly angler John Waller Hills described a Red Quill in his classic *History of Fly Fishing for Trout* (1921), although the English version, with its starling wings, quill body, and brown hackle, looked nothing like Flick's creation. What Flick was most proud of was his use of stripped Rhode Island Red hackle quill for the body on his Red Quill, writing, "To the best of my knowledge, I must plead guilty to being the first to use this material for bodies in flies."

In his *Streamside Guide*, he mentioned that he had looked everywhere for evidence of prior use of that material for flies but found none. He cautiously added, "If someone else used it prior to 1933, and I am taking credit that rightfully belongs to another, I extend my humble apology." Indeed, British fly tier H. G. McClelland's *The Trout Fly Dresser's Cabinet of Devices* (1898) mentions using stripped dark red hackle quill for a pattern named the Jenny Spinner; thus the Red Quill was not the first pattern to use that material.

Preston Jennings described the Red Quill in his *Book of Trout Flies* with all the materials that were true to Flick's pattern—including the stripped "Red Cock" hackle quill body—yet curiously he did not credit Art Flick for its creation. However, in describing the dry fly that was created to imitate the *Ephemerella subvaria* female, both Flick and Jennings credited Roy Steenrod, Theodore Gordon's student, as its creator. Flick altered both Steenrod's and Jennings's dressings for the Hendrickson dry fly.

Flick was partial to using "pink fur from vixen of red fox," the shade derived from urine burns. He liked the pinkish cast

Streamside Guide first-edition jacket cover.

He didn't have much use for the hundreds of garish trout fly patterns that were common in the fly boxes of most anglers in his era. I have a pleasant memory of the first time I met Art Flick in person, after having exchanged letters for two or three years. During the summer of 1972, when I was staying with Catskill fly tiers Walt and Winnie Dette, Flick came walking through the shop door with Art and Kris Lee, on their way to fish for shad on the Delaware River. Flick was passing around the cover of his soon-to-be-released *Master Fly-Tying Guide* when he spotted me, an enthusiastic 18-year-old fly tier, still geared up in my fishing vest from an early-morning outing on the Willowemoc Creek. "I'm happy to see that," he said as he approached me, pointing and smiling. It wasn't one of his Red Quills or Hendricksons that had caught his eye—it was the Trout Unlimited patch on my vest. "Have you ever caught a shad on a fly?" he asked. I replied that I had not. He confessed that he had not either. Then, with the same grin, he bent over and

the fur provided and reported better success catching fish on his version than on flies tied with the fawn-colored red fox fur preferred by Jennings.

The mention of urine-burned fox fur required for Flick's Hendrickson version sent many of his readers, including me, into a tizzy trying to find the material. Shortly after I purchased the reissue of Flick's *Streamside Guide* in 1969, my search started. Although most Catskill fly tiers paid little attention to actually tying with the pinkish fur, I felt it was something I had to have. Skipping out of school one day and walking a couple miles to downtown Binghamton, New York, I found myself at a local wardrobe fur shop called De Paris. In the backroom where the costly coats were sewn, among the proprietor's fur scraps were some fox pieces. I walked out with a bag of the stuff, some having the pink stain necessary for Flick's Hendricksons. The agreement was that I would return with some trout flies in trade for the prized pink fox remainders. I kept my side of the bargain, but to the owner's annoyance, all the flies I handed him were Hair-Wing Royal Coachmans—none tied with his fur. For me, parting with any of the pink gold was not an option.

An interesting side note to the story is that Flick probably would have shunned the Royals himself; Flick once commented that he had never tied a Royal Coachman in his life.

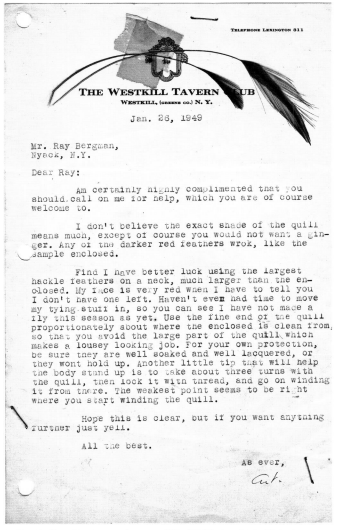

Letter to Ray Bergman, January 26, 1949, in which Flick described the stripped hackle quill used for his Red Quill dry-fly body. *Jill and Mark Schwarz collection*

added, "I'll tell you another secret—I've never tied a Royal Coachman!"

How I regret not having taken the time to run upstairs to my bedroom to retrieve my little *Streamside Guide*, purchased three years before Flick walked into the shop that day, so that he could sign it. The book still sits here on the shelf, its binding held together now with duct tape and its pages worn from over 40 years of companionship. I have other pleasant memories of corresponding with Flick from time to time after we finally met. Art Flick always returned letters, roughly typed on small stationery. Most of my inquiries had to do with his patterns and materials required to craft them.

It was interesting to study his tying style, which was somewhat different from that found among the tiers located in the southern Catskills on rivers such as the Beaverkill and Neversink. My 2009 book, *Tying Catskill-Style Dry Flies*, describes Flick's style of patterns compared with flies tied by Rube Cross, Roy Steenrod, Herm Christian, the Dettes, and the Darbees. Yet Flick's flies were equal in their beauty and craftsmanship, whether from his dry-fly series or the few sinking patterns he created and embraced.

Flick's book covered patterns beyond his dry flies, such as his effective Early Brown Stone wet fly and his Black-Nose Dace Bucktail. A few nymphs, imitating both mayflies and stoneflies, were also described in his book.

Most of Art's fly patterns emerged from my vise in the early years and still fill my fly box today. I'll always remember Art Flick as a great influence; others fondly remember his advice too.

Bert Darrow's introduction to fly fishing began decades ago on the historic Esopus Creek, which flows through the Catskills not all that far south of Flick's Schoharie. During the late 1970s, at a Trout Unlimited meeting along the Esopus's banks, Darrow had the opportunity to have his tying skills critiqued by Flick. Bert shared with me his thoughts on Art Flick and his tying style: "We had arranged to have Art give a tying demonstration that evening, but Art changed the plan—he really didn't like to tie in public. So, on his suggestion, I sat down at the table and tied some of his classic patterns. In the end, Flick's suggestion benefited me greatly; in essence I was able to get a tying lesson from him—and evaluation of my techniques. He told me that I was a very *consistent* tier—in terms of my dry-fly tail lengths, wing height, and hackle collar dimensions. The downside of Art's comments was that he said I was *consistently not adhering* to his recommended material proportions that combine to make a trout fly. Concerning hackle length, Art didn't base the barb length on hook gap width, as is common practice. He based hackle barb length on *wing length*; the wings were set, then hackle was measured against that dimension."

Bert Darrow has never forgotten the instruction he received from Art Flick that evening near the Esopus. Darrow's Catskill-style flies are beauties that are tied with consistency, just the way Art Flick would have loved to have seen them assembled. Darrow has told that story many times, always with a tone of admiration and reverence for his mentor at the vise, Art Flick.

Quill Gordon, tied by Art Flick. Flick used a Clorox solution to strip peacock eye feathers. This sometimes resulted in an overbleached, lightened quill body. *Catskill Fly Fishing Center and Museum collection*

Hendrickson, tied by Art Flick. *Catskill Fly Fishing Center and Museum collection*

Dun Variant, tied by Art Flick. Flick embraced the Dun Variant to imitate the *Isonychia bicolor* mayfly adults found on his home waters. It is still a popular pattern for that emergence. *Catskill Fly Fishing Center and Museum collection*

Cream Variant, tied by Art Flick. Flick liked this variant for imitating the late-season *Potomanthus* mayflies. *Catskill Fly Fishing Center and Museum collection*

Grey Fox Variant, tied by Art Flick. Although the Red Quill is considered his signature pattern, the Grey Fox Variant was his favorite.

Black-Nose Dace, tied by Art Flick. Flick commented that he wasn't much of a bucktail fisherman; this was the only pattern of that type he carried. He praised the pattern as a true fish getter. *Ted Patlen collection*

Early Brown Stone, tied by Mike Valla. Flick stated that the purpose of writing his *Streamside Guide* was to correlate dry flies to natural adult mayflies. However, he included a couple of stone-fly nymphs—the Stone Fly Creeper and this Early Brown Stone, which he fished wet.

March Brown, tied by Art Flick. Flick liked to use an orange thread for tying this pattern. The wings are tied with heavily barred lemon wood-duck flank. Flick altered his mentor Preston Jennings's dressing for the March Brown; Jennings favored mallard flank wings. *Catskill Fly Fishing Center and Museum collection*

Nymph patterns tied by Art Flick. Flick created nymph patterns that proved effective when the corresponding adult stage of the fly was on the water. From top: Dun Variant, Hendrickson, March Brown. *Ted Patlen collection*

Grey Fox, tied by Art Flick. This pattern was tied to imitate the lighter version of a March Brown. In Flick's time, the natural it imitated was labeled *Stenonema fuscum*. *Catskill Fly Fishing Center and Museum collection*

Blue-Winged Olive, tied by Art Flick. The fly pictured was sent to Catskill fly tier Walt Dette so that he could accurately tie the pattern for his customers. The BWO was left out of the original *Streamside Guide* because it had not been identified. *Mary Dette Clark collection*

CHAPTER 8

Edward Ringwood Hewitt
(1866–1957)

Edward Ringwood Hewitt sitting at his table tying flies. Hewitt was more a creator of trout fly designs than a prolific tier. He paid the Darbees and the Dettes to tie his own fly creations. *Catskill Fly Fishing Center and Museum collection*

Edward Ringwood Hewitt studied the mysteries of trout—and artificial flies that would entice them—with assiduous passion. It was an interest that began in his boyhood while roaming his grandfather's 20,000-acre estate at Ringwood Manor, New Jersey, his summer home. In his classic *A Trout and Salmon Fly Fisherman for Seventy-Five Years* (1948), he tells the story of fishing while he was still wearing dresses under the care of his nurse, at age four or five, from a bridge over the Ringwood River with a cut pole, string, and pin hook. He caught a chub, using a worm for bait, and it launched him into a lifetime of angling experiences that would follow. "All my life this early thrill has stayed with me and the incident is as vivid today as it was three-quarters of a century ago," Hewitt wrote.

Coming from a family of considerable means, Hewitt was able to explore the famous trout waters of the world while still a young man. He fished the rivers at Yellowstone when he was only 15, using both grasshoppers and flies. He visited the Nipigon in Canada and also fished throughout Europe, including France, Germany, and the British chalkstreams where he cast a

Brown Bivisible, tied by the Dettes in the late 1930s. Ed Hewitt wrote that the Brown Bivisible was visible to both trout and angler. It was the first in a series of Bivisible patterns featured and sold by both Ray Bergman and the Dettes.
Mary Dette Clark collection

line with G. E. M. Skues on the Itchen. The salmon rivers such as the Restigouche in New Brunswick also saw his fly line. Yet among all of his fishing travels and experiences, he seemed most passionate about Catskill trout streams, the Neversink chief among them.

Hewitt owned four and a half miles on the Neversink River, in the section that flowed between Hall's Bridge and Neversink, a long stretch that served as his laboratory. Given his background as a scientist and inventor who held many patents, it is no wonder that Ed Hewitt looked at trout habitat improvement theories, fly design, and fly fishing with an inquisitive eye. He tried to understand how trout might view a dry fly floating across its window and used the physics of light refraction and deflection to help him answer the question. There is a story about Hewitt and frequent fishing partner Jack Atherton, an illustrator and fly angler, getting down on their hands and knees and peering up at flies floating on the surface in an aquarium. The trout's perspective was always important, greatly influencing Hewitt's trout-fly designs and how he preferred them tied, whether by his hands or from the vise of another tier.

As Austin M. Francis noted in *Catskill Rivers: Birthplace of American Fly Fishing* (1983), Hewitt was more of a pattern creator and experimenter than a prolific fly tier. He did tie flies, but once the creation phase was completed, he often turned to commercial tiers to produce large numbers of his patterns both for his own use and for the pleasure of his fishing friends. Hewitt also had Catskill commercial fly tiers such the Darbees and Dettes provide flies; they tied such patterns as his Neversink Skater, Brown Bivisible, and flat-bodied nymphs.

The Skater was an interesting dry fly, a pattern that intrigued Atherton, who spent many a day on Hewitt's private Neversink water. The fly fell out of favor over the years because of the continued difficulty in locating the very large-barbed, stiff hackle required for the fly. Even in Hewitt's time, he said, "You won't find it on sale in any tackle stores, as few suitable feathers are available." Harry Darbee wrote in *Catskill Flytier* that he and Elsie put aside their longest and stiffest hackle for Hewitt's creations; they tied most of Hewitt's Skaters.

To create a Skater, they tied the 2-inch-diameter hackle, usually ginger, on a size 16 hook. The three large saddle or spade hackles were tied in just ahead of the hook point in a specific manner, the back hackle with the shiny side facing toward the hook bend, the front with the shiny side facing

The upper Neversink River in the Catskills. Hewitt's Neversink water was largely flooded upon the construction of Neversink Dam. The stream still serves as a reminder of Hewitt and his fly pattern contributions—flat-bodied nymphs, Bivisibles, and the famous Neversink Skater.

Ed Hewitt on the water. Hewitt spent a lifetime trying to understand the trout's perspective when designing flies. *Catskill Fly Fishing Center and Museum collection*

the hook eye, and the center hackle in either direction. The flies were tailless. While ginger was the most common shade, grizzly, dun, and brown were also employed.

Hewitt designed the fly to imitate butterflies; the large trout he had seen feeding on a fluttering natural inspired his creativity, if not his tale telling. His story about designing a new fly in response to the white or yellow naturals that tempted trout on his slow, still pools appeared first in the August 1937 issue of the *Sportsman* magazine, then later in an abridged form in his book *A Trout and Salmon Fisherman for Seventy-Five Years*, where he wrote, "It became evident to me that large winged flies in some way did not appear like butterflies to trout, and they therefore ignored them. I studied this problem carefully and came to the following conclusions. The butterflies did not rest on the water; they sometimes touched it but were always moving. When they did touch the water they only did so very lightly and were away again. I could not imitate this procedure with any flies I had in my box. How was I to do this? I went back to my camp and tied several flies, finally making what is known as the Neversink Skater."

Hewitt admitted that the Skater was not a durable fly and had to be put aside for a fresh one once it became waterlogged. Yet he stood by his concept, skipping and hopping the fly over his Neversink Big Bend Club waters. Fishing the big-hackled dry fly right in the middle of a July day, he managed to entice big trout. "The fly made only two jumps over the water, a large trout of about four pounds leaped right out of water right over the fly like a porpoise and missed it entirely, and before it had time to come again a smaller trout repeated the maneuver," Hewitt wrote.

After tweaking the method for best fishing the fly, moving it more slowly across the water, Hewitt and his son, whom he awakened from a nap to join the excitement, caught half a dozen fine trout. More experimentation, fishing the Skater right under his famous Neversink plank dams, brought promising results—enough to impress his angling friend Jack Atherton, who wrote about his own experiences fishing the pattern. In *The Fly and the Fish* (1951), Atherton said that his friendship with Ed Hewitt was "one of the most pleasant associations of my fishing career." He admired Hewitt's contributions to fly angling, citing the Neversink Skater as an example. Mollie's Pool was a favorite fishing spot; eating lunch on the high bank above the water, the two friends would watch big trout feeding in the pocketwater near their vantage point. Using his favorite red-brown hackle Neversink Skater, Atherton hooked a fish they nicknamed "Aunt Sally" several times but failed to land her. He also loved to fish the Skater under Hewitt's plank dams, working it in jerks right in the plunge pool foam. "One of the great attractions in fishing the large spiders, or skaters, is that frequently the trout clears the water in rising, taking the fly on the way down," Atherton wrote. He also said that whether or not he hooked the fish, or if the fish broke off, the experience was a "supreme thrill."

Besides impressing Atherton, Hewitt's Neversink Skater also intrigued other American fly anglers, such as Pennsylvania's Charles Fox, Vincent Marinaro, and Ed Shenk. Many fly tiers and anglers most associate Fox, Marinaro, and Shenk with patterns developed for hypercritical brown trout on their home limestone streams, particularly the Letort Spring Run. But all three fished Hewitt's skater pattern, and recognized its effectiveness in taking trout. The three crossed state lines, so to speak, when they adopted Hewitt's Skater. Fox was sniffing out Hewitt's creation in the early 1940s. In his March 1942 *Pennsylvania Angler* article titled "Some Dry Flies Up Close," a story that described Hewitt's Skater, Fox wrote, "If undue excitement has a bad physical effect on you, refrain from butterfly fishing. In the first place it will bring to the surface large trout, and that is a big order for a dry fly. In the second place the big trout frequently lunge and jump at the spiders without touching them, making a great surface commotion which is nerve racking."

Fox's sustained interest in the Skater led to a follow-up story that appeared in the May 1943 issue of the same magazine, titled "Skater Dry Fly Fishing," where he wrote, "Just received a copy of the intensely interesting book, *Telling on Trout*, written by the dean of American trout fisherman, Mr. Edward R. Hewitt, and in it is written a note which reads as follows: 'To Charles K. Fox, who has made the discovery that I told the truth about Neversink Skaters.'"

Charlie Fox's contemporary Vince Marinaro also chimed in on Hewitt's fly and how Fox first learned of it. However, readers wouldn't learn the whole story behind Hewitt, Fox, and the Skater for many years. In his June 1976 *Outdoor Life* article, "Secret of the Neversink Skater," Marinaro tells the story that Charlie Fox was sitting in his physician's office waiting room one day. He picked up a magazine and saw an article written by Hewitt titled "Butterfly Fishing." He was so intrigued by the story that he returned to the waiting room chair after his appointment and resumed reading. Fox fired off a letter to Hewitt and soon was in possession of a handful of the unique dry flies. Skating the flies on Spring Creek in Bellefonte, Pennsylvania, resulted in netting so many fish that Fox called the Neversink Skater "the greatest fish-finder in the world."

Fox took his last remaining fly with him to Penns Creek, where he fished it during a Green Drake hatch and enjoyed phenomenal results. He had to have more of them, but Hewitt couldn't supply them quickly enough. Fox, along with Marinaro and others, tried dissecting the flies with a razor blade to learn the secret of how they were constructed. But the technique Hewitt and his "mystery man tier"—probably Harry Darbee—used to create a "cupped" feature of hackle barbs facing each other, ending in a knifelike edge at top and bottom, eluded them.

Hewitt wasn't talking, but Marinaro finally figured out the technique. He showed a few friends he felt were trustworthy how it was done, provided they wouldn't disclose the secret for as long as Hewitt was living. Only one violated the promise, and Marinaro never trusted him again.

Now armed with ample Skater supplies in their boxes, Marinaro and Fox fished them to a variety of fish—trout, bass, and Atlantic salmon. Marinaro fished bass waters on his neighboring rivers, such as the Susquehanna, Juniata, and Conodoguinet. When fishing those streams, the Neversink Skater was the only fly he carried. Fellow LeTort spring-run fly angler Ed Shenk also kept a supply of Hewitt Skaters in his fly box from the late 1930s until the mid-1950s.

Shenk found the big-hackled flies to be great fish movers. If a big brown moved to the fly when Ed fished it, but he was unable to hook the fish, he marked the location and returned later with his standard favorite patterns, ants or small marabou streamers. Shenk's March 1988 *Fly Fisherman* magazine article, "The Skater Spider," describes his experiences with the fly both on home waters and out west on the Big Hole River below Melrose, Montana.

Beyond its effectiveness on New York and Pennsylvania waters, the fluffy-looking Skaters also surprised fly anglers across the great pond. Ed Hewitt carried it with him to Scotland, where a gillie informed him, "Ye will catch no fush with yon feather duster." Within short time, a 4-pound Loch Ordie trout smashed the Skater. After witnessing trout engaged in a feeding frenzy after Hewitt's fly, the gillie asked if he had any more "feather dusters." The Neversink Skater was effective in many different trout waters, both in America and abroad. Hewitt used them on the Test, the Snake River in Idaho, the Rogue in Oregon, and the Grand Lake Stream in Maine, where one of his angling friends took 80 landlocked salmon. However, many would disagree with Harry Darbee's comment in *Catskill Flytier* that this was the "best known of Hewitt's flies."

While some may not realize who first created the pattern, Hewitt's Brown Bivisible dry fly is far better known than the Neversink Skater.

Crafted entirely from hackle and thread, the Bivisible is relatively easy to tie. The extralong hackle barb needed for the Skater is not required for the two-toned Bivisible, which is tied by palmering brown hackle up the hook shank, finished off with a couple turns of white hackle just short of the hook eye. Hewitt based the pattern design on his theory concerning the trout's perspective. His theory was that dark colors, no matter what pattern, are more easily seen from the trout's vantage point from below the water surface than are light-colored flies. Such darker flies may be more easily noticed by the trout, but they are more difficult for the angler to see and follow as they drift along in the current. Hewitt's Bivisible, with its anterior wisps of white hackle fronting brown, got its name for its visibility to both trout and angler—the trout spots the brown, the angler spots the white.

In the early years, many notable fly tiers—such as the Dettes, Ray Bergman, and Rube Cross—highlighted Hewitt's Bivisibles, from the basic Brown Bivisible to many other variations. The Dettes listed Blue, Olive, and Gordon Quill Bivisibles in their first catalog, released in the early 1930s. Their second catalog, dating from 1935, was reproduced and printed in Eric Leiser's fine book about the fly-tying couple. A comprehensive pattern list shows a few more were added to the series, among them the Light Cahill, Gray Grizzle, and Royal Coachman Bivisibles. In the late 1930s, the Dettes also tied a Badger and a Black Bivisible.

Besides the Dettes, other Catskill fly tiers mentioned Hewitt's then very popular dry fly. In *Fur, Feathers and Steel* (1940), Rube Cross wrote, "A very good example and effective pattern of the hackle fly is the Bivisible Royal Coachman which I believe was brought out by the well-known author and angler Edward R. Hewitt. This pattern has the regular body and tail of a Royal Coachman, with brown hackle tied on the regular way and a white hackle wound in front. Bill Lawrence takes most of his fish from the Neversink on this fly year after year."

Catskill school tiers, including Rube Cross, the Dettes, the Darbees, and Ray Smith, tied and sold the Brown Bivisible. But well-known fly-fishing authors such as Ray Bergman also helped raise the profile of Ed Hewitt's creation. In *Just Fishing* (1932), Bergman featured the Brown, Black, and Badger Bivisibles in the color plates illustrated by Dr. Edgar Burke, who used samples obtained from the well-known Wm. Mills and Son supply house. A black and white illustration supporting Bergman's text also shows a Royal Coachman Bivisible. Along with the illustrations, Bergman made some favorable remarks concerning the pattern: "In my estimation the advent of the Bivisible flies marked a great improvement in flies for dry fly fishing. E. R. Hewitt, always a constructive pioneer in the art of trout fishing, is responsible for the introduction of this pattern. With it he solved the problem of floating a fly satisfactorily for many a tryo and also improved the game of many an old timer. These Bivisibles float high, it is hard indeed to sink them, they are easily seen when floating on the stream and

A TROUT
and
SALMON
FISHERMAN
For Seventy-five Years
by
Edward R. Hewitt
AUTHOR OF
TELLING ON THE TROUT, ETC.

CHARLES SCRIBNER'S SONS, NEW YORK
CHARLES SCRIBNER'S SONS LTD. LONDON
1948

Hewitt's 1948 *A Trout and Salmon Fisherman for Seventy-Five Years* introduced many anglers to his creations such as the Neversink Skater, Bivisible, and flat, hard-bodied nymphs.

the trout take them very well. Certainly one cannot ask for anything better than that."

In *Trout* (1938), Bergman gave additional enthusiastic coverage to the pattern, highlighting his first experiences with the Brown Bivisible. This was the first transitional dry fly he ever fished; up until then, he had relied on his regular "pet" patterns such as the double slip quill winged Whirling Dun and Royal Coachman. The color dry-fly plate in *Trout* featured six regular Bivisibles, with the white hackle just behind the hook eye, as well as a Pink Lady Bivisible, which featured green or yellow hackle behind the hook eye.

Bergman also made some brief notations in this book concerning Hewitt's nymph patterns. Just as Hewitt was not shy about dry-fly design, he had plenty to say about nymph patterns. Bergman showcased three Hewitt patterns, calling them "outstanding contributions" and featuring them in his nymph color plate illustrations. Hewitt was a proponent of flat-bodied nymphs, creations that were born on the Neversink River in 1933 while he was fishing with John Alden Knight.

In contrast to Oregon tier Polly Rosborough's fuzzy nymphs, the patterns that Hewitt and Knight created were flat, stiff, and hard. After attaching fur bodies to the hook shank, they dipped the completed flies in lacquer, then smashed them flat with small pliers. It was an interesting pattern, the result of careful observation onstream, but the flies never gained popularity and have been largely forgotten.

Although Hewitt's nymphs are rarely seen occupying a modern fly box, and his once cherished Neversink Skater is also long forgotten, Bivisibles may be moribund yet still hanging on for dear life. This pattern is still found in the most basic fly-tying manuals, especially those directed at youth, such as Dr. Ron Howard's popular 4-H publication, *Basic Fly Tying*, which includes step-by-step directions for the Brown Bivisible. Some contemporary fly anglers continue to rely on the pattern.

Cory Layton, a Catskill stream enthusiast, still casts the pattern on his favorite waters. Cory shared the following with me concerning the fly: "I fish a Brown Bivisible all the time on small Catskill pocketwater," he said. "Its abundant hackles keep it floating like a cork, as it tumbles through rippling seams, and, of course, it's easy to see. It does well on native brookies and browns." Teddy Patlen, a Lodi, New Jersey, fly angler who has tied the fly for decades, offered to me his own observations on the Bivisibles: "Way back when we had hair and eyes that focused in last light . . . everyone used that Bivisible. Everyone caught fish, of course, but then we got sophisticated and found 'new and better' stuff to throw at the fish. I didn't use them for a long time, but I went back to them the last couple of years. The fish still hit them. During a time of low water, during a very hot stretch we had in a recent season, I used them as a change-up from the micro stuff the fish have been feeding on. There were days that I caught fish on size 26 Bivisibles."

Cory Layton and Ted Patlen have not abandoned the famous Bivisible dry fly; their positive experiences with it on the water have given it an honored corner in their fly boxes. Catskill guide Walt Ackerman has not forgotten Hewitt's gem either. "I started tying Bivisibles in 1963," he said. "It was one of the first dry flies I tied. I still use them in several colors, although for some reason the classic brown with a twist of white at the head is far and away the most productive. I have found that the original Hewitt pattern that calls for a tail made of hackle points outfishes a fly with the standard hackle fiber tail. I have tested that theory many ways, including fishing two flies at the same time with one trailing the other, and then changing which is the lead or trail fly to eliminate the difference that position might make. This is also the fly I use

to teach people how to 'skitter' a fly. You know, dance the fly around on the surface of a riffle to entice fish up to hit it. It works amazingly well. I tie this fly like Hewitt, with the hackle packed on very tightly."

The famous Neversink Skater, which Ed Hewitt, Jack Atherton, and others once danced below the plank dam plunge pools at Big Bend Club, likely will never return to popularity. Nor will Hewitt's lacquer-soaked, plier-squashed flat-bodied nymphs, although the design concept was continued by tiers such as Ed Sisty of Denver, who once sold a series of flat nymphs tied with raffia. Others have carried on the flat nymph experimentations as well. However, many Bivisible fishers would not be surprised if this old pattern of Hewitt's made a comeback.

Hewitt's Neversink Skater, tied by Vincent C. Marinaro. Hewitt originally recommended tying the pattern on a size 16 dry-fly hook with ginger hackles. However, Pennsylvania great Marinaro tied it in larger sizes; it was a good salmon dry-fly pattern. *Pennsylvania Fly Fishing Association collection*

Royal Coachman Bivisible, tied by the Dettes in the late 1930s. *Mary Dette Clark collection*

Light Cahill Bivisible, tied by the Dettes in the late 1930s. *Mary Dette Clark collection*

Black Bivisible, tied by the Dettes in the late 1930s. *Mary Dette Clark collection*

Badger Bivisible, tied by the Dettes in the late 1930s. *Mary Dette Clark collection*

Olive Bivisible, tied by the Dettes in the late 1930s. *Mary Dette Clark collection*

Blue Dun Bivisible, tied by the Dettes in the late 1930s. *Mary Dette Clark collection*

Hewitt-Knight flat-bodied nymph, original fly tied by John Alden Knight in 1933. The duo developed this fly while fishing the Neversink River in the 1930s. The fur-bodied fly was dipped in lacquer, then squeezed slightly flat with pliers. *Catskill Fly Fishing Center and Museum collection*

CHAPTER 9

John Atherton
(1900–1952)

John Atherton, an accomplished illustrator, brought to his trout flies the tenets practiced by the impressionistic school of artists. *American Museum of Fly Fishing collection*

Atherton Number Five dry fly, tied by Mike Valla. The Number Five, from John Atherton's regular dry-fly series, exemplifies the use of mixed hackle shades, sparkling tinsel ribbing, and wood-duck wings, all of which cause the fly to project impressionistic qualities.

At a Museum of Modern Art exhibition in 1943, illustrator and fly tier John Atherton said, "Any painting lives or will last because it is well painted, regardless of whether it is a potato or a human body." These words could aptly be applied to trout flies: well-tied fly patterns that take fish will live and last. While it is unfortunate that Atherton's creative and effective fly patterns have lost popularity, the basic principles by which they were created are still employed today. However, fly anglers had only relatively short direct exposure to his fly design theories, as John "Jack" Atherton was only 52 years old when he drowned while fly fishing for salmon in New Brunswick. Atherton's fishing friends Lee Wulff and Walter Squires helped his wife Maxine bury his ashes under a small maple tree along one of his favorite pools on his beloved Battenkill River at Arlington, Vermont.

Battenkill River, Arlington, Vermont. Atherton owned a home not far downstream from this stretch. Atherton's ashes were buried under the root of a small maple tree on the bank of the Battenkill by his wife, Maxine, with the help of fishing companions Lee Wulff and Walter Squires.

Maxine, his wife, once wrote that Jack had said many times that when his last day came, he hoped he would be in his waders. It is remarkable what he accomplished in his short life, both as an artist and as a passionate fly tier and angler. Both endeavors were intimately interrelated; his perspective as a painter influenced how he looked at fly pattern design, taking into account how colors and tones, textures, and light reflections combined in natural insects. He was surprised that the dull, bland, solid-colored artificial flies took trout at all. Such thoughts were the essence of his seminal 1951 work, *The Fly and the Fish*, a landmark book that injected the principles of impressionism into fly tying. In a chapter titled "Flies and Impressionism," Atherton wrote, "If you look closely at a live dun (not one in a specimen bottle) you will observe that his coloring is 'impressionistic.' It is built up of many variations of tone such as we find in the paintings of Renoir, Monet and others of the impressionistic school of art."

With the keen eye of a talented artist, Atherton noted that natural insects are a kaleidoscope of colors, from head to thorax to tail, both dorsal and ventral sides. A natural fly's thorax might reveal yellows, blues, and even pink color tones when carefully examined. Veined mayfly wings often have dark

spots and often reflect sunlight, which accentuates those features. Atherton believed that trout flies should exhibit the appearance of life, and that tiers needed to take all the above characteristics of natural insects into consideration. He conveyed the importance of creating lifelike qualities with an example drawn from the principles of impressionism: "If an artist were to thoroughly mix certain colors to obtain a gray and then apply it to the canvas, the gray would be devoid of any life-like quality. But, if he should apply the same colors directly to the canvas without mixing them beforehand the result would have a great deal more vibration, light and life. At close range, the effect would be one of a mixture of colors. But at a slight distance they would appear close to the color and value of his original mixed gray, except that it would be alive and not dead." Creating "the appearance of life" was Jack Atherton's fundamental goal in crafting flies. Lifelike qualities were expressed in his patterns through careful material selection used for wings, body material, and hackle.

For wings on dry flies, Atherton liked wood duck, Bali duck, and hackle point feathers. Wood duck, although opaque, offered a "speckled look" and provided lifelike characteristics, breaking up the fly's outline. Bali duck was a much darker shade than wood duck and more closely matched the wings of some of the darker mayflies. Atherton believed that hackle points best represented the natural wings, although their biggest shortfall was their fragility. "There is nothing quite so good for imitating the very light pale duns," he wrote. "The glassy natural dun hackle point is amazingly life-like."

Atherton applied the same kind of careful analysis to the body materials. Many dry-fly patterns routinely fished in his era were beautiful, sometimes garish, but they were devoid of lifelike qualities. Atherton frowned upon silk flies, such as the old orange-bodied Queen of Waters, and wool patterns, like the sparkling yellow-bodied Flight's Fancy. Silk and wool darken when wet, cannot hold their colors, and soak in water, rendering them poor choices for dry flies. Atherton saw that natural fur provided qualities that wool and silk lacked; different fur shades, either natural or dyed, could be readily mixed and combined by hand.

He loved the sheen of seal fur and used it often in dry-fly as well as wet-fly patterns, writing, "Dubbing such as seal's fur is excellent for wet flies. It gives the effect of something alive which carries little bubbles of air. It adds a tremendous amount of life to any fly."

Natural or dyed seal combined with other furs such as muskrat and hare's ear provided texture along with bits of color and tone that suggested the qualities found in living things. Atherton felt strongly that fly bodies should "have a certain *authority*," the "juicy succulence of the natural." Seal fur added the quality of translucence that Atherton preferred in his patterns. He also liked his flies tied with enough body material to suggest a tasty food morsel, yet not so much as to make it overly clumsy in appearance.

Atherton nearly always ribbed his flies with bright oval gold tinsel, a material that added sparkle and shimmer such as is found in natural insects. He felt that flat tinsel was too weak and wire was too fine and easily buried under his mixed fur and seal fly bodies.

The overriding rule in Jack Atherton patterns—whether dry flies, wet flies, or nymphs—was that the final products should reflect the principles of impressionism. He achieved this not only through careful blending of furs accented with tinsel ribbing, but also through hackle shade selection and application. Hackle always created challenges for fly tiers in Atherton's era.

One can only imagine what Jack Atherton would have thought if he had lived in today's era of modern genetic hackle. He undoubtedly would have marveled at the vast array of hackle shades readily available, providing the qualities of barb stiffness and thin quills that made for easy wrapping on the hook shank. His words said it all when he wrote, "We all live in hope that by some strange turn of fortune we shall become the possessor of the ideal neck, the color being neither too light nor too dark, the suggestion of red in the dun of the exact proportion, and the stiffness dangerous to our fingers. It is something we can dream of to

the end of our lives as it will undoubtedly be still only a dream even then."

So insistent was he on having hackle of just the right quality and stiffness that Atherton traded one of his original paintings for a neck from a fly-fishing friend who allowed chickens to fly around his yard and roost in trees. Beyond the stiffness required for dry flies, he insisted on using the cross-bred variety of hackle with specks and splotches of browns, tans, and whites. He liked rusty duns that had brown streaks accentuating the gray tones and shades. Variegated hackle wedded to mixed-fur bodies enhanced the impressionistic qualities of Atherton's flies. His dry-fly, wet-fly, and nymph series exemplified the lifelike qualities he strived for in his creations.

Of all the flies that Atherton designed, from the tiniest drys to salmon flies, he is remembered primarily for his famous dry-fly series, with the flies simply labeled as Number One through Number Seven. No specific names were attached to these patterns other than the numbers. In designing the series, Atherton's goal was to create a comprehensive set that featured color progressions from light to dark, representing the gradations found in natural insects.

Number One in the dry-fly series was crafted to represent the lightest mayflies. Pale ginger mixed with very light grizzly hackle fronted pale cream fox fur ribbed with oval gold tinsel.

Pale dun hackle points served for wings. At the other extreme, Number Six is dark, its wings created from Bali duck or bronze mallard, its body formed from reddish brown seal and dark muskrat, and its hackle of rusty dun.

Atherton acknowledged that while the dry-fly series was a good basic set of floating flies, an angler's fly box should also contain a few standard patterns. It is not surprising that the Adams was among the standard dry-fly patterns he mentioned. The Adams had many qualities that he favored: mixed variegated hackle and tails, along with grizzly hackle point wings. The impressionistic, lifelike qualities found in the Adams blended perfectly with Atherton's requirements.

My own little Wemoc Adams, conceived years ago while fishing Willowemoc Creek in the Catskills, reflects Jack Atherton's influences and uses materials that give lifelike attributes to the pattern. The Wemoc Adams features cree hackle, which gives it tones and shades characteristic of Atherton's dry flies, along with gold wire or fine oval tinsel ribbing to provide sparkle and segmentation. The use of cree is an added advantage of the Wemoc Adams over a regular Adams. Cree provides all of the qualities obtained by mixing brown hackle with grizzly and serves as an "instant" Adams hackle. The gold wire also helps keep the muskrat fur body firmly attached to the hook shank.

Atherton also tweaked other standard patterns, such as the American March Brown, by blending fur with seal and hare's ear and accentuating with oval gold tinsel ribbing. His version of the American March Brown was based on the principles so prevalent in Jack Atherton's patterns.

Beyond dry flies, Atherton also applied impressionist principles to a short series of wet flies and nymphs he designed. Standard solid-color quill-winged wets did not display the impressionistic features that were so important to Atherton's theories. For winging, he relied on wood duck, bronze mallard, and pheasant feathers, which gave the fly the color splotches and variegations that helped make it appear more lifelike. Solid-colored hackle hanging off a wet-fly throat had no place in his flies either; nature did not create solid-shaded fly legs. Cree or grizzly hackles were his favorites for representing natural legs on wet flies. His wet fly Number Five exemplifies the mottled, lifelike buggy appearance Atherton loved, fulfilling all his impressionistic requirements. The same could be said for his series of three nymphs, in which Number One was light, Number Two was a medium tone, and Number Three was a very dark, rough-bodied nymph.

While Atherton strived to bring to his favored nymph patterns the same design scrutiny exhibited in his famous dry flies and wet flies, standard patterns filled his fly box when he pursued steelhead. Although Atherton's name is usually associated with trout and salmon fishing, steelhead were at the top of his list. He stated that the best fish species was whatever one he was fishing at that moment, but "if I could invariably have my choice of locality, river, and type of fishing I am inclined to believe that my favorite would be a fresh-run steelhead in a clear fast stream."

Atherton favored common steelhead flies like C. Jim Pray's Thor along with standards such as the Queen Bess and Van Luven. He knew these flies took fish but conjectured that "steelhead anglers who are fly tiers could find a large field for experiment in the direction of impressionism, and I'm sure their time would not be wasted." He liked the shimmer that tinsel added to the standard patterns and the sheen polar bear hair provided in flies like the Thor. Most appealing to Atherton were the colors that characterized many steelhead patterns. "And certainly 'color,' as such, is not lacking in steelhead flies!" he wrote. "They are truly gorgeous creations."

Gorgeous steelhead patterns were not the only flies Atherton tied for anadromous fish; Atlantic salmon patterns were also on his list. In addition to his May 1946 *Fortune* magazine color illustrations featuring classic trout flies (in the article "Fly Fishing and Trout Flies" by John McDonald), Atherton followed up in the June 1948 issue of the same magazine (in an article titled "The Leaper," also penned by McDonald), with paintings of salmon flies. He was well aware that thousands of patterns existed, but for the sake of practicality, he decided to focus attention on just a handful of examples.

In *The Fly and the Fish*, his approach involved reducing his list to a few patterns: light, medium, and dark representatives. The book featured color illustrations covering patterns such as the Jock Scott, Bastard Dose, and Blackville, presented from the simplest to the more complex.

Between the trout, salmon, and steelhead patterns featured in his book and the trout and salmon flies he illustrated in *Fortune*, it is not surprising that he was able to influence fly tiers everywhere, from the East Coast to the West. Among those he reached on the West Coast was a reclusive man who has been called one of the most talented steelhead tiers who ever lived: Edward Livingston Haas.

In a story Eric Leiser wrote on Haas for the *Art of Angling Journal*, we learn that Haas lived for nearly two decades in seclusion, "deep in the boondocks of the Klamath National Forest in the Salmon Mountains of Northern California." He lived a hermitlike lifestyle in a cabin that could be reached only by driving along a three-and-a-half-mile stretch of one-lane road with a sign that read, "Not recommended for campers, trailers, or drivers inexperienced in mountain driving." Leiser was one of the few who ever dared drive along the treacherous road, unprotected by guardrails, facing 500-foot drop-offs overlooking the Salmon River. Haas tied some 300 to 400 dozen flies every year in the remote cabin he had built with his own hands in 1966, selling them wholesale to André Puyans's Creative Sports fly-fishing shop. "We never met Haas in person," Jannifer Puyans told me in a recent chat, "but he and André spoke on the phone often. André admired his flies, and we sold lots of them."

The small heads on Haas flies are both beautiful and almost indestructible, the work of an artist, a man whom Scott Gingerich called in a 2001 *Art of Angling* article a very literate

Atherton on a trout stream. Atherton said many times that when his last day came, he hoped he would be in his waders. Indeed, he died by drowning while salmon fishing. *American Museum of Fly Fishing collection*

yet "eccentric genius." Scott also said that Haas's flies were "the best steelhead flies in the world, and most fishermen would agree that they are among the finest ties in existence." In his article, Gingerich offered insight into Haas's inspirations that resulted such stunning flies. Haas admired the work of C. Jim Pray and Peter Schwab, but John Atherton was cited as an influence.

Haas mentioned one of Atherton's favorite patterns, the Blackville, which Haas erroneously called a Blackwell in a quote that appeared in Gingerich's article: "I can't afford to tie the complicated flies like the Blackwell . . . the body of my flies are the same but I just put a different wing on it: hair wings and what have you. They (Atherton's) are much prettier, but the time involved in putting them together so that they are indestructible doesn't warrant it, so what I've done is simplify the fly as much as I can because it is strictly to catch fish with."

Ed Haas's steelhead flies are extreme examples of Atherton's influences on fly tiers, who created flies much removed from the delicate impressionistic dry flies tied to drift along eastern waters such as the Battenkill and Beaverkill Rivers. Yet both types of flies were crafted by artists. Atherton's and Haas's patterns no doubt will be remembered as art forms, as well as for being fish catchers.

John Atherton also liked variant dry flies, long-hackled patterns often tied with gold tinsel bodies and mixed-shade hackles. Furnace hackle, with its black center, was used in this fly tied by Atherton. *Bill Leary collection*

Atherton Number Two dry fly, tied by Mike Valla. This Atherton pattern used a mix of light cree and dun hackle, along with the characteristic narrow oval gold tinsel ribbing found in Atherton dry flies.

Atherton Number One dry fly, tied by Mike Valla. Pale ginger and pale cree hackles were mixed to create the lightest in the Atherton series of dry flies.

Atherton Number Six dry fly, tied by Mike Valla. Atherton sometimes used bronze mallard for dry-fly wings, as a substitute for Bali duck. Dun and brown hackle were combined in this pattern.

Atherton Number Three dry fly, tied by Mike Valla. Atherton called for a mixture of dun and ginger hackle in this yellow-bodied pattern.

Atherton dry fly, tied by John Atherton. Seal fur was a common material used by Atherton in many of his patterns. The fly pictured here is unidentified. *Bill Leary collection*

Atherton Number Four dry fly, tied by Mike Valla. Atherton created this pattern for pinkish-bodied naturals. The hackle is a mixture of dun and cree.

Atherton Number Five wet fly, tied by Mike Valla. Atherton designed wet flies using the same principles of color and shade applied to his dry flies. The tails and wings of this fly are bronze mallard, and the body is reddish brown muskrat mix.

Atherton applied red, pink, and buff shades to this unidentified variant he tied. Such shade mixtures were typical of Atherton flies. *Bill Leary collection*

Atherton Number Three dark nymph, tied by Mike Valla. Notice the body created by mixing different shades of seal and muskrat fur. Atherton's mixtures followed the same theories of impressionism as in his trout flies. The wing cases as tied in the original pattern called for the bright blue feather of an English kingfisher. Atherton recommended silk floss of the same color as a substitute.

Atherton Number One light nymph, tied by Mike Valla. This Atherton nymph combined the qualities, textures, and shades of natural seal fur ribbed with oval gold tinsel. Two tiny jungle cock eyes formed the wing cases.

Blackville Salmon Fly, tied by John Bonasera. Atherton loved tying salmon flies but tried to keep his list to a minimum. The Blackville was on his list of seven favorites.

Atherton Number Two nymph, tied by Mike Valla. Atherton liked the texture of this fly, with the picked-out hare's ear body simulating the gills of a natural nymph. Its wing cases use the same bright blue material as in the Atherton Number Three nymph pattern.

Wemoc Adams, created and tied by Mike Valla. This fly was created for fishing on Willowemoc Creek in the Catskill region of New York State. The shade mixture found in cree hackle combined with the sparkle from the gold wire ribbing make a very impressionistic pattern that meets Atherton's fly design aesthetic and fishes well.

CHAPTER 10

John Alden Knight
(1890–1966)

John Alden Knight was one of the most accomplished fly anglers of his era. He fished for everything from salmon to trout to bass. By no means a fly-fishing purist, he maintained that the black bass was a fish worthy of the fly rod. *American Museum of Fly Fishing*

John Alden Knight was a passionate sportsman who took full advantage of the natural world that surrounded him. His outdoor books and magazine articles were wide in scope, covering his hunting and fishing strategies that were based on careful observation and study in the field. Many primarily associate his name with his controversial solunar theory, which explained how animals move and behave depending on the location of the moon. Yet he was much admired by fly anglers, both warmwater and coldwater enthusiasts.

Knight loved bass fishing on the upper Delaware River as well as the streams flowing near his home in Williamsport, Pennsylvania, including the North Branch of the Susquehanna, where he fished Joe Messinger Sr.'s Hair Frog.

Bass angling also took him to Currituck Sound, North Carolina, where he fished bass bugs with Joe Brooks along the shorelines. Knight enjoyed casting for Atlantic salmon on Quebec's famed Matapedia, which he said reminded him of the Delaware, and fly fishing for trout with Ed Hewitt on New York's Neversink River. Besides Brooks and Hewitt, Knight surrounded

Mickey Finn, tied by John Alden Knight in 1937 in Canada.
Catskill Fly Fishing Center and Museum collection

himself with a veritable "who's who" of fly-fishing notables. Preston Jennings, who penned the now classic *Book of Trout Flies* (1935), shared water with Knight, as did George M. L. La Branche, author of *The Dry Fly and Fast Water* (1914).

John Alden Knight was not a fly-fishing purist by any means—he dabbled in bait and plug fishing as well—yet he made his mark with the long rod and the fly patterns he fished. His *Complete Book of Fly Casting* (1963), coauthored with his son Richard Alden Knight, was one of the first casting books that described techniques with descriptive photography. He popularized several fly patterns that he did not originate, such as the still popular red and yellow Mickey Finn Bucktail. However, it was Knight's interesting new fly creations, particularly nymphs that he and Ed Hewitt designed on the Neversink, that drew early attention from fly anglers as far back as the 1930s.

Concerning nymphs, Knight wrote in *Fishing for Trout and Bass* (1949), "There is nothing particularly new about nymph fishing. British anglers have been using artificial nymphs quite successfully on their chalk streams for thirty years or more. For almost that length of time the firm William Mills & Son of New York City has listed in their catalogues the American Nature Lures of the late Louis Rhead, among which are sev-

eral nymph patterns. However, on American waters the artificial nymph was never a good producer of trout until the flat nymphs were developed in 1932. So far as I know, I tied the first flat-bodied artificial nymphs—three of them at one sitting, at the work table of Mr. E. R. Hewitt at the camp on the Neversink River in New York State."

Knight took a great deal of credit for the new flat nymph influence on the fly-angling world, even to the extent of claiming, "as soon as we found out about tying flat nymphs, nymph fishing spread across the country like wildfire." In *The Modern Angler* (1936), he touched on the development of the flat-bodied nymph on Hewitt's water and provided rough step-by-step tying illustrations.

Both Knight and Hewitt wrote follow-up articles describing the new nymphs; Knight's appeared in *Sports Afield* and Hewitt's in *Field & Stream*. Knight also gave a complete account of the origination of his flat-bodied nymph in the 1964 *Fisherman's Digest*. The story, titled "Birth of a Nymph," explained how Hewitt became engaged in a discussion of nymphs with Knight, which led to the creation of the flat-bodied nymph.

Jack Knight and Dick Hunt, guests at Hewitt's Neversink River camp, were sitting around the woodstove with their

Susquehanna River not far from Williamsport, Pennsylvania, John Alden Knight's home. Knight fished his bass patterns on large rivers, such as the Susquehanna and Delaware.

host when the talk turned to nymph patterns. Hewitt opened his fly box filled with nymphs and lamented their failure as trout takers. He commented, "The trouble is all of us are all wrong in our approach to this problem. We fail to recognize the type, shape, size and coloration of the stream bottom bugs that we are trying to imitate."

Hunt and Knight listened as Hewitt pointed out that many natural nymphs are not round or cylindrical but flattened, yet the majority of artificial nymph patterns were not tied to reflect that shape. "And there's the rub," Hewitt said. "How are you going to wrap fly-tying materials around a fine wire hook and have the result come out flat and of different colors top and bottom?" Hewitt enjoyed expounding on the flat-bodied theme; in *A Trout and Salmon Fly Fisherman for Seventy-Five Years*, he observed that "most of the nymphs on our eastern American streams are brown on the back. They vary in the color of the belly where they are yellow, gray, cream, and some green although the green variety is rather rare and I have seen them only in a few streams." Hewitt recognized that some nymphs, such as burrowing nymphs that live in silt or gravel habitat, are primarily round. However, he placed much more emphasis on the greater variety of flat-bodied species.

Thinking he may have come up with a solution to the nymph problem based on Hewitt's observations, Knight retired to a tying bench near the window and rummaged for materials, choosing some reddish fox fur, oval gold tinsel, and Rhode Island Red rooster hackle. In *The Modern Angler*, however, Knight said that the first flat-bodied nymph was tied with mink fur on a size 13 hook (as opposed to the reddish fox fur he described using in his *Fisherman's Digest* "Birth of a Nymph" article). Using the fur for a body, ribbed with the tinsel for sparkle, Knight crafted new nymphs for each of the three to fish during the Red Quill hatch on the river.

After the hackle was trimmed top and bottom, leaving the barbs protruding from the sides to represent insect legs, Knight took one more bold step: he soaked the three prototypes in lacquer, allowed them to partially dry, then squeezed them flat with needlenose pliers. He then dabbed a bit of reddish brown lacquer on the top of the fur bodies to provide darker coloration along that area of the fly. "Well I'll be damned!" Hewitt exclaimed. "A flat-bodied nymph! Now why didn't I think of that?"

The three anglers headed to the water, each armed with one of the prototypes, to field-test Knight's flat-bodied creation. During the course of the hatch, Knight landed 74 trout before the 4X tippet and fly broke in the jaw of a big brown trout. Hewitt scored just as well before he lost his single fly and was so enthused about its effectiveness that he headed back to camp to fabricate one of the newfangled patterns himself, then returned to resume fishing. Hunt reported taking more than 50 trout. After the three left the water for a meal break back at camp, Knight took to the vise to replenish

Knight's 1949 *Fishing for Bass and Trout* explained the basics of fishing with dry flies, wet flies, nymphs, and streamers. The book also described the good qualities of bass bugs.

their flat-bodied nymph supplies. Hewitt insisted that Jack Knight have his sandwich at the tying table so that eating would not delay producing more of his nymphs for fishing later that day.

As seemed to be typical of Ed Hewitt, once he had a bee in his bonnet about some fly-tying or trout-fishing revelation, he couldn't wait for his genius to be recognized by others. In his 1938 book *Trout*, Ray Bergman wrote, "An outstanding contribution in the way of nymph imitations is Hewitt's Hard Body Nymph. It has a flattened body and is quite realistic although the opaque body does not imitate the translucent body of the natural." However, Hewitt's nymphs may have been developed from a completely different concept than Knight's prototype. Bergman made no mention of Jack Knight, nor of lacquer dipping as in Knight's creation. Yet it would be hard to argue that Knight didn't have something to do with the birth of Hewitt's three flat-bodied nymph patterns that were illustrated in *Trout*.

Moreover, Knight's concept of flattening nymphs with pliers after dipping them in lacquer was adopted by other fly tiers, Wendle Collins among them. In *The Fly and the Fish* (1951), John Atherton departed from his passionate adherence to the principles of impressionism as they applied to trout-fly designs.

His friend and angling companion Wendle Collins had provided him with some interesting new nymphs that he couldn't resist including in his book. "Mr. Collins also prefers the hard-bodied type," Atherton said. "My own experience has shown that the more impressionistic effect in the water is more successful. These differences of opinion are what make angling so fascinating, and it will only be proved to each angler whether one or the other is better by trying them himself." Atherton then provided step-by-step illustrated instructions for tying Collins's creations. Atherton's illustrations make it immediately clear that Collins must have had some exposure to Knight's technique, as the steps show the fly bodies being dipped into lacquer and then squeezed flat with pliers. Atherton and Collins often fished Hewitt's water, as did Knight; all three were in Hewitt's circle. There were a couple departures from Knight's technique in Collins's nymphs, however: the use of floss over fur and the addition of fuse-wire weight along the hook shank.

Jack Knight wasn't so rigid in his thinking as to believe that flat-bodied patterns were the be-all and end-all for nymphs. He realized that many nymphs were indeed round and cylindrical, and many smaller mayfly naturals could be well imitated with stripped quill bodies, which had already proved to be very effective trout takers. Knight recognized that his creation had worth in the early years, but few fly tiers today are dipping fuzzy fur nymphs into lacquer and squeezing them flat with pliers. The nymph design that so impressed Ed Hewitt 80 years ago has been abandoned, yet other innovative tiers have experimented with the flat-bodied nymph concept over the years. Some of these patterns have survived, while many others have not. George Grant had his large woven stonefly nymphs, and Chauncy K. Lively once lashed shaped thin sheet copper to a hook to provide substantial body width in tying a large dragonfly nymph. Those creations also were not well accepted, because they are tedious and time-consuming to tie. However, another fly that Knight popularized has never been forgotten and has survived to this day—the famed Mickey Finn Bucktail.

Tiers and fly anglers associate Jack Knight with the ever-popular Mickey Finn, although many wrongly assume that he originated the pattern. Yet without Knight's trumpeting of the garish red and yellow bucktail creation, it may never have gained its widespread popularity. Not many patterns have sustained popularity for more than 75 years, but one that has is the Mickey Finn.

In *Streamer Fly Tying and Fishing* (1966), Joseph D. Bates Jr. described the Mickey Finn history and included quotes from John Alden Knight. In a letter to Bates, Knight wrote, "In the spring of 1932, when I was living in Rye, New York, I was invited to fish the waters of a trout club a short distance out of Greenwich. My host, Junior Vanderhoff, gave

me a small bucktail which he had found most effective for catching stocked squaretail trout from this little stream (the Mianus River). It delivered the goods that day; in fact, it was the only fly that did so."

At the time the bucktail found its way into Knight's hands, it was unnamed yet available from the William Mills & Son supply house out of New York City, which simply called it a red and yellow bucktail. Knight continued to use the fly, finding it effective, but it wasn't until 1936 that its significance started to become fully realized. Knight traveled to Canada, where he was a guest of Frank Cooper on the Mad River. During that trip, Knight hooked and released 75 wild brook trout. Cooper and Knight christened the effective red and yellow bucktail the Assassin, but later that year a Toronto newspaper writer named Gregory Clark renamed it the Mickey Finn.

Then the fun really started; seemingly every fly tier around had to have Mickey Finns in his box.

Jack Knight got right to work promoting the Mickey Finn, both in his 1937 writings and by attaching it to the Weber Tackle Company in Wisconsin. After Knight's article appeared in *Hunting and Fishing* magazine, which also included an advertisement by Weber, its popularity escalated into a frenzy at the Sportsmen's show at Madison Square Garden in New York City. In his correspondence with Bates, Knight wrote that "the fly tiers at the show were busy for the entire week tying Mickey Finns. Each night, bushel baskets of red and yellow bucktail clippings and silver tinsel were swept up by the cleaning crew at Grand Central Palace and by Friday of that week not a single bit of red or yellow bucktail could be purchased from any of the New York supply houses."

The Mickey Finn's celebrity caused the Weber Company to go into fly-tying overdrive, trying to keep up with all the purchase orders that arrived daily. Knight went on to say that the Mickey Finn saved one supply house from bankruptcy proceedings once it turned its attention to "specializing intensively in the manufacture of Mickey Finns."

As *New York Times* "Wood, Field and Stream" columnist Ray Camp wrote in a February 1939 story, "There are bucktails and bucktails but according to the professor [Jack Knight] the Mickey Finn is just about the greatest thing since Tom Bosworth invented the Coachman." Knight thought so much of the pattern that he even tweaked it into a bass fly pattern, still using the yellow-red-yellow bucktail features. In his 1949 book, *Black Bass*, Knight's bass version of the Mickey Finn appears in the bass-fly color plate illustrations.

Other notable founding fly tiers, such as Ray Bergman, Rube Cross, and Keith Fulsher, couldn't ignore the Mickey Finn.

Bergman reported having used the then unnamed red and yellow bucktail since 1926. Yet the fly did not make it into the first edition of his book *Trout*, published in 1938. However, the Mickey Finn appeared in later editions, where Bergman wrote, "The pattern was made popular by John Alden Knight . . . it is a very effective pattern and well deserved the boost given it by Jack in his writings." Rube Cross, the once recognized dean of the Catskill fly tiers, wrote compellingly about the Mickey Finn in *The Complete Fly Tier* (1950). "All fish were taken on a 'Mickey,'" he wrote in describing a 1948 salmon outing on the Tabusintac River in New Brunswick. Keith Fulsher morphed the Mickey Finn into his Thunder Creek series. In *Thunder Creek Flies* (2006), he explained, "I originally worked up a Mickey Finn Thunder Creek because its color arrangement was right for the Thunder Creek style of tying." Fulsher later dropped this fly from the series, limiting the patterns to baitfish imitations, but still ties it occasionally because he likes the looks of it.

While the Mickey Finn and flat-bodied nymphs inspired many fly-tying and fly-fishing authors, Knight also created respectable dry flies, the Olive Badger and Cochy Knight among them.

The Olive Badger, the fly's original name, is a lovely pattern. With its olive green floss or dyed dubbing body with badger hackle, it lands gently on a placid water surface and can be skipped along riffles too. Knight noticed that the fly either took fish consistently or not at all, depending on the sun. In *The Modern Angler*, he wrote that he found the fly effective when fished in bright sunlight, but if fished along a shaded riverbank, it failed miserably. He first speculated—then, after repeated testing, firmly believed—that unless the fly was illuminated, trout could not distinguish the colors and shades that otherwise made it attractive. "It is a grand fly in sunlight but on a cloudy day it is carefully left in the fly box," he wrote. Jack Knight's theory led him to change its name to the Sunshine Fly.

Another Knight-created dry fly that Rube Cross also noted in his book *Fur, Feathers and Steel* is the Cochy Knight. Cross told the story of Knight fishing the Beaverkill one day during a hatch of brownish flies. His fly box had nothing that resembled the naturals, so he returned to his hotel room, grabbed his tying kit, and crafted a new pattern. Its red fox belly fur with coch-y-bondhu hackle palmer worked well for him that day.

The classic dry flies, nymphs, bass patterns, and bucktails that John Alden Knight either created or popularized show that he adapted his needs to the water he fished. But despite all the intrigue over the flat-bodied nymphs, and the creative dry flies and the theories surrounding them, it is the Mickey Finn that will always be considered Knight's signature fly, even though he was not its originator. Still today, it would be hard to find a major fly shop that does not carry this pattern that Knight made famous.

Wendle Collins's hard-bodied nymphs, tied by John Atherton. Atherton included the Collins-style nymph in his book, along with tying illustrations, but gave the patterns a lukewarm reception. *Bill Leary collection*

Mickey Finn, tied by Frank Cooper. Cooper and Knight fished the fly, then known only as a red and yellow bucktail, on the Mad River in Canada in the 1930s. It was so successful they christened it the Assassin. Cooper's friend Gregory Clark gave the fly its final name—the Mickey Finn. *Catskill Fly Fishing Center and Museum collection*

Mickey Finn, modern version, tied by Mike Valla. The contemporary version of the Mickey Finn looks much different from the originals tied by John Alden Knight and Frank Cooper. The yellow-red-yellow bucktail layers are neatly arranged on a long-shank streamer hook. The red stripe is clearly defined in the yellow hair sandwich.

Mickey Finn, tied by the iconic salmon fly tier Charles DeFeo. Tiers everywhere were tying this pattern once its effectiveness was made known. *Ted Rogowski collection*

Knight's Delaware, tied by Mike Valla. Knight was an enthusiastic bass angler who turned to both clipped hair bugs and fancy feather patterns to take bass on rivers such as the Delaware. The pattern was featured in the color plate illustrations in Knight's *Black Bass* book.

Mickey Finn bass version, tied by Mike Valla. The bass version was featured in Knight's 1949 book, *Black Bass*.

Knight's Brown Bomber, tied by Mike Valla. Large, gaudy feather bass patterns worked well for Knight on the Delaware and Susquehanna Rivers.

Cochy Knight dry fly, tied by Mike Valla. This fly was featured in Reuben Cross's *Complete Fly Tier* (1950). Cross called it a "good floater" and said it "works well in fast water." Knight did well with the pattern on the Beaverkill River.

Knight-Hewitt flat-bodied nymph, tied by John Alden Knight in 1933. Knight added dark markings along the top surface of the nymph to better imitate a natural immature aquatic insect. *Catskill Fly Fishing Center and Museum collection*

Sunshine Fly, tied by Mike Valla. This Knight pattern was originally called an Olive Badger. Knight changed the fly's name when he noticed it took fish more readily when fished in open sunshine, rather than along shaded bank stretches.

Knight's double-hook fly, tied by John Alden Knight. This unidentified pattern is tied with a second hook that emerges from beneath the body dubbing, at midshank. It's a very rare fly. *Catskill Fly Fishing Center and Museum collection*

CHAPTER 11

Joe Messinger Sr.
(1892–1966)

Joe Messinger Sr. at his tying bench. Messinger was best known for his Irresistible and bass hair frog patterns. *Photo courtesy of Joe Messinger Jr.*

Irresistible, tied by Joe Messinger Sr. in 1944. This fly was sent to John Alden Knight that year for field-testing. Note the two-toned hair body—dark on top, light on the bottom, characteristic of Messinger's pattern. Messinger tied his early Irresistibles with claret-colored hackle; later, he also tied them with dun shades. *Catskill Fly Fishing Center and Museum collection*

F
ly tiers are a resourceful group of individualists who constantly find new and innovative ways to attach fur, feathers, and hair to hooks. Every tier has a story about his or her early years and the circumstances that led to getting involved in the craft. And every fly tier can chronicle his or her imaginative attempts to create something a bit different, something inventive and even artistic, that would prove a better way to lure fish—a fly that would entice the most selective trout along a cold, fast-moving riffle or the most finicky bass among the lily pads in a tepid pond.

Joe Messinger Sr. was one such resourceful and talented fly tier. What tier today would not be impressed by a man who experienced serious war injuries and was told that he'd be confined to a wheelchair or crutches the rest of his life, yet brought to the fly-tying world creations still popular for

Joe Messinger Sr. chasing rainbows, of the "finny variety." *Photo courtesy of Joe Messinger Jr.*

nearly a century? When reflecting on Messinger's several years undergoing surgeries and rehabilitation after World War I, his son, Joe Jr., also a talented tier, explained it this way: "The doctors released him and told him to go chase rainbows, and that's just what he had in mind, but his rainbows were the finny variety." Catching fish and tying flies would be the focal point of Joe Messinger's life.

Messinger had been tying flies before his military duty, but after the war he found himself tying under different yet creative circumstances. His old Hudson automobile was remodeled—into a tying facility. The backseat was removed and replaced with a tying bench, with a dome light installed overhead. The car trunk held a coop of live roosters, enabling Messinger to pluck their hackles as needed. But hackle was not the only tying material he used; deer hair also was readily available and became his favorite for tying trout flies and bass bugs.

Bass flies were the focus in Joe Messinger's earliest involvement with fly tying. Recognizing that bass love frogs, Messinger went to work inventing his clipped deer hair Bucktail Frog, still known today as the Messinger Frog. Another early pattern, created in the 1920s, was the Nitehummer, a fly that was created to simulate moths, or millers, as they are sometimes called.

With its deer hair tail, wings, and clipped hair body, it was the precursor of one of the most famous trout flies ever tied—the Irresistible, a fly originally tied to imitate an egg-laden female drake fly.

In *Tying Catskill-Style Dry Flies*, I told the story of the time I asked Catskill tier Winnie Dette about a dry fly called the Irresistible and how to best spin and clip the hair to produce a nice, neat body. "It's not really a fly we prefer to tie," she said. "Here, take these Wulff patterns instead and fish the pocketwater." Walt and Winnie Dette were never fond of tying spun and clipped hair flies; they felt that tying such patterns was not cost-effective, considering the time it took to craft them. Irresistibles were not found in their fly bins, although they did tie a few very early in their careers. But their lack of enthusiasm for the pattern is largely an exception—tiers and anglers everywhere love that fly.

During a recent chat with Messinger's son, Joe Jr., he proudly explained the Irresistible's history. "It wasn't originally called the Irresistible," Joe told me. "It was just a deer hair drake pattern Dad was tying in the late 1930s." The fly wasn't christened with its name until a time when fishing friend and champion fly caster Art Neu wrote to Messinger inquiring about getting some new trout-fly patterns for a hospitalized friend, Ken Lockwood. Lockwood was an outdoor enthusiast and conservationist from New Jersey, a fly-angling figure who is still discussed by fly-fishing enthusiasts and for whom a gorge surrounding a couple miles of New Jersey's

Raritan River South Branch, known for its picturesque trout-fishing environment, was named.

Lockwood received some of the strange, new flies from Messinger. After he recovered and was released from the hospital, he headed to Canada on an angling excursion, where he tried out this new pattern. The flies proved so effective that Lockwood had to have more of them. In his words to Messinger, he described the new fly as "irresistible."

The name Irresistible stuck, although there have been some minor changes to the fly leading to variations in color shade, form, and even the way the hair is attached to the hook shank when tied. What may surprise modern fans of the Irresistible is that the original pattern was not tied with the now-popular single-shade, gray clipped hair body. Joe Jr. said his father originally tied the fly using natural blue-gray clipped deer hair on the dorsal aspect of the fly body, and white clipped deer hair on the underside. In tying the fly, Messinger used an original and unique method of attaching deer hair to the hook shank, for clipping, that allows for the lateral separation of hair colors.

RAY BERGMAN
GRACE BERGMAN
28 South Mill Street
Nyack 5, N.Y.

May- 13-1961

Mr.Jos.M.Messinger
15 Washington Ave.,
Morgantown,
West Virginia.

Dear Joe:-

Wrote you some days ago in answer to your Xmas card from Eddis. Just now cleaning up on correspondence that has piled up and came to your letter of April 10th.

Yes, I have retired from most of my business as well as from OUTDOOR LIFE but still make flies and leaders for a few old customers.

Re Dickerson. He has retired also, although he does make a few rods when he feels like doing so.

The last I heard from him he was in Florida. I am not sure about his present address. His old one was 3852 Bewick Ave., Detroit, Mich., the last one I have. CHECK- Just asked Grace about this. Dick and his wife visited us just after he went out of regular business, when they were on the way to Florida. At the time they told us that they had sold their home in Detroit and had moved to another location. After that and after they had come back from Florida Mrs. D.died. Unfortunately we didn't put the new address in a permanant address book so we can't find it now. Perhaps DETROIT P.O. has a forwarding address.
Simply Nyack, N.Y. will always reach us. We are both life-long residents of the town.

Would like to have a chat with you sometime, and meet your wife and ####### youngster.

Our very best to you both,

Ray

Letter from Ray Bergman to Joe Messinger Sr. Bergman featured Messinger's famous Irresistible in his books *With Fly, Plug, and Bait* and *Trout*. *Mark and Jill Schwarz collection*

Unlike the methods commonly used today for creating clipped deer hair bodies, Messinger placed the hook in the tying vise *vertically*. Each individual hair bunch increment was tied down to the hook with a knot, increment after increment; the hair was not "spun" around the hook shank, as is common practice today when creating clipped deer hair fly or bug patterns. Messinger's hair attachment method created a very durable fly or bug. The modern tier might assume that this method would lead to loosely compacted bodies, but such is not the case. The bodies on both the Irresistible and bass bugs are extremely compact, with pleasing lateral hair shade separation.

Beyond the differences in body construction, the hackle shades used for the Irresistible collar have also evolved. In the beginning, Messinger selected dyed claret or wine-colored hackle, something that might surprise the modern fan of the pattern. He later also tied the fly with brown or ginger hackle that matched the hair shade on top of the fly body.

In *The Complete Fly Tier*, Catskill fly-tying great Rube Cross mentioned the Irresistible as a popular salmon fly, collared with blue dun shade hackle.

The use of claret or wine hackle has been a head-scratcher for many. In a recent chat with Joe Jr., he offered some theories as to why his dad originally used hackle dyed claret. The Irresistible was routinely fished in faster-moving water, bouncing along over trout that might catch sight of the fly as it drifted near their holding area. The fish might lose brief sight of the fly in the fast-moving current, resulting in a short strike. The claret or wine shade might give the fly sustained visibility as it floated along through the rough water.

Contemporary fly tiers rarely, if ever, wrap claret hackle when tying Irresistibles. Brown, ginger, dun, or even mixes of those hackle shades are commonly employed. Modern versions of the pattern have been tied with a variety of wing types. Natural deer hair wings are still the most common, but the fly has also been tied using grizzly hackle tips, and it is sometimes tied wingless. Yet no matter what hackle shade or wing type, Joe Messinger's Irresistible has survived for many years.

Eric Leiser presented complete tying instructions for the fly in his *Complete Book of Fly Tying* (1977) and his later *Book of Fly Patterns* (1987). Leiser had it right when he wrote, "There is much room for experimentation. And no matter what the wing and tail materials, the pattern will lose none of its effectiveness, for what really makes the Irresistible, after all, is the clipped deer-hair body." Leiser presented a couple interesting variations of the fly, but they were still based on the original Messinger creation. It might have been logical to give the White Irresistible a completely different name, but given its generic features, the fly is still an Irresistible. The white version has a white deer hair (or calf) tail, clipped white deer hair body, a wing of white calftail or badger hackle points, and badger hackle.

The many different versions of the Irresistible have led other authors to chime in on the discussion. A. J. McClane, in his now-classic *Practical Fly Fisherman* (1953), featured the fly in his color plates but made this apt clarification concerning the pattern: "The Irresistible found in our dry fly plate is not the original pattern. The name has become synonymous with a type of fly rather than a specific dressing." However, McClane was quite liberal in his definition of the fly and the materials used. It is interesting that while McClane insisted that the fly he presented in his book be called an Irresistible, the materials used departed greatly from Joe Messinger Sr.'s original pattern. McClane's Irresistible used Impala wings, pheasant tails, a clipped caribou body, and dark ginger brown hackle. However, not all clipped hair body trout fly patterns with wings and hackle are labeled Irresistibles.

In *The Catskill Flytier* (1977), Harry Darbee included the Irresistible in his "Deadly Dozen." Along with the Irresistible, another fly on this list was the Rat-Faced McDougall, a spin-off from an earlier Darbee fly called the Beaverkill Bastard. Was there any connection between the development of the Rat-Faced McDougall and Messinger's Irresistible? Joe Jr. doesn't remember his father saying anything about a connection, or which fly came first. However, Joe told me, "Dad knew Harry Darbee and they corresponded with each other periodically. But the two are different flies in several respects. On the original Rat-Faced McDougall, Harry used ginger hackle fibers for the tail, and [cream] grizzly hackle tips for the wings. He later used calf tail for the wings on some of the flies he tied. Dad used deer hair for the tail and wings. The body of the Rat-Faced McDougall is spun brown deer hair. Dad's Irresistibles had dun-colored deer hair backs and white deer hair bellies." Also, Messinger did not use the common hair-spinning technique.

The relationship between the Irresistible and the Rat-Faced McDougall raised Ray Bergman's curiosity. In *With Fly, Plug, and Bait* (1947), Bergman wrote, "The principal difference between this fly and others is the body, which is clipped deer hair. While this particular combination, designed by Jos. M. Messinger, is new, other patterns with the same body have been used a long time. One of them, called the Rat Faced McDougall, I've used extensively since about 1939." Bergman mentioned the Irresistible in later editions of *Trout* and included the fly in his "new 1951 list," which covered additional dry flies not presented in his first edition of the book. The fly also appeared in Bergman's Plate #17 illustrations, which featured new dry flies. Bergman's notes concerning the Irresistible that accompanied the 1951 dry-fly list seem more qualified than his earlier statements. Here he wrote, "As far as I know, Joe Messinger, of Morgantown, West Virginia, was the originator of this particular combination of clipped deer body hair and deer hair wings. But I have also been told the first trout fly patterns made with this type

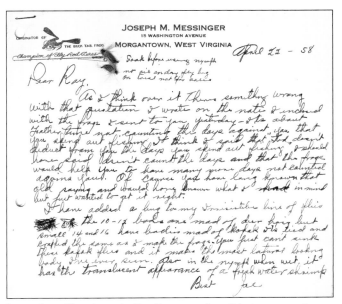

Letter from Messinger to Ray Bergman describing a new pattern he had added to his Irresistible line. The "nymph" was tied with clipped deer body hair for size 10s and 12s. Messinger experimented with kapok bodies in smaller sizes, which gave the fly a natural translucent look, as found in freshwater shrimp. *Mark and Jill Schwarz collection*

of body were made by Harry Darbee, of Livingston Manor, N.Y. I'm writing this as a reporter and nothing else."

However, Joe Jr.'s longtime acquaintance Larry Duckwall maintains that Messinger's clipped deer hair bodies inspired Harry Darbee. Catskill region fly-fishing aficionado Duckwall knew Darbee well and visited him often. They discussed two flies—the Irresistible and the Rat-Faced McDougall—and whether Messinger's fly influenced Harry's clipped deer hair body creations. In a recent chat I had with Larry Duckwall, he said, "I knew Harry well, and we talked about his Beaverkill Bastard and the Rat-Faced McDougall. Harry told me that he took the clipped deer hair body idea from Messinger. There was definitely a Messinger influence."

Duckwall's comments make sense. In his book, Darbee acknowledged that Joe Messinger Sr. created the Irresistible. Darbee also knew Art Neu, the individual who was responsible for getting Messinger's fly to his hospitalized friend, Ken Lockwood, and it was Lockwood who had named the fly the Irresistible. Neu had also taken a specialty fly tied by Messinger, called the Dogcatcher, to the Darbees to tie for him. The Dogcatcher exhibited the characteristic Messinger lateral separation of clipped deer hair colors—light yellow underside and dark brown back. So Darbee was definitely aware of Messinger's work and style.

Other clipped deer hair trout flies, besides the Rat-Faced McDougall, were created over the years. Don Martinez, the late western fly angler who crafted fly patterns from the 1930s until his death in 1955, credits Messinger for the development of his own clipped hair dry-fly series. However,

Joe Messinger Jr. demonstrating his craft to onlookers. Joe Jr. has carried on his dad's legacy and ties stunning patterns, bass frogs and Irresistibles among them. *Photo courtesy of Joe Messinger Jr.*

the Irresistible still stands above them all. Conversations about clipped deer hair trout patterns will undoubtedly bring up the famous Irresistible. In the contemporary fly-tying world, however, one rarely hears anything about the Beaverkill Bastard, Rat-Faced McDougall, Don Martinez's Rough Water dry flies, or Darbee's clipped white deer hair Coffin Fly.

As famous as the Irresistible is, many would be surprised to learn that Joe Messinger Sr. is as well known—better known, really—for his innovative clipped hair bass bugs and frogs, especially in bass circles. When Messinger returned home after World War I, he was not set on tying the pattern that would become the Irresistible, but instead was focused on creating a fly-rod bass lure that was christened the Bucktail Frog. In his November 1969 *Pennsylvania Angler* article, titled "Tying a Simplified Hair Frog," Pennsylvania fly tier Chauncy K. Lively expressed his admiration for Messinger and his frog patterns: "Frog bugs are many and varied but possibly the most artistic of them all is the Messinger Hair Frog, tied in former years by Joe Messinger of Morgantown, West Virginia. Old timers will remember the little masterpieces and the few still around are cherished by their owners like rare coins. Messinger's Frog has jointed legs, which kick when retrieved, an exquisitely trimmed body of spun deer hair, and protruding eyes. Its likeness to a real frog is startling; one almost expects it to jump right out of the box."

Messinger's inspiration for the clipped hair frog pattern came from his early love for bass fishing; his first bass was caught on a live frog. His clipped hair frog lure—which was not really created from "spun" hair as Lively described—was created in the early 1920s, using the same techniques to attach deer hair to the hook that Messinger later used for his

Irresistible. Spinning deer hair around a hook shank, the common technique used today for clipped hair patterns, had been invented back in the early 1900s, but Joe Sr. figured out a different method to craft his hair frogs.

Other styles of hair bugs from the hands of tiers such as Dr. James A. Henshaw, who crafted the Henshaw Bug, and Orley Tuttle, who invented the Devil Bug, were also gaining in popularity. But as William G. Tapply aptly wrote in *Bass Bug Fishing* (1999), it was Joe Messinger who "elevated the tying of deer hair bugs to an art form." The technique of *stacking* hair up the hook shank as the frog was tied, as opposed to *spinning* hair, was Messinger's own. As described above, bundles of deer hair were positioned along the hook to prevent it from rolling around the entire shank. This allowed for the lateral separation of shades, resulting in beautiful pale body undersides and colorful brown or green topsides on his frog patterns. The technique was very difficult to master, and its creator did not reveal it to anyone except family members. Even Joe Jr., who today crafts beautiful hair frogs, struggled at first with his dad's invention, his early attempts worthy only of a trash can.

Messinger's bass patterns grew in popularity, and by the mid-1930s, mention of him and his surface lures began to show in print. Myron E. Shoemaker from Laceyville, Pennsylvania, wrote extensive articles for the *Pennsylvania Angler* that described floating, clipped hair bass patterns and their use on his home North Branch of the Susquehanna River waters. In a 1935 story, he said, "Just who the originator of the surface lure is I do not know, but the first of these lures I used was made by Joe Messinger, Morgantown, W.Va.."

Admiration for Messinger and his now-classic frog lure, often simply called the Messinger Bucktail Frog, continues to this day. Many of fly fishing's most popular and well-known personalities have given the nod to Messinger and his patterns, particularly his frogs. The prolific outdoor writer John Alden Knight was an ardent bass angler who frequented rivers such as the Susquehanna and upper Delaware. In his 1949 book, *Black Bass*, Knight wrote about one of his favorite deer hair bugs: "We use Joe Messinger's hair frogs a great deal as these little masterpieces are looked upon with favor by the big smallmouths of the [Susquehanna's] North Branch." The book is tastefully illustrated with three Messinger creations: the Nitehummer, Popping Golden Frog, and Meadow Frog.

John Alden Knight wasn't the only high-profile fly angler to embrace Joe Messinger Sr.'s hair frogs. In the chapter titled "Landing Bass on the Fly," which first appeared in *The Complete Book of Fly Fishing* (1958) and was later reprinted in *Joe Brooks on Fishing* (2004), Brooks said, "Hair Frogs are great top-water lures for small-mouth bass. Although it is little used these days, I think that Joe Messinger's famous Hair Frog, tied many, many years ago, has probably caught more smallmouth bass than any other single lure. Fished fast across the surface, it looks like a swimming frog. Smallmouth tear into it with wild abandon."

Writing about bass bugs in *McClane's Angling World* (1986), A. J. McClane said, "One of the reasons I'm so careful about bass bugs I buy is that many of them don't cast well. I've used at least a dozen different frog bugs, for instance, and the only one that ever turned in a good performance on the water was the Messinger Frog." McClane felt that the bug cast easily, not as well as a dry fly, but better than its appearance would lead the angler to believe. He liked the balance between its bulk and weight, comparing it to casting a large Bivisible dry fly.

While other clipped hair bass bug aficionados may not use Joe Messinger's exact techniques in constructing the flies—many contemporary tiers prefer to spin hair—his impact has not been forgotten. In recent correspondence, tier Dave Whitlock wrote to me that although he had never met Joe Messinger Sr., "his hair frogs did play some part in my interest for tying deer hair bass flies. I did meet and know Joe Jr. and watched him create some of his dad's designs, over the last 20-plus years at various fly-fishing events. I don't really use any of their methods to tie deer hair bass flies, although I do admire them."

Irresistible, tied by Joe Messinger Jr. Note the two-toned hair body. *Mike Valla collection*

Meadow Frog, tied by Joe Messinger Sr. The golden brown, yellow, and white Meadow Frog was probably the most popular of Messinger's early clipped deer hair frogs. Soaking pieces of celluloid in acetone formed the eyes. Once softened, the eyes would adhere directly to the deer hair. The eyes were then painted. *Joe Messinger Jr. collection*

Irresistible, tied by Joe Messinger Jr. Early Messinger Irresistibles were tied with claret- or wine-colored hackle. *Mike Valla collection*

Bucktail Popper, tied by Joe Messinger Sr. The bug is a popping frog without legs. Messinger tied them in the same colors as he did frogs. *Joe Messinger Jr. collection*

Bleeding Bucktail Popper, tied by Joe Messinger Sr. The concave snout on this pattern produces bubbles and a popping sound when retrieved through the water. The red hair was used to simulate blood. *Joe Messinger Jr. collection*

Nitehummer, tied by Joe Messinger Sr. Nitehummers simulated moths, or "millers," as they are sometimes called. Bass bugger and trout angler John Alden Knight featured the Nitehummer in his 1941 book, *Black Bass*. Messinger's hair frogs and similar bass patterns, such as the Nitehummer, influenced Knight. The Nitehummer predated the Irresistible, and Joe Jr. believes that it was the inspiration for that fly. *Joe Messinger Jr. collection*

Bleeding Hair Frog, tied by Joe Messinger Sr. The use of dyed red hair simulates bleeding prey to a gamefish. *Ted Patlen collection*

Green, black, and white frog tied by Joe Messinger Jr. Joe Jr. has taken his dad's example to a higher level, crafting frog patterns worthy of both bass and a shadow box. *Joe Messinger Jr. collection*

CHAPTER 12

Ray Bergman
(1891–1967)

Ray Bergman was without doubt one of the most influential fly fishermen of his time. From East Coast to West Coast, Bergman fished flies created by others as well as his own patterns. *Jill and Mark Schwarz collection*

I t is no wonder that celebrated fly-fishing author and angler Ernest G. Schwiebert decided to title his 1978 two-volume encyclopedic book *Trout*; his entire introduction was devoted to the most prolific fly-fishing writer of the 1900s, Ray Bergman. Schwiebert wrote that Ray Bergman's 1938 book *Trout* was "a revelation that completely changed my life." Schwiebert's warmly written prose described how Bergman's *Trout* served as a substitute during times when it was impossible for him to be fishing. Bergman's writings sustained the then young Schwiebert's daydreams and hopes that he, too, would someday cast a line on the rivers in Ray Bergman's world.

Bergman lived his entire life along the Hudson River in Nyack, New York, not far from Manhattan. Yet in his mind, he undoubtedly lived along the banks of the famous eastern trout lakes and rivers and on occasion the noted waters outside of New York state. Bergman wrote often about north-country waters such as Cranberry Lake and the Ausable River. He frequented the Catskills, closer to his home in Nyack, as well. He explored and wrote about the Beaverkill and

Ginger Quill Wet Fly, tied by Ray Bergman. Bergman's greatest contribution to fly tiers may have been the inclusion in his books of Dr. Edgar Burke's color illustrations of hundreds wet, dry, nymph, and streamer flies. The wet-fly plates, in particular, have served as a valuable reference for tiers interested in that style of trout flies. *Jill and Mark Schwarz collection*

Ray Bergman at about 16 years old. Bergman devoted his entire life to fly tying, fly fishing, and writing about these passions. *Jill and Mark Schwarz collection*

Neversink Rivers, the Willowemoc and Callicoon Creeks. Bergman also enjoyed fishing some of the best-known western streams.

Ray Bergman fished streams such as the Umpqua in Oregon and the Firehole at Yellowstone. And following all of his fishing travels, whether on West Coast or East Coast waters, he described using flies that enticed trout, grayling, steelhead, and bass. Bergman corresponded with many of the best-known fly tiers and anglers of his era, and he introduced many of their favorite patterns in the many editions of his books *Just Fishing*, *Trout*, and *With Fly, Plug, and Bait*, as well as his numerous *Outdoor Life* magazine articles.

Fly tiers such as Don Martinez, Joe Messinger Sr., Elizabeth Greig, Buz Buszek, Len Halladay, Dan Bailey, Vince Marinaro, Charlie Fox, Art Flick, John Alden Knight, Mary Orvis Marbury, Lee Wulff, and others all appeared in his pages. The color fly plates in Bergman's books, painted by Dr. Edgar Burke, showcased patterns developed by many of those fly-fishing greats. In addition to these patterns, hundreds of other obscure patterns were illustrated by Dr. Burke. Fly-fishing tips found in Bergman's writings aside, the Burke

plates have proved highly helpful to many tiers seeking out dressings for the popular fly patterns of that time.

Fly tier Don Bastian devotes a considerable amount of time to tying the wet flies illustrated by Burke in Bergman's books. Although Bastian ties beautiful streamer flies, he is best known for tying wet flies featured in the Burke illustrations. Reflecting on Ray Bergman's influence, Bastian wrote in a November 13, 2011, blog entry titled "Ray Bergman-Some Clarification and Edification" (at http://donbastianwet-flies.wordpress.com):

"I am a Bergman fan, not solely of course, but like many anglers and fly tiers, I was influenced early on because his book *Trout* was my one and only source with illustrated fly patterns when I was still young. No other previously published book contained more flies to look at."

The Burke plates found in *Trout* also influenced many other fly tiers. Andrew Gennaro from New Jersey acquired his copy of *Trout* on one of his frequent trips to the old Reed Tackle shop in Fairfield, New Jersey. Fresh out of high school, his newly acquired 1954 Nash Rambler got him on trout streams and into Reed's store. "If my memory serves me right," Gennaro said, "Ray Bergman's *Trout* was the only book they sold, if not the most important. I bought my copy from them, and it was instrumental in my learning process during those early years when few books were available. I copied flies from Dr. Edgar Burke's color plates and digested Bergman's fishing lessons."

Rob Matarazzo, who first began saltwater fishing at age seven or so at his local pier in Brooklyn, also recalled being influenced by Bergman's *Trout*. In a letter to me he had this to say: "I started fly-fishing in my mid-twenties and was hooked deep. I read a few then-current books on the subject before remembering the "bible" of trout fishing and promptly obtained a copy. It wasn't long before I became a fly tier. Like most fishermen in the modern era, I avoided wet flies for quite some time. But at some point I became intrigued and went back to Bergman's book for patterns and techniques. I recall having thought early on about tying all those wet flies in the plates, but never took on the project."

The Burke wet-fly illustrations are indeed something nice to look at and influenced many tiers in their early years. However, many acknowledge that actual Bergman-tied flies are not examples of fine artistry; they were tied for fishing and not a shadow box. According to Don Bastian, "Ray was a production tier. He sold his flies through his mail-order business, which was essentially a mom-and-pop operation. Ray Bergman did not produce what we today seem to crave as presentation flies. Flies tied by Bergman himself are valued because of who he was, and because of his popularity, not particularly because of their quality as perfectly tied flies. I have a special feeling when looking at Bergman's flies—the historical significance of them. Even if certain elements lack perfection, this does not detract from their value."

While it is true that many fly tiers today have focused their attention on the hundreds of wet flies illustrated by Burke in Bergman's three popular books—*Trout, Just Fishing*, and *With Fly, Plug, and Bait*—Bergman was really a dry-fly man. He gave considerable attention in his books to floaters. Popular dry flies that Bergman tweaked to satisfy his own fishing needs included the Black Wulff, a spin-off from the famous Wulff series created by Lee Wulff and Dan Bailey. Bergman wrote in his 1952 2nd edition of *Trout* that his version was coincidental with and unconnected to the Black Wulff created by Dan Bailey. Bergman's version appears in *With Fly, Plug, and Bait*.

Beyond the influences of Wulff and Bailey, Bergman applied features found in patterns developed by other well-known fly tiers from his era that resulted in his own creations. The Hopkins Variant combined ideas gleaned from Don Martinez's Dunham dry fly and those provided by acquaintance Don Hopkins. Ray Bergman also assigned names to effective unidentified patterns. Such was the case with a fly that produced well for him on a favorite Catskill river. A dry fly mentioned in *Just Fishing*, which was illustrated by Burke but had no specific dressing, was unnamed when Bergman discovered it at the William Mills & Son store in New York

City. So productive was the fly during a mayfly hatch on the Neversink River in the Catskills that he labeled it the Bridgeville Olive, for a popular fly-fishing destination on that river. Bergman also found the pattern effective on a Pennsylvania stream, where he decided to try a "juicy looking fly." In 15 casts, he netted six fine trout.

Besides attaching names to flies that were nameless, as he did with the Bridgeville Olive, or creating pattern variations based on existing patterns, as with his Black Wulff, Ray Bergman also exhibited plenty of creativity at his tying bench. Many of his own dry-fly patterns appeared in Burke's plates or in his writings, often labeled with his initials "R.B." Included in the dry-fly mix described and featured in his books were several of his own, among them the Iron Blue Variant, Wake, Basherkill, Bataviakill, Paulinskill, R.B. Fox, R.B. Blue Fox, and R.B. Multicolor Variant, as well as the R.B. Black Angel, a fly that he mentioned in both *With Fly, Plug, and Bait* and *Trout*.

In *Trout*, Ray Bergman observed concerning black flies that "there is a need for them, and yet they are not in general use. I'll wager that if you took a census of the flies used on a dozen streams you would be lucky if you found one angler using a black fly. I know thousands of anglers who never use

Author on Firehole River, Yellowstone Park. In *Trout*, Bergman said he "never saw more beautiful or accessible dry fly water." Bergman noted that its currents were "just fast enough to float a dry fly." *Photo by Valerie Valla*

one, and I know that I neglect them from time to time even though I know from experience that they will often produce much better than other patterns to which we have become attached." Bergman's own Black Angel dry fly no doubt found a home in his fly box.

Along with the Black Angel, Bergman's Firehole dry fly would have been found in his boxes too. Tied in a few different variations, the Firehole patterns were born from necessity after Bergman fished the Firehole River at Yellowstone. The story of Ray Bergman's Firehole dry fly and his frustrations while fishing the river for which it was named is well told in *Trout*. Fish would not rise to his size 12 Adams flies; he learned in hurry that smaller patterns were required while fishing the Firehole during the part of the season when he was on the water. His new Firehole pattern, tied down to size 20, satisfied his needs while fishing the difficult flats on that western river.

The Firehole #1 and Firehole #2 both appeared in *With Fly, Plug, and Bait*, but only in the text; they were not illustrated in Burke's plates. However, an updated Firehole version appeared in the new color dry-fly plate added to Ray Bergman's 1952 edition of *Trout*. It appears that the restructured Firehole version allowed for liberal wing and tail choices: mallard, wood duck, and teal flank feathers were all okay. Its hackle collar blended natural grizzly with black, and its body was crafted from spun natural creamy fox fur. "This is one of my own," Bergman wrote. It was "so named because I had to invent a special pattern one year in order to take trout in the Firehole River. It was effective there mostly in the smaller sizes. However its mixture of black, grizzly and cream makes it a generally useful fly anywhere, and in all sizes ordinarily used for trout."

Beyond the Firehole River, Ray Bergman sampled other western rivers, where his own dry-fly patterns produced well for him. One of his patterns, the R.B. Blue Fox, brought good results on streams such as the Snake River in Idaho, Rio Grande in Colorado, and Encampment in Wyoming. The R.B. Blue Fox was a favorite; Bergman attributed its effectiveness to mixing two different hackle shades: grizzly and dun. Much like the Adams or dry flies designed by John Atherton, the combination of shades "promotes life in the fly," as Bergman wrote.

Bergman's words are reminiscent of Atherton's theories of impressionism. Another advantage of mixing grizzly with dun in the R.B. Blue Fox was that visibility was improved if anglers were fishing in poor light conditions or someone with poor eyesight was fishing a hatch of dun-colored mayflies. Solid-shaded gray dry flies were more difficult to follow as they floated along the water surface, yet Ray Bergman did not ignore popular dry-fly patterns with dun shades, Quill Gordons, Hendricksons, and Coty flies among them.

Standard dun-shaded patterns were always part of Bergman's fishing arsenal and commercial fly-tying endeavors. Yet Bergman was particularly fond of the Coty flies, spin-offs of the Iron Blue Dun and Blue Dun patterns, which were created in collaboration with Victor Coty and Bergman, for whom the Light and Dark Coty were named. Vic Coty was in search of a dry fly that would perform on the Ausable River flats in the Adirondack region of New York state. Coty experimented with blue-gray shaded Bivisibles, but when they failed to perform well enough, he continued his search for just the right pattern to suit his needs. "After that," Bergman wrote in *Trout*, "Victor and I experimented with different shades of blue-gray, both in bodies and hackle. The final result is shown in this book." Ray Bergman liked both patterns, but he again pointed out that the solid dun shades were difficult to following drifting along with the stream currents. "The only objection I have to it is the difficulty of seeing it on the water, in which respect it is as bad as the Quill Gordon."

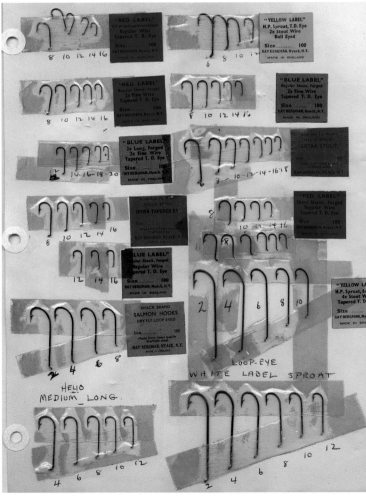

Bergman developed his own hook models, made in Redditch, England. Fly tiers interested in tying classic trout flies seek out Bergman-label hooks. *Jill and Mark Schwarz collection*

The Dark and Light Cotys, as well as the other inventive patterns discussed above, are perfect examples of Ray Bergman's willingness to experiment with new flies that would better serve anglers in fishing situations encountered on a variety of water types, in many geographic locations, east to west. No different, really, than what most fly anglers and tiers practice today.

There's always a better fly, it seems, to suit the situation at hand. Bergman loved experimenting with Variant and Spider dry flies, and they were extensively discussed in his writings and illustrated in Edgar Burke's color plates. His R.B. Multi-Color Variant was born after experimenting with different hackle shades. The original regular Multi-Color Variant, created by A.C. Barrell, called for cree hackle, which was becoming increasingly scarce. Bergman overhauled the original, mixing black, brown, and white hackles and tweaking the tails and wings.

Bergman also liked many different types of Spider patterns. A favorite Spider pattern mentioned in his writings was the Badger Spider, which or may not be original with him. The recipes provided in *With Fly, Plug, and Bait* included a couple versions of this fly. The body could be tied with either gold tinsel or peacock herl, whichever suited the tier, and with or without tails.

The wingless or tiny-winged, large-hackled patterns were undoubtedly favorites. Yet Bergman did not abandon the large-winged flies—the fan-wings. In *Just Fishing*, he wrote, "Without a doubt the fan wing flies have a peculiar attraction to trout, especially browns. This is possibly due to the fluttering action of the large wings, both when they are in the air and when they alight on the water." The Burke illustrations in *Trout* featured an entire fan-wing series, many based on the famous Royal Coachman Fan-Wing, which Bergman cherished. The series included the Silver Fan-Wing Coachman, Green Fan-Wing Coachman, Ginger Fan-Wing Coachman, and a very odd pattern named the McSneek, based on the Fan-Wing Royal Coachman. The McSneek was tied with dyed black peacock herl tufts surrounding a silver tinsel body, with black hackle and white wings. Among the fan-wings featured in Bergman's books, the Royal was a favorite. It is interesting that Ray Bergman selected the Fan-Wing Royal Coachman for his step-by-step dry-fly tying instructions that appeared in his March 1942 article in *Popular Science* titled "Fly Tying Made Easy."

Bergman wrote in *Trout* that he had previously scorned the Fan-Wing Royal Coachman, yet in *Just Fishing*, published six years before that book, he said, "Contrary to custom I highly recommend the frequent use of the fan wing Royal Coachman during the usual low water conditions of July and August." He quickly pointed out that many would consider using such a large dry fly in size 10 in low water ridiculous, but he insisted that "the practice of doing so has often brought me a great measure of success at times when other flies are ineffective."

While it is true that Bergman slanted his writings toward floaters such as the Fan-Wing Royal Coachman, Spiders, Bivisibles, and other creative patterns, he also discussed nymphs and streamers in his writings. He wrote about effective nymphs popularized by other fly tiers. Paul Young, who is probably better thought of as one of the most talented cane rod builders of his era, was also a fly tier. Bergman noted that Young's most famous pattern, the roughly tied Strawman Nymph, could be thought of as a cased caddis imitation, since it "looked nothing like a nymph."

Also tucked into his nymph discussion was an Ernie Maltz and Walt Dette creation called the Dickie. As was true of many fly patterns that found their way into Bergman's books, the Dickie was included because of correspondence from its tier, in this case Maltz, alerting Bergman to its effectiveness. Ed Hewitt's flat- and hard-bodied nymphs had some influence on Bergman's own R.B. Nymph series. (Bergman attached the letters "R.B." to the names of some of his nymphs, as he did with many of his patterns.) It appears that Bergman also experimented with small, hard-bodied, flat "creeper" type nymphs tied with stripped and lacquered hackle quill bodies, but he never named these. The Strawman and Dickie are largely forgotten today, along with many of Bergman's own nymph creations.

While tiny nymphs were favorites, Bergman's fly boxes also held plenty of large streamers and bucktails, many of his own design. Several Bergman-designed bucktails found their way into Joseph D. Bates Jr.'s *Streamer Fly Tying and Fishing* (1966), among them the Bucktail Silver Streamer, Ray Bergman Bucktail, and Gray Squirrel Silver Streamer.

The Gray Squirrel Silver Streamer is still a favorite pattern. It performed well for Bates, too, who wrote, "When the author visited the Gunnison River in Colorado in 1948, the most popular streamer fly on the stream was this one." Bates also presented the famed Jesse Wood Streamer, a pattern originated in 1926 by Jesse Wood of Warwick, New York. Wood actually collaborated with Bergman in developing the pattern, created to imitate minnows. The dressing for the pattern, as well as a photo of the fly, can be found in the Bates book.

Ray Bergman's influence on many fly tiers is unquestioned. Whether through the well-admired Edgar Burke color plates found in his books, the patterns described in his many magazine articles, or those featured in books by others, such as Bates's *Streamer Fly Tying and Fishing*, Bergman's works have not been forgotten and still serve as valuable resources for fly tiers. Don Bastian offered these thoughts concerning his high regard for Ray Bergman: "Ray remained modest, yet his professional profile was higher among American anglers than probably any other writer or fly tier of his time."

Firehole #1 dry fly, tied by Mike Valla. Bergman's pattern, featured in his *With Fly, Plug and Bait*, was developed for large trout feeding on midge hatches in shallow waters such as the Firehole River in Yellowstone Park. Bergman found that small dry flies—such as his Firehole patterns—"were a necessity on many occasions. Usually the somber patterns were best."

Coch-y Variant, tied by Ray Bergman. This variant used cut and shaped hackle wings and coch-y-bondhu hackle with black centers and tips. *Jill and Mark Schwarz collection*

Black Angel, tied by Ray Bergman. In *Trout*, Bergman observed that black flies were needed, although "they are not in general use. I'll wager that if you took a census of the flies used on a dozen streams you would be lucky if you found one angler using a black fly." *Jill and Mark Schwarz collection*

Cut-Wing Royal Coachman, tied by Ray Bergman. Using cut wings on the Royal Coachman is rare. *Jill and Mark Schwarz collection*

Badger Variant, tied by Ray Bergman. Bergman was very fond of Variant-style flies with long hackles relative to hook size. He often used gold tinsel for the bodies of his Variants, as was common in his era. *Jill and Mark Schwarz collection*

Fan-Wing Royal Coachman, tied by Ray Bergman. Bergman wrote in *Trout* that he had previously "scorned" this pattern, yet in *Just Fishing*, he said, "Contrary to custom I highly recommend the frequent use of the fan wing Royal Coachman during the usual low water conditions of July and August." *Jill and Mark Schwarz collection*

Yellow Spinner, tied by Mike Valla. The color fly plates in Bergman's *Trout* provided tiers with a reference including more than 100 dry flies. The Yellow Spinner was among them.

Green Body Cut-Wing, tied by Ray Bergman. Bergman frequently experimented with cut and shaped wings crafted from hackle tips. *Jill and Mark Schwarz collection*

Early Brown Stone, tied by Ray Bergman. This rare Bergman fly is tied using pheasant tail fibers for both tails and body. *Catskill Fly Fishing Center and Museum collection*

White Maribou Streamer, tied by Ray Bergman. This White Marabou is tied in salmon style, with double hooks—a rare tie for a salmon pattern. *Jill and Mark Schwarz collection*

Unidentified dry fly, tied by Ray Bergman. Bergman could have been experimenting with an alder, caddis, or stonefly imitation. *Catskill Fly Fishing Center and Museum collection*

Stripped Quill Variant, tied by Ray Bergman. Bergman corresponded with Catskill fly tier Art Flick about using stripped hackle from a Rhode Island Red rooster. This rare pattern shows that he put Flick's advice to good use. *Jill and Mark Schwarz collection*

Bucktail Royal Coachman, tied by Ray Bergman. *Jill and Mark Schwarz collection*

Hard Body Nymph, tied by Ray Bergman. Bergman took note of fly angler Ed Hewitt's fascination with nymphs, especially hard-bodied examples. This fly was tied in size 18. *Catskill Fly Fishing Center and Museum collection*

Gray Squirrel Silver Streamer, tied by Ted Patlen. Bergman created this streamer in 1933 and introduced it to Joseph D. Bates Jr. In 1948, Bates fished it on the Gunnison River in Colorado, where it proved to be the most effective streamer.

Strawman Nymph, created and tied by Paul Young. This roughly tied pattern was Young's most famous. Bergman noted that it could be thought of as a cased caddis imitation, since it "looked nothing like a nymph." *Bob Summers collection*

Dark Coty, tied by Walt Dette in late 1930s. Bergman was particularly fond of the Coty flies, spin-offs of the Iron Blue Dun and Blue Dun patterns created by Bergman in collaboration with Victor Coty, a fishing friend. *Mary Dette Clark collection*

CHAPTER 13

Lee Wulff
(1905–1991)

Lee Wulff is best known for his big, meaty Wulff series of dry flies. His original three Wulffs—Gray, Royal, and White—led to an entire series of patterns. *Courtesy of Joan Wulff*

To call Lee Wulff the consummate fly angler would be an understatement. Wulff would more aptly be described as a fly-fishing adventurer, innovator, theorist, designer, moviemaker, celebrity, conservationist, entrepreneur, and teacher. Yet even those words cannot fully convey Lee Wulff's lifetime passion for fly fishing. To attempt to profile Lee Wulff, as fly-fishing author John Merwin wrote in his introduction to *The Compleat Lee Wulff* (1989), would be to face "an impossible problem." This is because Lee Wulff lived an improbable fly-fishing life, a full life in which all the endeavors mentioned above were inextricably interrelated.

Lee Wulff was born in Valdez, Alaska, on February 10, 1905. He seemingly was destined to become a fisherman. In his *Lee Wulff on Flies* (1980) Wulff described his early fishing remembrances. His mother once said he was fishing "with a bent pin on a piece of string" as soon as he could "crawl the fifty yards to the crick behind the house." As an eight-year-old, Lee fished with a hand line, spear, or gaff, but in the next year or two, he tied some of his first flies. There was no stopping him from that time forward; fly fishing would prove to be his all-consuming passion.

Gray Wulff, tied by Lee Wulff. The Gray Wulff was first fished on the Esopus Creek with Dan Bailey in the 1930s. *Catskill Fly Fishing Center and Museum collection*

Lee Wulff was an accomplished trout angler but was probably best known for his skills catching Atlantic salmon. He created a "tailer" landing implement to quickly bag his catch. *Courtesy of Joan Wulff*

Wulff's accomplishments during his lifelong fly-fishing career are beyond impressive. He made forays into the Canadian wilderness in search of giant brook trout, reaching his destinations by piloting a small float plane. He fished for Atlantic salmon with a 2-ounce rod and size 28 dry flies.

He filmed Labrador fishing adventures that left audiences at sportsmen's shows, as far back as the late 1930s, awestruck. He invented the first fishing vest, salmon tailers, and special fly lines.

Lee's early adventures included fishing on New York's Esopus and Ausable Rivers with Dan Bailey, in the years before Bailey's permanent departure to Montana. Among all of Wulff's myriad accomplishments, the majority of fly anglers today associate his name with the famous beefy, heavy-water dry flies he first fished with Bailey in the spring of 1930. But his innovations did not end there. From 1941 to 1962, Wulff lived on the Battenkill River at Shushan, New York, where he fished with local characters like Al Prindle, the postmaster for whom Lew Oatman named his Shushan Postmaster pattern. It was during his Shushan years that Wulff invented an interesting new way to craft trout flies, fabricated by embedding materials in plastic bodies, made without thread or typical tying procedures; these flies were known as the "Form-A-Lures."

In a recent sit-down chat with Joan Wulff, whom Lee had called "my finest catch of all," we discussed the history behind the Wulff series. Much of what Joan described is also found in Wulff's own books, *Lee Wulff on Flies* (1980) and *The Compleat Lee Wulff: A Treasury of Lee Wulff's Greatest Angling Adventures* (1989). "Lee was responsible for three of the Wulff dry flies—the Gray Wulff, White Wulff, and Royal Wulff—but it was Dan Bailey who insisted that Lee attach the name 'Wulff' to the flies," Joan told me. "There was a collaboration and friendship between Dan and Lee, which resulted in the series that is today so well known."

In *The Compleat Lee Wulff*, Lee Wulff commented, "Among the great memories of my very early days of angling are those shared with Dan Bailey. Dan and I fished a great deal back in the early 1930s. Dan was a science teacher at Brooklyn Polytechnic, and I was a free-lance artist. We both lived in the Greenwich Village section of New York City. It is hard to imagine two more dedicated anglers. We opened the season in the Catskills even if there was snow on the banks of the Beaverkill, or the winds of the Esopus Valley froze our fly lines in the guides of our rods. We fished every free moment, and I can remember how great the fishing was."

In *The Compleat Lee Wulff*, Lee wrote about his early experiences using Wulff flies, the Gray Wulff being the first fished. "I used them first on the Esopus in that spring of 1930 with Dan Bailey, my regular fishing companion," Wulff wrote. "Results were dramatic. Hendricksons were hatching and the Gray Wulff was extremely effective."

Wulff caught 50 trout that day on a single fly. He had equal success with the White Wulff during Coffin Fly fishing, and it also proved to be a good searching pattern in poor light conditions. The Royal Wulff worked well during varied conditions and was easy to spot on water—by both angler and fish. Wulff's reasoning behind assembling the meaty dry flies with animal hair was validated that day on the Esopus Creek, as well as on other heavy-current rivers such as the Ausable and Salmon Rivers in New York state.

Lee Wulff's rationale for crafting a dry fly with animal hair, along with a fly body that had some substance to it, was based on observations of the patterns available back in the 1920s and '30s from angling supply houses such as Hardy Bros. in England. Wulff thought that the dry flies, slender silk bodies daintily dressed on fine wire hooks, were rather "anemic." He theorized that the bodies traditionally tied that way, to lessen the amount of material that would soak up water, instead caused the fly to sink when it was supposed to float. Wulff wrote, "If I were a trout, I'd be darned if I'd come up from the depths to the surface to get a skinny bug like that. For a hatch maybe, but for one bug?" Revisiting dry-fly design was in order.

Besides the slenderness that was typical of the British dry flies, they had one other flaw: after catching a fish, the tail and wing feathers tended to become slimy and gummed up. This required either changing the fly or grooming and drying it before it was again ready to fish. Wulff wanted a wing and tail that were durable and easily readied for the next cast after removal from a fish's mouth. Bucktail seemed to have the performance combination Wulff was looking for; it was sturdy, and the hair tail offered improved flotation over flimsy hackle feather barbs. With the added floatability, a heavier body on the hook shank could be used. Bucktail wings also increased visibility while the fly drifted along heavy, fast-flowing currents. The Wulff series was born, first tied with bucktail tails and wings along with angora or rabbit fur bodies.

Lee Wulff thought the new hardy, well-floating flies should be called the Ausable Gray, Coffin May, and Bucktail Coachman. Bailey, however, insisted that the three new dry-fly patterns be named for their originator. But it didn't stop with the original three flies; Lee and Dan designed several more Wulff patterns in the fall of 1930.

Wulff and Bailey were busy tying flies to supplement their meager earnings in the Depression years, and the new series gained attention from fly anglers searching out new patterns. In cogitating what fly material shade combinations could be added to enhance the original fly design list, Wulff first considered a pattern based on the Grizzly King fly. Bailey and Wulff collaborated and added the Blonde Wulff, Brown

Wulff, and Black Wulff. Ray Bergman, who embraced the new dry flies, introduced the Black Wulff in his 1952 edition of *Trout*. Bailey told Bergman the Black Wulff "looks like nothing under the sun to me but the trout love it. It is used more on the lower Yellowstone and Boulder than any other dry fly pattern." By coincidence, Bergman also crafted a Black Wulff "quite without any connection" to Bailey's pattern. Bergman added his initials, "R.B.," to the name to differentiate between the two versions.

The big boost for the newfangled patterns undoubtedly came via Bergman. Wulff fished the Ausable in the summer of 1930 with Vic Coty, catching trout between 2 and 3 pounds on the original Wulffs. Like Wulff, Coty was also a fishing friend of Bergman's, and it wasn't surprising that the Gray, White, and Royal Wulffs all made an appearance in Bergman's *Trout*. Wulff handed the three patterns to Bergman, who also found success fishing the new creations on his favorite streams.

Dan Bailey soon started fishing the Wulffs on his favorite Montana streams during his summers off from his teaching position at Brooklyn Polytechnical Institute. He was so enthused by the Wulffs that he provided some of the flies to

Dan Bailey collaborated with Lee Wulff in developing what became the Wulff dry-fly series. Bailey encouraged Lee to attach the name "Wulff" to the high-floating, effective flies. *John Bailey collection*

Catskill region notable Preston Jennings when the two fished together on Montana waters. Jennings admitted that the Wulff patterns were fish getters, but because they didn't imitate any natural insects, he had a tough time justifying including them in his *Book of Trout Flies*. In his *Lee Wulff on Flies*, Lee writes: "Although the Montana fishing convinced Preston that they would take fish, he didn't put them in his well-known *A Book of Trout Flies*, published in 1935."

Jennings was all about hatch matching, his book an early American fly-fishing work that correlated artificial flies with natural insects. The effectiveness of Wulff patterns no doubt went against his grain. In *Lee Wulff on Flies*, Wulff wrote that Jennings "told me he couldn't figure out why trout liked them so well. It was, he said, one of the unreasonable things about fly fishing." It would have been interesting to witness Jennings's reaction if he had lived in the era that Lee Wulff wrote about in his story "The Essential Fly Box," which appeared in *Fly Fisherman* magazine in October 1977.

Concerning his Royal Wulff, Lee Wulff wrote in his article, "Carry some Royal Wulffs in #10-14 (I don't get royalties on them!). They look like strawberries-and-cream to a lot of trout that seem to have been waiting all their lives for just such a fly. Trout will sometimes take a Royal right in the middle of a hatch they're working, and it's also the best exploratory fly in the field to use when the trout aren't surfacing." The Royal Wulff has survived some 80 years since it was first born on eastern waters.

East Coasters no doubt accepted the Wulffs as legitimate patterns. Talented fly tiers and authors mentioned the flies in their writings. Even Rube Cross, the iconic Catskill fly tier known for his sparsely tied and delicate dry flies, mentioned the Wulffs in his book *Fur, Feathers and Steel* (1940). In the chapter titled "Favorite Patterns," he wrote, "Lee Wulff, originator of the flies that bear his name, sticks, naturally enough, to the Wulff type of fly with deer hair wings and tail." Cross provided dressings for two of the patterns.

All the Wulff patterns are especially popular on western rivers, no doubt thanks to Dan Bailey's efforts to promote the flies that he had something to do with. Western tiers and fly anglers continue to embrace the Royal Wulff and its siblings; the Wulff series has never lost its appeal. Wulff flies are tied in many versions today, varying in materials used for both body and wings. While bucktail was the preferred wing material, calftail wings are also very popular. Wulff stated that although he "failed to try calf-tail back in the early days of testing," he recognized the hair had good floating properties and made it easier to match wing lengths and position attitudes on the hook. However, he believed it lacked the "elegance of bucktail."

When using bucktail for wings, Lee Wulff recommended evening up the hair tips. Although it is common today for tiers to use hair stackers for even and uniform wings, Wulff said that if calf tail was used, it wasn't necessary to even the

hair tips. The disheveled appearance of the flies tied by Lee Wulff is not surprising, since, amazingly, he tied the flies with only his hands and didn't use a tying vise. Wulff recognized the bedraggled appearance of his cherished high-floating dry flies, as he called his variations the Grizzly Scraggly, Bumble Bee Scraggly, and White Moth Scraggly.

Lee Wulff defined his Wulffs as a generic pattern, rather than an inflexible fly calling for strict adherence to materials and form. He wrote in *Lee Wulff on Flies*, "The Wulff flies almost seem made to be tied in various patterns. I like to think of flies such as the Wulff as categories, in the same manner as trout and salmon form a category with the first name of *Salmo*. Not only popular for trout the Wulffs have been fished for bass and are effective salmon flies." Wulff welcomed variations created by other fly tiers, such as flies tied with front- or rear-slanting wings, or short- or long-shank hooks. He also tied a variation with slim bodies and sparser hackle for use on some mayfly emergences, such as the Hendrickson (*Ephemerella subvaria*) hatch on eastern waters. In fact, he tied one variation with no hackle at all, instead tied spent-winged. Even today the Wulff dry-fly family continues to grow; Dan Bailey's Fly Shop sells a Baetis Wulff and an Adams Wulff along with the classic patterns.

Keith Fulsher, best known for his own Thunder Creek bucktail series, is a Wulff fly aficionado and enjoys tying and fishing the pattern. "I think the Royal, Gray, and White Wulff patterns are among the very best dry flies ever designed, not only for salmon but also for trout," he said to me recently.

"The Royal is my very favorite dry-fly pattern for salmon. For years it was also my favorite for trout, and I fished it constantly until I discovered Nelson's Caddis, and then the two patterns became equal favorites. For trout, I tied them from 18s on up; for salmon, usually 8s and 6s. The Royal will take fish when no other pattern will work, and I always felt its floatability and silhouette was the reason. I tie it a bit differently than Lee did. I make the tail and wings with white calf tail, while Lee uses deer hair. I don't fish drys for salmon very often, but most of the fish I have taken on the surface have been taken on a Royal Wulff or Green Machine, with the Royal accounting for the most action. I remember sitting on a TGF [Theodore Gordon Flyfishers] panel one time with several other tiers, and each of us was asked what dry-fly pattern was our very favorite. Harry Darbee and I both answered, 'The Royal Wulff.'"

While the Wulffs continue to please many a fly angler and a variety of fish species, other flies Lee Wulff created are less known and understood. Some creations date back to 1951, when Wulff was living on the Battenkill River at Shushan, New York. Chief among the most interesting patterns are Lee Wulff's "Form-A-Lure" plastic-bodied flies. The idea behind these flies was to simplify conventional fly making.

In *Lee Wulff on Flies*, Wulff explained, "I figured that tying flies by hand with thread was the equivalent of drilling

Lee Wulff's Form-A-Lures were advertised as a "new and better method" of making flies.

Catskill Fly Fishing Center and Museum collection

holes and riveting sheets of steel together as the construction workers used to do before the process of welding made rivets obsolete. I saw that imbedding materials in a plastic body would permit making flies to become, to a large extent, an assembly line procedure, and I started a business."

The Form-A-Lures covered a range of fly types—streamers, wet flies, and an interesting plastic-bodied Surface Stonefly tied with a parachute hackle. The sell line read, "More Durable . . . Catch More Fish." Wulff fabricated cold steel molds in which polystyrene fly bodies could be made. Using plastic solvents enabled traditional feathers and hair to be embedded in the bodies. The embedding idea was patented, yet the hoped-for acceptance by fly anglers did not materialize. There was a degree of acceptance of the unique stonefly pattern, yet fly fishers were disappointed that more conventional streamers were not offered. Wulff and his hard-working partners in the venture did produce some traditionally named streamers, such as the Mickey Finn, Gray Ghost, and Black Ghost, but even so, the flies never caught on. In a 1986 *Rod and Reel* magazine article by Silvio Calabri titled "Flies of the Future," Wulff was quoted as saying, "The same thing happened back in the '30s when I came up with my bushy Wulff patterns. No one was interested—they were just too different."

Once the molds were lost in a flood, "the business went to hell," Wulff wrote in *Lee Wulff on Flies.* He didn't totally give up on the idea, but had a couple new molds manufactured and purchased a new plastic machine.

Now he placed emphasis on manufacturing the Surface Stone Fly, which maintained a degree of popularity on North Shore Atlantic salmon rivers in Nova Scotia. Wulff's "Flies of the Future," as they are still called today, continue to be discussed on trout streams such as the Beaverkill, and some anglers even fish them. However, the creations are moribund at best.

During my enjoyable afternoon chat with Joan at the Wulff home on the upper Beaverkill River, she showed me the pneumatic injection machine that still occupies a corner of her basement. "Lee was a bit disappointed that his Flies of the Future never caught on to the degree he had hoped," she said. "Traditional fly tying, with thread neatly attaching traditional materials to a hook shank, maintained its popularity. We sold Flies of the Future do-it-yourself kits, but those never really caught on either."

There was a period of time in the 1980s when the injection machine was producing large numbers of fly blanks and flies. Catskill fly tier Dave Brandt, a close friend of the Wulffs, stepped in to help upgrade the mold designs. Wulff friend Agnes Van Put, the mother of Catskill fly angler and historian Ed Van Put, now in her 90s, fondly recalls those days when she was busy attaching material to the plastic blanks: "It was an enjoyable time manufacturing the Flies of the Future," Agnes said to me recently over coffee and conversation. "Once the plastic fly bodies came off the injection machine, my job was to finish the patterns." Examples of Agnes's flies are on display at the Catskill Fly Fishing Center and Museum in Livingston Manor, New York.

While the Flies of the Future may not have been the most popular fishing flies created, they are certainly interesting to study and admire. "Here, take these with you; I want you to have them," Joan Wulff said as she handed me an old, tarnished tin film canister loaded with examples of the plastic blanks and completed flies. They are indeed something unique, a historical testament to Lee Wulff's creativity.

The Royal Wulff, tied by Lee Wulff. This is the most colorful of all the Wulffs. *Catskill Fly Fishing Center and Museum collection*

Fly of the Future streamer. Wulff experimented with molded plastic-bodied flies such as this streamer, but the concept never really caught on with anglers. *Mike Valla collection*

The White Wulff, tied by Lee Wulff. This fly is a good fish taker during Coffin Fly fishing, the spinner stage of the eastern *Ephemera guttulata*. Like all of Lee's Wulffs, this one is tied in a scraggly manner. *Catskill Fly Fishing Center and Museum collection*

Fly of the Future optic streamer. Lee created a number of different streamer patterns using a variety of materials to finish off the fly. Optic patterns were typical of his new streamers. *Mike Valla collection*

Size 28 midge, tied by Lee Wulff without a vise. Lee was known to have fished for Atlantic salmon with a 2-ounce rod and size 28 dry flies. *Mike Valla collection*

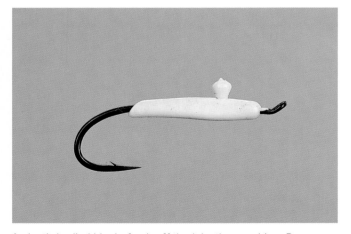

A plastic-bodied blank, fresh off the injection machine. Parachutes such as the Surface Stonefly hackles could easily be tied onto the plastic post. *Mike Valla collection*

Surface Stone Fly, tied by Lee Wulff. Lee called this plastic-bodied fly the salmon fly he'd most hate to give up. He used it mostly as a dry fly but said it could also be fished as a bucktail. Lee was partial to stoneflies ever since he used natural live ones, in the 1920s, for trout bait. *Mike Valla collection*

Royal Wulff, tied by Keith Fulsher. Fulsher and Harry Darbee once sat on a question-and-answer panel at a Theodore Gordon Flyfishers gathering. When asked which dry fly was their favorite, both replied, "The Royal Wulff." *Keith Fulsher collection*

Fly of the Future Riffling Hitch Fly, tied by Lee Wulff. Wulff also developed plastic-bodied salmon flies that could accommodate the riffling hitch. Lee didn't invent the hitch, but he popularized it in an article he wrote for *Outdoor Life* in 1946. Tying the leader with two half hitches behind the hook eye resulted in the fly skittering across the water surface. *Mike Valla collection*

CHAPTER 14

Fran Betters
(1931–2009)

Fran Betters, tying Ausable Wulffs. The Wulff-type dry flies influenced Betters in the development of his Ausable Wulff. Ray Bergman, who frequently fished the Ausable River, also influenced him at the vise. *Photo by Jan Betters*

The name Fran Betters is synonymous with the West Branch of the Ausable River, the stream he loved and fished for virtually his entire life. It is next to impossible to mention fishing that river, in the Adirondack region of New York, without also mentioning fly tier Betters, who was to the West Branch what the Dettes and Darbees were to the Beaverkill and Art Flick was to the Schoharie. And to cast a line on Fran Betters's stream without thought of the trout flies he developed on those waters over several decades would be equally difficult.

"He knew that river like no one I ever met knew a river," his longtime friend and fly fisher Bob Mead said a couple of years ago, shortly after Fran's death. Mead, who first met Fran Betters in the late 1960s and was a frequent visitor to his shop, was quick to attribute Fran's love for the Ausable to the influences of his father. Victor Betters, who with his wife, Margaret, adopted Fran at birth, had been fishing the Ausable for some 30 years before Fran was born. Victor introduced his young son to the Ausable, sharing with the boy his own love for trout fishing. Yet beyond trout, Fran's father also had something to do with introducing his son, albeit indirectly, to the art of fly tying.

The Ausable Wulff, tied by Fran Betters. Most fly tiers who admired Betters remembered him primarily for his Ausable Wulff, his signature pattern he developed in 1964 for fishing the Ausable River in New York's Adirondacks. *Bob Mead collection*

While Victor Betters was not a fly tier himself, fellow members of the Green Drake Club, which included Victor's friends and fishing companions Red Wilbur, Ray Bergman, Lou Kirtzknocker, and Bill Rawle, first exposed Fran to the craft in the late 1930s. Wilbur provided Fran with his first bits and pieces of fly-tying material and encouraged him to learn to tie flies. It was Wilbur, along with fishing author and tier Ray Bergman, who first taught the young Fran Betters to tie trout flies. In *Fran Betters' Fly Fishing, Fly Tying and Pattern Guide* (1986), Betters wrote, "Even though I was still a lad, I was sort of accepted in that inner circle of fly fishermen and had by then learned much about fly fishing and was in the learning process of fly tying. Most of my fly tying technique had been learned from Ray Bergman, and one of my dad's best friends and a master fly tyer, "Red" Wilbur from Rennsalaer [*sic*], N.Y."

In the same book, Betters also said that his father had served as the "catalyst" that greatly influenced the course and destiny of his life. Victor Betters successfully fished dry flies in some of the most turbulent stretches of the West Branch, with the younger Betters in tow. He observed that his father on many occasions returned home with trout so large that their "tails would hang over the sides of my mother's large dishpan." His father's success in fishing these difficult waters with complex currents left a lasting impression on Fran, who likewise learned to aggressively approach such waters with floating flies.

The geomorphology of the river presented fly-fishing challenges vastly different from those found on other New York trout streams, and Fran Betters was always eager to help those who came through the doors of his Adirondack Sport Shop in Wilmington seeking advice. While sitting at his tying bench there, he enjoyed talking about the time-tested fly patterns he had developed over the course of decades.

Some dry flies Betters tied and fished were quite different from what would be found in the boxes of most fly fishers. Fran experimented with and improved on a wide range of styles. Each freshly created pattern carried with it an interesting story, conceived through the philosophy that form follows function. Most fly tiers who have admired Betters remembered him primarily for his Ausable Wulff dry fly, which is no doubt his most famous pattern, perfect for the swift, strong currents found on its namesake river.

Catskill region fly tier Dave Brandt knew Betters for more than 40 years. Despite his attachment to Catskill waters and history, Brandt made frequent pilgrimages to the famed Ausable and Betters's home and shop. During a chat I had with Brandt shortly after Fran's death, he recalled, "It was an omnipresent fly. I can remember stopping in to see Fran, at his home, a couple of days after Christmas over 30 years ago. He tied a lot of flies during the winter, and of course that Ausable Wulff was always around his tying area. There was a simple card table there that day. Every square inch of that table was

The Ausable River, near Wilmington, New York. Fran Betters designed his trout flies for the turbulent currents that flowed through the stream that he fished and studied all of his life.

just covered with Ausable Wulffs, all standing upright on their noses. There were so many flies he had to push them up against each other to squeeze in yet another fly."

It is not surprising that Betters attached Wulff's name to the fly. Lee Wulff had already field-tested his own original Gray and White Wulff flies on the Ausable in the summer of 1930 with his fishing companion Vic Coty, and he had originally planned to name the Gray Wulff the Ausable Gray. Betters's Ausable Wulff is tied in the same vein as Lee's famous Wulff flies.

Betters first created the Ausable Wulff in 1964 after observing some unusual characteristics found in insects inhabiting the Ausable River. He noticed that many of the immature mayflies and stoneflies had a slight orange tinge on their thorax and head areas, which he attributed to the mineral content of the streambeds. In his *Fly-Fishing, Fly Tying and Pattern Guide*, he wrote, "My objective was a fly that would float well on the rough, heavy currents of the river, as well as in the riffles and white water pockets where large

Fran Betters's Adirondack Sport Shop was a gathering place for fly anglers fishing the West Branch of the Ausable River. Despite declining health, he was in his shop almost daily in his final years. *Bob Mead collection*

trout would hide. It needed to be highly visible to the trout and the angler alike, and I wanted to incorporate the rusty orange coloration of the mayfly and stonefly nymphs into the pattern. I decided that a Wulff pattern was the answer since the hair wing would provide both buoyancy and visibility to the fly. I settled on white calf tail for the wings."

Fran's characteristic rusty orange Australian opossum fur body that defined the pattern joined Betters's roughly shaped white calf wings on the Ausable Wulff. He also liked hot orange heads. Betters loved woodchuck guard hair for tailing, a material fly tier and author Eric Leiser also fell in love with. Almost echoing Leiser's words, Betters wrote, "If I were asked to select the two animals or materials from the two animals I believe most valuable to the fly tyer, I would have to pick the deer and that little animal known to us as the groundhog or more commonly the woodchuck." Like Leiser, Betters loved the barred effect the hair provided. Given that both Leiser and Betters agreed so adamantly on the attributes of woodchuck guard hair, it is no wonder that the editors at *Fly Fisherman* published articles by Betters and Wales along with an article by Lieser under the one title, "How Many Flies Can a Woodchuck . . ." in the June 1978 *Fly Fisherman*. Both Betters and Wales presented interesting and unique information about using woodchuck for highly effective flies.

In the story, Betters wrote, "In truth, there probably is no ultimate material, and perhaps we wouldn't really want to find one. For our search would then be ended, but the woodchuck is certainly a contender for the title." The first two patterns in which Betters employed woodchuck guard hairs were not floating flies; he used the hair on both his Dark and Light Stonefly Nymphs. However, in the *Fly Fisherman* article, Betters quickly got right into woodchuck as a valuable component for his Haystack dry flies, both light and dark versions.

The Haystack patterns are considered the precursors of the Compara-dun dry flies developed later by Al Caucci and Bob Nastasi. At first glance, they might be likened to small twigs. The prototype fly that Betters created in June 1949, while still a high school senior, later became one of his more popular creations. Betters felt that the effectiveness of the fly had to do with its versatility—it could be used to imitate several species of aquatic insects. The original fly, made from Key deer hair hackle or wings combined with muskrat or opossum dubbing, was a serious trout tempter.

In the *Fly Fisherman* story, Betters wrote, "These forerunners of the Comparaduns were tied with bleached Key deer hair and bleached Australian opossum for the Light Haystack, with gray whitetail deer hair forming the tail and fanning wings of the Dark Haystack, while the body fur was originally muskrat. Since Key deer hair is all but impossible to obtain, we started looking to another material." Betters found just what he wanted in woodchuck. "It not only produced a good-looking fly that floated well, but in many instances it outfished Haystacks tied with Key deer," Betters said. While he fully recognized the value of deer hair, calftail hair, and woodchuck hair as valuable components for good floating dry flies, he performed something of an about-face when it came to another of his popular patterns, the Phillips Usual.

The Phillips Usual, commonly called simply the Usual, was so effective that the fly soon colonized Catskill region shops, such as Dette Trout Flies, where it found a home with traditional wood-duck winged Catskill dry flies. Although the Ausable Wulffs and Haystacks are favorites on Ausable waters—and beyond—the Phillips Usual is also quickly associated with Betters's name. The Phillips Usual is also an odd-looking pattern; some would have difficulty accepting it as a trout fly. But it works.

The pattern, named after Bill Phillips, the fly fisher who first test drove it, is to many fly fishers an ugly-looking fly. Many of us wondered, after first fishing the fly, how something that looked like nothing more than lint out of the clothes dryer could be so effective. It looks like someone simply lashed a gob of hair from the pad of a rabbit's foot to a fishhook. But its ability to skitter along the water, sink, and pop back up again defined the fly as something very versatile: it could be fished as a hop-and-skip dry fly or a nymph.

It's an interesting dry fly, one that was sometimes surrounded by confusion as to who exactly first created the pattern. Betters's friend Bob Mead explained to me the controversy that swirled around the fly's creation: "The Usual, or Philips Usual as it was originally called, always created a controversy concerning who originated it. That's easy—Fran originated it. A hunter friend had left a couple snowshoe rabbit feet with Fran, and they'd been on his desk for a while. Fran had been tying Haystacks and was taking a break from tying. He spied the rabbit feet and decided to experiment with them. He tied maybe a half dozen Haystacks but substituted snowshoe rabbit feet fur instead of deer hair. I remember Fran sharing with me that they were originally tied in size 16s. The flies Fran tied were still on his desk when

Bill Phillips came in the room. The chatter came around to flies, and Bill noticed the different looking "Haystacks" and asked what they were. Fran said to Bill that there was no name attached to them; the flies were just experiments using rabbit feet." Mead, who loves to share stories about Fran Betters, continued describing the story of the Usual. "Fran suggested that Bill should give them a try on water. Bill was the first to try them out, and when he came back that evening, he said to Fran, 'You'd better name that fly, because it caught a lot of fish today.' A couple anglers asked Bill what he was using; he replied, 'The usual.' Fran said, 'Okay, the Usual it is—the Phillips Usual.'"

Mead explained that 25 or more years ago, Bill used to kid people, telling them he developed it. "'Why else would it have my name on it?' Bill used to say. It was a running gag. Newer people in the game would hear only one side and get into arguments about who created it."

The Phillips Usual and Haystack patterns are "must-have" trout flies on the Ausable River. Yet in addition to dry flies such as the Ausable Wulff, Haystack, and Usual, as well as some parachute patterns, Betters also tied plenty of subsurface patterns. "Mini" Muddlers, bucktails, and picked-out body nymphs tied with woodchuck guard hair tails were also in demand on the Ausable and other trout waters.

Anglers walking into his Adirondack Sports Shop during fishing season would no doubt catch Fran at his throne, surrounded by materials scattered on his bench, tying his favorite creations. During the last couple months before his death at age 78 on September 6, 2009, Fran appeared increasingly frail and required morphine injections for the pain he was experiencing. Admirably, he still insisted on spending time at his fly-tying table. Almost daily, his wife, Jan, and friend Pat Allen would bring him to the shop, where Pat had to lift him into his tying chair. That's where he wanted to be.

Ausable Bomber, tied by Fran Betters. The Ausable Bomber was a spin-off of the Ausable Wulff, tied with the same orangeish body and fluorescent orange thread. *Bob Mead collection*

Mini-Muddler, tied by Fran Betters. In his writings, Fran gave full credit to Don Gapen for the original Muddler Minnow. Betters tied the fly down to size 16 on Mustad 9671 hooks. *Bob Mead collection*

Light Haystack, tied by Fran Betters. At first glance, the Haystacks could be likened to small twigs. Haystack flies are considered the precursors of the Compara-dun dry flies developed later by Al Caucci and Bob Nastasi. The prototype fly that Betters created while still a high school senior in June 1949 later became one of his more popular creations. Betters felt that the effectiveness of the fly had to do with its versatility. *Mike Valla collection*

The Usual, tied by Fran Betters. The Phillips Usual, commonly called simply the Usual, was so effective that the fly soon colonized Catskill region shops, such as Dette Trout Flies, where it found a home with traditional wood-duck winged Catskill dry flies. The fly created a controversy over whether Betters or Bill Phillips had originated it. Bob Mead said to me during a discussion of the pattern, "That's easy—Fran originated it." *Mike Valla collection*

CHAPTER 15

Eric Leiser
(1929–)

Eric Leiser is known as one of the pioneers in making fly-tying materials available to tiers through his supply house, Fireside Angler. He is also a well-known fly-tying and fly-fishing author and talented tier. *Catskill Fly Fishing Center and Museum collection*

An advertisement in the "Buy-Sell-Exchange" section of *Field & Stream* magazine in the 1960s caught many a fly tier's eye: "HACKLE! Gamecock necks, feathers, furs, bucktails, tying materials—Catalog. Fireside Angler, Box 823, Melville, New York 11746." It was a simple time when only a dozen or so mail-order fly-tying supply houses existed across the United States. The few options available for purchasing materials included establishments such as E. Hille in Williamsport, Pennsylvania; Reed's in Caldwell, New Jersey; Bud Wilcox in Rangeley, Maine; Herter's in Waseca, Minnesota; and Buszek's in Visalia, California. These mainstay fly-tying material businesses served the needs of fly tiers everywhere. Yet Eric Leiser's Fireside Angler soon became the preferred supply house for many East Coast fly tiers, including me.

The H. J. Noll fly-tying kit that I received as a Christmas present in December 1967 contained barely enough feathers, flosses, and hooks to tie even the simplest fly patterns. The free catalog

Llama Streamers, tied by Eric Leiser. The Llama was not original with Leiser, but he popularized the largely unknown pattern. The pattern is an example of Leiser's fondness for using woodchuck guard hairs in trout flies. *Mike Valla collection*

I obtained thanks to Fireside Angler's striking advertisement in *Field & Stream*'s classified section proved the solution to acquiring quality materials.

And for Leiser, the idea of dabbling in the commercial enterprise of selling fly-tying materials seemed just the solution, too, for enhancing his growing interest in the hobby, which was sparked a few years earlier when he met iconic tiers such as Charlie DeFeo at New York Sportsmen's shows. Leiser needed tying materials, and he also needed a better career path. Fireside Angler served as the launching pad for his life-long involvement in the fly-tying and angling industry, an endeavor that proved much more lucrative and fulfilling than the music career he had hoped for.

In a draft of his memoir, *Woodchucks and Windknots*, Leiser recalled his formative years, explaining, "My aim in life was simple. I loved the outdoors. I loved fishing and hunting, but I couldn't afford it to the degree I wanted to pursue it. I decided to become a songwriter." As a first-chair violinist at Brooklyn's Most Holy Trinity High School in 1948, Leiser assembled a country-western band called the Rocky Mountain Serenaders, though none of the band members had been west of New Jersey. It wasn't long before music writer Fred Rose, who coauthored Gene Autry's and Hank Williams's songs, noticed Leiser. Leiser submitted a song or two to Rose, and eventually Rusty Gabbard recorded one of his creations on the MGM label.

Leiser's dream of raking in the money from his music career faded, however, when the first royalty checked arrived—it was for a meager $13.41. His second royalty check statement said, "No sales reported." Perhaps the fly-fishing industry was a better fit for Eric Leiser, talented songwriter or not. The vast number of tiers that were influenced by Leiser's fly-tying endeavors were undoubtedly thankful that he traded the music business for the fly-angling industry. His influences went far beyond supplying hairs, hooks, and hackle to fly tiers eagerly waiting for packages to arrive on their doorsteps.

Eric Leiser penned several important fly-fishing and fly-tying titles, among them *The Complete Book of Fly Tying*, *The Caddis and the Angler*, *Stoneflies for the Angler*, *The Book of Fly Patterns*, *The Metz Book of Hackle*, and *The Dettes: A Catskill Legend*. Many fly tiers regard his *Complete Book of Fly Tying* (1977) as his most influential. The book, which has sold more than 100,000 copies, is still cherished by tiers entering the hobby today. Lou Kasamis, a fly tier who picked up the book in the early 1980s, was a three-time overall winner of the Mid-Atlantic Fly Tying Classic and the 2010 winner of the Southern Appalachian Fly Tying Championship, said to me, "Eric's book was every bit like having an in-person expert instructor."

The book was published under the keen eye of Angus Cameron at the Alfred A. Knopf publishing company, and Leiser held Cameron in such high regard that he named a

Eric Leiser throwing loops. *Photo by Lefty Kreh, Catskill Fly Fishing Center and Museum collection*

fly in his honor—the Black Angus. This fly, one of a few Angus patterns that Leiser developed, was originally crafted when Cameron asked Leiser if he could tie a fly that was a cross between a Leech, Woolly Bugger, and Muddler to suit his needs while fishing for big Alaska rainbows. Cameron wanted a dark fly that would hug the stream bottom. Leiser created the fly by adding a mix of black feathers and hair to a lead-weighted Mustad 79580 hook.

The Black Angus is tied with four jet black hackles protruding rearward from the hook bend and several black marabou plumes wrapped up the hook shank, like folded hackle, which give the fly a "feather duster" effect. The feathery fly features spun and clipped deer hair at the head, Muddler style. In describing the pattern, Leiser wrote in *The Book of Fly Patterns* (1987): "I used marabou as the main ingredient simply because it has more movement than any other material and secured it like a wet-fly to the shank since it was the one way I could get an abundance without losing the action or creating an imbalance in the way it rode the current." Later versions of the Black Angus tied by Leiser in 2008 show a bit of flash, colorations added to the clipped hair head, and a bit of gray marabou.

The Black Angus produced well when field-tested for rainbows, and it became a standard on the Alaska waters

Angus Cameron fished. Complete step-by-step instructions for tying the Black Angus are found in Leiser's *Book of Fly Patterns* (1987).

Leiser also created the Bass Angus and Moray Angus, both tied in the same feathery style. The Angus flies also provided reasons for laughter at fly shows decades ago.

The Suffern Show, on Long Island, New York, was once one of the most popular fly-fishing gatherings on the East Coast. Eric Leiser could be found at the table, tying his Angus patterns. His good friend Lefty Kreh was right there with him, casting and instructing. Leiser's table was covered with the fluffy marabou feathers, just waiting to become airborne. Longtime Leiser friend Larry Kennedy, who now resides in Georgia, shared the following with me in during a recent chat about Eric: "Lefty would sneak up behind Eric while crowds were watching him tie Angus patterns. Smiling behind Eric's back, he'd motion to the crowd with his fingers, conveying a silent message to watch for Leiser's reaction. Lefty would then blow as hard as he could on the marabou sitting on the table, sending the fluffy feathers everywhere. Eric would then mutter his annoyance to the crowd—but it was all in fun." Lefty's prank made Leiser's Angus pattern tying demonstrations all the more entertaining.

Eric Leiser's Angus flies, especially his Black Angus, are considered his signature patterns. Yet other significant flies are closely associated with Leiser as well, although he did not originate them. Much as John Alden Knight is associated with the famous Mickey Finn Bucktail, which he did not invent but merely popularized, Eric Leiser is associated with two patterns he promoted: the Llama and the Chuck Caddis. Many collectors seek out not only the Angus patterns, but also these other two patterns tied with woodchuck guard hair.

While Leiser made it clear in print that he did not invent the Chuck Caddis and the Llama, tiers still consider these two highly productive patterns "Eric's flies." Woodchuck guard hair has a nice way of behaving on hook shanks, whether for dry flies or streamers, although it remains underappreciated for fly-tying qualities not found in other animal hair. As Leiser wrote in his 1987 *Book of Fly Patterns*, "The hide from this animal may be the most underrated and underused of all furs and fibers, though it does seem to be gaining more popularity in recent years."

Although woodchuck hair is not hollow, it floats a fly well. Leiser also liked its variegated color and suppleness, allowing it to be used for reasonably long-winged bucktails and streamers. Fran Betters liked woodchuck for tails on his Ausable Wulffs. In the June 1978 article that appeared in *Fly Fisherman* titled "How Many Flies can a Woodchuck . . ." Leiser argued the case for using woodchuck guard hair.

In the article, Leiser began the story of his love affair with woodchuck this way: "The speed limit was 50 miles per hour and I know I was not doing less. The furry creature that dashed in front of my station wagon didn't have a chance."

That wasn't the first time Leiser reported harvesting roadkills, and he could not leave this one behind either. After pulling over on Route 30, where the fatality occurred that day along the Pepacton Reservoir in the Catskills, Leiser went to work. "I opened the rear door of the wagon and removed a knife and a large plastic bag," he said. "I gutted the carcass and put it into the bag. The chest cooler in the station wagon would keep it cool until I got home where I could do a more efficient skinning and cleaning." His companion on the trip, George Hocker, who was driving right behind him, was bit perplexed why Leiser had suddenly pulled over on the winding, narrow road. He asked his friend what he was going to use the woodchuck for. "Almost anything" was Eric's reply.

The more he used woodchuck hair, Leiser said, the more he appreciated and recognized its potential as a great fly-tying material. "For me," Leiser explained in the article, "it is the most desirable piece of fly tying material I own, other than basic rooster necks." This was a significant statement from a man who probably had more experience with fly-tying materials than any other purveyor at the time. His *Fly Tying Materials* (1973) was considered the best book available at the time of its publication. Leiser's comments that woodchuck was his top-drawer material sent many tiers scurrying for the hair, although it was hard to come by in those years.

Given Eric Leiser's admiration for the attributes of woodchuck hair—its manageability, floating qualities, strength, and versatility—it is no wonder that he tied the Chuck Caddis and Llama by the hundreds. There was a time when Eric provided large supplies of both of these patterns, tied by him, to Dette Trout Flies shop in Roscoe, New York. Even today, the bins at the Dette shop stock the two patterns, and the Chuck Caddis remains a favorite of many.

The Chuck Caddis is an offshoot of the Eddy's Fly, a pattern that Gary Borger sent to Leiser. Leiser changed the fly's body material from the original burnt orange monocord to natural fur dyed in any of a few different shades. The final version of Leiser's Chuck Caddis could be tied in a variety of fur body shades—orange, gray, brown, olive, black, tan, and yellow. The orange and olive shades are still very popular; Leiser preferred the orange. He used hairs from the woodchuck's back for larger hook sizes and from the legs and tail for very small flies. Using the shorter hairs found on the legs and tail for smaller flies ensured that both white and black guard hair bands would show on the finished fly wings. Streamer patterns, such as the Llama, however, require the longer guard hair found on the back of the pelt.

The Llama has been a favorite pattern for years. Leiser popularized the fly, which was first created by Miles Tourellot, a Wisconsin Native American who died in the mid-1970s. When Eric Leiser handed out flies as gifts to friends, chances were that they would be Llamas, tied in the original red floss body shade. Other versions have been tied with black or white floss.

In *The Book of Fly Patterns*, Leiser wrote that when selecting a hook for the Llama, the hook-shank length, and thus the model used, was linked to the hair length available. He felt it important, just as in the Chuck Caddis, that all the guard hair color bands—black, tan, black—show in the wing. To ensure that all bands would appear in the wing, he suggested using hooks from 3XL to 6XL. Leiser preferred the Mustad 9575, 79580, and 38941 in sizes 6 to 12. He also liked to use weighted hook shanks. The Llama, with its long guard hair wings, likes to float, so Leiser wrapped the hook shank with lead wire to get the fly down when fishing it, casting it slightly upstream. Woodchuck guard hair has many uses in a variety of fly patterns, not just those tied primarily for trout. It's used as wing material in some salmon fly patterns, such as the popular Rat series.

Eric Leiser liked to experiment with fly-tying techniques and was always intrigued by the myriad new patterns developed by others. From his early years admiring Charlie DeFeo tying trout and salmon flies to the time he spent with every noted fly tier in the country over the course of his remarkable life in the industry, Leiser has seen it all. His books covering every facet of fly tying will continue to influence many new tiers who join in the fascinating pastime. Even a U.S. president had something to learn from Leiser. "By the way, I bought your book," President Jimmy Carter told the renowned tier at a Camp David barbecue that Leiser was invited to attend so he could demonstrate fly tying for the group. "Would you mind signing it?" Leiser asked Carter how he would like it inscribed. The president replied, "Oh, just inscribe it to Jimmy Carter."

Black Angus, tied by Eric Leiser. This pattern was originally crafted when Leiser's Knopf book editor, Angus Cameron, asked if he could tie a fly that was a cross between a Leech, Woolly Bugger, and Muddler to suit his needs while fishing for big Alaska rainbows. Cameron wanted a dark fly that would hug the stream bottom. *Mary Dette Clark collection*

Bass Angus, tied by Eric Leiser. *Mike Valla collection*

Black Angus, tied by Eric Leiser. For this later version, Leiser added some color and flash to the pattern. *Mike Valla collection*

Moray Angus, tied by Eric Leiser. Leiser can't recall the reason for this pattern's name. His friend Larry Kennedy of Georgia suggested that the fly may have been named after the moray eel. *Mike Valla collection*

Wet flies, tied by Charles DeFeo. Eric's first interest in fly tying stemmed from observing DeFeo, among others, tie trout flies such as these. *Ted Patlen collection*

Chuck Caddis, orange version, tied by Eric Leiser. The Chuck Caddis is an offshoot of the Eddy's Fly, a pattern sent to Leiser by Gary Borger. Leiser changed the fly's body material from the original burnt orange monocord to dyed natural fur. Like the Llama, it featured one of Leiser's favorite materials, woodchuck guard hair. *Mike Valla collection*

Chuck Caddis, green version, tied by Eric Leiser. *Mike Valla collection*

Chuck Caddis, gray version, tied by Eric Leiser. *Mike Valla collection*

Chuck Caddis, tied by Lou Kasamis. Kasamis, a frequent winner of fly-tying competitions, said Leiser's *Complete Book of Fly Tying* "was every bit like having an in-person expert instructor." *Mike Valla collection*

CHAPTER 16

Elizabeth Greig
(1902–1996)

Liz Greig at her tying table. Greig was a talented tier who created everything from trout wet flies to salmon flies to early saltwater patterns.
Photo courtesy of Bill Stuart.

John McDonald's now classic May 1946 *Fortune* article titled "Fly Fishing and Trout Flies" provided readers with one of the most comprehensive American fly-fishing histories to date. In his article in the large-format publication, McDonald told the story of how British fly-fishing author Frederick Halford influenced our own Catskill river fly tier Theodore Gordon. "The art of fly tying opens a treasure box of antiquity," he wrote, "full of fish stories, views of embattled theorists, memories of immortal fly-fishers, and all the numberless books that have made fly-fishing the most literary of sports."

He also introduced a new generation of fly-tying artists, accompanied by their favorite fly patterns that were cast on American waters in those years. These were the era's "who's who" in American fly-tying know-how. All the big names were there, their flies tastefully portrayed in Jack Atherton's captivating color illustrations. These trout flies represented the fundamental flies of that era, captioned with the name of the fly tier who helped make them famous. They were our "founding flies," tied by the old-school masters.

Paramachene Belle, tied by Liz Greig. Greig took complicated old patterns such as this one and reduced them to versions that even beginners could tie. With its single red duck quill slip on white, this is perhaps the simplest version of the pattern, which appeared in the *Noll Guide to Trout Flies*.

McDonald featured fly tiers Dan Bailey, Rube Cross, Walt and Winnie Dette, Harry and Elsie Darbee, Don Martinez, C. Jim Pray, Charles Kewell, and Paul Young. Among these better-known tiers was a woman named Elizabeth Greig, "a Scottish poacher's daughter, who learned her art at age seven." McDonald dubbed her the "First Lady of U.S. Fly Tying." The 12 wet-fly patterns that Greig tied for the Atherton illustrations combined what fly tying was at that time—half were of British stock, half were American creations.

Growing up in Scotland, Greig watched her father tie flies, standing on her toes by his tying bench. He knew at that time that she would grow up to be a "flee tyer." When she was 14, before she immigrated to the United States, Greig worked as a fly-tying apprentice under Robert Turnbull in Edinburgh, Scotland. She was a quick study, had a good eye, and worked quickly, making her an asset to Turnbull's fly factory.

She learned from the old Scottish ways, yet after immigrating to America in the late 1930s, it was here that she made her name. Greig tied salmon and trout patterns at one of the most popular fly and tackle shops in the country at that time, Jim Deren's Angler's Roost in New York City. John McDonald described Deren as a "gun-toting angler—he kills trout eating snakes—once met a shotgun-toting farmer whom he surprised by returning his fire in a stream shattering dual."

Even today, there are those fly anglers still living who turn red when Deren's name is mentioned, given some behaviors that his mother would not have been proud of. But like him or not, fly tiers gravitated to the Roost in search of tying materials, fishing flies, and just about any other type of tackle an angler would need. Greig was known as a kind and temperate woman who no doubt helped balance out Deren's personality. Her attachment to Deren's operation resulted in added exposure at New York Sportsmen's shows where the both of them shared a booth.

A great number of fly-fishing notables attended these shows, held at Madison Square Garden. Walt Dette was one of them, and like others, he became intrigued that Liz Greig could tie beautiful flies without the aid of a vise. They became good friends during those war years. Walt eventually offered to help out at the Roost, to keep it going after Deren got drafted. Walt frequently told amusing stories about his times helping out at the Roost, especially when Deren was home on leave. In Eric Leiser's book *The Dettes* (1992), Walt Dette described Greig's frustration with Jim Deren: "When Jimmy came home on leave he'd get a little pushy and have Liz doing all kinds of work in the shop. One day Liz got fed up and told him, 'Why don't I just put a broom up me arse and sweep the floor while I'm doin' whatever it is you want.'"

Yet however difficult it might have been for Liz Greig to tolerate Jim Deren, the association gave her a great deal of exposure, and many other fly tiers as well as writers took note of her talents. A. J. McClane, Joe D. Bates Jr., Rube Cross, Ray Bergman, Ray Camp, and Willliam F. Blades all brought Liz Greig and her flies into their writings. But her first major exposure came through McDonald's *Fortune* piece.

If Greig's trout flies looked anything like John Atherton's color trout-fly illustrations that were associated with her name, it would have been no surprise that McDonald desired to include her in his story. The wet flies that she created for Atherton were tied in the style of that era. These flies that included the Parmachene Belle, Butcher, and Wickham's Fancy, as well as mallard flank winged wet flies, such as the Rube Wood.

Greig's wet-fly style was simple; she avoided the material clutter found in the wet flies tied by others. Her Paramachene Belle, for instance, was tied without an ostrich herl butt tag, a feature found in older American pattern recipes such as those described by Mary Orvis Marbury and illustrated in the color fly plates by Dr. Edgar Burke in Ray Bergman's books. Greig simply married a single red quill strip to the top of the white wing quills. She also simplified other wet-fly patterns such as the Butcher and Silver Doctor, ordinarily complicated patterns that were time-consuming to tie, making her versions easier for a beginning fly tier to master.

It is interesting that the now-classic *Family Circle's Guide to Trout Flies and How to Tie Them* (later reprinted as the *Noll Guide to Trout Flies and How to Tie Them*), a pattern reference guide that first appeared in 1954, featured illustrations of wet flies tied in Greig's simple style. The Butcher and Silver Doctor patterns have numerous variations, some very complicated. Theodore Gordon, in his 1907 writings, said

Elizabeth Greig with her tying team at Eger Bait Company in Bartow, Florida. Greig didn't use a vise, but she obviously encouraged her crew of tiers to use one. *Photo courtesy of Bill Stuart*

that "the various patterns of the Silver Doctor are wondrous to behold." George Parker Holden, in his 1919 *Streamcraft*, similarly called the Silver Doctor "much diversified."

The *Guide* presented the Butcher and Silver Doctor in the same uncomplicated form as depicted in Atherton's illustrations of the Greig-tied flies that appeared in John McDonald's *Fortune* article. This was undoubtedly no coincidence; Jim Deren had a lot to do with the *Guide*. In the manual's preface, *New York Times* outdoor editor Ray Camp wrote, "All in all, it may be that Jim knows more about flies and fly patterns, and where they produce best, than any man in this country. Thus it was logical for the publishers of this book to choose Jim to select the classic trout patterns. And supplementing his knowledge, he has one of the finest collections of original patterns in the country. These he drew on for the illustrations that follow."

Deren selected representative patterns from those sold at his Angler's Roost; seven of the streamer illustrations that appeared in the *Guide* were Oatman patterns. It is likely that Elizabeth Greig's simple wet-fly versions also influenced Deren's selections. Indeed, all 12 of the wet flies that Greig tied for John Atherton's *Fortune* illustrations were found among the 72 wet flies featured in the manual. Greig's style and pattern versions doubtless influenced thousands of fly tiers over the years, given that the *Noll Guide* was the companion manual for the H. J. Noll fly-tying kit, the most popular kit available during the 1960s and early 1970s.

Nevertheless, however simple Elizabeth Greig's wet-fly style may have been, she was fully capable of tying complicated patterns. Greig's salmon flies, such as the Silver Doctor and Jock Scott, retained the older, more complex traditional styles. Many anglers, including Joseph D. Bates Jr., admired Greig's salmon-fly art, and Bates commented on her talents in *Streamer Fly Tying and Fishing*. In writing about fly tier Alex Rogan, he mentioned that Rogan was "generally considered to be one of the two greatest American Dressers of salmon patterns (the other being Elizabeth Greig, also of New York City)."

Bates's book also featured one of Elizabeth Greig's favorite fancy streamer patterns, the Campeona Streamer.

The fly looked more like a salmon fly, tied on a traditional up-eye salmon-fly hook. The photograph of the striking Greig-tied Campeona left no doubt that she was a great salmon-fly tier. The Campeona was not original with Greig, but she helped popularize the fly. Bates wrote, "This fly originated in Chili [*sic*] and is widely used in South America. The pattern was sent to Mrs. Greig, famed New York City dresser of salmon flies, for duplication of South American customers. Mrs. Greig has found it successful on New York State streams for all trout."

Elizabeth Greig's success on trout streams with the Campeona is interesting, given its salmon-fly characteristics. Yet it was the Greig Quill, a Catskill-style dry fly sometimes

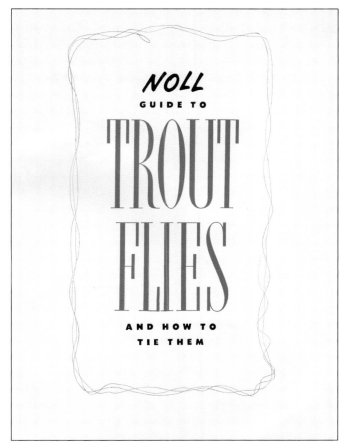

The *Noll Guide to Trout Flies and How to Tie Them* featured flies provided to illustrator G. Don Ray by Jim Deren of the Angler's Roost in New York City. Liz Greig tied flies for Deren at the Roost. The book influenced thousands of tiers from the 1950s to the early 1970s.

tied as a wet fly, that was most admired by fly anglers fishing streams such as the Beaverkill River. Ray Bergman included both dry- and wet-fly forms of the Greig Quill in the updated 1952 edition of *Trout*; both forms appear in Edgar Burke's color illustrations in that edition. Bergman called it "a variation of the divided Mandarin-winged flies, nearly all of which are good fish takers." Wood duck was largely unobtainable in those years, hence the mandarin duck substitute, which is nearly identical. The Greig Quill also found a place in William F. Blades's *Fishing Flies and Fly Tying* (1951), both in his black and white photo plates and in the dry-fly recipe section.

Many tiers liked peacock quill-bodied, wood-duck winged Catskill dry flies but years ago became frustrated with the unavailability of natural dun hackle to the amateur fly tier. Dyed hackle was mediocre at best and often of such poor quality and color that many of us used it only because we had to for patterns such as the Quill Gordon. Badger hackle was much easier to come by, in both good quality and color. Stripped peacock quill lovers embraced Greig's pattern, although she also stood by British dry-fly standards such as the Greenwell's Glory.

Jim Deren (far left) and Walt Dette (right at vise) tying at Deren's booth at a Sportsmen's show in 1937. Greig also tied flies at Deren's booth at shows. *Mary Dette Clark collection*

Rube Cross, the finicky Catskill fly tier who set the standard for dry flies in his region, met Elizabeth Greig at New York City sporting shows and became impressed with her talents. In his 1940 book, *Fur, Feathers and Steel*, Cross said that Greig, "the Scotch Lass who came across the Atlantic several years ago with a wealth of fishing and fly-tying knowledge under her curly locks, sticks to the Greenwell's Glory and has been a high-rod angler for the day many times on some of the Catskill streams." Cross included photographs of both dry and wet Greenwell's Glory flies.

While Rube Cross praised Liz Greig for standard wet-fly patterns such as the Greenwell's Glory, many still mention her name as a salmon-fly tier as well. Two years after John McDonald's *Fortune* trout-fly story was published, a follow-up article titled "Atlantic Salmon" appeared in the June 1948 issue of the same magazine. Artist John Atherton featured a few of Greig's favorite salmon-fly patterns: the Black Dose, Silver Wilkinson, and a beauty called the Durham Ranger, a very popular salmon pattern.

But salmon flies were not the only colorful fishing flies Greig was known for; she soon delved into the saltwater world as well. Bill Eger, a fishing lure maker in Bartow, Florida, eventually recruited Elizabeth Greig to supervise saltwater fly production. Tarpon, bonefish, and barracuda flies such as the Cornelia Fancy, Xmas Finery, and Lizzie were produced under Greig's direction.

Butcher, tied by Elizabeth Greig. Greig's Butcher is a simple version of a complicated pattern. This simple version that a beginner can handle is featured in the *Noll Guide*. *Catskill Fly Fishing Center and Museum collection*

Rube Wood, tied by Elizabeth Greig. Notice the beautifully formed mallard quill flank wings. It is difficult to make mallard flank behave the way Greig mastered it here. This pattern is featured in the *Noll Guide*. *Catskill Fly Fishing Center and Museum collection*

Wickham's Fancy, tied by Elizabeth Greig. This pattern also appears in the *Noll Guide*. *Catskill Fly Fishing Center and Museum collection*

Greig Quill, tied by Mike Valla. Ray Bergman included this pattern in both dry-fly and wet-fly forms in the updated 1952 edition of *Trout*. The Greig Quill also appeared in both the plates and dressings section of William F. Blades's *Fishing Flies and Fly Tying*.

Alder, tied by Elizabeth Greig. *Catskill Fly Fishing Center and Museum collection*

Lizzie saltwater fly, tied by Lee Schechter. Greig created this pattern while directing the tying team at the Eger Bait Company in Florida. She was one of the early saltwater fly tiers. Her signature saltwater pattern was the bright red and white Lizzie, a simple tie by today's saltwater standards. Greig's involvement with Eger's enterprise made her a pioneer in directing a commercial saltwater fly-tying operation. *Lee Schechter collection*

Olive Quill, tied by Elizabeth Greig. Greig was a master at tying mallard quill slip wings, and she precisely wrapped olive dyed stripped peacock quill bodies and hackle throats. *Catskill Fly Fishing Center and Museum collection*

Campeona, tied by Lee Schechter. In *Streamer Fly Tying and Fishing*, Bates featured one of Elizabeth Greig's favorite fancy streamer patterns, the Campeona Streamer. The fly looked more like a salmon fly, tied on a traditional up-eye salmon-fly hook. *Lee Schechter collection*

CHAPTER 17

Helen Shaw
(1910–2007)

Helen Shaw, fly tier. Shaw's book *Fly-Tying: Materials, Tools, Technique* instructed many first-time tiers in the critical steps necessary to craft a fishing fly. *Mike Valla collection*

While the title "First Lady of U.S. Fly Tying" was assigned to Elizabeth Greig in the mid-1940s by author John McDonald, another talented tier was worthy of a similar crown. In a tribute to Helen Shaw that appeared in the Fall 2011 issue of *The American Fly Fisher* after her death, the late Arnold Gingrich, founding editor of *Esquire*, was quoted as having once proclaimed Helen Shaw the "First Lady of Fly Tying;" hence, the fly-tying world was blessed by two first ladies of the craft. Many fly tiers owe their first lessons to Helen Shaw's classic book; they surely would echo Arnold Gingrich's words. The step-by-step tying lessons, captured in black and white photography by her husband, Hermann Kessler, took a lot of mystery out of simple procedures. It was Hermann who said to Shaw, "If you can show me and have me understand how to tie a fly, you will be able to show others."

Thanks to Shaw, many of us learned how to set hackle tip wings on dry flies, tie fan-wing patterns, spin and clip deer hair bodies, and wind hackle. The vantage point of the photography was such that fly tiers following her directions felt as though they were sitting right behind the

Red Shiner, tied by Mike Valla. This rare Helen Shaw streamer was presented in the first installment of "Match-the-Minnow Streamer Fly Series," in the July 1968 *Field & Stream*. Shaw was promoting barbless hooks more than 40 years ago.

vise themselves. The book's simple, clear, and uncluttered tying suggestions were perfect for beginning tiers.

Ed Ostapczuk, known as "Dean of the Esopus Creek" in the Catskill region of New York state, was one of the many tiers who appreciated Shaw's work. Ed recently shared his thoughts with me concerning Helen Shaw and her first book. "When I was a young teen back in the 1960s," he said, "there were no VCRs or DVDs on fly tying, no TU classes to attend, no one else in the neighborhood that tied flies, and very few books on the subject. I often wandered over to the town library after school, looking through the stacks for any and all information on fly tying and fly fishing. Helen Shaw's book, *Fly-Tying*, was the only one that included photos to visually show what she was trying to instruct, which was a monumental help to a 13-year-old kid like me."

Fly-Tying, the book that helped so many eager youngsters like Ed Ostapczuk learn the craft, had its roots in a passion that began when Helen Shaw was just a youngster at her father's side on the Lake Michigan shores in Sheboygan, Wisconsin. By the time Shaw was in high school, she began tying flies for a local shop called Art Kade Flycraft. Once she graduated from high school, Shaw worked at the shop full-time, not only tying flies to fill the bins, but also teaching others how to tie. Her talents at the vise grew, along with her reputation, and eventually she opened her own shop in the same town.

Shaw's reputation as a talented fly tier led to her participating at International Outdoor shows in Chicago during the late 1930s and early 1940s. It was after she married Hermann Kessler on September 10, 1953, that she relocated to New York City. It wasn't long before Shaw was part of the New York City fly-tying crowd, demonstrating her craft at New York Sportsmen's shows alongside other greats such as streamer tier Lew Oatman. Shaw was the first woman invited, in 1953, to a luncheon held in her behalf at the prestigious all-men's Anglers' Club of New York. Many of the members became clients, seeking out her trout flies.

Shaw's move to New York and her husband's position as art director at *Field & Stream* provided more contacts, including A. J. McClane, who served as fishing editor for the magazine. The association with McClane led to Shaw's selection as a contributor to the fly-tying section in *McClane's Standard Fishing Encyclopedia*. Her book *Fly-Tying*, along with her presence in McClane's writings, further influenced thousands of fly tiers around the globe. In his first installment of the "Match-the-Minnow Streamer Fly Series" in the July 1968 *Field & Stream*, McClane called Helen Shaw "without question one of the most artistic fly tyers in the world today," saying, "A professional of long standing, her attention to detail is at times awesome." The article included her favorite patterns alongside others by many of the best streamer tiers of that era, among them Keith Fulsher, Art Fusco, Sam Slaymaker II, Merton J. Parks, and Dave Whitlock.

Helen Shaw tying flies with talented streamer tier Lew Oatman at the *Field & Stream* booth at an annual New York Sportsmen's show. *Catskill Fly Fishing Center and Museum collection*

While Shaw did not include streamer patterns as her focal point in *Fly-Tying* or her later book *Flies for Fish and Fishermen: The Wet Flies* she did present some interesting streamers in both McClane's article and *Art Flick's Master Fly-Tying Guide* (1972). McClane's streamer article included color illustrations by Richard Evans Younger of Shaw's Emerald Shiner, Warpaint Shiner, Johnny Darter, and Red Shiner. It is interesting that Shaw tied the Red Shiner using a kinked barbless hook, a hook type that she characteristically used for many of her dry flies.

Shaw's patterns that appeared in McClane's article are not commonly tied today and are largely unknown.

Although a couple of Shaw's streamers in the McClane article, such as the Red Shiner, are fairly complex patterns to tie, beginning fly tiers can tackle her Golden Furnace Streamer presented in Flick's book. It's a simple pattern, tied in classic style, with red-gold furnace hackle wings. Helen Shaw's *Fly-Tying* focused on mastering tying the components

Helen Shaw's book *Flies for Fish and Fishermen* (1989) has no doubt inspired many wet-fly tiers.

that make up a fly; it did not feature complete step-by-step instructions for tying a specific pattern from start to finish. However, many tiers who purchased Flick's book were able to read and follow Shaw's step-by-step instructions for the Golden Furnace, enabling them to complete one of her suggested patterns. Shaw also presented an interesting bass pattern in the same book.

In describing bass flies, Shaw made some interesting observations, among them a comparison between bass flies and trout flies. Bass-fly aficionados have tackled fly pattern design with the same fervor as the most ardent trout angler and tier, developing new patterns specifically for that fish species. Yet, as Shaw so aptly wrote, "many trout-fly patterns greatly enlarged make excellent flies for bass fishing, and perhaps it

would be safe to say that any trout fly of a size large enough to entice a bass would be a good fly to use." And the converse was true as well, the Bubble Pup being a good example.

While Helen Shaw's Bubble Pup was developed for bass, it might prove useful for trout fishing on larger streams, and perhaps even for night fishing. The yellow clipped deer hair Bubble Pup was named for its ability to gurgle or bubble when twitched on water. It's a simple bass fly to tie, one that many Shaw fans would be surprised to learn was one of her favorites. It serves as a perfect example of Shaw's diversity in the art of fly tying, although it is widely felt that her real talents lie with wet flies.

Shaw's *Flies for Fish and Fishermen* is probably one of the best wet-fly tying books ever written and is a "must have" for any tier interested in crafting wet trout flies. It has no doubt inspired many wet-fly tiers. Shaw included many of the standard wet flies in her book—Coachman, Leadwing Coachman, Governor, Rio Grande King—and a large majority of those that appear in her color plates were tied following the flies that appeared in Edgar Burke's illustrations in Ray Bergman's *Trout*. Some flies that Shaw presented in her book would be called old-school "fancy flies"—vibrant-colored patterns, some with small jungle cock eyes at the shoulders as in the Golden Drake. One of Shaw's own wet-fly patterns has jungle cock eyes, giving the fly a decorative appearance.

Shaw's dry flies were also striking. She tied standard dry-fly patterns, such as the Cahills, Hendrickson, Whirling Dun, Lady Beaverkill, Rat-Faced McDougall variations, and Hopper flies. Some were tied on up-eye, kinked barbless hooks, heavily hacked and with interesting proportions, such as very short tails. Such patterns demonstrate Shaw's willingness to experiment.

Helen Shaw will always be known as a gifted fly tier who was ever mindful that trout flies are works of art. In celebration of Shaw's finest work, *Flies for Fish and Fishermen*, Dick Talleur's thoughts were included on the book jacket cover: "As a life-long wet-fly aficionado, I greatly admire Helen's work." Talleur praised the book and said he was certain that its readers would "achieve mastery of techniques that have challenged and frustrated aspiring wet-fly tiers for years." Helen Shaw's books have influenced many fly tiers, and there is no doubt that they will continue to do so in the years to come.

Bubble Pup, tied by Mike Valla. The yellow clipped deer hair Bubble Pup was one of Shaw's bass patterns. It was named for its ability to gurgle or bubble when twitched on water.

Golden Furnace Streamer, tied by Mike Valla. Shaw provided step-by-step instructions for tying this streamer in *Art Flick's Master Fly-Tying Guide*. The pattern can be easily tackled by beginning fly tiers.

Lady Beaverkill, tied by Helen Shaw. Shaw wasn't afraid to tie Catskill patterns with a little different slant, adding her own interpretations to this old standard fly. She substituted gray floss for the natural fur body the original dressing called for. The wings were set in the British style, heavily hackled. *Bill Leary collection*

Hopper, tied by Helen Shaw. Shaw's Hopper was heavily hackled to ensure adequate floating capability. *Bill Leary collection*

Rat-Faced McDougall, tied by Helen Shaw. This Harry Darbee Catskill favorite was tied using a kinked barbless hook. *Bill Leary collection*

Abe Munn wet fly, tied by Helen Shaw. Shaw often tied wet-fly patterns that were not standards. Many were of her own design. *Mike Valla collection*

CHAPTER 18

Lew Oatman
(1902–1958)

Lew Oatman at his tying bench in Shushan, New York, on the Battenkill River. Oatman is recognized as a pioneer in the development of streamer patterns that closely imitate specific baitfish and juvenile fish. *Photo by Herb Eriksson*

Brook Trout, tied by Lew Oatman. Oatman tied this pattern for fishing waters inhabited by large brook trout that prey on juveniles. It proved effective in Quebec, Canada. *Ted Patlen collection*

When Joseph D. Bates Jr.'s *Streamer Fly Tying and Fishing* was published in 1966, fly tiers regarded the book as the most complete reference ever written about that type of fly. The book's history of streamers and bucktails, the complete pattern survey it provided, and information describing the talent behind the flies made the work an instant classic. The full-color fly plates that highlighted the most important streamers and bucktails of that era were a ready reference for fly tiers everywhere. Anyone desiring to craft streamers and bucktails would turn to Bates's book first.

Streamer Fly Tying and Fishing introduced tiers to streamers that they never would have been aware of otherwise, talents hidden in local regions where they may already have stamped their mark of excellence. Many of the streamer patterns featured originated from talented tiers on Maine

lakes. Yet a number of other flies were created by individuals who were well known on their home waters but hardly heard of elsewhere. Lew Oatman fell into that group. It was Bates's book that raised his profile as one of the first fly tiers who focused most of his attention on baitfish imitations.

Sadly, Oatman's name and his baitfish imitations were not widely recognized until after his death in April 1958 and the subsequent release of Bates's book. Oatman wrote two articles for *Esquire* magazine—"The Shushan Postmaster" in the March 1956 issue and "Streamer Flies from Nature's Patterns" in the August 1956 issue—but it was Bates who helped elevate Oatman's profile as an innovative fly tier. Prior to that, A. J. McClane mentioned Lew Oatman and a couple of his patterns in his 1953 *Practical Fly Fishermen*, and the 1954 *Family Circle's Guide to Trout Flies and How to Tie Them* featured seven of Oatman's streamers: the Doctor Oatman, Male Dace, Brook Trout, Golden Darter, Yellow Perch, Golden Smelt, and Silver Darter. However, tier originator names were not included alongside any of the 152 trout flies illustrated in color by G. Don Ray in this slender reference manual. For many tiers who used the *Guide*, the creator of those seven beautiful streamer patterns remained a mystery.

Once Bates's book was published, six years after Oatman's death, the significance of Lew Oatman's contributions to fly tying became apparent, and he received greater recognition for his baitfish imitations. Plate VI in the 1966 edition of Bates's book showed 17 imitator patterns created by Oatman: the Golden Shiner, Red Fin, Silver Darter, Cut Lips, Brook Trout, Red Horse, Gray Smelt, Golden Smelt, Trout Perch, Yellow Perch, Male Dace, Golden Darter, Mad Tom, Ghost Shiner, Doctor Oatman, Shushan Postmaster, and Battenkill Shiner. The book also listed complete pattern dressings for each of these flies. Shortly before Oatman died, he sent Bates a letter including background notes and dressings for 12 of the 17 patterns that eventually appeared in the book. Fly tier and angler Keith Fulsher supplied the information for the others. Excerpts from Oatman's letter also appeared in Bates's book. Keith Fulsher recently provided a copy of the historic letter.

"One point is that while many flies were designed for landlocked salmon and have also been effective for trout, very few have been designed especially for trout and on heavily fished waters, while at the same time resembling forage fish common to trout streams," Oatman wrote. "Some of my patterns such as Silver Darter, Golden Darter, Gray Smelt, Ghost Shiner when tied in small sizes will often take rising trout when they won't take a dry fly and apparently these must resemble small fry or nymphs."

Bates had the dressings for Oatman's flies but lacked a complete set of flies for his upcoming book. That's when talented fly tier Keith Fulsher stepped in to help. Keith corresponded with me, providing additional insight into Oatman's

Lew Oatman and Shushan's colorful postmaster, Al Prindle. Besides Oatman, Prindle gained the admiration of Lee Wulff, artist Norman Rockwell, and local resident Herb Eriksson, who snapped this photo in the 1950s. Oatman named a fly after him, the Shushan Postmaster.

connection with Bates. "I had first corresponded with Joe Bates in June 1965 and first met him in July of that year," Fulsher wrote. "He sent me a list of the Oatman patterns he knew existed and earmarked the four for which he had samples. He asked me to loan to him the [Oatman] patterns I had, for photography. I couldn't do that as they were all framed up, etc., and anyway I didn't have all the missing ones but offered to tie any patterns that he wanted. We had a lot of correspondence back and forth and a few meetings, and in September 1965 he asked me to tie six of the patterns, which I did. Then he asked me to tie six more of the patterns, and finally in a letter dated September 21, 1965, he asked me to tie all the patterns he didn't have copies of, which I did. You can see from all of this that Lew had been dead for seven years when Bates was working on the book, and Bates had to either shop around to locate all of the patterns (an impossible task) or ask someone else to tie them. The book was published in 1966."

Fulsher had known Oatman well and occasionally turned to him for suggestions concerning fly-tying problems. In Judith Dunham's *Atlantic Salmon Fly* (1991), Fulsher wrote, "I cut apart a lot of flies, including some of Lew's—I wish I still had those flies. I did buy materials from him. He had the best custom-dyed saddle hackle I've ever seen."

Keith Fulsher's assistance to Joseph D. Bates Jr. provided readers and fly tiers a glimpse into Lew Oatman's baitfish imitations. Streamer fly tiers interested in Oatman's patterns still use the pictures of the 17 flies in Plate VI of the 1966 edition, along with the accompanying notes, as reference.

Several of Oatman's pattern names reflect his intimate association with his home Battenkill River waters. The Doctor Oatman was named after his father, Lewis R. Oatman, a well-respected Greenwich, New York, physician who died in 1944 after practicing in the community for 43 years. Greenwich is a small village situated on the lower Battenkill River, a couple miles upstream from its mouth with the Hudson River. It is no wonder that Lew named a trout fly after his father, a very active community member whom his hometown newspaper, the *Greenwich Journal*, called "an example of the highest type of country doctor," saying, "Through all the years of his life in Greenwich and up to the hour of his last illness any call for his services met with a prompt response."

It is obvious that the Battenkill River played an important role in Lew Oatman's development as a fly angler and tier. In an August 12, 1951, letter to Ray Bergman, Oatman wrote, "I was born and raised in Greenwich, New York on the Bat-

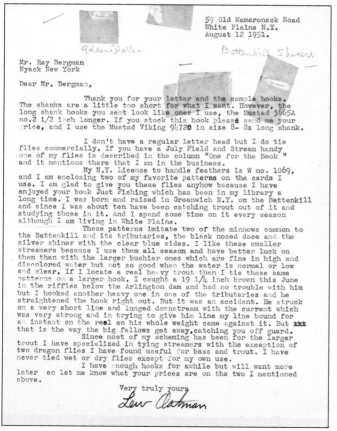

Lew Oatman corresponded with such notables as Ray Bergman, with whom he shared information about his experiences with his baitfish patterns. *Jill and Mark Schwarz collection*

tenkill and since I was about ten have been catching trout out of it and studying those in it. And I spend some time on it every season although I am living in White Plains."

Although Greenwich is situated on the lower few miles of the famous trout stream that arises in the Green Mountains of Vermont, trout still inhabit the river just upstream from where the Oatman family once lived. Lew Oatman eventually relocated to White Plains, New York, where he worked in the banking industry. However, he never cut his ties with the Battenkill and eventually acquired a small home on Roberson Road in the town of Shushan, on the west side of the river, where he tied his flies.

"He was working as a banker downstate; he came back up here for his health," 89-year-old Herb Eriksson told me during a recent chat. "He had a big table in the living room, and that's where all his tying materials were arranged." Eriksson grew up in Shushan and spent time in the 1950s following Lew Oatman and the local postmaster, Al Prindle, one of the more colorful town residents, around with his camera. Eriksson photographed Oatman at his tying table at his Roberson Road home. "I saw Lew Oatman every week," Eriksson added, recalling his fond memories of those years.

Oatman's house was within walking distance of the well-known Buffum's Bridge pool and the Spring Hole pool. A small shop called the Tackle Box served as the perfect place to enjoy cracker barrel discussions with town residents and sell his streamer patterns. Postmaster Al Prindle was so highly regarded by just about everyone that Oatman believed he was worthy of his own fly, and hence the Shushan Postmaster "streamer" (technically a bucktail) was born. The gold tinsel ribbed, yellow floss bodied pattern with fox squirrel tail hair for the wing was created in 1953.

In *The Compleat Lee Wulff* (1989), Lee called Prindle "the most memorable of all my fishing companions." He first met Prindle in 1931 while fishing the Battenkill. Wulff was living in New York City at the time. When Wulff walked through the Shushan post office doors after a five-hour drive from the city, Prindle dropped everything, turning his postal duties over to his wife, Anna, and headed to the river with his friend. They fished together in those years almost every weekend. Wulff wrote warmly about the times Prindle sat on the riverbank discussing the works of Hewitt, La Branche, and other important fly-fishing authors.

Norman Rockwell, who lived not far from Shushan at the time, used Prindle as a model for numerous paintings, some of which appeared in calendars. Lew Oatman also felt all the world should know about Prindle, and he wrote an article published in the March 1956 issue of *Esquire* magazine titled "The Shushan Postmaster." Oatman's "streamer" bearing Al Prindle's name was a fitting tribute to the postal worker who won many hearts, both onstream and off.

As was true with his Shushan Postmaster and Doctor Oatman, Lew Oatman's streamer pattern names were not arbi-

The Spring Hole on the Battenkill River, Shushan, New York. Oatman tied his famous streamers at his home, which was within walking distance from this famous pool upstream from Buffum's Bridge in Shushan, New York.

trary. They had some connection to an individual, an actual baitfish or juvenile fish, or a stream. Oatman's notes to Joseph Bates indicated that he had created the Mad Tom to represent the small, dark catfish species. Mad Toms are tiny catfish that grow only a couple inches long. Although Oatman and Bates didn't mention it, a Battenkill River tributary is called the Mad Tom Brook. The Mad Tom is a good example of how Lew Oatman used observation and reasoning in tying his creations. Black hackle represented catfish whiskers, and the tricolored marabou tails gave the fly plenty of action in the water.

Oatman tied his baitfish imitations with the same degree of observation that he applied to the Mad Tom. He often nested saddle hackle shades in an attempt to better simulate the reflective colors found in shimmering baitfish or juvenile fish such as yellow perch. Oatman's Cut Lips and Red Horse patterns were tied with olive saddles nested inside a pair of dun saddles. His Battenkill Shiner was tied using two silver badger hackles nested over a pair of medium blue saddles. The Male Dace used olive hackle surrounded by golden badger. Not all of Oatman's streamers had mixed feather shades in their wings, tails, and throats—the Doctor Oatman wing, for example, was tied with four white saddles—but combining colors was a common theme. Yet no matter how

his beautiful flies were tied, no matter how effective they proved when fished, Oatman's baitfish imitations served as the foundation for other streamer patterns that followed.

In *Trout* (1978), Ernest Schwiebert wrote about fishing with Lew Oatman at Buffum's Bridge pool, which had the reputation of harboring large trout. The hook-jawed 6-pound brown that smashed the Yellow Perch streamer pattern that Oatman handed Schwiebert that day proved the point.

Schwiebert said that Oatman tied his streamers "so beautifully that they were as exquisite as the most elegant dry flies of the Catskill school, and his imitative theories made him the father of the scientific approach to baitfish patterns." Schwiebert also noted that Oatman was "perhaps the first streamer expert to embrace the theory of baitfish imitation systematically. . . . Oatman's example has been expanded in the imitative patterns of contemporary fly dressers like Keith Fulsher, Dave Whitlock, Roy Patrick, Polly Rosborough, Don Harger and Gary Howells." Lew Oatman has not been forgotten; his founding patterns are still admired by followers of his craft who have embraced his theories.

Chris Del Plato, a New Jersey streamer aficionado and one of Oatman's greatest admirers, firmly believes that Oatman's theories have validity.

Lew Oatman and postmaster Al Prindle cleaning trout. Oatman and Prindle were close friends in Shushan, New York. *Photo by Herb Eriksson*

Chris shared the following thoughts with me: "Over the decades, the big fish's desire for big meals has been well documented. Oatman's broad efforts of 'matching the baitfish' and his exact imitation designs have stood the test of time, as effective now as they were in his heyday. Natural colorations and key characteristics make these patterns easily identifiable to large fish as prey they're accustomed to feeding on. Those fishing these patterns today may have a distinct advantage. Dedicated (classic) streamer fishers are few and far between, and a majority of onstream competition and pressure will likely come from bug slingers."

There are other streamer-fly aficionados who have tied Oatman patterns for decades. As a youngster, Teddy Patlen learned the basics of Lew Oatman streamers from his father back in the 1960s. "My lifelong love affair with Oatman patterns started very early," he said to me. "My dad, a bricklayer by profession, tied bucktails and streamers for a local shop. He had the eye for precision that all bricklayers have, but he also had the rough hands that accompanied that type of work. It was difficult for him to wrap a nice, smooth floss body up a long hook shank. When my tying skills were proficient, I took over dressing the floss bodies on bucktail and streamers; he finished the rest of the fly. We tied Oatman's Silver Darters and Male Daces. We admired Oatman's color schemes created to imitate specific baitfish. Only his Doctor Oatman could be considered a fanciful fly, an attractor."

Lew Oatman's patterns are still fished today on the Battenkill River waters where he first studied baitfish and crafted his streamers and bucktails to imitate them. While some may consider his flies antiques, they are still highly effective and worthy of a place in any fly angler's vest. In *Thunder Creek Flies: Tying and Fishing the Classic Baitfish Imitations* (2006), Keith Fulsher reminded readers of Lew Oatman's significance: "The exceptional progress Lew made in the field of baitfish imitation was cut short by his untimely death, but the dozen and a half patterns he developed will long remain favorites of fishermen who prefer close copies of natural baitfish."

Other baitfish tiers followed Lew Oatman's example, as Joseph D. Bates wrote in his book *Streamer Fly Tying and Fishing*: "Following in the footsteps of the revered Lew Oatman, a knowledgeable angler from Lancaster, Pennsylvania, named Sam Slaymaker II, adopted a different but equally sensible approach to the development of exact imitations. Knowing that trout in streams where they spawn have no compunction against devouring their young, Sam developed three bucktails to imitate their young: the Little Brown Trout, Little Rainbow Trout and Little Brook Trout." Slaymaker's classic bucktails continued the trend first set by Lew Oatman, who helped divert attention from matching the insect to matching the baitfish and juvenile gamefish.

A triplet of Shushan Postmasters, tied by Mike Valla.

Mad Tom, tied by Lew Oatman. The Mad Tom was described in a letter Oatman sent to Joseph D. Bates for inclusion in Bates's *Streamer Fly Tying and Fishing*. Oatman created the Mad Tom to represent a small catfish species of the same name. Mad Toms are tiny catfish, growing only a couple inches long. Although Oatman and Bates didn't mention it, a Battenkill River tributary is called the Mad Tom Brook. *Jill and Mark Schwarz collection*

Golden Shiner, tied by Ted Patlen. Oatman created this pattern to imitate the minnow of the same name. He called it a "clear water fly" and tied it down to very small sizes.

Male Dace, tied by Ted Patlen. The pattern imitates the male Black-Nose Dace minnow in its spawning colors. Back in the 1960s Patlen helped his father tie batches of the pattern.

Silver Darter, tied by Chris Del Plato. A New Jersey streamer aficionado who is one of Oatman's greatest admirers, Del Plato firmly believes that Oatman's theories have validity.

Yellow Perch, tied by Lew Oatman. The fly was designed for large-mouth bass fishing. Oatman's patterns also imitated juvenile fish that large fish prey upon. However, Ernie Schwiebert once took a 6-pound brown on the pattern while fishing on the Battenkill River in Shushan, New York. *Bill Leary collection*

Red Horse, tied by Ted Patlen. Oatman designed the fly as a bass pattern to fish waters inhabited by the red horse sucker.

Cut Lips, tied by Ted Patlen. Oatman tied the pattern to imitate the cut lips minnow, a dark minnow found in trout streams around fast-moving water.

Doctor Oatman, tied by Ted Patlen. Lew's father was a respected family doctor in Greenwich, New York, on the Battenkill River. This pattern was named in honor of Dr. Lewis R. Oatman.

Red Fin, tied by Lew Oatman. This pattern was created to imitate the red fin shiner. Keith Fulsher advised Joseph D. Bates that in its original form, the red marabou used for the throat and tail was longer. Oatman decided to clip both in its final form, which he later preferred. *Bill Leary collection*

Battenkill Shiner, tied by Ted Patlen. Oatman tied this pattern for his home stream, the Battenkill River, where he had fished for trout since age 10.

Trout Perch, tied by Ted Patlen. This is another streamer tied for warmwater fishing. Pike perch feed on schools of trout perch when the minnows run to creeks to spawn.

Little Brown Trout, tied by Mike Valla. Joseph D. Bates wrote in *Streamer Fly Tying and Fishing*, "Following in the footsteps of the revered Lew Oatman, a knowledgeable angler from Lancaster, Pennsylvania, named Sam Slaymaker II, adopted a different but equally sensible approach to the development of exact imitations."

Ghost Shiner, tied by Ted Patlen. This Oatman streamer is also recommended as an effective pattern in the very low, clear water typical in late-summer fishing.

Gray Smelt, tied by Lew Oatman. This pattern was tied for the minnow that bears its name. It has proved effective on waters inhabited by smelt and has been used as a trolling pattern on Cayuga Lake in New York state. *Bill Leary collection*

CHAPTER 19

Keith Fulsher
(1922–)

Keith Fulsher, creator of the Thunder Creek series of flies. Fulsher's creativity resulted in new approaches to imitating baitfish and juvenile fish that serve as prey for bass, trout, and other fish species. His talents at the vise, however, go well beyond his famous Thunder Creek patterns. *Keith Fulsher collection*

Redlip Shiner, tied by Keith Fulsher. Featured in Fulsher's 1973 book, this pattern imitates a small minnow found in Virginia and North Carolina. Fulsher cut off the black floss at the tail as a continuation of the black lateral stripe.

J oseph D. Bates Jr. sent a letter to talented fly tier Keith Fulsher on September 2, 1965, commenting on his beautiful baitfish imitations, which were going to be represented in Bates's upcoming book: "I surely admire your expertness in dressing flies. They are beautiful. I think I've done a good job in writing up your 'Thunder Creek Series'—and your name will also appear elsewhere in the book. Awfully busy trying to get the manuscript completed by October 1st spin fishing."

Bates's 1950 *Streamer Fly Fishing in Fresh and Salt Water* was out of print by this time and considered a collector's item. However, his new title, *Streamer Fly Tying and Fishing*, was nearing completion for its release in 1966. Bates said that the new, expanded version would incorporate "the better parts of the older one and much new material besides." It would include the most exhaustive list of streamer tiers ever assembled into one work, covering the "who's who" in streamer-tying know-how. Fresh names would be introduced, along with comprehensive and detailed histories of all the patterns that were presented. And among the new tiers and patterns was Keith Fulsher and his newfangled Thunder Creek flies.

Fulsher, a native of north-central Wisconsin, spent his early years fishing for wild brook trout with his father and uncle during the 1920s and 1930s. It was during that period that he first dabbled in fly tying, his earliest creations crafted from yarn or cloth scraps—anything that might entice the panfish that he fished for with his cousin. Those were the years of 9½-foot, three-piece cane rods, gut leaders, and snelled wet flies. Service to his country during World II interrupted Fulsher's trout fishing. After discharge, he enrolled in Brooklyn College, where he met his wife, Lois, and then took a more serious interest in fly tying, starting with a simple kit and instruction sheet.

Many of the country's finest and most talented fly tiers, including Rube Cross, Herb Howard, Lew Oatman, and Alex Rogan, became good friends and mentors and helped Fulsher develop his craft. They were there to answer his tying questions. Such resources had a positive impact on Fulsher's artificial fly creations, their beauty and form crafted with attention to every detail, each addition of material having purpose.

Fulsher's Thunder Creek series, formally created in 1962, was born from design concepts that master tier Carrie Stevens experimented with for saltwater patterns. The flies used Stevens's reverse-tied bucktail concept, which Fulsher had become aware of through Bates's *Streamer Fly Fishing in Fresh and Salt Water*. In recent correspondence, Fulsher explained, "I did not know Carrie Stevens, nor did I ever meet her, although I did know of her reputation as a streamer fly tier. Back in the mid to late 1950s and into the 60s, I was tying a lot of streamer flies for the Angler's Cove in New York City. I was tying the New England type streamers, including some of Carrie's patterns and also some of Lew Oatman's. It was during this period that I started to experiment with some patterns that would come closer to a minnow in appearance. I was familiar with the old reverse-head wet flies of the 1800s, and I knew from Joe Bates's first book on streamers that Carrie had experimented with a saltwater fly that had a reversed head of bucktail, although apparently she didn't tie many of them, which leads me to feel she didn't care for them compared to the beautiful streamers she tied. It was from that background that the Thunder Creek patterns evolved."

The Stevens Reverse-Tied Bucktail, as Bates described it, combined saddle hackles with bucktail tied down so that the hairs were pointed beyond the hook eye. The bucktail was then gathered backward tightly, projecting the hairs toward the hook bend.

A few thread wraps lashed down the hair, creating a striking band and a well-defined hair head. The band and head were flooded with varnish.

Prairie River. Fulsher tested improved versions of his first Thunder Creek flies on this Wisconsin River that flows just a few miles from his hometown of Tomahawk and not far from Thunder Creek.

Keith Fulsher used Stevens's basic reverse-hair head concept, yet his own flies were unique. As Bates wrote in his new book on streamers, "Keith's series of four primary patterns and three secondary patterns are so unusual and enjoy such an impressive record in taking game fish in so many regions that they deserve special attention as a notable contribution to American Angling."

Bates gave Fulsher quite a bit of acreage in his book. The primary and secondary patterns were listed, along with detailed dressings for the hook-shank covering (tinsel), lateral stripe, back hair shade, stomach hair shade, and eye/pupil lacquer color. The primary patterns were Black-Nose Dace, Golden Shiner, Red Fin Shiner, and Silver Shiner; the secondary patterns were Emerald Minnow, Satin Fin Minnow, and Spotted Tail Minnow. A "Sentimental Pattern," the Mickey Finn Bucktail, was also described. The simple Silver Shiner was the first in Fulsher's series and had been field-tested in northern Wisconsin trout waters.

Keith Fulsher enjoyed fishing a small brook called Thunder Creek on his excursions to Wisconsin's north woods regions. Thunder Creek winds and turns through meadows and swamps; its brook trout find refuge among the deadfalls and beaver ponds. It's an isolated stream, well off main roads. There are a couple of different creeks in Wisconsin bearing the same name; Keith assisted me in finally finding "his" Thunder Creek, in the summer of 2012. In the spring of 1962, Fulsher took along a few prototypes of the reverse-tied bucktails, somewhat overdressed, on downturned-eye hooks to Thunder Creek. He wasn't entirely pleased with the bulky appearance but decided to take them along on the trip anyway.

Fished above a beaver dam, the brown and white fly with its silver tinsel body took a number of brook trout, convincing Fulsher that the fly design had potential. He made a couple design changes, decreasing the amount of bucktail, which gave the fly a more streamlined appearance, and switching to straight-eyed bait hooks. The straight-eyed hooks provided

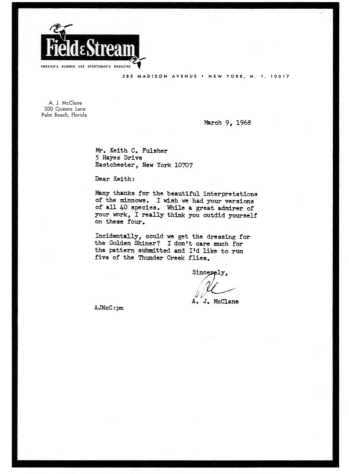

Two years after Bates's book featuring Fulsher's unique Thunder Creek flies was published, A. J. McClane followed up with a July 1968 *Field & Stream* article that was the first in the "Match-the-Minnow Streamer Fly Series." Fulsher's Thunder Creek flies were featured in the series, along with patterns by the top streamer tiers in the country.

a better continuum, causing the eyes to almost become part of the head.

The fly heads and added-in details such as red "gills" are particularly important in the Thunder Creek design. Fulsher made the point that the head contributed around one-fifth of a minnow's total length. Traditional streamer and bucktail designs did not recognize the relationship of head size to total length. The small, red gills added realism to the flies. In recent correspondence, Fusher explained his red gill feature: "In early times I made the gills from the red tying thread that I used in tying the whole fly. The problem was that I had to use more white hair for the belly of the fly so the red wouldn't bleed through under the head when I put on the finishing coat of lacquer. I solved this problem by tying the fly with white thread and adding the gills with red lacquer. This let me tie the fly more sparsely; if there were any small openings between the reversed hairs in the head, the white tying thread blended in. I painted the gills only on the bottom sides of the head to make them appear more realistic; I thought

Joseph D. Bates Jr.'s 1966 letter reveals his excitement over the book that helped raise the profile of Keith Fulsher and his soon-to-be-classic Thunder Creek series of patterns.

there was too much red when it circled the head." The tightly pulled-back hair heads with their neatly painted eyes created from little dabs of red enamel define Fulsher's Thunder Creek series.

When compared with Thunder Creek patterns, most bucktails and streamers, as Fulsher pointed out in his writings, are crafted with heads made entirely from built-up thread, inadequate in size. Even when eyes are painted on the thread heads with enamel, the fly's proportions do not approximate those found in a natural baitfish, and the eyes overwhelm the small heads. Carrie Stevens's reverse-hair bucktail concept provided Fulsher with the head proportions he desired, creating plenty of head margin surrounding painted eyes that were later added to the basic design. It also improved the fly's behavior while fished.

Traditional saddle hackle streamers behave much differently when trolled or quickly retrieved in fast-moving water. The saddles most often streamline themselves along the top of the hook shank, moving slightly side to side as the fly moves through the water. In *Thunder Creek Flies*, Fulsher wrote, ". . . when these flies are fished slowly—and especially when they are sinking or being gradually moved up and down—the wing becomes entirely separated from the body, leaving the imitation looking like anything but a minnow."

Fulsher also recognized that some of the other traditional streamer design characteristics did not simulate natural minnow morphology. One of the most basic features in traditional baitfish imitations is a floss body with tinsel ribbing. While the tinsel wraps added a bit of flash, an attempt to imitate a minnow's sheen and sparkle, the tapered floss fell short of representing overall baitfish profile shapes. As Fulsher added, "Unfortunately, bodies of tapered floss or other material just don't give the desired oval cross-section." Streamer and bucktail fly design needed to be changed, and Fulsher took on the challenge.

The Bates book popularized Keith Fulsher's new approach to baitfish imitations, creating almost instant fly pattern classics. The Thunder Creek flies found their way into *Field & Stream* fishing editor A. J. McClane's writings in the magazine's July 1968 issue concerned with baitfish imitations. McClane wrote a letter on March 9, 1968, to Fulsher, commenting, "I wish we had your versions of all 40 species. While a great admirer of your work, I really think you outdid yourself on these four."

Bates had introduced the Thunder Creek patterns, and McClane's writings helped the momentum. The growing popularity of the patterns was further enhanced when Keith Fulsher's *Tying and Fishing the Thunder Creek Series* was published in 1973. Fulsher's Thunder Creek series grew from the 8 flies introduced in Bates's *Streamer Fly Tying and Fishing* to the 15 freshwater patterns he presented in his own book. By the time *Thunder Creek Flies* came out in 2006, Fulsher's list had grown to 22 freshwater and 6 saltwater flies.

All but a couple patterns that appeared in Fulsher's book were designed to imitate specific baitfish or immature gamefish. Fulsher created the Marabou Shiner as a fish "locator."

The Mickey Finn is an attractor pattern, a spin-off from John Alden Knight's famous creation. The Marabou Shiner is a generic pattern, intended to imitate a wide variety of silver-sided, dark-backed, white-bellied baitfish. Fulsher added modern materials such as Krystal Flash to the patterns, creating a bit more sparkle than found in the originals he first tied. Thunder Creek flies that represent immature gamefish patterns are particularly interesting. Among those represented in Fulsher's 2006 book are the Yellow Perch, Blueback Trout, Brook Trout, Brown Trout, Rainbow Trout, Smallmouth Bass, and Largemouth Bass (the last three are shown on page 123).

All capture the shades and hues found among the fish in their early stages of development. They are as beautiful as they are effective.

Thunder Creek. Located in northcentral Wisconsin, near Willow Lake, this tea-colored stream flows through woods, swamps, and meadows. Fulsher named his now classic patterns after the creek that holds a good population of baitfish.

The six saltwater flies Fulsher introduced in his book also represent Thunder Creek pattern versatility. Thunder Creek style saltwater flies were created as interest in saltwater fly fishing grew. At the time Fulsher's *Tying and Fishing the Thunder Creek Series* was first published, in 1973, not all that many fly anglers, in relative terms, were hitting the salt. Keith Fulsher took note of saltwater fly-fishing opportunities and turned his attention to new patterns that could entice a variety of large-water species. In his 2006 book, he wrote, "Rather than abandon my ideas about creating patterns to imitate baitfish, I discovered that my theories and the traditional Thunder Creek designs were easily adapted to salt water. By selecting stainless-steel or rust-resistant hooks of the correct size and choosing materials in the appropriate colors, you can create Thunder Creek patterns that match the most important types of saltwater baitfish."

Snook, sea trout, striped bass, small tarpon, and other saltwater fish were attracted to Fulsher's salt patterns. The Silverside Thunder Creek pattern blended silver Krystal Flash with olive and white bucktail. The 4- to 6-inch silversides that the pattern imitates are baitfish that run in schools and are indigenous to East Coast waters from Maine to Florida. The Silverside is tied with the same basic principles and techniques Fulsher applied to his Thunder Creek patterns—sleek and slim. Fulsher's longtime fishing friend Gardner Grant took both snook and tarpon on this pattern. Grant wrote to me, "I asked Keith to tie me a few of his signature Thunder Creek flies on saltwater hooks, hoping they might work on the snook and small tarpon I chase every winter in Florida. I needn't have worried. They loved them just like their freshwater brethren."

Beyond his creative saltwater flies, Fulsher also dabbled with tying hair-wing salmon flies with Thunder Creek style heads. Flies such as the famous Rusty Rat, Blue Charm, and Silver Blue didn't escape the style.

Fulsher's reason for adding the Thunder Creek heads to some hair-wing salmon flies was to create an enhanced water surface disturbance, which is often tempting to salmon. A salmon-fly leader attachment called the Portland Creek hitch or riffling hitch, popularized by Lee Wulff, caused flies to riffle along the water surface, often attracting fish strikes. Fulsher wrote in his *Atlantic Fly Tyer: A Memoir* (2008), "I reasoned that by putting a larger head on a fly, it should riffle higher in the surface film causing increased turbulence that would be more tempting to salmon."

The big-headed flies were tested on the Grimsa River in Iceland during a July 1977 fishing trip by Gardner Grant and Grant's son Gary. The Thunder Creek–headed Blue Charm and Blue Reynard resulted in many fine salmon taken by the Grants. Fulsher also fished the Thunder Creek–headed patterns without the riffling hitch attachment on rivers like Quebec's Matapedia, with good results. However, his experimentation with hair-wing salmon flies is not limited to those

with Thunder Creek heads. Fulsher is also an excellent traditional hair-wing salmon-fly tier and has designed his own patterns. Among his original hair-wing salmon-fly patterns is the Squimp, a cross between a squid and a shrimp.

Yet as beautiful as Fulsher's original hair-wing salmon flies are, he is still primarily associated with his Thunder Creek flies and the techniques he developed to craft the patterns. Some consider the techniques required to tie Thunder Creek patterns very time-consuming. As Eric Leiser pointed out in his *Book of Fly Patterns* (1987), they take a bit more time to finish than standard bucktails and streamers such as Flick's Black-Nose Dace or a Marabou Muddler. As Fulsher wrote in *Thunder Creek Flies*, "I have heard these patterns aren't more widely available because professional fly tiers consider them too time consuming to make." There was a time when they were more readily available, but as Leiser suggested, the decline probably had to do with the lack of commercial tiers willing to spend the time required to craft the flies. Leiser's book provides step-by-step instructions for tying the Thunder Creek Black-Nose Dace, and three of the patterns tied by Fulsher are shown in the color plates.

However, Fulsher's 2006 book addresses everything the fly tier needs to know concerning tying his classic patterns. Full-color step-by-step instructions cover four fundamental patterns: the Black-Nose Dace Thunder Creek, Emerald Shiner Thunder Creek, Marabou Shiner Thunder Creek, and Silver Shiner Thunder Creek. The book has brought a resurgence of interest in Keith Fulsher's creative Thunder Creek series. Attention to detail is necessary in tying them, but they are such highly effective fish takers that they are worth the time and effort it takes to tie the patterns.

Keith Fulsher has been somewhat stereotyped over his career. He's always been considered the "Thunder Creek guy," but his talents at the tying vise go well beyond his famous series of Thunder Creek style patterns. His fishing friends, such as Gardner Grant, have done well with a variety of Fulsher-tied flies, whether using his classic Thunder Creek patterns or unique dry flies. As Grant commented in a recent note to me, "Keith is not as well known for his dry flies for trout, but I would not venture on a stream without a few of his ties of Nelson's Caddis [first created by Nelson Ishiyama a few decades ago]. This multiwing fly, which I find impossible to tie, is the 'go-to' fly on the eastern waters we often fish together."

There probably isn't a fly Fulsher can't tie, and tie well. His dry flies are well crafted and appear almost unsinkable. Some of his dry flies are old Catskill patterns, such as the Light Cahill and Wulffs. Yet his dry-fly style is uniquely Fulsher, heavily hackled, tied typically in thorax style, with neat, well-formed, almost indestructible heads. Perfect for heavy-water fishing. But all in all, it's not such a bad thing that Fulsher was the guy who took streamer designs to a new and interesting level in the history of American fly tying.

Spottail Shiner, tied by Keith Fulsher. This minnow is found across a broad range in Canada and the northern United States. Fulsher used clipped black floss at the tail to represent the minnow's black caudal spot.

Largemouth Bass, tied by Keith Fulsher. As is true of the Smallmouth Bass Thunder Creek pattern, this fly imitates the young of the fish for which it was named.

Smallmouth Bass, tied by Keith Fulsher.

Brook Trout, tied by Keith Fulsher. This is an earlier example of the pattern. Modern versions feature pearl red Krystal Flash under the hackles. *Ralph Graves collection*

Rainbow Trout, tied by Keith Fulsher. Rainbow trout fingerlings are preyed on by many fish species.

Golden Shiner, tied by Keith Fulsher.

Wedgespot Shiner, tied by Keith Fulsher. Bass prey on this minnow, which is found in some central and south-central states.

Redfin Shiner, tied by Keith Fulsher.

Marabou Shiner, tied by Keith Fulsher. This streamer was tied as a general-use Thunder Creek pattern.

Steelcolor Shiner, tied by Keith Fulsher. When the material became popular and proved effective in other fly patterns, Fulsher incorporated Krystal Flash in his Thunder Creek streamers.

Striped Jumprock, tied by Keith Fulsher. Many species of gamefish prey on this small sucker.

Silver Shiner with Tail, tied by Keith Fulsher. Fulsher tied this modern version of the common shiner with Krystal Flash. He experimented with a variety of feathers to craft the tail in order to make the fly more realistic. For this pattern, he used hen pheasant covert feathers.

Green Raynard, tied by Keith Fulsher. Fulsher's talents go far beyond his Thunder Creek series; he is a gifted salmon-fly tier as well.

Sulphur Dun, tied by Keith Fulsher. Fulsher tied neat, heavily hackled dry flies. He was far from being just the "Thunder Creek guy."

Fulcro, tied by Keith Fulsher. Fulsher created this salmon pattern in a motel room in Doaktown, New Brunswick, with Charlie Krom back in 1967. A bottle of Glenfiddich helped their creativity.

Rusty Rat, tied by Keith Fulsher. A talented salmon-fly tier, Fulsher loves tying and fishing Rat series salmon patterns such as this one.

Nelson Caddis, tied by Keith Fulsher. Fulsher and his fishing companion Gardner Grant embraced this Nelson Ishiyama caddisfly pattern.

Squimp, tied by Keith Fulsher. Fulsher created this pattern as a cross between a squid and a shrimp. *Mike Valla collection*

CHAPTER 20

Carrie Stevens
(1882–1970)

Carrie Stevens tied her famous patterns without the aid of a tying vise. *Rangeley Lakes Region Historical Society's Outdoor Sporting Heritage Museum collection*

Gray Ghost Streamer, tied by Carrie Stevens. Stevens's signature fly, the Gray Ghost is perhaps the most famous streamer pattern ever tied. The unique thread band is an identifying feature of her ties. *Rangeley Lakes Region Historical Society's Outdoor Sporting Heritage Museum collection*

The gravel road to Upper Dam winds and turns through woodlands belonging to Maine's Rangeley Lakes region, terminating at a short row of old fishing cottages along one of the most famous fly-fishing waters in the country. The clockwise-swirling Upper Dam Pool, the tailrace that connects Mooselookmeguntic Lake and the Richardson Lakes, is steeped in fly-fishing history. From its waters, an enthusiastic angler named Carrie Stevens netted her record 6-pound, 13-ounce brook trout that took second prize in the 1924 *Field & Stream* fishing contest.

Taken on a self-tied fly with aid of a 9-foot Thomas rod and Hardy reel, the fish and the story surrounding its capture propelled Stevens from relative anonymity to national significance in the sporting world. The event also launched Stevens into the world of commercial fly tying, and her colorful patterns stamped the Rangeley region as streamer country, with the

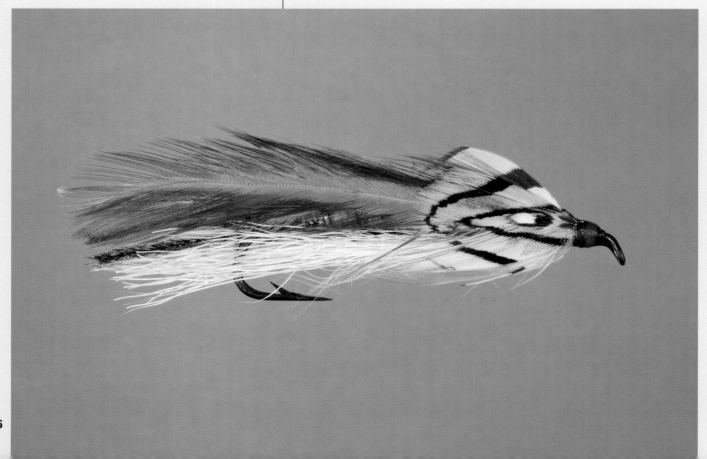

craft becoming a local heritage that is still practiced today. Upper Dam Pool will forever be associated with Carrie Stevens and the long-feathered jewels she once tied a few steps from its turbulent currents.

The little cottage where Carrie and her angling guide husband Wallace stayed for some 30 fishing seasons still stands among white pines and spruce just down the simple portage road that runs along the top of the dam—at least for now, as the historic dam, first constructed in the mid-1800s as an aid to logging drives, is scheduled for replacement. In their well-researched book *Carrie Stevens: Maker of Rangeley Favorite Trout and Salmon Flies* (2000), Graydon and Leslie Hilyard tell us that the Stevenses first arrived at Camp Midway, as the cottage is still called, sometime before 1919. Carrie was introduced to the fly-tying world in 1920, when Charles Wheeler, a longtime friend and visitor to Upper Dam, sent the Stevenses a long-shank feather and hair streamer to try in Upper Dam Pool. Along with the British-tied fly were a few feathers and a hook, and Wheeler, better known as "Shang," suggested that Carrie try fly tying. Using the feathers together with hair from an old camp floor deer hide, Carrie Stevens tied her first fly, known as the Rangeley Favorite.

The Rangeley Favorite led to other patterns, some suggested by fly fishers who paraded to Midway with their ideas on color combinations that could prove effective for both salmon and trout. Numbers rather than names identified her first patterns, the orange silk-bodied No. 9 among them. By the 1930s, her list included patterns with names such as the Don's Delight, Blue Devil, and Green Beauty.

Among her early patterns was the Gray Ghost, one of the most popular fly patterns ever created, regardless of style and form. There are also examples of interesting Stevens-tied streamers that have yet to be identified, but the Gray Ghost is such a fundamental streamer pattern that it would be rare to find an accomplished fly angler who has never heard of it. The fly falls into the same circle of historic patterns as the Royal Coachman, Quill Gordon, the Blondes, Adams, Woolly Worm, and Muddler Minnow. Its history is equally interesting, but there has been some confusion surrounding the pattern.

Anglers taking the short walk from Upper Dam down the portage road will notice a tribute plaque erected along the dirt path directly across from Midway Camp. Carrie Stevens's friends erected the plaque on August 15, 1970, "to honor a perfectionist and her original creations which have brought recognition to her native state of Maine and fame to the Rangeley Lakes region." The plaque served as well to remind visitors that the Gray Ghost streamer made both Stevens and the region famous. However, it also led readers to mistakenly believe that the Gray Ghost was the fly that took her record 6-pound, 13-ounce record brook trout.

The tablet reads, "On July 1, 1924 while engaged in household tasks in her home across the portage road, she

Carrie G. Stevens, "Maker of the Rangeley's Favorite Trout and Salmon Flies."

was inspired to create a new fish-fly pattern. With housework abandoned, her nimble hands had soon completed her vision. In less than an hour the nearby Upper Dam Pool had yielded a 6 pound 13 ounce brook trout to the new fly that would become known throughout the world as the Gray Ghost streamer."

This contradicts Carrie Stevens's own words that she took the fish on a Rangeley Favorite. The confusion rests in the wording; most would interpret the sentences to mean that the Gray Ghost, in its historic final appearance and form, took the fish. But it did not. Perhaps Harold H. Smedley's *Fly Patterns and Their Origins* (1944) was used as a reference for the wording on the plaque. Smedley stated in describing the Gray Ghost, "First fished by Mrs. Stevens, it took a prize-winning trout of almost seven pounds in the 1924 season."

In their book on Stevens, Graydon Hilyard and Leslie Hilyard removed some of the confusion, drawing on the work of Austin S. Hogan and his 1967 monograph, *An Angler's American History: Streamers*. Hilyard and Hilyard quoted Hogan's explanation of the evolution of the Gray Ghost, of which the Rangeley Favorite was the progenitor. In describing the Rangeley Favorite, Hogan noted that there were three different dressings. "Apparently this was the Gray Ghost in embryo," Hogan said, "but obviously other patterns were designed before the refined Gray Ghost appeared on the scene with its sophisticated dressing."

The Gray Ghost indeed has a sophisticated dressing, as do other historic and contemporary versions that were inspired by both the pattern and its creator. Like the morning mist arising from a pristine Maine lake, other wraith-named streamers emerged from the hands of other Maine fly tiers. Bert Quimby, a fly tier and guide from South Windham, Maine, created his Green Ghost streamer, a pattern that closely imitates the Gray Ghost aside from its green saddle hackle wings. Quimby also contributed the Lady Ghost and Galloping Ghost.

While Quimby is considered an important figure in Maine's streamer heritage and is still discussed in contemporary streamer-fly aficionado circles, his streamers often lacked the sleekness of Carrie Stevens's patterns. Quimby's streamer heads were often large and prominent, the wing feathers wide and sometimes clumsy. Nevertheless, he is mentioned in many early fly-tying books, and some patterns that were actually created by other tiers, such as the Chief Needahbeh, were attributed to him.

In *The Practical Fly Fisherman* (1953), A. J. McClane erroneously attributed the Black Ghost pattern to Carrie Stevens. It was Herbert L. Welch of Mooselookmeguntic Lake, Maine, who created the Black Ghost in 1927. It is also

Carrie Stevens netted her record 6-pound, 13-ounce brook trout from Upper Dam Pool. It took second prize in the 1924 *Field & Stream* fishing contest.

common for fly anglers to assume that the Green Ghost was a Carrie Stevens creation. Given the myriad spectral creations that emerged from the hands of Maine's fly tiers, it is no wonder that there is often confusion as to what tier created what pattern. The current—and growing—list of Gray Ghost spin-offs alone is a head-scratcher.

In their book on Stevens, Hilyard and Hilyard list other apparitional patterns: the Red Ghost originated by Ray Salminen, Brown Olive Ghost by David Goulet, Blue Ghost by Gardner Percy, Pink Ghost by Paul Kukonen, Rainbow Ghost by Ernest Bodine, Red-Green Ghost by Kyle McCormick, and Rogan Royal Gray Ghost by Alex Rogan. Jim Warner offered his Babbs Ghost, and Leslie Hilyard jumped right in and created the Jungle Ghost, a beautiful pattern sporting a row of jungle cock eyes protruding underneath a traditionally tied Gray Ghost.

To say that Carrie Stevens's Gray Ghost influenced other tiers is an understatement. Besides all the other Ghosts, some tiers used the Stevens streamer style as a model for their fly-tying practices. There are fly tiers who have attributed their early interest in streamers to Carrie Stevens's patterns that appeared in Bates's *Streamer Fly Tying and Fishing*. One such tier is Mike Martinek Jr., a superb streamer tier who studied Stevens's patterns and then used them as a template for his own beautiful creations.

Martinek is a gifted fly tier from Massachusetts who has tied streamers for nearly 50 years. As was true for many tiers, the 13 Stevens-tied streamers that appeared on Plate IV of Bates's 1966 book inspired Martinek. Together with actual examples of Stevens's work in front of him, at a time when her flies were more easily available to collect, Martinek acquired an appreciation for her work. "She was a major influence in my tying," Martinek said during a recent chat.

Mike Martinek's passion for the Stevens style, and his insistence on better representing Stevens's patterns that came from his own vise, led to the introduction of a new hook. Carrie Stevens commonly tied her streamers on the old Allcock 1810 model, a hook that is difficult find even in small quantities. The Redditch-based Allcock factory was bombed in World War II. However, talented hookmakers still residing in Redditch have duplicated the hook once favored by Carrie Stevens, closely following the original specifications. Martinek teamed up with Grahame Maisey of Gaelic Supreme Hooks to manufacture the new Redditch-made Mike Martinek's Carrie Stevens Streamer Hook, which closely matches the Allcock 1810 aside from its half-down-eye feature. Its creation ensured a ready supply of hooks well suited for Carrie Stevens's patterns, as well as for Martinek's own creations.

Among Martinek's original streamer patterns are the Blue Bird, Crow Warrior, Ice Out Princess, Mandarin Prince, and Flying Dutchman. Martinek's work has helped ensure that Carrie Stevens's style and the Rangeley tradition will not be forgotten. Mike Martinek has inspired others to take an in-

The clockwise swirling Upper Dam Pool, the tailrace that connects Mooselookmeguntic Lake and the Richardson Lakes, is steeped in fly-fishing history. Carrie Stevens tied her famous streamers in a small cottage on the far side of the dam.

terest in the craft that captured his imagination for nearly half a century.

Jim Quimby is an enthusiastic streamer tier from Rangeley, Maine, who was greatly influenced by Martinek and benefited from his instruction. Quimby's interest has helped maintain Carrie Stevens's streamer style at its birthplace. He had this to say to me in a recent note: "At a very young age growing up in Rangeley the name Carrie Stevens was very well known (1960s) and somewhat mythical, as was Herbie Welch. My grandfather Field was a Maine guide at the Oquossoc Angling Association for many years. He also guided for the Reed family on Richardson Lake for years. My other grandfather Ellis built the Rangeley Boat from 1938 (a craft he learned from the Barrett Brothers themselves) to about 1986, when he built his last boat. So I do have very firm roots in Rangeley's rich fishing history—not to mention my last name, Quimby, and being a direct descendant of one of Rangeley's very first settlers. I have always fished the rivers, ponds, and lakes in the Rangeley region.

"It was not until I retired from the military in 1998 that I really got interested in fly tying and the Rangeley Streamer tied in the Carrie Stevens tradition. This interest came through my association working at the Saddleback Ski Area in Rangeley. All our trails are named after fishing flies, most of them Carrie Stevens patterns, including our flagship premier trail, the Gray Ghost; we also have the Blue Devil, Green Weaver, America, Firefly, and others. When I took over as the mountain manager of Saddleback, I wrote a brief history of the original patterns associated with our trails. I gained an extreme passion for fly tying associated with our heritage. I was able to spend some very quality time with Mike Martinek at the L.L. Bean sporting show a couple of years ago, and he really took me under his wing and helped me redefine the way the way I tied Carrie Stevens patterns. It was instruction that I'll never forget. I will continue to tie and fish Carrie Stevens patterns in the Kennebago, Magalloway, and Cupsuptic Rivers. Her influence on me is lifelong."

Beyond individuals who devote their tying efforts to the Maine streamers, with Carrie Stevens placed front and center, even the occasional classic streamer fly tier has no doubt tackled the Gray Ghost, since it is such a high-profile pattern.

The *Noll Guide to Trout Flies and How to Tie Them* (formerly *Family Circle's Guide*), an illustrated slender volume used as a reference by many tiers new to the hobby from the 1950s through the early 1970s, featured two Carrie Stevens streamers, the Gray Ghost and Colonel Bates. The two patterns featured may not have been arbitrary; Stevens wrote to Bates that the Gray Ghost and Colonel Bates were the two most popular patterns requested by her customers.

Massachusetts fly anglers quickly embraced the Colonel Bates, a landlocked salmon and smallmouth bass fly created during World War II for Joseph D. Bates Jr., who was a colonel. In his book, Bates wrote that Frank Mooney of the Andover (Massachusetts) Fly Fishers reported, "This beautiful streamer has been so consistently successful for me that if I had to settle for one streamer pattern I would be content with the Colonel Bates."

Carrie Stevens also named other streamers after individuals that she was close to or who requested a custom-tied pattern. The Don's Delight was featured in both Bates's and Hilyard and Hilyard's books. The striking white-winged pattern was named for fly angler G. Donald Bartlett of Willimantic, Connecticut, a friend of Carrie and her husband. Don and his father, George, were Upper Dam enthusiasts for many years. The Shang's Favorite is also covered in Bates's book, named in honor of Charles E. "Shang" Wheeler of Stratford, Connecticut, a state senator and champion duck decoy maker.

Wheeler not only inspired Carrie Stevens to delve into fly tying, but also suggested dressings for a number of her flies.

According to Hilyard and Hilyard, the Judge streamer was likely named after another Stratford resident, Judge Charles H. Welles, one of Wallace's clients.

However, saddle hackle streamers were not the only patterns Carrie Stevens tied. A bucktail pattern, the FRS Fancy, was named for Francis Reast Smith. Research by Hilyard and Hilyard indicated that Smith, from Garden City, Long Island, was involved with real estate and the coal industry. Bucktail patterns were rare, but Carrie Stevens did experiment with those types of flies, including what could be described as a reverse-tied bucktail, a concept that influenced Keith Fulsher and led to his famous Thunder Creek series style.

In tying the reverse bucktails, Stevens attached saddle hackles in the wing position behind the hook eye. Bucktail was attached in the same area, with the tips pointing *forward*. The hair was then gathered and pulled *back*, uniformly surrounding the hook shank, then tied down. Carrie Stevens occasionally tied saltwater flies using the reverse-hair method; she believed the method resulted in a strong fly. Yet it is clear that bucktails were not her favorites; she is most remembered for her colorful, long saddle hackled streamers and the self-taught methods she used to tie them.

The unusual methods that Carrie Stevens used to tie her streamers were much different from the typical sequence of

Upper Dam Pool tailrace. The pool is still a favorite fly-fishing destination enjoyed by many who hope for a large brook trout or salmon.

Cottage where Carrie Stevens tied her flies. The little cottage still stands among pine and spruce trees just beyond the dam.

attaching materials to the hook shank used by contemporary fly tiers today. She crafted fly wing sections separately off hook, then attached the completed sections—left and right—to the hook shank. Using the Gray Ghost as an example, as depicted in the Bates book illustration, she selected a silver pheasant shoulder feather, then cemented a jungle cock eye on top of its surface. Next, Stevens selected two olive-gray saddle hackles and cemented all four feathers together. She made a number of right and left assembled sections at one time, placing piles of left and right sections to the side. After the remainder of the body materials were attached to the hook, she tied in the sections, left and right, one side at a time.

Carrie Stevens's technique would seem tedious to the modern tier, but her flies were known for both their beauty and strength. The Gray Ghost will forever be known as her signature fly and will likely remain widely known among fly anglers, regardless of region. Other favorite patterns may fade away, but her legacy will continue to live on through the hands of her followers. Carrie Stevens's signature fly heads, finished off with three bands—black, reddish-orange, black—defined her patterns, the exception being some of her very first flies, as was true with her No. 9. The final fly that came from her hands wore a gold center band, her "trademark," reserved for her most beautiful flies of utmost quality.

Hilyard and Hilyard's opening sentences in their fine *Carrie Stevens* book described the sobering final moments on December 4, 1953, when Stevens tied her last fly. In a 1990 letter to the Hilyards, H. Wendell Folkins described the circumstances that led to Carrie's final fly. Folkins visited Stevens in her Madison, Maine, home along with George Fletcher, who had supplied fly-tying materials to Stevens. Folkins was interested in acquiring her business. The deal was concluded over tea, cookies, and cake. Then Carrie Stevens took to her feathers one last time and tied her grand finale—the Pink Lady Streamer, her last fly, wearing the band of gold.

Pattern No. 9, tied by Carrie Stevens. Numbers rather than names identified her earliest patterns, the orange silk-bodied No. 9 among them. *Rangeley Lakes Region Historical Society's Outdoor Sporting Heritage Museum collection*

The Judge, tied by Carrie Stevens. Hilyard and Hilyard conjecture that the pattern may have been named for Connecticut judge Charles H. Welles. *Rangeley Lakes Region Historical Society's Outdoor Sporting Heritage Museum collection*

Don's Delight, tied by Carrie Stevens. The fly was named after Don Bartlett, a Connecticut fly angler. Bates called the pattern an "Upper Dam Pool Favorite." *Rangeley Lakes Region Historical Society's Outdoor Sporting Heritage Museum collection*

Morning Glory, tied by Carrie Stevens. *Rangeley Lakes Region Historical Society's Outdoor Sporting Heritage Museum collection*

F.R.S. Fancy, tied by Carrie Stevens. Hilyard and Hilyard's book tells us that Carrie named the fly after Francis Reast Smith, who spent summers in the Rangeley Lakes region. Stevens tied some bucktails, such as this classic. *Rangeley Lakes Region Historical Society's Outdoor Sporting Heritage Museum collection*

Rapid River, tied by Carrie Stevens. This pattern was named for the 6-mile-long Rapid River, which flows from Lower Richardson Lake to Umbagog Lake in the Rangeley region. *Rangeley Lakes Region Historical Society's Outdoor Sporting Heritage Museum collection*

Unidentified pattern, tied by Carrie Stevens. *Rangeley Lakes Region Historical Society's Outdoor Sporting Heritage Museum collection*

General MacArthur, tied by Carrie Stevens. Stevens tied this fly in honor of Gen. Douglas MacArthur, as a patriotic gesture. *Rangeley Lakes Region Historical Society's Outdoor Sporting Heritage Museum collection*

Unidentified pattern, tied by Carrie Stevens. *Rangeley Lakes Region Historical Society's Outdoor Sporting Heritage Museum collection*

Ebden Fancy, tied by Carrie Stevens. This fly is another very colorful example of Stevens's work. *Rangeley Lakes Region Historical Society's Outdoor Sporting Heritage Musuem collection*

Pink Lady, tied by Carrie Stevens. This was the very last fly tied by Carrie Stevens, a gem bearing its gold head band. *Rangeley Lakes Region Historical Society's Outdoor Sporting Heritage Museum collection*

Indian Rock, tied by Carrie Stevens. The namesake Indian Rock lies at the confluence of the Rangeley and Kennebago Rivers and was said to have been inhabited by very large brook trout. *Rangeley Lakes Region Historical Society's Outdoor Sporting Heritage Museum collection*

Gray Lady, tied by Carrie Stevens. This striking Stevens pattern is flanked by dyed blue feather shoulders. *Rangeley Lakes Region Historical Society's Outdoor Sporting Heritage Museum collection*

Shang's Favorite, tied by Carrie Stevens. According to Bates, the fly was named for Charles E. "Shang" Wheeler, a former Connecticut senator who summered at Upper Dam. *Rangeley Lakes Region Historical Society's Outdoor Sporting Heritage Museum collection*

Flying Dutchman, tied by Mike Martinek. Martinek has been a follower of the Stevens style for decades. He created many of his own gems based on the Rangeley style and inspired by his own creativity.

Gray Ghost, tied by Bert Quimby. Bert Quimby, a fly tier and guide from South Windham, Maine, created his Green Ghost streamer, a pattern that closely imitates the Gray Ghost but has green saddle hackle wings. Quimby also contributed the Lady Ghost and Galloping Ghost.

Colonel Bates, tied by Mike Valla. In Bates's book, we learn that the fly was second only to the famed Gray Ghost streamer. Bates was a colonel in the Second World War.

CHAPTER 21

Joe Brooks
(1901–1972)

Joe Brooks was called "the world's best fly fisherman." He traveled the world in search of new and exciting waters where fish could be caught on the fly. *Bill Leary collection*

The Blondes—Black, Pink, Platinum, Argentine, Honey, and Strawberry—tied by Ralph Graves. Joe Brooks said, "If I had only one pattern for all big fish in both fresh and salt water, I'd choose the Blonde." *Mike Valla collection*

I t was the story that raised fly anglers' brows everywhere. The strange, new "no-hackle" dry flies that Carl Richards and Doug Swisher created in 1967 and Joe Brooks reported on in an *Outdoor Life* story sent fly tiers scrambling to their vises. It seemed impossible that dry flies tied without hackle could float and be kept on the water surface with the aid of body dubbing and outrigger tails alone. Some readers were skeptical; others were just intrigued by the Swisher-Richards fly design concept. But many fly anglers embraced the new dry-fly architecture and gave it the benefit of the doubt. If Joe Brooks wrote about a new fly-fishing concept or a new type of fly, we stood at attention—he gave innovations tremendous credibility.

Whether his creations or those of other anglers or fly tiers, Brooks did fly fishers a tremendous service by popularizing many fly patterns he found to be productive in all types of waters. His experience with the long rod

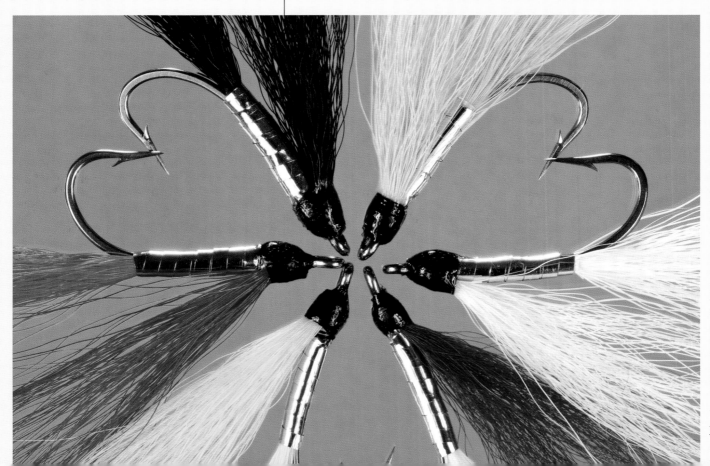

was vast: he fished waters around the globe—both fresh and salt—with every conceivable type of pattern dangling off his tippet for every imaginable fish species. From the landing of a 29-pound striper on Oregon's Coos Bay waters taken on his little shrimp popper to netting monster brown trout like his 18-pounder in Argentina, Brooks enlightened us with his stories. The little creeks were on his list, like Letort Spring Run in Pennsylvania, where he fished tiny terrestrials with the iconic Vince Marinaro. Counterpoint big rivers in Montana were favorites. Brooks convinced fly anglers that Don Gapen's Muddler Minnow was worthy of their tippets. Brooks fly-fished everything from midges to traditional dry and wet flies to large saltwater streamers to gargantuan bass bugs. And as his friend Lefty Kreh once wrote, "Brooks opened up the world to all those who followed."

In the foreword to *Joe Brooks on Fishing* (2004), a collection of Brooks's writings edited by Don Sedgwick, Kreh reviewed the climb his friend had made from writing a small outdoor newspaper column in Towson, Maryland, in 1945 to his eventual role as fishing editor for *Outdoor Life* magazine. Brooks made his statement with the fly rod during a Florida Keys fishing trip in 1947 with noted area fishing guide Jimmy Albright. Holding to a promise he made in the *Miami Herald* outdoors column, he caught two bonefish on a fly.

Although Joe Brooks was not the first fly angler fishing the salt—others such as Harold Gibbs came before—it was considered rare in those years. Accomplishments on both salt and fresh water earned Joe Brooks the titles of "the world's greatest angler" and "the world's best fly fisherman." His books and collection of magazine stories describe the flies that Brooks used in his adventures.

One series of flies, the Blondes, no doubt helped raise Joe Brooks's profile as a great fishing fly innovator. In "Those Deadly Blondes," an article in the December 1963 issue of *Outdoor Life*, Brooks wrote, "If I had only one pattern for all big fish in both fresh and salt water, I'd choose the Blonde." The photos accompanying his article were both striking and convincing, adding to his intriguing story that proved the fly's effectiveness on any water. Whether he fished them for land-locked salmon on the Trauful in Argentina, northern pike in Saskatchewan's Middle Lake, or albacore off the coast of Africa, the Blondes performed for Brooks. Brooks said that the big Atlantic salmon on the Aurland River in Norway "busted their spots going for the Blondes."

Added to Brooks's Blonde scorecard were 8-pound tiger-fish on the Limpopo River in East Africa, false albacore near Paradise Island in the Indian Ocean, and 100-pound tarpon that "powdered" the pattern in the Florida Keys—as did striped bass on Chesapeake Bay. Large brown trout hammered Brooks's Blondes, too. Reading Brooks's *Outdoor Life* story no doubt led many to believe that the Blondes—all six of them—were the patterns of choice for large fish, regardless of species. The Blondes that captivated fly anglers every-

where were originally designed for stripers, the Platinum Blonde being the first.

In 1939, Brooks was fishing his striper beat on the Susquehanna River near Port Deposit, Maryland, when the new fly was conceived. Brooks landed plenty of fish on his size 1/0 white bucktails, but nothing over 6 pounds. Striped bass were feeding on baitfish larger than his artificial: 6- or 7-inch alewives, herring, and anchovies. Brooks's hunch was that the large fish wanted something longer than the fly he was using. As Brooks described it, "I tied a three-inch long white bucktail wing right in back of the eye of a 1/0 hook, another three-inch wing at the bend of the hook, then wrapped the body with silver tinsel. That was the Platinum Blonde, the first of the series. It raised the average weight of the stripers I took."

Brooks's Platinum Blonde remained nameless until his second trip to Argentina, accompanied by *Toledo Blade* outdoor editor Lou Klewer. Up until that Rio Grande trip, Brooks referred to the fly, which the big Argentina brown trout hammered, as simply a two-winged white bucktail. It was Klewer that suggested the name Platinum Blonde, a fly that evolved into an entire series: the Argentine Blonde, with the first wing blue, second wing white; the Strawberry Blonde, first wing red, second wing orange; then the mono-color-winged yellow Honey Blonde, Pink Blonde, and Black

Joe Brooks with his first fly-caught permit in the Bahamas in the 1960s. *Catskill Fly Fishing Center and Museum Photo by Lefty Kreh*

Blonde. Gold tinsel is sometimes used for the fly bodies of the Strawberry and Honey Blondes, but the usual flash is silver tinsel for all of the Blondes.

It was the Platinum Blonde that resulted in Joe Brooks's largest Argentina brown trout taken on his cherished streamer. The renowned Chimehuin River, noted for its clear waters that offer big browns and rainbows, was a Brooks favorite. He looped out 60 feet of line, dropping his enticing palm-size 1/0 Platinum just above the pool tail. Then in mid-strip, the river blew up. "Flying water blotted out everything, then I saw the crocodile-like jaws of the fish, the massive head, the long thick body as he cleared the water and smashed down the fly," Brooks wrote. His 16½-pounder proved to Brooks that big Argentina trout like big flies. Yet it's not only Southern Hemisphere browns that smash the pattern; Montana browns tear them apart, too.

It was Pennsylvanian Al Troth who, like many anxious fly tiers, headed to his vise after reading Brooks's "Those Deadly Blondes." However, Troth went up to 3/0, following Catskill region fly tier Harry Darbee's advice that western waters could be better fished with big bucktails tied on salmon-fly hooks. Troth's excursion to the Big Hole River, fishing a big Platinum Blonde, resulted in some mighty large trout—ranging from 4 to 8 pounds.

Beyond Al Troth, Brooks's flies also inspired other contemporary fly anglers. In *Saltwater Fly Tying* (1991), Frank Wentink devoted his first chapter to the Blonde series, writing, "I feel it's appropriate that we begin with a type of fly on which most tyers of my generation have cut our teeth, that is, the fly with which we started our fly fishing careers. Actually, it's not one pattern but a series of streamer-type flies known collectively as 'the Blondes.'" Wentink's first fly-caught saltwater fish, a striped bass, was taken on a Blonde. For Wentink, the Blondes served as the foundation for his interest in salt patterns, and Brooks's writings surrounding the series "fired up" his imagination.

Yet many other writers before Wentink helped popularize the Blondes. Those readers who missed reading Brooks's classic 1963 *Outdoor Life* piece may have been exposed to the Blondes in Joseph D. Bates Jr.'s *Streamer Fly Tying and Fishing* (1966). In his book, Bates devoted plenty of acreage to the Blondes and included a color photograph of a Brooks Blonde, attributing the pattern to both Brooks and Homer Rhode Jr. In describing the Blondes, Bates wrote that Rhode was "probably the father of this type" of fly. Before 1950, Rhodes had given Bates examples of the Homer Rhode Jr. Tarpon Bucktail. That same year, a sketch of the fly appeared in Bates's book *Streamer Fly Tying and Fishing*. Its morphology is closely aligned with Brooks's Blondes.

Despite Bates's observations concerning Rhode's bucktail, the colorful Blondes remain synonymous with Joe Brooks and are considered his signature patterns. They've been tweaked slightly over the years, with some tiers adding a

Joe Brooks first thought about creating the big fly that ultimately became his Platinum Blonde while striper fishing in 1939 on the Susquehanna River near Port Deposit, Maryland, and on Chesapeake Bay. However, Brooks fished for a variety of saltwater species, including bonefish. *Bill Leary collection*

shade or two and more body material. In *Saltwater Fly Patterns* (1995), Lefty Kreh mentioned that he preferred to add a bit more flash to his Blondes—a few strands of Flashabou or Krystal Flash. Those materials were not yet available or even developed when Brooks crafted his original patterns. Kreh also added a couple more Blondes to the family: the Blushing Blonde, with white lower wing and red upper wing, and Hot Orange Blonde, with orange lower and upper wings. Joe Brooks likely would have nodded his head to friend Kreh's additions and added them to his fly box arsenal.

Brooks liked his big, colorful Blondes, yet his expansive fly pattern preferences did not leave out smaller traditional wet flies, dry flies, and streamers. While these were not flies he created, he mentioned the classic patterns in his writings, which helped keep many of the old standards alive. In *The Complete Book of Fly Fishing* (1958) and *Trout Fishing* (1972), Brooks gave a list of his favorites. His fly boxes included classic wet-fly patterns like the Royal Coachman, Black Gnat, McGinty, Cowdung, Alexandra, and Ginger Quill.

But his favorite wet fly was the common Coachman, about which he wrote, "I can readily believe that a trout will see that white wing sooner than any other color. I believe the trout like a combination of brown and white, and I am sure that when I retrieve that fly in short jerks, it looks exactly like small minnows so often found in trout streams." Brooks also thought that the ancient Alexandra, with its flashy silver tinsel body and peacock sword wings, also imitated minnows. However, one strange, ugly-looking fly that was tied to imitate the ugly, big-headed, minnowlike sculpin really caught Brooks's attention—and he did everything he could to promote it.

The famed Mudder Minnow, a Don Gapen creation, was first tied in 1916 for use on the Nipigon River in Ontario, Canada. The big brookies devoured the fly. Brooks carried the fly with him west to Montana where, he said in *Trout Fishing*, "I caught more big trout than with any fly I had ever used." Brooks dropped the fly into Dan Bailey's hands, and from there it rocketed in popularity. As was true of many flies Brooks promoted in his writings, the Muddler was not original with him—he popularized it just as he had done in 1970 with the Swisher-Richards no-hackle dry flies.

Brooks brought the ugly Muddler into armchair fishing excursions when he wrote "Best All-Round Trout Fly," which appeared in *Outdoor Life* in October 1963. Commercial operations like Dan Bailey's shop massaged the fly into many variations, but it was Brooks who made anglers aware of the original pattern and its worth. Brooks built on the early exposure the Muddler received when A. J. McClane presented the fly in his October 1954 *Field & Stream* article "Presenting the Muddler Minnow." As Lefty Kreh said about his friend Brooks in a 1974 recorded remembrance, "He merely was the first person to recognize the value of these things, and to bring them to the attention of people through his writings, his travels, his meetings with many people. . . . Joe was not the first man to fish in Peru and Chile. Joe was not the first man to fish salt water in Central America. Joe was not the first man to fish in Africa. But it was Joe who was the man who came home and said, 'Use these flies, go to these camps, fish for these fish at these times of the year.'"

It's tragic that many contemporary fly tiers don't know much about Joe Brooks and the flies that helped him "put salt water on the map," as Lefty Kreh also said in his recorded remembrance. He didn't sit at a vise and crank out hundreds of Blondes to fill fly bins. He really wasn't a great innovator. He was a good fly angler who found out what worked for him, and then reported to the angling world his findings. It is fitting that his signature patterns, the Blondes, are still known as "Joe's flies."

Honey Blonde, tied by Ralph Graves. *Mike Valla collection*

Argentine Blonde, tied by Ralph Graves. *Mike Valla collection*

Pink Blonde, tied by Ralph Graves. *Mike Valla collection*

Black Blonde, tied by Ralph Graves. *Mike Valla collection*

Joe Brooks's favorite wet flies, from top to right—the McGinty, Alexandra, Black Gnat, Ginger Quill, Cowdung, and Coachman, with Royal Coachman at the center—tied by Mike Valla. Brooks did not abandon traditional patterns; he promoted the old standard flies in his writings. The simple Coachman wet fly was his favorite.

Strawberry Blonde, tied by Ralph Graves. *Mike Valla collection*

Lefty's Deceiver, tied by Lefty Kreh. Kreh said that Joe Brooks "put salt water on the map." Kreh and Brooks were very close friends. *Ted Patlen collection*

Platinum Blonde, tied by Ralph Graves. *Mike Valla collection*

CHAPTER 22

Don Gapen
(1907–1986)

Don Gapen, creator of the Muddler Minnow, on the Albany River in Ontario, October 1973. *Ted Patlen collection*

I n his September 1970 *Field & Stream* article titled "The Sculpin and Its Imitations," noted fly angler Dave Whitlock wrote of Don Gapen's extraordinary Muddler Minnow pattern, "The fly and the idea spread across the country like a windblown prairie fire." Joe Brooks, who had a lot to do with its early popularity, said in *Trout Fishing* (1972) that it was "like the Adams dry fly—everywhere I have taken it in foreign lands, anglers and tiers have been enthusiastic about it." Yet long before Whitlock and Brooks made those accurate statements, A. J. McClane wrote about the fly in his book *The Practical Fly Fisherman* (1953) in the chapter titled "Fly Fishing for Bass," where he cited his August 1949 *Field & Stream* article, "Bass Flies, Old and New." He was hot on this new pattern, calling it without reservation the "prima donna of smallmouth flies." The Muddler Minnow, one of the most famous and effective flies ever crafted, served as the foundation for many other flies that were created out of its mold.

Don Gapen first tied the pattern while fishing in Nipigon, Ontario, in the late 1930s. He intended it as a darter minnow imitation, but it soon became known as an excellent fly for taking

Original Gapen Muddler Minnows from the Gapen Company in Minnesota. Joe Brooks called the Muddler "the greatest streamer-bucktail fly of all time." The general morphology of the Muddler has changed over the years from loosely compacted hair heads to well-compressed styles. *Mike Valla collection*

large brook trout. In *The Practical Fly Fisherman* (1953), Mc-Clane described his success with the Muddler while fishing with his friend Guy Kibbee on a small pond in Quebec, Canada. He caught more than 20 brook trout over 5 pounds fishing the Muddler as a dry fly. While McClane acknowledged that Gapen had created an excellent trout fly, he was even more impressed with its use as a bass pattern.

"There was something about the Muddler, though, that smacked of smallmouth, and that was the reason why this pattern was introduced in an article on bass flies," McClane wrote in *The Practical Fly Fisherman*. Whether on a Connecticut pond or on placid West Branch of the Delaware River pools in New York state, McClane proved to himself that the Muddler was meant for bass as much as for brook trout. McLane's now classic October 1954 *Field & Stream* article "Presenting the Muddler Minnow" also described his success fishing the Muddler from rainbow trout on the White River in Vermont and browns on the Beaverkill while fishing with Catskill fly tier Harry Darbee. With time, Gapen's Muddler Minnow proved to be a versatile pattern that was effective for a variety of species, including large brown trout, and it enjoyed global popularity.

Dan Gapen Sr., Don's son, who currently heads the Gapen Fly Company in Becker, Minnesota, described the Muddler in his company catalog as "the world's leading trout fly, sold in as many countries as there are sporting fish which swim." Various conflicting accounts have been written over the years describing the birth of the Muddler Minnow. Dan Gapen, in June 2011 correspondence, gave me his version of the Muddler's creation: "Virgin Falls on the Nipigon River in northern Ontario plummeted vertically some 24 feet into deep crystal-clear water at its base. Dozens of colorful brook trout swam lazily about. Don Gapen, accompanied by two guides, paddled slowly up within 50 feet of thundering falls. John Cheboyer pointed with his crudely cut cedar paddle. 'Mr. Gapen, see that trout? It's about 8 pounds. Try for him!' The try failed. Even though the Royal Coachman streamer passed within a foot of its mouth, the big trout didn't seem interested. 'They like cockatush! I'll catch you a live cockatush, Don. We must go to shore to find one under the rocks,' instructed Dan Mausso, the canoe's bowman. Thirty minutes later the trio returned with three live sculpin minnows in a campfire pot used to heat tea in. Replacing his fly with a single hook and a small weight, one of the minnows was hooked through the lips and allowed to descend into the 15-foot-deep water. The guides skillfully had relocated the large trout, and it was this fish Don led his live bait to. The moment the bait got within two feet of the trout, it darted forward and swallowed the favorite trout food on the Nipigon. Once landed, the trout was estimated at a bit over 7 pounds.

"'Fellows, I think I can tie a fly which will imitate the cockatush of yours. Let's go to shore where it is quieter,' Don Gapen suggested. Not believing that anyone could build a fly

Dan Bailey fly shop, 1939. Bailey's shop grew in popularity as a result of its offerings of flies and tackle for anglers fishing western waters. The shop helped popularize the Muddler Minnow once it was made apparent that the fly was so effective. *John Bailey collection*

to imitate their beloved cockatush, yet not wanting to offend their boss, the Indian guides complied with the request. As he'd done for years, while fly-fishing the streams near Monroe, Wisconsin, where he grew up, Don retrieved all the gear needed to tie a fly to match the hatch from within his small backpack. With a fly vise he attached to the front thwart of the 20-foot freighter canoe, Don Gapen began his creation. An English 4X Allcock hook in size 2 was chosen to work the magic. Mottled brown turkey wing feathers were selected, as well as gray squirrel tail. Next, a patch of deer hair was retrieved from deep within the pack. All these, when placed side by side, took on the colors of the cockatush. With only wide, flat gold tinsel in his backpack for body material, Don Gapen had no choice; the new creation would be garnished in gold."

Don Gapen's original Muddler, created that August 1936 day, looked a bit different from numerous variations that followed over the years. The original fly head, created from spun deer hair, was tied somewhat loosely, much different from the well-compacted, neatly trimmed hair heads that typify modern Muddlers. Modern fly dressers take great pains to ensure bullet-shaped heads that have not a hair out of place, but these are a great departure from the pattern first created by Gapen. The morphologic changes occurred once entrepreneurial fly tackle dealer Dan Bailey of Livingston, Montana, got his hands on the pattern. And fishing writer Joe Brooks had something to do with helping the Muddler colonize Montana.

Brooks enjoyed great success with the pattern on Montana waters. In *Trout Fishing*, he wrote of the Muddlers, "With them, I had caught more big trout than with any fly I had ever used. In the water it seemed to come alive, sparkling, somehow managing to resemble all kinds of fish food—grasshoppers, stoneflies, other minnows as well as the minnow it was designed to represent." So enthusiastic was Joe Brooks about Don Gapen's creation that he showed the Muddler to Dan Bailey. Bailey took a keen interest in the pattern, setting his shop tiers into action to produce the fly on a commercial level. It is likely that the Muddler Minnow's steep rise to national prominence was due to a combination of several important factors: the pattern was effective in taking a variety of fish species, nationally recognized fishing writers were more than eager to promote the fly together with the great fly-fishing potential that existed in western states, and

Bailey's lady fly-tying team in Livingston, Montana, tied Muddlers by the hundreds to meet growing demand. *John Bailey collection*

Dan Bailey's fly shop had the capability to produce the fly commercially in great numbers.

The Bailey fly shop had modest beginnings. Shortly after Dan and his wife, Helen, moved from the East Coast to Livingston in 1938, they opened a fly shop at the Albemarle Hotel. In his fine book *Fly-Fishing Pioneers & Legends of the Northwest* (2006), Jack Berryman described Bailey's early endeavor as mostly a wholesale and mail-order operation. However, Bailey soon brought in two teenage fly tiers, Red Monical and Gilbert Meloche, and eventually he hired his first female tiers. By the 1940s, the number of commercial women tiers Bailey hired grew. Bailey experimented with a number of new patterns, and his modification of Gapen's original Muddler occurred around this time. In the 1950s, Monical's wife, Louise, coordinated 12 women production tiers, surely enough hands to produce sufficient Muddlers to meet the growing demand spurred by national writers who endorsed Montana's waters.

Once Joe Brooks, who began writing for *Outdoor Life* in 1953, made his summer home in Livingston, Bailey's shop capitalized on the flocks of East Coast anglers that followed him. Berryman aptly summarized the impact on Gapen's Muddler: "Brooks and Bailey began to popularize big streamers and long casts for western trout fishing, and added the double-haul and weight-forward lines to the trout fisher's arsenal. Along with this type of fishing, Brooks highlighted Bailey's variants [flies] and the Muddler Minnow." Berryman quoted well-known outdoor writer Charles Waterman, a longtime friend of Bailey's, as saying, "It was this fly that got Dan Bailey's Fly Shop as much recognition as anything else he ever produced."

It was not only the regular Muddler Minnow that gained Bailey growing recognition. Other Muddler spin-offs soon found their way into Bailey's fly bins, created by Dan himself or with the help of other tiers connected to his shop One Muddler variation Dan created is the Missoulian Spook.

The Missoulian Spook (or sometimes labeled the Mizoolian Spook) was introduced in Joe Brooks's October 1963 *Outdoor Life* story "Best All-Round Trout Fly." Bailey designed the fly by crossing Theodore Gordon's Bumblepuppy with Gapen's Muddler. He called it a White Muddler at first, but once Alley Oop comic strip artist V. T. Hamlin found success with it near Missoula, Montana, it acquired a new name. As Brooks explained in his story, "The strip that ran on Wednesday, October 24, 1956 shows a leaping trout, and hanging from its mouth is a big White Muddler, labeled by Hamlin the Missoulian Spook."

Beyond the Missoulian Spook, Bailey also created the White Marabou Muddler and the Spuddler spin-off patterns. Bailey used Don Gapen's basic Muddler design but switched out the turkey quill wings for white marabou, giving the fly an entirely different action while fished. The Spuddler, according to Joe Brooks, was a crossbred streamer designed by

Dan Bailey and Red Monical. Eric Leiser and Dave Whitlock said that fishing guide Don Williams also helped with the design. Whitlock's article "The Sculpin and Its Imitations" mentions the Spuddler, which he said "came as a hybrid of the Dark Spruce and my imitation [the Whitlock Sculpin]."

The Spuddler combined Gapen's spun and clipped hair head concept with a popular Pacific Northwest pattern called the Spruce Streamer, hence the name. However, other than the saddle hackles used on the Spruce Streamer as winging, it takes a bit of imagination to accept that any of that pattern's attributes were combined with the Muddler Minnow to create the new fly. Whereas the Spruce Streamer has badger saddle wings along with a red wool and peacock herl body, the Spuddler has dyed brown grizzly saddles and a cream wool body, and there is no resemblance between the two. It is interesting to note that William Bayard Sturgis described a Hair Head Minnow in his 1940 book, *Fly-Tying*. The fly featured in the black and white photo plate, with its saddle hackle projecting rearward from a clipped hair head, has morphological features similar to a Spuddler. At any rate, Gapen's Muddler influence is clearly recognized in the Spuddler's spun and clipped hair head, a design feature that has found its way into many other spin-off patterns that followed.

Eric Leiser's *Book of Fly Patterns* (1987) lists five variations of Gapen's Muddler Minnow: Muddler Minnow Green, Muddler Minnow Orange, Muddler Minnow White, Muddler Minnow Yellow, and Ralph Graves's Golden Muddler Minnow. All feature the basic Muddler design but have some variation in body materials or wing shades. The Graves pattern is identical to a regular Muddler aside from the dyed golden yellow turkey quill wings. Beyond Leiser's Muddler variation list, today we have Conehead Muddlers, White Muddlers, and a unique pattern called the Kennebago Muddler, a Maine favorite.

The Kennebago Muddler is a slimmed-down version that uses natural or dyed deer hair with mallard or sometimes wood-duck flank wings. Brett Damm, owner of the Rangeley Region Sport Shop in Rangeley, Maine, uses it for *Hexagenia* emergences on his local waters. "The Kennebago Muddler, a Mike Arsenault creation, was designed to copy the drake emerger on Kennebago Lake," he told me. "The lake is known for drake and Hex hatches throughout the summer. The closely trimmed head lets it sink more easily than the traditional Muddler, and the long, sparse deer hair collar resembles legs. The mallard feather overwing gives it a real buggy appearance. It is also good in rivers as a streamer. In the larger sizes and olive color, it has been used as a dragonfly/stonefly nymph; even greased up with floatant, it has been effective in imitating stoneflies as a dry fly. I've even used the smaller sizes as a top nymph in a double-nymph rig."

Other fly tiers throughout the country embraced the Muddler design, with its characteristic ugliness. Adirondack region fly tier Fran Betters developed his own Muddler variations. In *Fran Betters' Fly Fishing, Fly Tying and Pattern Guide* (1986), he wrote, "As so often happens with a proven pattern, variations are often derived that prove more valuable and productive than the original pattern." What Betters did was simply scale down the size, rather than change the basic pattern. He tied the fly on size 12, 14, and 16 Mustad 9672 hooks, labeling his fly a Mini-Muddler. Like the Gapen pattern, the standard Mini-Muddler had turkey quill wings. However, Betters also tied a Brook Mini-Muddler with yellow duck quill wings, a Mini-Muddler Nymph with a clipped turkey wing, and a wingless Stone Mini-Muddler.

Other noted fly tiers changed the morphology of the Gapen Muddler, resulting in completely new patterns. One was the Whitlock Sculpin, which A. J. McClane featured in his July 1968 *Field & Stream* article in the "Match-the-Minnow Streamer Fly Series." Dave Whitlock's creation used some of the Muddler's features but enhanced them into a more realistic likeness of the natural minnow it was intended to imitate. Inspired by the Muddler yet an entirely new creation and not simply a variation, Whitlock's Sculpin is so far advanced beyond a standard Gapen Muddler that the fly is worthy of its own label. While Whitlock eventually brought the original Muddler to greater heights by building on its original design, he also expressed admiration for Gapen's creation. In *Art Flick's Master Fly-Tying Guide* (1972), Whitlock wrote, "My hat off and a deep bow to Don's wonderful creation—and one more bow to Dan Bailey for adapting the original a bit to suit western conditions."

Don Gapen's original fly, in its simple form, was the foundation for many other patterns that followed. Both similar patterns such as those created by Fran Betters and unique ones like Dave Whitlock's are part of the Muddler's lineage. But despite all the variations, the original Muddler Minnow remains a very popular fly. Given the worldwide reputation of Dan Gapen's Muddler, it is no wonder that Joe Brooks wrote, in *Trout Fishing*, "I class it as the greatest streamer-bucktail fly of all time."

Spuddler, from the Bailey Fly Shop. The Spuddler, according to Joe Brooks, was a crossbred streamer designed by Dan Bailey and Red Monical. Gapen's original Muddler, in part, inspired the creation of this pattern.

Don Gapen's original Muddler continues to evolve into new spin-off patterns like the White Muddler and Conehead Muddler. *Mike Valla collection*

Dan Bailey's White Marabou Muddler, from the Bailey Fly Shop. This was a spin-off pattern influenced by Don Gapen's Muddler.

Missoulian Spook, created by Dan Bailey. Sometimes labeled the Mizoolian Spook, or White Muddler, this Muddler spin-off was made famous by fly angler and cartoonist Vince Hamlin, who drew the fly in one of his *Alley Oop* comic strips. Joe Brooks helped popularize the fly when he wrote about it in *Trout Fishing* and his October 1963 *Outdoor Life* article titled "Best All-Round Trout Fly." *Mike Valla collection*

Kennebago Muddlers, tied by Brett Damm of the Rangeley Region Sport Shop in Rangeley, Maine. This Muddler spin-off "was designed to copy the drake emerger on Kennebago Lake," Brett said. "The closely trimmed head lets it sink more easily than the traditional Muddler, and the long, sparse deer hair collar resembles legs."

Early Muddler, from the Dan Bailey Fly Shop. Bailey's shop once sold the Muddler attached to cards.
Mike Valla collection

Missoulian Spooks (sometimes labeled Mizoolian Spooks) were also attached to fly cards at the Bailey shop.
Mike Valla collection

CHAPTER 23

Dave Whitlock
(1934—)

Dave at his vise tying one of his colorful bass bugs. The same level of innovation found in Whitlock's trout patterns can be found in his bass and saltwater flies.
Dave and Emily Whitlock collection

The article titled "The Four Seasons River" in the May 1968 issue of *Field & Stream* was fascinating, and many of us who grabbed the magazine off newsstands and from our mailboxes have never forgotten it. The author's story concerning improbable trout water in Arkansas was filled with anecdotes describing fishing a variety of flies—Marabou Muddlers, Woolly Worms, fuzzy weighted nymphs, and traditional dry flies such as Light Cahills, Irresistibles, Jassids, and Joe's Hoppers. The water described was the White River, a tailrace stream created by the construction of Bull Shoals Dam in 1952. The fish were big, colorful rainbows, wide-girthed and plump. The beautiful photograph of a striking rainbow that appeared in the article was proudly held by a little-known smiling fly angler named Dave Whitlock.

The story was Whitlock's first fly-fishing article, providing readers with a glimpse of the author and his favored patterns on the unique Arkansas trout stream. After that article came other stories written for publications such as *Fly Fisherman*, *Fly Fishing and Fly Tying Journal*, *Trout*, *In Fisherman*, and *Field & Stream*. Over the years, Dave Whitlock has written and illustrated

Dave's Hopper, tied by Dave Whitlock. Whitlock strove to improve the standard hopper patterns of his era. For the Dave's Hopper, he borrowed some of the favorable features of Joe's Hopper and added missing characteristics that would enable the fly to behave better when fished. *Mike Valla collection*

five books and contributed to many others, and in these writings, readers have been exposed to some of the most creative fly patterns ever crafted.

Some of Whitlock's fly pattern designs evolved from his early experiences on the White River, where ugly, big-headed sculpin minnows thrived in abundance in its fertile waters. Two years later, Dave Whitlock once again addressed *Field & Stream* readers with an in-depth September 1970 feature titled "The Sculpin and Its Imitations," a story that further addressed a July 1968 article by the magazine's fishing editor A. J. McClane in his "Match-the-Minnow Streamer Fly Series." McClane had introduced a new fly called the Whitlock Sculpin, predicting that it would oust Gapen's Muddler Minnow for deep-water fishing. Whitlock responded, in the gentlemanly way he is still known for today, "I don't think it can ever replace the now legendary Muddler fly, but it certainly has proven its effectiveness wherever a sculpin population exists."

Sculpin-gulping trout were clearly facing many new Muddler variations that would take them to net. In his article, Whitlock listed patterns such as Dan Bailey's Marabou Muddler, the Gordon Dean Muddler, and the Searcy Muddler. Whitlock, like other tiers, had become intrigued with the sculpin and potential fly pattern design possibilities. He followed suit with his newfangled fly, an improved version of the highly popular original Gapen Muddler Minnow. "Fishing the various existing imitations on the sculpin loaded White River in Arkansas, I had only limited success," Whitlock wrote. "The Brown Marabou Muddler worked best, but it still fell short of my expectations for the stream's big browns and rainbows. Bait fishermen and spin fishermen scored me twenty to one on the large fish. I studied the sculpin's characteristics and experimented at the vise for several seasons before I hit upon a successful fly and method of fishing it."

Whitlock had progressed in his fly-fishing ability to be able to catch smart trout, but the ultimate quarry—a big, 10- to 15-pound brown trout—required a large fly that would hug the water bottom. He studied a large fly called the Troth Bullhead, tied by his Pennsylvania friend Al Troth, embraced its large-profile characteristics, combined it with some of the Muddler Minnow's features, and created his own sculpin imitation. Whitlock's original sculpin featured a well-mottled deer hair head, as well as cree hackle, which offered additional coloration that closely resembled the natural minnow.

With his new sculpins in hand, Dave Whitlock headed to Montana, where he field-tested them on the Yellowstone and Madison Rivers. The fly performed well, catching not only above-average-size browns and rainbows, but also the attention of Dan Bailey and Red Monical, who gave the fly its name: Whitlock's Sculpin. The new pattern gained momentum and enjoyed added exposure in *Art Flick's Master Fly-Tying Guide* (1972). Joining many notable tiers of the era in its pages, Whitlock contributed tying instructions for several favorite patterns. In the book, he expressed reverence for Don Gapen's famous Muddler Minnow, calling it a "fantastic pattern," and provided tying instructions for the Dan Bailey version. The Whitlock Sculpin was also one of the patterns described, once again introduced to fly tiers, this time along with detailed step-by-step tying instructions. Whitlock reinforced its design rationale, writing, "The sculpin's shape, color and habits are centered on the fact that it lives on the stream bottom. Any good sculpin imitation must display these characteristics in its design or you won't take many sculpin-eaters for your effort."

Dave Whitlock's hope that his new pattern would result in catching his dream fish—big, spotted brown trout—was realized when he landed his first big brown, a 10½-pounder out of the Missouri River, on his Sculpin fly. It also performed well on his home White River.

The Whitlock Sculpin also influenced other patterns, such as Dan Bailey and Red Monical's Spuddler Minnow. Ed Shenk created the popular Shenk's Sculpin to fit his needs on his Pennsylvania waters. Whitlock also continued to tweak

Dave Whitlock and a striking rainbow trout. Whitlock scrutinized fly patterns, always mindful of improvements that could be made. The old axiom "form follows function" steered him to new fly designs. *Dave and Emily Whitlock collection*

his basic sculpin design, improving and enhancing the pattern. His excellent July 1994 *Fly Fisherman* feature story titled "Fishing Sculpins" provided a review of the many different sculpin patterns available at that time. The Matuka Sculpin and NearNuff Sculpin were discussed in the story.

The Matuka Sculpin, tied with straight eyes or sometimes upturned eyes, is a big beast. Whitlock's Sculpin performed well but needed some tweaking. The cree-shaded hackles that projected toward the hook bend sometimes became wrapped around the hook-gap area. About the same time, another effective fly called the Matuka made its appearance. The Matuka's hackle feathers are lashed to the fly body, allowing the feather to create motion in water without wrapping around the hook. Dave Whitlock liked the Matuka's design feature and incorporated it into his own pattern, resulting in his new and improved, more trouble-free Matuka Sculpin. Whitlock recommended tying the pattern on 4XL to 6XL streamer hooks up to 5/0.

Sculpin design was obviously dear to Dave Whitlock's fly-tying heart, and his fertile imagination led to other versions such as his NearNuff pattern. Regular Matuka Sculpins are a bit time-consuming to tie, especially if the goal is to fill a fly box with them. The NearNuff Sculpin is just what its name implies—a suggestive imitation that is quicker to tie yet near enough in appearance to the natural that it is still very effective, maybe even more so than the Matuka Sculpin. Whitlock ties the fly in a couple different shades: an olive version and

one with a golden-brown hue. The NearNuff proved itself on the White River as well as other trout streams that Whitlock fished. His NearNuff Crayfish was also born from the same necessity—a fly that could be tied more quickly yet still retained the fish-taking effectiveness of his Softshell Crayfish, which performed well but took a while to tie.

Whitlock's creativity led him to invent other flies, in addition to his sculpin and crayfish patterns, that are equal in fly-fishing significance. His Hopper patterns, Dave's Hopper and Whit Hopper, are among the most popular. Whitlock's love affair with deer body hair is expressed in those patterns as well. As is characteristic of Dave Whitlock's design strategies, he studied the functionality of a traditional Hopper fly to determine whether it best suited its intended purpose on water. The traditional Joe's Hopper underwent Whitlock's scrutiny; for the resulting Dave's Hopper, he borrowed some of the favorable features of Joe's Hopper and added missing characteristics that would enable the fly to behave better when fished.

Dave Whitlock produced an excellent video titled, "Dave's Hopper and Whit Hopper." The video explains Hopper design rationale and gives tying instructions for both. What Whitlock noticed about Joe's Hopper was that although the hackle collar helped the fly float, it made casting difficult in western winds. One other problem with Joe's Hopper was that it landed on the water too lightly, almost parachuting down, whereas natural hoppers plop onto the water, causing

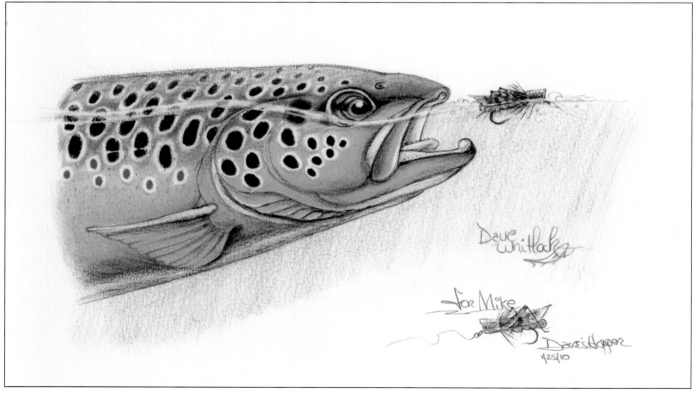

Dave Whitlock's artistic talents can be seen in the fly patterns that he developed over many years. Many feel that Dave's Hopper is his signature pattern, although he is equally associated with Sculpins. *Mike Valla collection; Art copy by permission of Emily and Dave Whitlock*

a small wake. Whitlock discussed this with Joe Brooks, who said that using a Muddler Minnow instead of the regular Hopper pattern would remedy the problem. Whitlock tried Muddlers for hopper fishing and had somewhat encouraging results, but the Muddler didn't look like a natural grasshopper. The large, clipped hair head caused a good plop on water, but changes to the design were needed to give the fly a more hopperlike appearance. Dave explained in his video, " I sort of married the Joe's Hopper, which to me looked an awful lot like a natural hopper, with the head of the Muddler Minnow, which looked a lot like a hopper's head."

The Whit Hopper also has a unique head, made of folded hair with projecting antennae. Its design enables the fly to plop down on the water, causing a disturbance that triggers fish strikes. As with the Dave's Hopper pattern, nothing was arbitrary in its design. Both Hoppers were the result of Whitlock's careful study of natural insects. In creating the designs, he paid particular attention to component material selection, proportions, and how the flies would fish on water.

This is the common theme among all of Dave Whitlock's creations: *design after careful observation*. The Red Fox Squirrel-Hair Nymph, for example, is an impressionistic fly yet still looks alive and edible. Readers may be surprised to learn that the fly Whitlock fished most consistently was not a Muddler, Hopper, or Sculpin. Whitlock wrote in a *Fly & Field* webpage article (http://www.flyfield.com/whitart.htm) titled "Red Fox Squirrel-Hair Nymph," "My Red Fox Squirrel Nymph (RFSH) is the most consistently effective fly I have ever used for all species of trout, char, and whitefish, both in numbers caught and size."

The fly had accidental beginnings. Dave Whitlock's early nymph inspirations came from the masters, including Thom Green, Ted Trueblood, and Polly Rosborough. However, the furs recommended by those tiers—otter, mink, seal, and beaver—were often unobtainable. Whitlock used what he could get his hands on, such as gray and red fox squirrel, which he could easily get locally. At first he was not sure whether fox would be as effective as the blends used by the masters, but his uncertainty vanished over years of field-testing. "I am convinced from my experiments that there is no single nymph pattern superior to my squirrel-hair patterns as an all-purpose nymph," he wrote in *Fly & Field*.

Besides the Hoppers, Sculpins, and fuzzy squirrel hair nymphs, the growing Whitlock fly family also included warmwater patterns, which captured the imagination of many fly tiers. With the modern development of his clipped deer hair bass creations, Whitlock sent a message to anglers who restricted themselves to the salmonids that bass-bug fishing provided fine sport as well.

The social elitism surrounding fly fishing, as the sport grew in popularity through the 1960s and into the 1970s, opened an already widening gulf between traditional bass anglers and fly anglers. As Jack Ellis aptly wrote in *Bassin' with a Fly Rod* (2003), fly fishing "was no longer simply a fun way to catch bass when conditions were right. It had become a statement of social caste, a way of life, a means of defining oneself philosophically, socially and economically."

Fly fishing with a long rod had somehow evolved away from the early years when Joe Messinger Sr. developed his clipped hair frog patterns that iconic fishermen such as John Alden Knight and Ray Bergman grabbed, promoted, and fished with enthusiasm. Fly-rod bugging articles that appeared throughout the 1930s in fishing magazines such as *Pennsylvania Angler* exemplified the sport's popularity in that era, but this eventually began to wane. A few well-known fly anglers, fly tiers, and writers, such as Tom McNally and Chauncy Lively, continued a nonelitist stance well into the 1960s and '70s. Both developed bass popping bugs, with Lively creating an interesting clipped hair tadpole imitation.

However, as Jack Ellis eloquently argued in his book, it was "the Whitlock Revolution" that recaptured the dignity in fly fishing for warmwater species. According to Ellis, "Dave made bass bugging respectable. Solid coldwater credentials and exceptional fly-tying skills gave him credibility with this new breed of well-educated, affluent, sometimes 'yuppie' fly fishers, and his warmwater advocacy received a degree of approbation that had been denied to many of his predecessors."

Dave Whitlock brought the same artistry and careful attention to bass-bug functionality as he did with the best of his trout flies. Whitlock's reputation convinced even the most idealistic "match-the hatch" fly anglers that they were missing out on fine sport. His pattern inventiveness also helped persuade many an elitist fly angler to put their fine British Wheatley trout-fly boxes aside during the summer months and grab patterns such as his Whit Hairbugs and Diving Frogs.

Dave Whitlock's continual fishing-fly development led to other patterns, such as his Sheep Minnow series, flies that can catch many fish species. However, he will always be primarily associated with his Sculpins and Hoppers—flies that no doubt have inspired others to tie new patterns using the same keen eye for detail characteristic of all Whitlock patterns. Frank Johnson, creator of the Partridge Sculpin and the 1984 winner of the prestigious Federation of Fly Fishers Buz Buszek Memorial Award for outstanding contributions to the art of fly tying, had this to say to me about Dave Whitlock's pattern innovations: "Dave's Hopper and other patterns made us start thinking in new directions. His innovative approach got us all thinking more 'out-of-the-box.' Dave is such a fine man and so willing to share with others that I'm always in awe of him. We have fished together, tied together, and he has visited my home. I always learn something from him."

The Whit Hopper, tied by Dave Whitlock. Its design enables the fly to plop down on the water, causing a disturbance that triggers fish strikes. As is true with its sister Dave's Hopper pattern, nothing was arbitrary in its design. *Mike Valla collection*

Matuka Sculpin, tied by Dave Whitlock. Dave decided to improve his original Sculpin pattern by borrowing some of the excellent features found in the popular Matuka fly. *Mike Valla collection*

Sculpin, tied by Dave Whitlock. This 1960s-era fly is simple in its design. *John Capowski collection (formerly belonging to Jim Bashline)*

NearNuff Sculpin, tied by Dave Whitlock. The NearNuff Sculpin is a suggestive imitation that is quicker to tie than the Matuka Sculpin, yet near enough in appearance to the natural that it is still very effective. *Mike Valla collection*

Sculpin, tied by Dave Whitlock in the 1960s. Sculpins proved highly effective for landing very large trout. *John Capowski collection (formerly belonging to Jim Bashline)*

NearNuff Crayfish, tied by Dave Whitlock. Dave's NearNuff can be tied more quickly than other crayfish patterns yet still retains the fish-taking effectiveness of his Softshell Crayfish, which performed well but took a while to tie. *Mike Valla collection*

Red Fox Squirrel-Hair Nymph, tied by Dave Whitlock. According to Dave, the fly "is the most consistently effective pattern I have ever used for all species of trout, char, and whitefish, both in numbers caught and size." The fly had accidental beginnings. *Mike Valla collection*

Joe's Hopper, tied by Mike Valla. Dave Whitlock used some features of this famous pattern in creating his Dave's Hopper. He found the large hackle collar to be too wind-resistant, a characteristic that hampered casting. The fly also failed to plop on the water as natural hoppers tend to do.

Whit Fruit Cocktail Hairbug, tied by Dave Whitlock. Whitlock's pattern inventiveness helped persuade many an elitist fly angler to put their fine British Wheatley trout-fly boxes aside during the summer months and grab patterns such as his Whit Hairbugs and Diving Frogs. He is credited with trumpeting the worth of warmwater fly fishing. *Mike Valla collection*

Matuka Sculpin variation, tied by Poul Jorgensen. While Jorgenson was known for his striking salmon flies, he also experimented with a variety of popular patterns. *Ralph Graves collection*

CHAPTER 24

Art Winnie
(1880–1966)

Art Winnie, the Traverse City, Michigan, barber, at his tying bench. Winnie was responsible for creating a better Hopper imitation. *Gary Miller collection*

Mary Orvis Marbury wrote in *Favorite Flies and Their Histories* (1955), "Everyone who attempts artificial flies sooner or later undertakes an imitation of the grasshopper. Some of these imitations bear close resemblance to the originals, and have been made with bodies of wood, cork, or quills and covered with silk, wool, rubber, and silkworm gut; but they are apt to be clumsy, lacking as they do the spring and softness of the real insect." The Hopper she featured was a simple attempt to craft something that resembled a grasshopper, but one would have to use liberal imagination to equate the fly with a natural insect. Harry Pritchard of New York tied the fly for Marbury, who called it "generally known." She reported excellent results with the fly for large trout and bass, yet it is hard to imagine that a large fish would think it was a real hopper.

Tiers eventually started experimenting with Hopper patterns that were more imitative than Pritchard's attempt. In *Streamcraft* (1927), George Parker Holden introduced readers to a Hopper crafted by Dr. J. E. Storey of Beaumont, Texas. The fly was described as one of Holden's

Michigan Hopper, tied by Art Winnie. Winnie's Michigan Hopper influenced the development of many other turkey wing patterns that followed. It led to Joe's Hopper and then to the hoppers created by Dave Whitlock. *Bob Summers collection*

"pet bass-bugs." Holden also wrote about cork-bodied patterns that were very popular in his time. In *A Modern Dry-Fly Code* (1950), Vincent C. Marinaro described a Hopper, roughly designed by Charlie Craighead and tweaked by Bill Bennett, that was fabricated from goose or turkey quills. However, the early attempts of Pritchard, Storey, Craighead, and others seemed to fall short of an easily cast and fished yet suggestive pattern. Then the fly-fishing world discovered a pattern first called a Michigan Hopper, later popularized as Joe's Hopper, conceived and tied by a Traverse City barber named Art Winnie.

Gary L. Miller, who I had the great pleasure to personally meet and spend time with in the summer of 2012, is a Williamsburg, Michigan, resident and recognized authority on fish decoys, wrote an article called "The Winnies: Traverse City's First Family of Fishing," published in the December 2006 issue of *NFLCC Magazine*. Miller's article presented a fascinating history of the Winnie family, based on exhaustive research and filled with anecdotes and intrigue. It would be hard to find another family so involved with the outdoors, particularly fishing, and it gained them great admiration and reputation within their community. Of the six family members Miller researched, he called Albert and Arthur, both town barbers, "the principal stars in the Winnie family story."

Miller offered entertaining insight into Art Winnie, describing what he was like and the enjoyment he experienced among similar-minded folks. Readers can almost hear the laughter coming from the Shack on the Boardman, a clubhouse on that famous Michigan river that was built from salvaged materials and used by the famous Traverse City Casting Club. Art recorded stories from the Shack in a diary, which fed many a regional outdoor writer with plenty of material to satisfy their readers. Yet Miller wrote that humorous happenings in the Shack were only second to what went on inside Art's barbershop. His role as a commercial fly tier and a barber for more than 60 years no doubt initiated many fly-fishing discussions within the shop walls, too. According to Miller, it is estimated that Art Winnie tied over 200,000 flies during his career, and his home at 415 State Sreet in Traverse City was labeled by Jay Smith, editor at the *Traverse City Evening Record*, as "the house that flies built." Smith, an Art Winnie barbershop hang-around, wrote in 1916, "Winnie has completed a modern bungalow on one of the nicest residential streets in the city and while the flies did not have much to do with the actual construction work, they financed the job."

Art Winnie advertised that he tied some of the old classics, including the Royal Coachman, Wickham's Fancy, McGinty, and Professor, along with some of his own patterns, such as the red, white, and blue Victory Fly, a patriotic pattern created during World War II and described in the February 7, 1942, issue of the *Grand Rapids Press*. He was not only productive at the fly-tying vise, but he was also creative, and out

This colorful 1931 calendar served as a great advertisement for Art Winnie and his famous Hopper. *Gary Miller collection*

of that creativity came his Fore and Aft, Stonefly, Caddis, and his famous Michigan Hopper, the patriarch of many Hopper patterns that followed. Joining the hundreds of natural species that have been known to swarm and infest western states like Montana, Art Winnie's creation caused quite a commotion—not with farmers, but with fly anglers.

During the height of its popularity on western streams, before the explosion of more contemporary Hopper patterns, some assumed that Art Winnie's Hopper had been created by a western tier. George F. Grant wrote in *Montana Trout Flies* (1981), "It would be difficult for most Montana fly fisherman to concede that 'Joe's Hopper' did not ride the riffles of the Madison of the Big Hole before it was used elsewhere, but the original of this fly was known as the 'Michigan Hopper' and was created by Art Winnie of Traverse City, Michigan. It is consoling to realize that we adopted another's child, gave it a new name, dressed it quite well, provided it with an

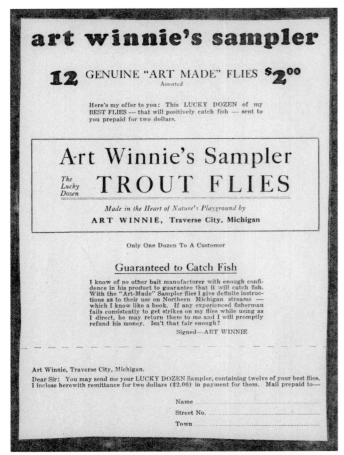

Art Winnie tied other patterns besides his Michigan Hopper and Michigan Caddis. His "Art Made" sampler consisted of flies recommended for northern Michigan streams. *Gary Miller collection*

exciting place to live, and proudly presented it as though it was our own. When the fly moved out west, where the trout are, it was evidently first used with success by 'a guy named Joe.' It is possible, however, in some western states to find this same pattern assuming the name of 'Jack's Hopper' or 'Jim's Hopper,' but as has been said, 'a rose by any other name would smell as sweet.'"

Some assume that the "Joe" was Joe Brooks, who has been credited with helping popularize the fly, but there's no real proof that there even was a "Joe." In *The Complete Book of Fly Fishing* (1958), Brooks mentioned Joe's Hopper with an asterisk, noting that it was also called Dan's Hopper. It is interesting that this pattern is among the illustrations painted by Jack Atherton for John McDonald's classic piece on trout flies that appeared in the May 1946 issue of *Fortune*. The caption there reads, "Joe's Hopper, by Dan Bailey, Livingston, Montana." However, in *Trout Fishing* (1972), Joe Brooks credited Joe's Hopper as a Michigan pattern, writing, "Grasshoppers, which are also terrestrial insects, are certainly high on the list of any trout's favorite foods, and you will find the artificials in a myriad guises, from the renowned Joe's Hopper of Michigan to the Pontoon Hopper tied by Charlie

Fox." A few paragraphs later, Brooks brought in Dan Bailey: "Hoppers have always been an old standby in the streams of the Middle West and the Rocky Mountains, and many of the top fly tyers have produced their own versions. Dan Bailey's of Livingston, Montana, sells a Bailey's Hopper that takes its full share of fish."

Other Hopper patterns were influenced by Art Winnie's creation. In his book *Trout Fishing*, Joe Brooks also mentioned a Rebel Joe Hopper, and the photo of this fly alongside Joe's Hopper shows the striking resemblance. It is clear the design is of Art Winnie lineage. Other Hopper patterns belong to the Michigan Hopper family tree, such as Dave Whitlock's Dave's Hopper, which resulted from the crossbreeding of the Muddler Minnow and Joe's Hopper. Beyond those creations, Winnie's design may have influenced other Hopper tiers in Michigan. Or perhaps new Hopper creations coming out of Michigan were coincidental.

In *Fly Patterns and Their Origins* (1944), Harold Hinsdill Smedley described another famous Art Winnie pattern, the Michigan Caddis. At the tail end of that description, Smedley mentioned Winnie's Hopper: "The Michigan Hopper is also one of Art Winnie's designs and original with him, and is often referred to by his name. It has a yellow chenille body, brown mottled turkey wings and brown hackle. It is supposed to imitate a grasshopper."

Smedley's words make it clear that Art Winnie's Michigan Hopper was known among Michigan anglers in the 1940s. However, a fly tier by the name of Ken Cooper, a "Michigan tier of note," sent his new Hopper and a letter to Ray Bergman describing the pattern. Bergman updated earlier editions of his popular book *Trout*, adding an additional color plate of regional dry-fly patterns. Notes describing the flies in plate 17, which includes a fly called Cooper's Hopper, followed his "new 1951 list." Cooper wrote that he designed the Hopper after camping on Michigan's Au Sable River. He had collected natural hoppers, studied them, and then crafted his pattern. Cooper's Hopper used tan chenille for the body and had a dark red tail, brown hackle, and mottled turkey wings. As with Winnie's pattern, there is no mention of hackle palmer along the body.

Many hopper fly fishers assume that Joe's Hopper and Winnie's Michigan Hopper are one and the same. However, sometimes a distinction is made between the two names based on the body and the presence or absence of a hackle palmer. In his *Book of Fly Patterns* (1987), Eric Leiser noted the similarities but presented the flies as two distinct patterns, listing them separately. Leiser also wrote of Art Winnie, "He may be best known for the Michigan Hopper, which may have been the first fly that used a turkey feather wing."

The Michigan Hopper gave Winnie renown as a fly tier, but he was also known for his Michigan Caddis. Smedley's book devoted ample attention to the fly, whose name has often caused confusion. Most maintain it was created to imitate the large *Hexagenia limbata* hatch, which provides excitement on some of Michigan's trout streams. Even today many refer to the anticipated emergence as the "caddis hatch," a big event that begins around mid to late June. Smedley wrote, "History has it that the so-called Caddis-fly, which has found favor with the Michigan fisherman, was first tied by Art Winnie, of Traverse City, ex-king of the National Trout Festival held every year at Kalkaska, Michigan. He tied a fly which found favor with the trout and just gave it the name of 'Caddis' and the name stuck, both for the fly and the hatch."

Michigan fly-fishing historian Tom Deschaine, who loves to research and tie important Michigan dry flies both classic and contemporary, described the Michigan Caddis IV, a fore-and-aft hackle fly with large mallard quill wings, gold yarn body, and gold tinsel ribbing. Three natural shade deer hair strands form the long tails. In describing the large fly tied on a size 8 long-shank hook, Deschaine wrote on the Michigan Dry Flies webpage (www.michigandryflies.net), "This beautiful pattern was created by Art Winnie back in the 1920s. It is also called 'Winnie's Michigan Caddis' or 'Winnie's Fore-and-Aft.'" Bob Summers, a superb cane-rod builder from Traverse City, mailed me two examples of Winnie-tied Michigan Caddis in a fore-and-aft hackle style, with very large quill wings, maybe goose. The fly has similarities to Deschaine's Michigan Caddis IV interpretation, based on the pattern that originated from Art Winnie's hands.

Art Winnie also experimented with his original Michigan Caddis, creating the Albino Caddis. In a 1951 story that appeared in the *Grand Rapids Press*, George Wells wrote, "Art Winnie, Traverse City barber, ex-trout king, and fly tyer ex-

Art Winnie loved to advertise his famous Hopper pattern. This ad was printed in 1926. *Gary Miller collection*

traordinaire, may be expected to pull something new out his vise from time to time to startle fly fishermen. This time it's a Blond version of the famed 'Michigan Caddis' fly in fore-and-aft pattern (which means it has hackle on each end) mounted on a formidable No. 6 hook." Winnie said the new fly was field-tested before he announced it to eager fly anglers, who ordered many of them.

Art Winnie's Caddis is still admired and discussed by Michigan fly-angling enthusiasts, such as Tom Deschaine and Bob Summers, yet as Eric Leiser wrote in *The Book of Fly Patterns*, "Winnie is probably best known for his Michigan Hopper." Indeed, his Hopper has enjoyed continued mention in many fly-tying and fly-fishing books, as well as in articles that appeared in his hometown newspaper. Another Hopper version, Winnie's Texas Hopper, was described in the July 22, 1949, issue of the *Traverse City Evening Recorder*, as Winnie was nearing his 70th birthday. The fly was similar to his original Hopper, but it has a white body instead of a yellow one and a red underwing. The first large order for this fly came from the Lone Star State, giving it its name.

Beyond Winnie's Michigan Hopper and Texas Hopper, as well as those Hoppers crafted by Dave Whitlock, other patterns that use turkey quill wings have continued to evolve. Among these are Ed Shenk's Letort Hopper, René Harrop's Spring Creek Hopper, and Ed Schroeder's Para Hopper, which tier Charlie Craven has called "one of the most popular hopper patterns around."

Many contemporary Hopper patterns are available to the modern fly fisher; some are entirely synthetic, while others combine the attributes of natural materials, such as turkey quill, with man-made products, such as Antron dubbing. Most have abandoned the water-absorbing yellow chenille body once used by Art Winnie in his Michigan Hopper. Winnie's original Hopper has no doubt vanished from the arsenal found in many fly boxes. But his long turkey quill wings still live, reminders of the colorful character who once amused fly anglers at his barbershop in Traverse City, Michigan.

The Winnie barbershop in Traverse City, Michigan. Brothers Albert (left) and Art (right) ran the shop, which was just as much a gathering place for tale-telling as it was a place to get a haircut. Winnie family historian Gary Miller called the two "the principal stars in the Winnie family story." *Gary Miller collection*

Michigan Caddis, tied by Art Winnie, was a popular dry fly for fishing Michigan's hatch of *Hexagenia*, a large mayfly. *Bob Summers collection*

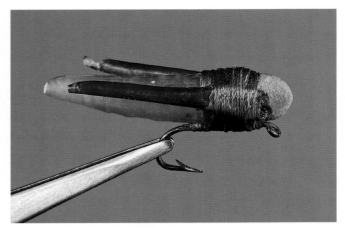

Pontoon Hopper, tied by Vince Marinaro. The Hopper was born out of a crude design crafted by and tweaked by Bill Bennett. Marinaro popularized the pattern through his *Modern Dry-Fly Code* and magazine stories. Marinaro once hooked and lost a gargantuan Letort trout, which he dubbed "Vesuvius" on the Hopper. *Pennsylvania Fly Fishing Museum Association collection*

Joe's Hopper, tied by Mike Valla. Joe Brooks helped popularize the Hopper, but what "Joe," if any, that the fly is named after is still unknown. Winnie's Hopper influenced the development of this popular pattern. Joe's Hopper, in turn, influenced Dave Whitlock in creating his Dave's Hopper.

CHAPTER 25

Len Halladay
(1872–1952)

Len Halladay. In 1922, Halladay named the famous Adams fly at Mayfield Pond in Michigan. He tied the pattern for fishing the Boardman River in that same state. *Gary Miller collection*

The Boardman River is a trout stream gem that flows some 40 miles through Grand Traverse and Kalkaska Counties in northwest lower Michigan, emptying into Grande Traverse Bay at Traverse City. Its waters once held large populations of grayling, their disappearance still lamented by those passionate about Michigan's rich outdoor heritage and history. However, the story of Len Halladay and his Adams—a pattern first cast on Mayfield Pond and the Boardman—will never vanish from discussions centered on fly-fishing history.

Many consider the Adams the most popular and effective dry fly ever created. Tom Deschaine, a Michigan dry-fly history buff, wrote in an online *Hatches* magazine article titled "The Adams: History Revisited" that he considers the Adams to be "probably the most famous fly in all of history." Whether or not the fly has attained that level of importance, few would argue that the pattern is widely fished and widely known. It is a dry fly that has evolved into many variations, beginning with its simple form first tied by Len Halladay, who once lived in the township of Mayfield, Michigan, where he named the Adams at Mayfield Pond in 1922.

Original Adams, tied by Len Halladay. Many consider the fly the most famous and effective dry fly ever created. As far back as the 1930s, Halladay tied it with red, yellow, and gray bodies.
Bob Summers collection

The fly has been discussed, debated, argued, and admired ever since Charles F. Adams said it was a "knockout," as quoted by Harold Smedley in his book *Fly Patterns and Their Origins* (1944). Friendly chats have pondered the reasons for its effectiveness in taking trout. Yet there have also been disagreements over the years concerning the role Charles Adams played in its creation. Some have debated its original design—its appearance at the time Halladay first tied the fly—and exactly what insect the fly was tied to imitate. But as Deschaine aptly said in his Adams history article, "History is not always as clear and uncluttered as we would like it to be." However, there are several written historical references to the fly, as well as personal accounts, that give us some insight into Len Halladay, Charles F. Adams, the Adams dry fly, and the circumstances surrounding the fly's creation.

In *Fly Patterns and Their Origins* (1944), Michigan author Harold Hinsdill Smedley offered a brief glimpse into "Michigan's favorite fly." He quoted Halladay as saying, "The first Adams I made I handed to Mr. Adams, who was fishing in a small pond in front of my house, try [*sic*] on the Boardman that evening. When he came back the next morning, he wanted to know what I called it. He said it was a 'knock-out' and I said we would call it the Adams, since he had made the first good catch on it."

Charles F. Adams, 1958. He called the fly that Len Halladay tied for him a "knock-out." *Charles Felix collection*

Charles Adams, described by Smedley as an ardent trout fly angler who fished the Boardman for many years, had a summer home on Arbutus Lake. He and his son Lon, both attorneys from Loraine, Ohio, fished with Halladay, who tied flies for them. He later became a judge, and many in the area referred to him as Judge Adams.

Leonard Halladay was originally from New York but left the area early in his life when his family moved to Mayfield. Halladay and his wife, Rilla, known as Mary, operated a hotel in Mayfield, a small town near the Boardman River. It was there that he supplemented his income by tying trout flies and guiding anglers. "I have been tying flies since 1917," said Halladay in Smedley's book. "I haven't caught a fish on a baited hook for the last thirty-five years. I use the fly only." Halladay was a custom fly tier, catering to anglers like the Adamses.

In a 1996 letter to the editor of *Michigan Natural Resources*, Edith Halladay Blackhurst, then the only living member of the Halladay family and who was living at home when the fly was created, told the story of how the Adams fly was first created for Charles Adams. "Judge Charles Adams, as he was known to all of the people at Arbutus Lake and surrounding area, enjoyed night fishing on Mayfield Pond. Mrs. Adams did not permit her husband to fish alone. She or her daughter Thelma always accompanied him. Mrs. Adams often came over to visit with mother and I, if one of his friends from Kingsley came to fish also. Bert (Lon) seldom came as he was of high school age and enjoyed the activities of the young people at the lake and surrounding area. One evening when the Judge came to fish, the fish were jumping more than usual and he noticed that there was a different hatch on the water. He came over to the hotel and asked my father to tie a fly for him. My father, also an avid dry-fly fisherman, told him he knew what it was, and sat down and tied the fly for him. Later that evening, the Judge returned and said, 'Len, it's a killer. I got my limit in no time. Will you please tie one for Bert (Lon) so we can fish the Boardman in the morning?' My father sat down and tied a second. The next day the judge returned to report the results. He said, 'Bert and I each got our limit. What are going to name it?' My father thought for a moment and replied, 'Since I have already tied a "Halladay Fly," which wasn't too successful, I am going to name this one "The Adams" since I first tied it for you and we have been very good friends ever since you arrived in our area.'"

Some 60 years before the publication of Edith Halladay Blackhurst's letter, however, R. J. Blackhurst tried to clarify the Adams fly's origins in a letter to Ray Bergman on April 15, 1937. In research for this book, Jill and Mark Schwarz, who inherited Ray Bergman's belongings, offered documents pertaining to the Adams fly history, including this letter. In it, Blackhurst described the history behind the Adams fly as he remembered it. Bergman apparently had referenced the Adams fly in his May 1937 *Outdoor Life* article titled "Flies

Len Halladay (right) with son-in-law Roswell Blackhurst in front of Halladay's Hotel. *Gary Miller collection*

for Odd Situations," but stated that its origination was unclear. "Its history is unclear. I'm sure that it originated in Michigan, but I can't get authentic data concerning its history," Bergman wrote in his story. In response, Blackhurst shot off a letter to Bergman dated April 15, 1937: "I am taking the liberty of send you a bit of unsolicited information regarding the origination of the Adams fly. Mr. Leonard Halladay made the first Adams fly and he now lives at Mayfield, Michigan. In fact, Mr. Halladay has lived in this village for more than sixty years and it was he who pioneered the art of dry fly fishing when there were still grayling in the nearby river.

"The first Adams fly was, of course, an experiment and Mr. Halladay gave it to Mr. Charles Adams, an attorney, who now lives it Loarain, Ohio. Mr. Adams reported that the fly was a 'killer' and 'Len' said that he would call it the 'Adams.' Mr. Halladay also ties a hair stone fly which I consider the best dry fly I have ever used. I am sending a photograph of 'Len' and also a 'genuine' Adams fly."

Bergman quickly responded to Blackhurst with a letter dated April 27, 1937: "Dear Sir: Thank you very much for your information on the Adams fly. I wanted to have an authentic first hand dope and that was the reason I mentioned the fact that I did not have it in *Outdoor Life*."

However, another letter concerning the creation of the Adams, written by Charles Adams's son Lon but undated, was sent to Ray Bergman concerning Bergman's *Outdoor Life* article, telling a different story: "Dear Sir: In the May issue I notice a reference to the 'Adams Fly'—together with a statement that its origin is uncertain—It is not. My dad has been a rabid fly fisherman for the last twenty years—fishing mostly in the Boardman River Michigan. About eight years ago he asked Mr. Len Halladay of Mayfield, Michigan—who makes most of our fly's [*sic*] to make him a variation of Mr. Halladay's 'Gray Palmer' fly by putting wings on that fly which was originally solely a hackle fly—the result was the original 'Adams fly' which was named after dad. The fly has been much changed and refined since that time and Mr. Halladay now makes it with red, yellow and gray bodies—the most successful being the gray body with a sort of quill stripe—we have used the fly in all its variations and found it to be a most consistent fish 'getter.' Mr. Halladay makes the best dry fly's I have ever seen—most of them original patterns—the best of which is a spread wing 'stone fly' tied out of deer hair which I use most of the time I'm in the river. It is so well-made that one fly has lasted me an entire season and it will be well-worth your time to try a few of his patterns."

Decades later, in a letter Lon wrote to Kenneth L. Peterson, he was still sticking to his story about the Adams fly being crafted from tweaking a Gray Palmer dry fly, but this time he said it was he and not his father, Charles, who presented the Gray Palmer to Halladay for tweaking. Lon's story creates more confusion about the fly's birth, implying that he had something to do with its creation. An article by Peterson titled "The Adams Family" appeared in the March 1992 issue of *Michigan Out-of-Doors* magazine, in which he included excepts from Lon Adams's letter to him. The story tells us that Lon first fished the Boardman around 1913 with his father, and by 1920 he was well into dry-fly fishing. According to Lon Adams, "About 1922 or 1923 we were using a Gray Palmer almost exclusively . . . but we were also trying to find something which might be more attractive to the browns. We had most of our flies tied by Len Halladay of Mayfield, and one day I asked Len if he could come up with a winged variation of the Gray Palmer, which I thought might be effective. He tied two or three samples and eventually came up with what was the first Adams fly. That fly had hackle similar to the body (hackle) of the Gray Palmer. The body was bulky and of rough gray yarn. It was a male fly and had two rather small tail feathers, which I think may have been little slivers of peacock feathers."

Peterson noted that although it may have been true that the tails described by Lon Adams were as stated, it was well accepted that by 1930, golden pheasant tippet barbs were used for tailing. Peterson quoted others in his article who supported that fact. The late Hans L. Peterson, an operator at the Grayling, Michigan, fish hatchery was introduced to the fly in about 1930 and was quoted in the article as saying, "At that time the male version was tied with mixed dark ginger and dark grizzly (Plymouth Rock) hackle and had a gray

The Michigan Outdoor Writers Association paid tribute to Len Halladay and his famous Adams fly.

wool-yarn body, golden pheasant tippet tail, and spent wings of grizzly hackle tips."

The fact that one of the earliest Adamses, if not the original, was tied spent-winged with golden pheasant tails and wool yarn body is well documented; muskrat fur for the body entered the design later. The dressing that Len Halladay gave Harold Hinsdill Smedley (that appeared in the updated 4th edition published in 1950) was as follows: "Body: gray wool yarn. Tail: two strands from a golden pheasant neck feather. Hackle: mixed, from neck feathers of Barred Plymouth Rock and Rhode Island Red roosters. Wings: narrow neck feathers of barred Plymouth rock rooster, tied advanced forward and in a semi-spent manner."

The April 1938 issue of *Pennsylvania Angler* magazine featured an article by R. W. McCafferty titled "Trout Tackle Suggestions." A large illustration of a spent-wing Adams, sporting its sparse golden pheasant tippet tails, was shown on the opening page. An article by Ed Brasseur titled "Experimenting with Artificials for Trout" in the June 1943 issue also showed an Adams in the same spent-wing form. However, there was confusion concerning who did what when during the fly's creation.

R. E. Stinson, who wrote an August 1993 editorial to *Michigan Out-of-Doors*, no doubt would have refuted Lon Adams's letter to Kenneth Peterson in which he said that he was the one who had approached Halladay about creating a winged version of the Gray Palmer. Stinson, since the age of 15, was a good friend of Halladay's. He told the tale this way: "One day when we were relaxing on a bank of the Boardman River after a morning's fishing he [Halladay] told me how he named the fly, and I quote him: 'I had tied up a couple of dozen of these new flies when Charlie Adams and his son stopped by on their way to go a-fishing on the river. I showed them to Charlie, and he thought they looked pretty good, so I gave him a few to try out. After three or four hours he came

back with a grin on his face and a whole basket of fish. He said it was the best fly for brown trout that he had ever seen. I told him, well, since you are the first man to catch trout with it, we'll name it the Adams.'"

Stinson also pointed out that Len Halladay had used small boxes to merchandise his flies that were plainly marked, "Originator of the Adams Fly," and that Len was "scrupulously honest—Halladay would have never put that statement on his boxes if that wasn't the 'pure truth.'"

Whatever mix of circumstances ended with the creation of the Adams fly, the "pure truth" is that the pattern is omnipresent. Many anglers wouldn't think of being without a few onstream, no matter what its original purpose, whether to imitate insects or to serve as an attractor. It's hard to find agreement on just why the fly is so effective, however.

Since it was first fished in Michigan, many fly anglers and tiers have chimed in on the Adams, each with his or her own theories concerning the fly. Back in the 1940s, Harold Hinsdill Smedley attributed its lasting popularity to its combination of "what I personally regard as the two basic colors of flies, brown and gray," saying that "the mottling blends the two colors in a most natural way." Smedley reported that Lon Adams believed it was most effective for flying ant emergences and that Lon and his father, Charles, "thought it is the bug that it apparently simulates."

In an article fly tier Dick Talleur wrote for *Fly Fisherman* magazine titled "The Adams Family," he said he believed that Len Halladay "was thinking mayfly when he conceived it." He also wrote, "I've often said that if I had to fish for my supper and I was allowed only one pattern, it would be the Muddler Minnow. However, if it were further decreed that the fly had to be dry, I'd opt for the Adams." History is filled with similar admiration for the Adams.

The late western fly tier Don Martinez also loved the pattern. In his June 1953 *Field & Stream* article titled "The Right Dry Fly," he wrote, "On first thought, I'm of the school that considers fly pattern unimportant, but on first reflection I have to confess that like all other anglers I'm a sucker for some. The Adams and similar flies combining brown and Plymouth Rock hackle will get my vote every time." Martinez was well known for his Quill Adams dry fly.

Catskill fly-fishing historian Ed Van Put, an accomplished angler who lives on the banks of the Willowemoc Creek in Livingston Manor, New York, began fishing the Adams in the 1960s, and there has probably never been a more passionate cheerleader for the pattern. Beyond the fine Catskill fly-fishing history books he's written, Van Put is perhaps most closely associated with the Adams. Some have called him "the vacuum cleaner," owing to the large number of Catskill trout he's taken on the Adams over the years. In recent correspondence, Ed offered interesting thoughts on Halladay's gem: "I began using the Adams in the 1960s. As is the case with many fly fishers, for the first several years I was hooked on 'matching the hatch' and carried around a number of flies in many different sizes, tied to imitate the great variety of aquatic insects found along trout streams. I started to keep a diary of my experiences and recorded my catch: the species, whether the fish were wild or stocked, what they were taken on, water temperatures, and a general description of what flies were on the water. Interestingly, the more I fished, the more I found that I was catching the vast majority of trout on flies that imitated no specific hatch but were proven standards that had withstood the test of time, such as the Adams, Royal Coachman (both the hair wing and bivisible), Pheasant Tail Midge, Elk Hair Caddis, and a couple of others. I did not set out to prove anything by using these flies; but in using them with success, it changed my philosophy about matching the hatch.

"It was also in the early 1960s that I began fishing the Delaware River for its large rainbow and brown trout. The fishing was demanding, mostly because the best way to fish it was with dry flies; and being a big river, long and accurate casts were necessary for success. The fish often worked only in the late evening, rising to spinnerfalls, beginning a half hour to an hour before dark and continuing into the night. I began using an Adams at this time, at first tied 'spent-winged,' believing this was necessary during the spinnerfall, but soon tied the more traditional upright-winged pattern. The fly was a great success on the Delaware—and I also began using it on all the streams I fished.

"I tie the Adams in sizes 18 through 12, though 14 is my favorite. I am very particular about the wings and use a well-shaped, fairly stiff hackle tip. I once fished the upper Beaverkill on a day that was exceptionally good and caught 37 trout on the same fly. During this spree, I lost the tail of the fly, then the body; and after a few more fish, the hackle came off—and with just the wings remaining, the fly took a couple more fish.

"It is my belief that the Adams works exceptionally well because of the mixing of hackle—the red/brown hackle mixed with a grizzly hackle gives the fly a 'broken' or distorted image, not a solid one; and this causes the trout to see an optical image that is more consistent with a natural fly. The Adams has a general blue/gray/brown appearance that is prevalent in many mayfly hatches. When cast among Hendricksons riding the water, the Adams blends in nicely with the naturals; the same is true with *Isonychias* that hatch a couple of times a year, or the many Blue-Winged Olive hatches that occur on our streams. I also think that in the evening, when it is com-

Mayfield Pond, near Traverse City, Michigan, birthplace of the Adams. The man-made pond formed by the damming of Swainston Creek, a tributary of the Boardman River, was just outside the hotel where Len Halladay tied his trout flies. *Photo by Valerie Valla*

mon for fly fishers to switch to a lighter fly for visibility, the Adams actually works better; being a dark fly, it shows up well against the lighter sky, and trout looking up can see its shape better than that of a light-colored fly."

While Van Put believes the Adams doesn't represent any one insect type, others, such as Michigan's dry-fly aficionado Tom Deschaine, theorize that Halladay tied the fly to represent a specific insect. Deschaine wrote an online article titled "The Adams and the Alder" that appeared on the Michigan Dry Flies webpage: "It has been said that the Adams was originally designed to represent a mayfly, some say a caddisfly and still others say a stonefly. I present to you today a different theory—I suggest to you that the Adams was designed to imitate an alderfly." This caddislike insect has grayish brown wings and is found on Michigan rivers like the Pine, Au Sable, and Boardman. If one prefers the popular version of the Adams creation story that Charles Adams brought several insects to Halladay so that he could custom design an imitation, Deschaine's theory seems interesting and plausible.

"Mr. Adams was no stranger to fly-fishing," Deschaine explained. "By all accounts he was a very accomplished and knowledgeable fisherman. It would make sense that he was aware of the local hatches and had at least some knowledge of insect names. Why would he bring the insects to Halladay when all he had to do was to say, 'Tie me up something that resembles a Little Black Caddis, or a Brown Drake'?" Deschaine theorized that it was more likely that Adams brought Halladay an insect he was not familiar with after encountering them on the water, and an Alderfly was the perfect candidate. It makes for interesting discussion around a campfire after a long day on the water, as do all the other theories concerning the Adams.

Len Halladay's fly packaging boxes had labels that said he was the originator of the Adams fly. *Box from Bob Summers collection*

But even more thought-provoking are the fly's longevity, popularity, global acceptance, and the intrigue that follows it everywhere. And it is still revered by those in Michigan who have their own memories of the fly. *Michigan Outdoor* writer Dave Richey fondly recalled, "My first personal exposure to this famous fly came at the hands of my teenage mentor, Max Donovan of Clio, Michigan. He felt the Adams fly tied on a size 10, 12, 14, 16, and 18 hook was perhaps one of the steadiest-producing flies used on the Manistee and Au Sable Rivers near Grayling. 'A person could give me a fly box filled with different flies, and if it contained only one Adams, that is the fly I'd use,' Donovan told me back in the 1950s. 'I don't get too many chances to wade the river, but when it comes time to wade the river, I want to be casting a dry fly that produces trout. I'm told it matches a number of emerging flies, and that is one reason for its popularity—it produces good trout catches.'

"Donovan was a hemophiliac and an amputee, and he could wade the Au Sable River and flick casts here and there under and alongside the sweepers, and would catch 10 trout for every one I caught. Since he was my mentor, and I was trying to learn from this master sportsman, I secretly began carrying a half dozen Adams flies in various sizes. When we would meet again at the end of the fishing day and compare catches, my success rate made a major jump, and suddenly I was catching as many fish as my teacher."

Michigan fly anglers like Richey and Deschaine still cherish the pattern. And it seems to pop up in almost every book ever written on fly tying and fly fishing. Big names like Ray Bergman, Joe Brooks, Rube Cross, Eric Leiser, J. Edson Leonard, A. J. McClane, Ernie Schwiebert, and many others have all discussed the fly. Jack Atherton loved the idea of the mixed brown and grizzly hackle shades, which fit perfectly with his ideas concerning impressionism. Outdoor writer Ted Trueblood wrote about the Adams in his May 1963 *Field & Stream* article titled "Flies for Sophisticated Trout," in which he theorized that although the Adams didn't imitate any bug in particular, it possessed the important quality he termed "insectness."

It seems there is an Adams for every conceivable situation and taste. Fly anglers everywhere have embraced many different versions: the Parachute Adams, Female Adams, Adams Irresistible, Adams Midge, Silhouette Adams, Thorax Adams, Adams Wulff, Spent-Wing Adams, and Upright-Wing Adams. My own Wemoc Adams was featured in my book *Tying Catskill-Style Dry Flies*. Pennsylvania fly tier Gerrard Zazzera ties a green-bodied Adams-like parachute. Even Halladay tied a few variations. We know from Lon Adams's 1937 letter to Ray Bergman that even back then the fly was tied with red, yellow, and gray bodies. It is a pattern that will likely be around as long as fly lines loop over water—a true gem coming from Len Halladay, the originator of the Adams fly.

Side view of a Halladay-tied Adams. Halladay's Adams flies were roughly tied but effective trout takers just the same. *Bob Summers collection*

Adams Female, tied by Don Lieb. The Adams took on many forms and styles, such as this parachute example tied with a yellow egg sac.

Another Adams, tied by Len Halladay. Notice the sparse golden pheasant tippet tails and spent wings, which are characteristic of the original Adams. *Bob Summers collection*

The author tying an Adams fly on the remains of what was once the porch of Len Halladay's hotel in Mayfield. The hotel, once called Kelly Boarding House, was located on Mayfield Pond. *Photo by Valerie Valla*

Boardman River near Traverse City, Michigan. Charles Adams's success with the Adams on this famous trout stream launched the pattern, one of the most effective trout flies ever tied. *Photo by Valerie Valla*

CHAPTER 26

George Griffith
(1901–1998)

George Griffith tying a Gnat after having his eyesight restored. He had lost his vision in one eye 30 years before, in 1953, when a streamer caught his eye on a backcast.
Bob Summers collection

Georgeorge A. Griffith was a giant among conservationists, admired everywhere for his foresight in pulling together a small group of Michigan outdoorsmen who shared his concern for the dwindling wild trout populations in his state. He had witnessed his own favorite stream, the Au Sable, in precipitous decline, its trout habitat threatened by increased stream habitat degradation. In-stream deadfalls that provided habitat for trout were removed by canoeing enthusiasts. Poorly treated wastewater being dumped into the stream resulted in overproliferation of aquatic vegetation. The impacts to the stream also led to changes in the local insect populations, to the further detriment of the fishery. George Griffith, who was currently serving as the state commissioner of natural resources, had witnessed too much devastation to sit back and do nothing about it. Out of his concern, an organization devoted to the well-being of trout was born on the banks of the Au Sable River.

It was a rainy Saturday morning, July 19, 1959, when Griffith and 15 other sportsmen met at the Barbless Hook, George's cabin on the river. The group elected Griffith temporary chairman

Griffith's Gnat, tied by George Griffith. While fly anglers routinely tie the fly in very small hook sizes and fish it in the surface film, George and his friend Bob Summers commonly fished it in size 14. In some instances, they fished it with a small split shot attached to the tip-pet for subsurface fishing.
Bob Summers collection

of the new organization, which they named Trout Unlimited. Griffith was elected chairman of the board in the early 1960s, and from that point forward he enjoyed a life of trout fishing on the Au Sable and devoted an enormous amount of time to the important cause of preserving the trout fisheries.

Under the leadership of George Griffith and the other founding members, Trout Unlimited became one of the most successful conservation organizations ever created. For years, Griffith had been an outspoken critic of widespread stocking of hatchery trout. Catching wild trout over hatchery-raised fish was becoming increasingly rare. Within a short time, the group was successful in revamping Michigan's regulations. It wasn't long before other states were beginning to take notice of Trout Unlimited's good work, largely through the efforts of Art Neumann, another founding father of the organization.

Those who never met George Griffith can only imagine the wonderful times he must have experienced at the Barbless Hook, a name that Joe Brooks gave this summer retreat that Griffith acquired in the late 1930s. We can only picture in our minds what it must have been like sitting in the living area of the cabin on that July day in 1959 when Trout Unlimited was first conceptualized or accompanying Griffith on his frequent floats on the Au Sable, fly rod in hand, seeking out the wild trout he worked so hard to protect.

Cane fly-rod maker Bob Summers of Traverse City, Michigan, was Griffith's closest friend and fishing companion. Summers and Griffith fished the Au Sable together many times, casting flies out of an authentic Au Sable riverboat, a 24-foot flat-bottom craft that dates back a century or more to the early days of guiding for grayling on the river. One of the most effective flies they fished on their floats was the Griffith's Gnat.

It is interesting that this simple, diminutive trout-fly pattern bears the name of a titan, an individual responsible for what is now one of the largest conservation organizations in America. Whenever the Griffith's Gnat is mentioned, fly fishers are quick to identify it as one of the most effective flies. This little pattern, with its simple peacock herl body and grizzly hackle palmer, often appears on published lists of the top-10 flies ever created.

Many fly flickers know the name of George Griffith primarily as someone who fathered the Griffith's Gnat. Some have no idea of Griffith's role in the founding of Trout Unlimited, but they are familiar with the Gnat and its effectiveness on waters everywhere. Numerous publications cite George Griffith as the creator of the Griffith's Gnat, but this is not the case. In a couple recent chats with Bob Summers, he cleared up some of the confusion surrounding the popular fly. "We were using the fly quite regularly and it was effec-

George Griffith and his fishing companion Bob Summers floating the Au Sable in early 1990s. *Bob Summers collection*

tive," he said to me during a discussion of the pattern's history. "You could compare it to why an Adams fly worked well. There's no Adams bug out there; it was the same way with that Gnat. We fished it dry, but we also fished it beneath the surface by attaching a very tiny split shot on our leaders—that was done as a last resort. Most of the time we were fishing the Gnat in size 14—right around that size—not the real small sizes popular today with others. George shared with me that he wasn't the one who created the Griffith's Gnat—he wasn't the first one to tie it. A fishing buddy of George's was the one who first designed and tied the fly."

Both George and his friend fished the Gnat with great success, but it lacked a name. "George's buddy suggested that the fly be named the Griffith's Gnat, a name that both of them agreed to call the effective pattern. It was by mutual agreement that George's name was attached to the fly," Summers explained to me. "It wasn't like George's buddy handed the fly to him, then George went off on his own and named it after himself. It didn't happen that way at all. It was a mutual agreement to name it using George's name, because the fly didn't have a name. All this happened on the Au Sable River."

Other fly anglers who came to the Au Sable were introduced to the Griffith's Gnat. Its popularity continued to grow when the fly started appearing in print. In his 1973 book *Nymphs*, fly-fishing author and angler Ernie Schwiebert shared with readers his introduction to the Griffith's Gnat while fishing the Au Sable River in the 1960s with George Griffith and Art Neumann. It was an early-season outing on the stream that ended with evening chats concerning natural aquatic insects and artificial flies. Discussion turned to smutting rises and how to approach those situations. Griffith handed Schwiebert half a dozen flies that he said worked well for him and his friend Neumann. Art Neumann laughed when he commented to Schwiebert, "It's called a Griffith's Gnat."

Somewhat flushed and embarrassed, Griffith interjected, "It's called a Griffith's Gnat—but it works!" Schwiebert questioned whether the fly would perform well for midge activity. "It's really good," Neumann acknowledged, but he added that they "barely" fished the fly dry; it was commonly fished in the surface film. Schwiebert left with the flies Griffith gave him, tucked into a corner of his Wheatley fly box, where they sat for a year until he tried them on the Musconetcong River in New Jersey.

That day, Schwiebert and Arthur Morgan were on the river, which seemed comatose in the afternoon. Once evening came, trout began feeding in the flats on minute insects. Nothing Schwiebert threw at them worked until he tried the strange peacock-bodied, palmered grizzly hackle Gnats that Griffith had handed him a year before. The flies imitated the small midge pupae before they shed their skins in transforming into adults.

George Griffith and his wife, Peri, at their Barbless Hook cabin on the Au Sable River. That cabin saw the beginnings of Trout Unlimited. *Bob Summers collection*

Impressed by the original Griffith's Gnats, Schwiebert altered the pattern slightly to cover the entire range of shades and colors displayed by natural tiny midges. He substituted synthetic floss, muskrat fur, and seal fur bodies for peacock herl in shades from light to dark. His box also continued to hold flies with peacock herl bodies "in deference to the original Griffith's Gnat." There is no doubt that Schwiebert embraced the pattern and helped popularize the fly. The fact that George Griffith's name was attached to the pattern, given his well-known achievements with Trout Unlimited, also helped popularize the fly, its effectiveness aside.

The Griffith's Gnat's popularity continued to rise, and the pattern soon began to appear in print everywhere. Other noted authors, such as Tom Rosenbauer, Gary Borger, and Mike Lawson, embraced the original pattern. Rosenbauer has consistently placed the Griffith's Gnat on his top-10 fly list. In *Naturals: A Guide to Food Organisms of the Trout* (1980), Borger called the Griffith's Gnat "the finest imitation of emerging midges I've ever used." Borger was also inspired by Schwiebert's description of the fly in *Nymphs*. In *Spring Creeks* (2003), Mike Lawson advised anglers concerning the Gnats, "Don't be on any spring creek or tailwater without an assortment of them."

Tailwater aficionado Pat Dorsey favored the pattern with a twist. In his fine book *Tying and Fishing Tailwater Flies* (2010), Dorsey said, "You'd be hard-pressed to find a more versatile midge pattern than the Griffith's Gnat." Dorsey rec-

George and Bob Summers on the Au Sable, early 1990s. *Bob Summers collection*

ognized that fishing the pattern in very small hook sizes, 22 to 26, during crepuscular hours presents a visibility problem for the angler. Water surface glare during those last few hours before darkness adds to the problem. He addressed sighting the small fly on water by using a Hi-Viz Griffith's Gnat, similar to the original pattern but with a fluorescent orange, pink, or chartreuse McFlylon post. The bright post greatly improves the fly's visibility in foam mats and riffles. Dorsey also tied the Griffith's Gnat in larger sizes—up to size 12—when fishing among midges clustering in slow-water tailouts and backeddies.

Like Dorsey, Henry's Fork angler René Harrop also recognized the visibility issue when fishing small Griffith's Gnats. In *Learning from the Water* (2010), Harrop wrote, "The Griffith's Gnat comprised of grizzly hackle palmered over a compact body of herl is a simple but effective way to imitate midge clusters. However, certain deficiencies in flotation and visibility have prompted me to tie a CDC version of this popular fly. Sparse white CDC tied at the head of the fly corrects the problem." Because he essentially altered the fly with CDC, Harrop called the new pattern a CDC Cluster Midge.

Aficionados of the original pattern might take exception to calling a fly tied with a fluorescent post or cul de canard a Griffith's Gnat. But any variation of the original is no doubt tied and named out of reverence for George Griffith and the highly effective pattern he popularized and fished on his beloved Au Sable for many years.

Hi-Viz Griffith's Gnats, tied by Pat Dorsey. Dorsey addressed the problem of sighting the small fly on water by using a Hi-Viz Griffith's Gnat. The Hi-Viz variation is similar to the original pattern but uses a fluorescent orange, pink, or chartreuse McFlylon post.

CHAPTER 27

Jim Leisenring and V. S. "Pete" Hidy
(1878–1951; 1914–1983)

"Big Jim" Leisenring, the tool-maker from Allentown, Pennsylvania, who fished streams such as the Brodhead Creek and Little Lehigh, brought new vigor to subsurface fly patterns. *Lance Hidy collection*

V. S. "Pete" Hidy in 1973. Ernie Schwiebert called Hidy "perhaps the best-known of Leisenring's disciples." Hidy met Leisenring in the mid-1930s. *Lance Hidy collection*

It was a little book by Jim Leisenring and V. S. "Pete" Hidy that helped save the wet fly from being completely overshadowed by a growing enthusiasm for the floater over the sinker on American trout waters. Theodore Gordon's promotion of the dry fly on Catskill streams in the late 1800s and early 1900s contributed to anglers' increased eagerness to put sinking flies aside. With the publication of Emlyn Gill's prodigious *Practical Dry Fly Fishing* in 1912 and George M. L. La Branche's *Dry Fly and Fast Water* in 1914, the pounding continued. Preston Jennings's *A Book of Trout Flies* arrived in 1935, and on the heels of that work came Art Flick's *Streamside Guide to Naturals and Their Imitations* (1947). The emphasis in the pages of these works was on dry-fly patterns.

Mahogany Flymph, tied by V. S. "Pete" Hidy. It's not a wet fly and it's not a nymph; it's a hybrid of the two. Hidy called such soft-hackle flies "flymphs." This pattern is tied with brown mohair, tinsel ribbing, and badger hackle. *Lance Hidy collection*

Despite the growing interest in dry-fly fishing, fueled by the Catskill-centric fly-fishing authors who authored those influential titles, the wet fly still hung on, moribund but not yet completely dead. Not all fly anglers were caught up in the dry-fly craze—a tall, slim man from Pennsylvania called "Big Jim" Leisenring made that clear in his slender *Art of Tying the Wet Fly* (1941), a landmark book devoted to Leisenring's wet-fly theories, as told to V. S. "Pete" Hidy, who was responsible for its publication. The toolmaker from Allentown, Pennsylvania, who fished streams such as the Brodhead Creek and Little Lehigh, brought new vigor to subsurface fly patterns.

Leisenring's fresh approach to wet-fly design was both enlightening and inventive, with designs completely different in form and function than the large, garish attractor wets promoted by Mary Orvis Marbury in the late 1800s. He minimized the worth of commercially tied flies from the hands of those who knew nothing about fishing, and of tiers from his own era who crafted patterns with inferior materials. Leisenring felt that not knowing or understanding the be-

Not all fly anglers were caught up in the dry-fly craze that occurred in the early 1900s. Jim Leisenring made that clear in his slender *Art of Tying the Wet Fly* (1941), a landmark book devoted to Leisenring's wet-fly theories, as told to V. S. "Pete" Hidy, who was responsible for its publication.

havior, form, and colorations of natural insects put the wet-fly tier at a great disadvantage when facing the tying vise. The essence of his belief was that "the art of tying the wet fly rests upon a knowledge of materials used for imitating the insect life, and an ability to select, prepare, blend, and use proper materials to create neat, durable, and lifelike imitations of the natural insects."

For Jim Leisenring, the proper use of materials started with the very basics. First on his list was something often thought of as the least important material used in tying fishing flies—the thread. Leisenring called thread "a most important and necessary item for a fly tier." Without the proper thread, the tier could not create a wet fly that was both neat and durable. Thread also served another important function in Leisenring-tied wet flies: he felt that the tying silk shade should "harmonize" with the fly body, projecting out as an undercolor that reflected and showed through the body dubbing in the completed fly. He used colored tying threads treated with beeswax, turpentine resin, and fresh lard; his thread was well waxed.

Leisenring gave equal attention to the materials that the colored silks would bind to the hook shank. He wanted hackles that would "look alive" to trout, simulating insect legs that appeared to be kicking and struggling as the morsel drifted through stream currents. Not all water currents were the same; some stretches were swifter than others, and the stiffness of the hackle barbs should be varied according to those differences. Body materials were of paramount importance to Leisenring, who insisted that fly bodies should imitate the naturals' qualities of translucence, texture, and flash. He embraced natural furs such as fox, opossum, muskrat, and hare's ear, as well as peacock herl. He also liked simple buttonhole twist for bodies and ribbing, a material he used for the Tups Nymph.

To Leisenring, the durability of the fly body was as important as its color, texture, and translucence—trout can rip a fly to shreds with their sharp teeth. He used a specific technique for spinning body material to thread that in his opinion rendered the fly "practically indestructible." He stretched a length of tying silk along a pant leg at the knee and placed dubbing along its top. Half the thread was folded over the dubbing, trapping the material between the two layers of thread. By twisting both ends of the thread in opposite directions, with the dubbing nested inside, he produced a strong, thread-reinforced body. Leisenring stored the prefabricated bodies on celluloid cards for later use. Because the dubbing is integrated tightly with the tying thread, it wears well with heavy fishing.

Leisenring believed that wings were "the least important part of a fly." He acknowledged that some fly patterns would not perform as well wingless as they would with wings. But he also insisted that he could bring more fish to net with a wingless fly. When he did attach wings to his patterns,

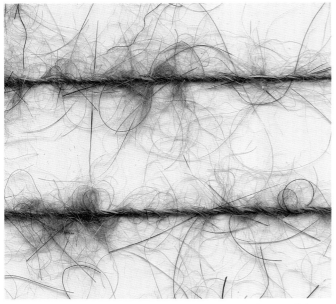

⅓ Hare's Face, ⅓ Muskrat, ⅓ Mole Mohair

Hidy learned from Leisenring how to craft spun bodies, or dubbing loops, on waxed silk. Here is an example of one of Pete's favorite texture blends. His preferred tying silk colors were Pearsall's Primrose, Ash (no longer available), Crimson, and Hot Orange. *Lance Hidy collection*

Leisenring selected materials that matched the qualities found in the naturals. A natural insect has transparent wings, and that same quality should be found in the type of material selected. He favored transparent feather sections over the popular thick and stiff mallard quill wing material. He considered hackle points good wing material for patterns such as stoneflies, which Leisenring believed "cannot be well represented unless tied with wings."

Jim Leisenring also took note of wing feather subtleties in tying his patterns and was particular about details that few other fly tiers were concerned with. The way he tied the Hare's Ear wet fly, an old British pattern, is a good example of Leisenring's fastidiousness when it came to material selection, in this case wing feathers. He held the Hare's Ear in high regard, commenting that it could represent natural aquatic insects well, but only if tied well. He liked the fly when sedges were on the water. In tying the pattern, Leisenring used woodcock slips taken from wing secondary feathers. But it had to be English woodcock, which "has a bar lacking in our American woodcock." Some would debate whether the buff tips found on English woodcock secondary feathers made a big difference in netting trout. Such insistence might be viewed as a dogmatic stance, but obviously

Leisenring felt that the shade band feature was important and added to the pattern's effectiveness.

Besides the Hare's Ear, Leisenring adopted other British-named patterns. The Cowdung, Gray Hackle, Blue Dun, Brown Hackle, Iron Blue, and Spider patterns were among his favorites. Leisenring praised British fly angler W. C. Stewart's Spiders, patterns Stewart had introduced in his epic 1857 book, *The Practical Angler*. The three Spiders introduced by Stewart in his book—Black, Red, and Dun—were represented in Leisenring's book. Of Stewart's Spiders, Leisenring wrote, "I have found W. C. Stewart's spiders to be a deadly combination on every stream I have ever fished. If a fisherman presents them carefully, he can soon acquire the reputation of a fish hog!" Stewart had also praised the effectiveness of the flies in his book, his only complaint being that "the feathers are so soft that the trout's teeth break them off." But it was the soft, lifelike hackle barbs dancing and turning in the water current that undoubtedly made the Spiders attractive to both fish and Leisenring.

Patterns promoted by other British titans found their way onto Jim Leisenring's tying vise as well, including the Tups, a

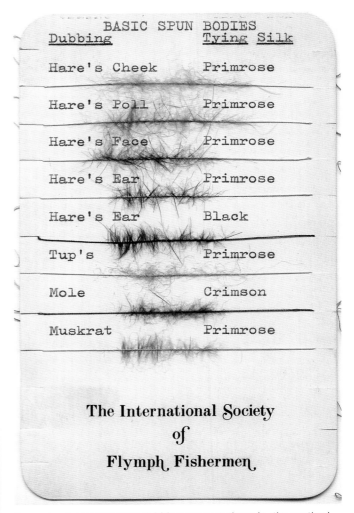

BASIC SPUN BODIES	
Dubbing	**Tying Silk**
Hare's Cheek	Primrose
Hare's Poll	Primrose
Hare's Face	Primrose
Hare's Ear	Primrose
Hare's Ear	Black
Tup's	Primrose
Mole	Crimson
Muskrat	Primrose

The International Society of Flymph Fishermen

Example of prefabricated dubbing spun on threads, the method used by Leisenring and Hidy. *Photo by Lance Hidy*

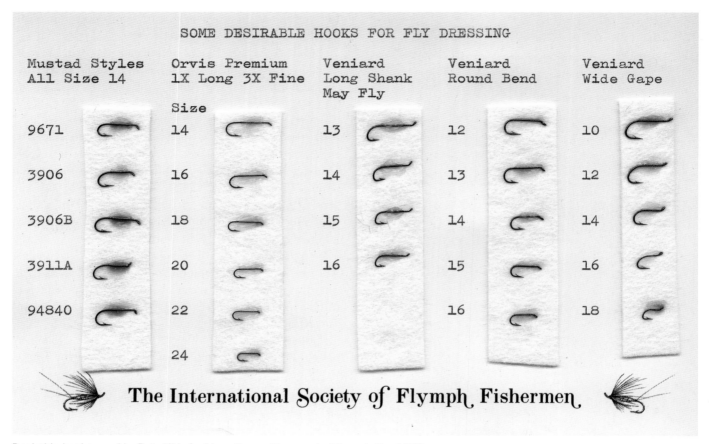

SOME DESIRABLE HOOKS FOR FLY DRESSING

Mustad Styles All Size 14		Orvis Premium 1X Long 3X Fine Size		Veniard Long Shank May Fly		Veniard Round Bend		Veniard Wide Gape	
9671		14		13		12		10	
3906		16		14		13		12	
3906B		18		15		14		14	
3911A		20		16		15		16	
94840		22				16		18	
		24							

The International Society of Flymph Fishermen

Desirable hooks used by Pete Hidy for his patterns. He mounted them in the 1970s. *Photo by Lance Hidy*

peculiar fly admired by wet-fly and nymph defender G. E. M. Skues. The Tups Indispensable caused much commotion in the British chalkstream region of Devon and Cornwall, and not many were privy to its secrets. Few knew the dubbing mix ingredients first put together by its creator, R. S. Austin.

G. E. M. Skues was one of the few who knew its formula, and he later disclosed it in the early 1930s with the permission of Austin's daughter. The original mix included highly translucent wool from the "indispensable" part of a tup, a British term for a male sheep. Added to the material obtained from a ram's private parts were reddish mohair, cream-colored seal, and lemon yellow spaniel fur. The Tups fly had a pinkish cast. Jim Leisenring embraced the British-born Tups, commenting, "It is a nymph that catches fish throughout the season." Leisenring used a different material mix, as did nearly every other American Tups tier, but his fly was similar in general form and coloration to the original fly.

There is no doubt that the mention of the Tups and many other British subsurface trout-fly patterns in Leisenring's *Art of Tying the Wet Fly* helped keep the dry-fly craze in check. As fly-fishing author Ernie Schwiebert aptly wrote in the introduction to the 1971 edition of Leisenring's book, "American anglers have largely forgotten James Leisenring who quietly adapted the wet-fly tactics of Stewart and Skues to the fly hatches of American waters, just as Gordon and La Branche transplanted British dry-fly methods to the swift rivers of the Catskills."

Yet long before Leisenring presented his fly design theories and patterns in his book, others benefited from his knowledge directly. Pete Hidy was, as Schwiebert also noted, "perhaps the best-known of Leisenring's disciples." Leisenring and Hidy became close fly-fishing friends after a chance meeting in the mid-1930s, and their fly design axioms are so intimately interrelated that it is difficult to separate the two like-minded fly anglers. When Leisenring's name surfaces, Hidy's typically is mentioned in the next sentence.

When Crown Publishers reissued Leisenring's 1941 work 30 years later, in 1971, it included a second section written by Hidy, titled "The Art of Fishing the Flymph," a treatise that expanded on Leisenring's aquatic insect simulation concepts. It was Pete Hidy who helped and encouraged Jim Leisenring to organize his thoughts concerning trout-fly design, putting *The Art of Tying the Wet Fly* between covers. Lance Hidy, Pete's son, who has worked diligently to ensure that Leisenring's and his father's contributions to fly design theory and practice are not forgotten, wrote a short piece in the spring 2012 issue of *Freshwater* titled, "In Tune with Trout." In the story, Lance described how his dad was the driving force behind getting Leisenring's wet-fly theories published. He writes, "A budding journalist, Pete cajoled Jim into writing down his knowledge—and then single-handedly edited it, found a publisher, and art-directed the illustrations." Pete Hidy's efforts helped ensure that Leisenring and his wet-fly theories would not be overlooked as the popularity of dry-fly fishing continued to escalate. In the new book, Hidy's own ideas concerning subsurface fly patterns supplemented Leisenring's original contributions. Its title, *The Art of Tying the Wet Fly & Fishing the Flymph*, put Leisenring and Hidy side by side, just as they had both stood decades before on Brodhead Creek in Pennsylvania's Poconos.

This edition also introduced Hidy's concept of the flymph, a hybrid of a wet fly and a nymph. Pete Hidy defined the flymph, a name he coined in 1962, as "a wingless artificial fly with a soft translucent body of fur or wool which blends with the undercolor of tying silk when wet, utilizing soft hackle fibers easily activated by the currents to give the effect of an insect alive in the water, and strategically cast diagonally upstream or across for the trout to take just below or within a few inches of the surface film."

Hidy's wingless fly couldn't exactly be classified as a nymph or a wet fly; it was something in between the two types of trout flies. The manner in which flymphs are tied, then fished, also set them apart from wets and nymphs. The excitement experienced by the dry-fly angler is not lost in flymph fishing. In his Autumn 1974 *Anglers' Club Bulletin* article, "The Origins of Flymph Fishing," Hidy wrote, "You fish flymphs close to the surface and trout take them with visible swirls."

The practice of tying and fishing flymph-style flies has spread around the globe. Passionate flymph followers, including names such as Jim Slattery, Mark Libertone, and Allen McGee, came together to found the International Brotherhood of the Flymph, an organization born out of Hidy and Leisenring's patterns. Libertone recently explained his early influences in correspondence with me: "In 1972, my fly-fishing perspective shifted from dry-fly fishing to wet-fly fishing. It was all due to a little book, *The Art of Tying the Wet Fly & Fishing the Flymph*, by James Leisenring and his friend and student, Vern Hidy. Leisenring took me into

Pete Hidy's fly book—loaded with his flymphs. *Photo by Lance Hidy*

the realm of the wingless wet fly, and from that point on, my focus was upon his beautiful flies and the techniques used to dress them. The idea of blending materials to culminate in an overall representation of the natural insect was inherent in Leisenring's approach to tying. His insightful discussions on body materials and hackle selection demonstrated how a good wet fly is constructed, and I followed his lead. The overall translucence and light-reflecting qualities of the natural insect were stressed. Leisenring's dubbing technique was new to me, but I quickly learned it and found it produced strong and long-lasting bodies. While this technique may seem time-consuming today, I believe it gives results which are unmatched by other dubbing methods. I still use the technique today. By combining the underlying tying silk with the dubbing fur or wool, I feel the overall effect is more akin to the appearance of a real insect.

"In addition to the well-constructed body, the hackles selected for tying were soft and movable in the currents, adding 'life' to these flies, which I feel contributes to their success. In addition, hackles like starling, which possess a natural iridescence, also contributed to the more lifelike appearance of the flies. Each dressing was carefully created to adequately bring the fly to reality. The idea of using various stiffnesses of hen hackle for different water speeds also helped make my fishing more successful. Leisenring liked hackles with a different colored list. He felt that this was representative of both wing and legs of natural insects. I often select hen hackles based on this idea and construct the thorax of the fly to match the color of the list of the hackle. The result is a fly that gives a lifelike appearance. It was obvious to me by the number of fish I was catching that the ideas put forth by Leisenring were effective. Leisenring considered all in the construction of these flies, and in doing so changed my fishing focus on tying wet flies completely."

John Shaner, a well-known East Coast fly angler who has tied and fished Leisenring-Hidy style flies extensively, corresponded with me recently and made clear his admiration for Jim Leisenring: "As an avid young fly fisher, I devoured that little book. The straight forward but gentle prose, the simple line drawings and black and white photos seemed to belong to a different era. But even as a teenager, I understood how much wisdom was contained in those pages, and my boxes were soon filled with flies such as the Red Hackle and Iron Blue Dun. Leisenring's insistence on the use of proper materials, the sparseness of his dressings, and the lovely simplicity of his patterns made an impression on me that still marks my own flies today. Over the years, my interest in the humble wet fly has become almost an obsession, and I've studied everything from the earliest Yorkshire Spiders to the most modern variations of soft-hackles, but there has been no greater influence on my tying and fishing than that slim little book written so many years ago by 'Big Jim.'"

Leisenring-Hidy patterns were effective in their years on the trout stream. They are still effective but have somehow been lost in the explosion of all the new types of fishing flies that are available to fly anglers today. It would not be surprising if the effective subsurface patterns designed and fished by Big Jim Leisenring and Pete Hidy enjoyed a new discovery, however, as fly tiers have and always will be searching for something a little different in fly design.

Hare's Ear, tied by Jim Leisenring. Leisenring liked fishing the Hare's Ear when sedges were on the water. In tying the pattern, Leisening preferred woodcock slips taken from wing secondary feathers. *Lance Hidy collection*

The Tups, tied by Jim Leisenring. The Tups Indispensable, a peculiar fly coveted by British wet-fly and nymph defender G. E. M. Skues, found its way onto Leisenring's tying table. *Lance Hidy collection*

Old Blue Dun, tied by Jim Leisenring. The currents easily activate the soft hackle found on this Old Blue Dun, giving the effect of an insect alive in the water.

Golden Stone, tied by Jim Leisenring. He considered hackle points good wing materials for patterns such as stoneflies, which he believed "cannot be well represented unless tied with wings." *Lance Hidy collection*

Red Spider, tied by Jim Leisenring. Of this pattern by an early British fly angler, Leisenring wrote, "I have found W. C. Stewart's spiders to be a deadly combination on every stream I have ever fished. If a fisherman presents them carefully, he can soon acquire the reputation of a fish hog!" *Lance Hidy collection*

Pale Gold-Ribbed Olive Flymph, tied by Lance Hidy. A perfect example of the soft-hackle patterns Leisenring and Hidy were known for. *Lance Hidy collection*

Leisenring Spider, tied by Pete Hidy. Leisenring favored Spider patterns, and these were found among his soft-hackle fly arsenal. *Lance Hidy collection*

Hare's Cheek and Light Honey Dun Flymph, tied by Pete Hidy. Hidy defined the flymph as "a wingless artificial fly with a soft translucent body of fur or wool which blends with the undercolor of tying silk when wet, utilizing soft hackle fibers easily activated by the currents to give the effect of an insect alive in the water, and strategically cast diagonally upstream or across for the trout to take just below or within a few inches of the surface film." *Lance Hidy collection*

Iron Blue Dun, tied by Jim Leisenring. Featured in Leisenring's book, this pattern is a good example of how colored thread integrated with body dubbing can create an interesting final fly shade. *Lance Hidy collection*

Mole and Black Flymph, tied by Pete Hidy. Hidy wrote of his creations, "You fish flymphs close to the surface and trout take them with visible swirls." *Lance Hidy collection*

Lance Hidy, son of Pete Hidy, demonstrating techniques for tying patterns created by his dad and Jim Leisenring.

Mark Libertone at the tying vise with fellow Leisenring-Hidy aficionado Jim Slattery looking on. So influenced by Hidy's vision for an "international society" dedicated to the Flymph, Libertone and Slattery—along with Allen McGee and others—established the International Brotherhood of the Flymph and the flymph forum.

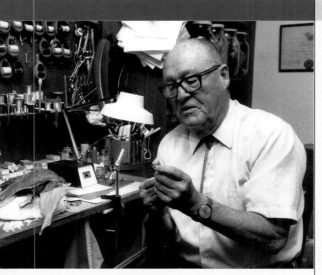

George Harvey at his tying bench. Harvey tied flies for some 80 years and taught thousands of students his craft. *Catskill Fly Fishing Center and Museum collection*

Night Fly, tied by George Harvey. Harvey's signature pattern, the Night Fly, was kept a closely guarded secret for many years. He caught more big fish on this pattern than on all his other flies combined. The side wing "kickers" cause a pulsating effect in the water that is irresistible to big trout lurking during darkness. *Brad Gates collection*

CHAPTER 28

George Harvey
(1911–2008)

George Harvey was a teacher and a conservationist, as well as one of the most passionate fly tiers and anglers who ever lived. His time at the tying vise spanned some 80 years. Few fly tiers could make the claim that they placed thread to hook shank for that length of time. Harvey's passion and influence reached thousands of students who were eager to learn fly tying under his tutelage.

In *Limestone Legends: Papers and Recollections of the Fly Fishers' Club of Harrisburg* (1997), Norm Shires and Jim Gilford included a piece that George Harvey wrote in 1994. In it, Harvey revealed that between 1934 and 1972, he taught 24,175 students through the Pennsylvania State University angling program. Many fly fishers roaming rivers, creeks, ponds, and lakes today learned their fly-tying and angling skills from George Harvey, affectionately called "Mr. Trout" and "the dean of American fly fishing."

Harvey's experience on trout waters in his home state of Pennsylvania was vast; he was known by many as an accomplished fly angler. President Jimmy Carter and Rosalynn, with whom Harvey fished on Spruce Creek, admired him: "He has always provided us with flies we need on our fishing trips," Carter wrote as a testimonial in Harvey's memoir, titled *George Harvey: Memories, Patterns and Tactics* (1998).

It is no wonder that Carter turned to George Harvey for flies and fishing advice. Harvey brought to the sport some interesting fishing techniques, such as the tuck cast, a method that allows the caster to get a nymph down deep into the water column quickly. Yet fly-fishing techniques aside, Harvey is most remembered for his fly-tying skills, along with the interesting patterns that he developed to fish his favorite streams, both day and night. As is true of many fly tiers, Harvey's first experience with feathers and hooks occurred very early in his life.

George Harvey's memoir is filled with information about his boyhood years, exploring central Pennsylvania mountain streams, fishing, and trapping rattlesnakes. He also recalled his first time at the tying vise. Harvey was only 10 years old when he snipped hair from the family cat and lashed it to a hook. He discovered that his uncle Ira's dry flies were tied

George Harvey, in 1943, with his students and faculty members, including the dean of Pennsylvania State University, at his side learn to tie flies. Between 1934 and 1972, Harvey taught 24,175 students through the university's angling program. *Pennsylvania Fly Fishing Museum Association collection*

George Harvey and his friend and colleague Joe Humphreys, 1977. Humphreys, accomplished fly angler, author, and instructor, wrote in his foreword to Harvey's book that his mentor Harvey was in his view "Dean of Flyfishers for Trout" and the "teacher's teacher." *Lefty Kreh and Pennsylvania Fly Fishing Museum Association*

with hackle, not hair, by untying one. He then got a supply of hackles from the live chickens that were butchered for his uncle's meat market.

Harvey was soon fishing bass bugs and trout flies, including some of the most popular patterns of his time. When he was 15, his uncle Ira introduced him to George M. L. La Branche's Pink Lady, a fly that dates back to the early 1900s. Over time, other standard dry-fly patterns filled his boxes as well. Quill Gordons, Red Quills, Adamses, Skaters, and Light Cahills were all there, but often tied with a different twist. Harvey applied a degree of inventiveness and experimentation in tying standard dry-fly patterns, sometimes taking suggestions from fishing friends; he also tweaked them to his own liking.

In his memoir, Harvey described a fly he called the Yellow Adams, which he tied for his friend Bob Harpster in 1946. Harpster embraced the standard Len Halladay Adams dry fly but approached Harvey about adding yellow dubbing instead of the standard gray body shade, with the idea of fishing it during Sulphur hatches. Harvey altered the Light Cahill, a tremendously popular dry fly tied with buff- or cream-colored fox fur, by applying different body dubbing shades. His rationale was well founded. "There are different shades of natural Light Cahills, so I tie different shades of artificials to match them," Harvey wrote. He used body shades from pale yellow to cream to orange-yellow, with hackle that varied from very pale to very dark ginger, depending on the natural he was imitating.

While George Harvey enjoyed tying and fishing old standards, his fertile imagination led to dozens of his own creations, many labeled with his own signature. Among his ties are the Harvey's Green Drake Dun, Harvey's Brook Trout Dry Fly, Harvey's Male Trico, and Harvey's Female Trico. But the most famous of his signature patterns is the Night Fly, commonly called Harvey's Night Fly or sometimes a "Pusher Fly."

In his memoir, Harvey said that his "secret" pattern, the Night Fly, was one of his best creations. "I caught more big trout on it than on all my other flies put together," he confided. So effective was the pattern that he kept it close to his chest for many years. "The only person I showed that fly to, besides Tom Sowers, was Joe Humphreys. I fished that fly for 15–20 years before I showed it to him," Harvey wrote. They had an agreement at that time that they would keep the pattern a secret, which they did. Eventually the coveted pattern was shared with the public after Harvey felt some guilt concerning the secrecy, since he was a teacher. After he wrote an article about the fly, he openly discussed its effectiveness on Spring Creek. The Night Fly, anglers finally learned, accounted for some very large catches—including a 25½-inch brown trout.

Harvey liked the Night Fly in sizes 2/0 to 8, tied in a couple variations. The predominant feature of the fly is its "kickers," feathers such as stiff-quilled goose or pheasant tied with concave sides directed toward the hook eye. These create a "pusher" effect as the fly is fished. Stiff quills are important so that the fly can pulsate yet spring back into position. Harvey didn't tie the pattern with any particular attention to proportions and typically tied it unweighted. Although he tied it as a dry fly, Harvey admitted to fellow Pennsylvania angling author and night fisher Jim Bashline that 90 percent of his fish taken on the Night Fly were taken as he slowly retrieved the fly subsurface.

In *The Final Frontier: Night Fishing for Trout* (1987), Bashline devoted an entire chapter to the Night Fly and the circumstances that led to his receiving a few from George Harvey. Jim was already an accomplished night fisher. Bashline's earlier book, *Night Fishing for Trout* (1973), had fallen into Harvey's hands since he, too, enjoyed night fishing. Harvey took note that Bashline fished in the blackness with large wet flies and suggested that he try the large "dry-fly" patterns he had been experimenting with. He sent a letter to Bashline along with a few samples of the Night Fly. At first Bashline wasn't convinced that the "Pusher Flies" would perform for him, but Harvey urged him not to give up on the Night Fly. Bashline's doubts concerning George's pattern soon vanished when a 21-inch "bull headed male brown" took Harvey's unique fly. Other fly anglers who embraced the Night Fly took even larger fish; Joe Humphreys, for example, took his record 15-pound, 5-ounce Pennsylvania brown trout on Harvey's "Pusher" Night Fly.

While the Night Fly may have been Harvey's most imaginative pattern, it wasn't the only fly that came with a story.

In his book, he provided interesting anecdotes along with the descriptions of many of his patterns, such as his Spruce Creek dry fly. Harvey created his Spruce Creek fly in 1940, when he was a member of the Tyrone Club on the stream that gave the fly its name. It was late in the season and Harvey noticed the trout rising to small black flies. He tied a new dry fly, in size 16, to imitate the naturals. The very dark dun hackled fly was so successful that he eventually tied the pattern in sizes 12 to 20. The same stream also gave its name to Harvey's Spruce Creek Streamer, a silver tinsel bodied fly with red yarn tail, red bucktail belly, silver badger wing, wood-duck flank shoulder with jungle cock eyes, and red yarn throat.

George Harvey's Spruce Creek flies were favorites, and he thought enough of them to include the patterns in his memoir. Yet he included other interesting patterns in his book that provide the reader with a glimpse of his versatility at tying flies, something he continued to do even during his final years. The flies he showcased also send a strong message that George Harvey never abandoned experimenting with new types of materials. Even in the 1990s, he continued to report his findings concerning different approaches to fly tying and the development of new and unique patterns.

Harvey's December 1990 *Fly Fisherman* magazine article, titled "New Dry-Fly Wings," alerted readers that genetic hackle breeding resulted in saddle feathers that made for very suitable wings for all sorts of dry flies. The fly photos in his book included an interesting caddis pattern, the Grannom Caddis, tied with mottled hen saddle feathers. Harvey also was quick to incorporate new materials in his patterns. When he discovered Krystal Flash, for example, he soon used the added sparkle in his Female Trico Krystal Flash Spinner, a fly also featured in his book. There was al-

George Harvey's tying room. At this bench, Harvey tied for the average angler as well as a U.S. president and his family. *Pennsylvania Fly Fishing Museum Association collection*

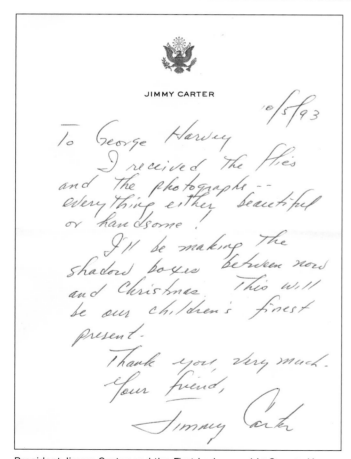

George Harvey stretch, Spruce Creek. Harvey named some of his favorite patterns, such as the Spruce Creek Dry Fly and Spruce Creek Streamer, after his beloved creek in central Pennsylvania. *Photo by Valerie Valla*

JIMMY CARTER

10/5/93

To George Harvey
I received the flies
and the photographs --
everything either beautiful
or handsome!
I'll be making the
shadow boxes between now
and Christmas. This will
be our children's finest
present.
Thank you very much.
Your friend,
Jimmy Carter

President Jimmy Carter and the First Lady were big George Harvey fans. The Carters fished with Harvey on Spruce Creek. *Pennsylvania Fly Fishing Museum Association collection*

ways something new to discover and apply to tying fishing flies, and Harvey's followers were eager to learn about his new patterns and innovations.

My friend and fellow fly-fishing author Eric Stroup of Spruce Creek, Pennsylvania, is well aware of George Harvey's influence on hundreds of fly tiers and anglers. He offered the following thoughts concerning Harvey: "It would be impossible to be from central Pennsylvania and not be influenced by the tying and fishing of George Harvey," he said, "and though my major influence came from Joe Humphreys, he was in many ways an extension of what George developed and taught about flies. When I consider my tying style today, I can trace nearly everything I do back to George. Harvey, through a number of sources, has influenced all my proportions, hackling style, and general thoughts on impressionistic tying. I am fortunate to have a number of friends that knew George very well and spent an enormous amount of time with him. I have been the gracious recipient of years of personal instruction from many of these folks. When discussing various techniques or theories with regard to tying and fishing, many whom I know in the business will argue a point feverishly until someone steps forward and says, 'George did it this way.' The reply is usually, 'Oh, okay.' End of discussion."

It was Monday evening, March 24, 2008, when Stroup heard Harvey had died that day. He thought long and hard about George and his legacy. Stroup planned to fish the next day and decided to honor George Harvey in his own way. Eric also shared with me his feelings when he had learned of Harvey's death: "I pulled my old Thompson AA vise off the mantle and took out the Night Fly that George had given me when I was 15 years old. I blew the dust off of it and stuck it in my chest box for the next day. When we got to the stream, I tied the fly onto some heavy 1X Maxima tippet and told my client to toss it out there. On the second cast, we caught a wild 18-inch brown. I took the fly out, cut it off, placed it back in my Richardson, and winked at the sky. Thanks, George."

Spruce Creek Dry Fly, tied by George Harvey. Harvey created his Spruce Creek fly late in the season in 1940, after noticing the trout rising to small black flies. At the time, he was a member of the Tyrone Club on the stream that gave the fly its name. *Pennsylvania Fly Fishing Museum Association collection*

Adams variation, tied by George Harvey. George was also known to have tied the Adams with a yellowish body. *Pennsylvania Fly Fishing Museum Association collection*

Harvey Sulphur, tied by George Harvey. Harvey wrote, "There are lots of different sulphurs. Just try different combinations of color and size until you get it right for the stream that you're fishing." He sometimes tied Sulphurs with light pinkish bodies and fluorescent wings. *Pennsylvania Fly Fishing Museum Association collection*

Caddis imitation, tied by George Harvey. Harvey experimented with trimmed mottled hen saddle feathers for caddis dry flies. This green-bodied pattern is a fish getter for sure. *Pennsylvania Fly Fishing Museum Association collection*

CHAPTER 29

Vincent C. Marinaro
(1911–1986)

Vincent C. Marinaro, in 1959. His 1950 book *A Modern Dry-Fly Code* examined new dry-fly design theories as well as the importance of terrestrials in fly fishing.
Pennsylvania Fly Fishing Museum Association collection

In a simpler time, when fly-fishing trade magazines were nonexistent, anglers relied on the occasional fly-fishing stories that appeared in one of the big three outdoor magazines: *Outdoor Life*, *Field & Stream*, and *Sports Afield*. The March and April 1969 issues of *Outdoor Life* had just provided Cecil Heacox's now classic two-part article on the "Charmed Circle of the Catskills" when the same magazine hit hard again in the July issue with one of the most profound fly-fishing articles ever written in that era: a thriller by Vincent C. Marinaro titled "The Hidden Hatch." Marinaro had written other articles for *Outdoor Life*, but for those who entered the sport in the late 1960s, "The Hidden Hatch" may have served as their first introduction to the man known to many as the "dean of Pennsylvania's Letort Spring Run."

Vincent Marinaro was born in Reynoldsville, Pennsylvania, in 1911, the son of Italian immigrants. In *Split & Glued by Vincent C. Marinaro* (2007), Bill Harms and Tom Whittle divulge much about Marinaro's early life. Fly fishing was very close to Vince's heart ever since his high school years, when he'd bike or hitch rides to area streams. "During many summers, there

Thorax style mallard quill slip wing dun, tied by Vince Marinaro. The fly is tied following Marinaro's basic thorax style design axioms: prominent wings set well back from the hook eye, small fur ball thorax to better anchor the cross-wrapped hackle, no abdomen, and tails set at right angles to the hook to act as "outriggers" that keep the fly upright on water. *Pennsylvania Fly Fishing Museum Association collection*

were weeks on end—day and night—when Vince was more likely to be found on the local streams than anywhere around the neighborhood," Harms and Whittle wrote. He was also an enthusiastic split-cane rod builder, inspired by the early work of George Parker Holden and *The Idyl of the Split-Bamboo* (1920). Beyond rod building and rod design, Marinaro's inquisitiveness led to his developing fly patterns that were better suited to the slow-moving, cold, and clear limestone waters of the Cumberland Valley in Pennsylvania, such as the Letort.

"The Hidden Hatch" was one of Marinaro's most intriguing magazine articles. It told the story of what Marinaro called the "Caenis" hatch, the tiny mayfly that British fly anglers termed "the white curse." The article's photos showed Marinaro's diminutive fly imitations, stuck in his thumb above his nail. The size 22 and 24 duns and spinners were simple British-vintage patterns promoted by Frederick M. Halford and G. E. M. Skues. The photo of Marinaro, squatting next to the placid flow of his limestone stream on a bright summer day playing his trout, has been imprinted in anglers' minds for more than 40 years; many other anglers can easily recall the story.

Marinaro's "Hidden Hatch" was such an influence on me, inspiring my first attempts at tying tiny flies, that it seemed only natural for me to contact him by letter and seek out his other writings. It was surprising that he sent me letters in return, handwritten and gracious in his kind remarks. Many fly anglers today who knew him describe Marinaro as an irascible man, a person quick to correct anyone who might debate his theories. His return letters to me certainly didn't indicate that type of personality; maybe he looked kindly on kids who shared his passion.

I had some success in locating some of his earlier writings, although it took another year for his epic work, *A Modern Dry-Fly Code*, to reach my mailbox. The library shelves were empty of the 1950 Putnam edition of the book. It wasn't until 1970, when Crown reprinted the narrative, that Marinaro's book finally occupied a place on my tying table next to other Crown reprints fresh off the presses: Preston Jennings's *Book of Trout Flies* and Art Flick's *New Streamside Guide*.

Marinaro's work was different and absorbing; his *Code* was far more sophisticated than his story of "The Hidden Hatch." The book, a fly-fishing literature classic, departed greatly from the mayfly-centric Catskill fly design themes found in Jennings's and Flick's works. In it, Marinaro presented radically different mayfly dry-fly design theory, tying his philosophy into the important mayfly hatches on his Pennsylvania streams—Green Drakes, Hendricksons, and Sulphurs. Marinaro fully recognized the important contributions of early American dry-fly anglers who studied and fished on Catskill waters in New York State. But his waters were different.

Individuals such as Theodore Gordon, Emlyn Gill and his *Practical Dry Fly Fishing* (1912), and George M. L. La Branche and his epic *Dry Fly and Fast Water* (1914) were given adequate mention in Marinaro's book. Marinaro also found delight in Edward Ringwood Hewitt's wingless Neversink Skater fly, and La Branche's Bivisible pattern. Those authors built their works around the central theme that the swift-moving rivers in the eastern United States were different from the slow-moving British chalkstreams where titans such as Halford and Skues developed and fished their dry flies. The new American dry-fly school helped sever the dependence on British floating-fly designs that were created for placid streams. American dry-fly fishers, especially Catskill anglers, would no longer continue to be constrained by British theories.

But some American trout streams do have similarities to Britain's slow-current flows, and Marinaro recognized that fact. He found that the big clipped hair dry-fly patterns, such as Harry Darbee's Rat-Faced McDougall, were ill suited on his waters. "There are calm waters as opposed to rough waters," he wrote, "the rich weedy waters as opposed to the rocky, barren waters; thin underfed trout against fat well-fed fish, and limestone waters versus freestone streams, all of which is sharply contrasted and plainly reflected in the attitude of the trout and their feeding habits."

Marinaro believed that the character of a stream and of its resident trout should be what dictate the best fly to fish and how to fish it—not the fly angler. Through careful observations on his home waters, Marinaro completely rethought dry-fly design, placing an emphasis on how the trout might view a fly as it drifted over the fish's observation post. Marinaro wrote compellingly that a dry fly's *wing* was of paramount importance in pattern design: "for the wing, its height and breadth and flatness, is the most important part of a floating dun!"

In discussing the importance of the wing in dry-fly design Marinaro acknowledged that in patterns composed entirely of long hackle tied in a flat plane, such as Hewitt's Spider (Neversink Skater), the hackle "forms a surprisingly good wing." Anglers fishing the emergence of the Green Drake, one of the largest mayflies, on central Pennsylvania limestone waters reported good success using the Hewitt pattern. Catskill fly tier Art Flick used his long-hackled Grey Fox Variant with similar success to fish the Green Drake emergence on his home Schoharie Creek. However, Marinaro described what he believed was the best wing design of all—a cut and shaped wing that was more similar in width and form to a natural mayfly's profile.

In *A Modern Dry-Fly Code*, Marinaro argued that as a natural mayfly floats along and approaches the fish's observation post and window, it is the wing that comes into view first. In order to best give the suggestion of a substantial wing, he fashioned wings from cut and shaped hackles or duck breast feathers, which maintain their shape when wet. However, when Marinaro wrote *In the Ring of the Rise* (1976), he qualified his previous statements concerning cut-wings and their use in mayfly patterns. In the section titled "Notes on Dry-Fly Construction," Marinaro wrote, "The cut-hackle wing that I recommended and used for so many years remains a very fine wing; it is durable and shapely and will not turn or spin the fly if it is cut at the soft tip of the hackle. Cut wings are absolutely worthless unless they can be cut uniformly so that the pairs are perfectly matched." Marinaro used a pair of commercially available rocker-type wing cutters to ensure a good matched set.

In his 1976 book, Marinaro also considered a very old wing construction method: matched duck quill slip wings. With such wings, Marinaro strongly advised that the quill slips be first attached to the hook shank with—and not against—the grain of the quill fibers. The slips should then be rotated into an upright position and secured with thread. A tiny drop of cement along the quill fiber tips can improve durability. Marinaro used a fairly complicated method of wrapping cross turns of hackle at the wings. He used a "little ball" of spun fur around the hook shank very close to the wings; there was no body to speak of, just the thorax. Marinaro wrote, "The little ball will function as anchoring shoulders to hold the cross turns of hackle." Properly wound hackle floated the fly; the tails on Marinaro's thorax flies served primarily as stabilizers. As Marinaro also explained in his earlier book, true thorax-style flies do not require support from tails; the widely split fibers merely function as "outriggers" or "governors" to prevent the fly from falling as it drifts along the current. He liked the tail fibers tied at right angles to the hook shank.

In *A Modern Dry-Fly Code*, Marinaro also emphasized the importance of wing height, not just wing breadth, on his dry flies. Trout are interested in feeding on mayfly bodies, not wings, Marinaro explained. But it is the wing that signals to the fish that food is fast approaching the feeding station, and thus the height of the wing above the water surface is of primary importance. "The term 'high-riding' is a misnomer," Marinaro said, "and ought to be replaced with the term 'high winged' as being a more accurate description of the requirement for the wings of duns; it does not matter if they float 'on their toes' or not, so long as the effective height of the wing above the surface is the same as that of the natural!"

Marinaro's convictions concerning the importance of the wing led him to boldly state that ". . . the imitation of bodies on the *dun* or *subimago* of the mayfly is meaningless and superfluous." He gave the example of some tiers who made a distinction between the male and female Hendrickson, leading to the creation of two versions with different body shades. Marinaro saw no good reason for making such a distinction and suggested that "others are honestly mistaken in their appraisal of this matter." For Marinaro, it was all about the wing and another important aspect in dry-fly design: fly balance on the water surface.

Marinaro believed that the fly would achieve better balance if the hackle and wing were shifted more toward the hook bend, a position that offered greater on-water support and stability. Additional stability could be obtained by using short-barbed hackles wound on each side of the wing in an X fashion. The shorter barbs, Marinaro believed, should be positioned more in the fore part of the fly, creating a tendency for the fly to tip slightly forward, elevating the tails. Hackle and wings in that position on the hook shank also provided for a profound body thorax, something Marinaro maintained was more important than the posterior body aspect, since the thorax tended to hug the water surface.

Out of Marinaro's design came the "thorax" dry-fly prototype, a style embraced by many fly tiers and anglers. In a December 1987 *Fly Fisherman* article titled "The Thorax Dry," Eric Peper described his enthusiasm for Marinaro's thorax design. Peper tweaked Marinaro's original design, winding hackle in the traditional dry-fly manner instead of an X fashion, then clipping it on the fly's underside. He recalled his interaction with Marinaro concerning the "perversion of his pattern" by Peper and Larry Solomon. In correspondence with me, Eric described what Marinaro said to him: "I sent Vince a letter telling him how we were approaching thorax ties and asked what he thought of this bastardization of his thorax style flies. I expected a typically crusty, 'You're doing it all wrong' response. Instead I got a very polite letter, outlining why he did what he did, but also suggesting that we were on to something and that he probably was overly complex in his approach and that he was rethinking the design somewhat." Yet concerning the hackle-winding technique, Peper wrote in his article that Marinaro "still thought I ought to use his hackling method."

Well before Eric Peper embraced Marinaro's design elements, Pennsylvania fly tier and angler Chauncy K. Lively was consumed with creating unique dry-fly patterns based on cut and shaped wings tied in thorax style. Following Marinaro's axioms, Lively also hackled his dry flies for maximum stability on the water. Marinaro's influence is quite recognizable in Lively's dry-fly designs. "Thinking about people who might have inspired and influenced Dad, I'd say that would have to be Vince Marinaro," Chauncy's daughter Anne Lively said in correspondence with me. "Early in his fly-fishing career, Dad read Marinaro's *A Modern Dry-Fly Code*. Marinaro's thorax style, imitating the way a fly sits on the water, intrigued him. He started thinking in terms of light patterns as seen from below by the fish. Pretty soon he'd built a glass slant tank that he could fill with water and float various insects, both real and artificial, to study and photograph from below. From those observations, Dad worked out a mayfly pattern with a sparse parachute hackle under the body. The slant tank also led to his reverse palmered style hackle with a V clipped on the bottom. The flies floated well and almost always landed upright. Dad thought from a trout's point of

Marinaro on a trout stream. He crafted his own split cane rods and netted many a fine trout with his long-handled net. He once lost a large trout on the famous Nineteenth Hole Pool on the Letort after difficulty bringing the fish to net. From that point forward, he always used a long net to ensure this would never happen again. *Pennsylvania Fly Fishing Museum Association collection*

view and tried to tie flies that would create light patterns on the surface of the water that they were familiar with."

Besides his concepts concerning winged thorax style dry-fly designs, which greatly influenced anglers such as Peper and Lively, Marinaro also developed an interesting flush-floating spinner pattern that used a porcupine quill. He wrote about the large Green Drake mayflies that aroused much attention on the limestone streams in northern Pennsylvania—Penn's Creek, Spring Creek, Spruce Creek, and Fishing Creek. Of the Green Drake spinners, commonly referred to as the Coffin flies, Marinaro said in his *Modern Dry-Fly Code* that even if the trout were not rising, "the journey to see one of the grandest sights in nature" was worth the effort. He attached a hollow, lightweight, buoyant, and durable porcupine quill to a short-shank hook. He then wound hackle on the thorax and clipped the top and bottom, leaving a flat, broad plane "wing" that floated the fly well. In his book *In the Ring*

of the Rise Marinaro admitted that the use of porcupine quills for spinners never really caught on with other fly tiers, but maintained that he stood by the design. He wrote, "I could not abandon porcupine quill entirely for I still do not know a better way to get a good floating spinner in very large sizes such as for the big eastern green drake or the huge Michigan *Hexagenia limbata*."

While porcupine quill offered good flotation characteristics for the big mayfly drakes, Marinaro approached smaller mayfly spinners differently. *In the Ring of the Rise* makes a big point about using seal fur as body material, but unlike tiers such as Jack Atherton, Marinaro scoffed at the idea of blending it with other materials. He also expressed disdain for "rolling it around the tying thread," the method employed by Jim Leisenring and Pete Hidy. He called it a "minor crime to pollute this material." Wings on his small spinners, such as Hendricksons, were tied with hackle fibers, which he said can

Letort Spring Run at Carlisle, Pennsylvania, attracted many well-known fly fishers to its waters. Bankside benches were convenient resting spots where anglers could exchange fish stories and tales about the creek. Left to right: John Goddard, Charlie Fox, Lefty Kreh. *Courtesy Lefty Kreh and the Catskill Fly Fishing Center and Museum*

"gather and condense light" like the wings on a natural mayfly on the water.

Beyond dry-fly dun and spinner design and theory, Marinaro also explored terrestrial insects and patterns, an important fly-fishing facet woefully underrecognized in his era. Many consider Marinaro's early promotion of terrestrial patterns his greatest contribution to modern fly fishing. In *A Modern Dry-Fly Code*, he described strange new land-bug patterns that were well suited to his beloved Letort: beetles, ants, hoppers, and Jassids, minute specks that he fished along its placid waters. Many consider the unique Jassid, made from a jungle cock eye, his signature pattern.

Jungle cock eyes, or nails, the small feathers revered by streamer and salmon-fly tiers, found their way onto Vince Marinaro's hooks in his search for materials best suited to fabricate a good pattern to imitate the nonindigenous Japanese Beetle. By the early 1940s, *Popillia japonica* had become apparent on Pennsylvania limestone streams in "great hordes," as Marinaro described the infestations. The pesky beetle, which first invaded the United States around 1916, was an agricultural disaster yet opened up interesting fly-fishing possibilities on streams such as the Letort. Floating along the drift lines, the big Letort browns took the beetles "quietly and unobtrusively."

Marinaro's partner in the Letort terrestrial laboratory, Charles K. Fox, tried a variety of imitations when fishing bee-

tle drifts on his home waters. He experimented with small dry flies, hair bugs, cork bugs, and an interesting imitation crafted from a single coffee bean. In an article titled "Coffee Bean Jap Beetles" in the February 1944 issue of *Pennsylvania Angler*, Fox described how he filed a groove on the flat side of a bean, then glued it to a size 14 or 16 hook shank with Duco Cement. The bean fly produced reasonably well for Fox on the Yellow Breeches Creek, yet Marinaro was unable to achieve equal results with the bean creation on the Letort. After much experimentation, Marinaro found that a jungle cock nail offered advantages over the heavy coffee bean imitation, which was difficult to cast.

The bulky Japanese Beetle could be imitated with a single large eye tied over palmered black hackle. Marinaro theorized that trout peering upward at a beetle imitation see only the dimensions of length and width, and not its thickness. The jungle cock eye offered the necessary ovoid dimensions and was very light, making casting much easier. Clipping a wide V from the hackle underneath the hook shank allowed the imitation to sit flush on the water surface.

Marinaro's fly design concept employing jungle cock eyes also proved effective for the smallest of insects—leafhoppers. Charlie Fox's article "A New Kind of Fly," which appeared in the March 1958 issue of the *Fisherman*, described the problematic situation anglers faced on streams such as the Letort when trout were sipping leafhoppers: "Trout feeding on leafhoppers are among the choosiest, for they are difficult to deceive with the standard dry-fly. Almost every flat section of stream has such feeders, and frequently in some quarters they enjoy the reputation of being impossible to catch."

Fox described how his friend Vince Marinaro strained the water surface on the Letort with a cloth to ascertain exactly what the sipping trout were feeding on; they were the tiny leafhoppers, commonly called Jassids.

Traditional small dry flies proved useless as imitations. Fox recalled Marinaro's investigative work: "For one week Vince camped in the meadow. When he was not fishing, he was either conducting a series of water tests or tying more flies in his experiment to imitate this natural. It was my custom to join him in the late afternoon to check on operations, replenish his diminishing larder and to fish. About the fifth evening he was bubbling over with enthusiasm. 'I have a fly,' advised the maestro. 'Show me a jassid-eater and I think I can hook him.'"

Charlie Fox took on the task; he showed Marinaro a difficult, "untouchable" trout that was an incessant surface feeder. His friend took the fish on the first cast with the new Jassid fly. Success at hand, Marinaro handed Fox three of the effective flies. Fox went right to work field-testing the Jassid on a pod of six feeders that he had been unable to entice with anything else. "It took no more than half an hour to deceive trout which I previously could not touch and which were held in high regard as being ultraselective," Fox wrote. The Jassid was a success. Marinaro began tying the pattern in small sizes, 18s to 22s. At the time of his story, Fox preferred to use two eyes, concave sides together, with clipped hackle on the belly. The original Jassid had orange tying silk with ginger hackle, but other combinations of silk and hackle shades were used later. Praising the Jassid, Fox wrote: "As far as I'm concerned, the Jassid is indispensable for meadow streams and the larger flats of mountain streams, and its usefulness commences each year with the first hot days, continuing throughout the remainder of the season."

Charlie Fox wasn't the only Letort fly angler who adopted Marinaro's new fly. Letort regular Ed Shenk also embraced the pattern. Shenk, a member of the Letort school of fly anglers, contributed his terrestrial-fishing know-how in writings in various sporting magazines, such as *Sports Afield* and *Field & Stream*. While Shenk didn't catch a mammoth trout on Marinaro's Jassid, he did embrace the pattern as an excellent Letort trout taker.

Shenk penned an article that appeared in the June 1968 issue of *Field & Stream*, titled, "Sublime to the Ridiculous: The Miniature Jassids." The story's opening photo—a line of size 28 Jassids and ants along the top of a ruler, for scale—captured the imagination of many readers in that era. Fishing 28s was almost unheard of then. The old gold

Mustad 28s were the smallest hook sizes available at that time, and few tiers dared to bother with them. Even Shenk admitted that when Mustad started manufacturing them in the early 1960s, tiers tackled the minute hooks as a joke. However, Shenk successfully broke the hook size barrier, proving that 20-inchers could be taken on such small flies fished off 8X tippets.

Jassids worked for Shenk; they also gained the admiration of fly-fishing notables such as Joe Brooks and Ernie Schwiebert, who cast the little specks on streams many miles away from the Letort. In *Trout Fishing* (1972), Brooks displayed a color photo of six Jassids along with another of Marinaro fishing along a Pennsylvania stream. Of the Jassid, Brooks wrote, "With that fly Vince took trout after trout from the midsummer Letort, and since then the Jassid has continued to take fish in many streams when all other flies fail. I have used Jassids successfully in nearly every part of the United States where trout are found, and in European streams as well, always with the same success." Brooks fished Marinaro's creation on the Bann River in Ireland and also on the River Dove in England.

Ernie Schwiebert expressed equal admiration for Vince Marinaro's little Jassids. In *Remembrances of Rivers Past* (1972), Schwiebert's chapter titled "Legend and the Letort"

Letort Spring Run, Carlisle, Pennsylvania. The Letort served as Marinaro's laboratory in the development of many of his classic trout flies.
Photo by Jay Nichols

describes the times he fished to dimpling trout on the stream made famous by Marinaro and the contingency of other south-central Pennsylvania fly fishers. By the time the book was published, jungle fowl capes were banned from entry into the United States, yet that did not deter Schwiebert from reminding readers, "Jassids have proved excellent, and their development will make Marinaro an angling legend wherever big midsummer browns feed quietly in flat water."

The diminutive Jassids, which had gained increasing popularity through the 1960s, began to wane once importation of the Asian bird was prohibited. Supplies of capes began to diminish, and prices rose steeply. The once readily available $5 capes began to vanish. About the only way Jassid tiers could get their hands on new jungle cock capes was through the black market. Once jungle cock again became available, thanks to new importation controls, Marinaro's little creation had been long forgotten. Newer flush-floating terrestrial patterns had been created that filled the void. Good jungle cock is now very expensive, and there's little hope that Marinaro's leafhopper imitation will see new life on the Letort and other slow-moving spring creeks. Yet the memory of Vince Marinaro and the patterns he developed during his years on the Letort—his flush-floating terrestrials and his thorax dry flies—will always hold a special place in fly-fishing history and in the hearts of those who knew Marinaro well.

One such person is Tom Baltz, a popular Cumberland Valley, Pennsylvania, fishing guide and fly tier with 50 years of tying experience who said he became "a limestone fly tier by osmosis." Limestone icons such as Charlie Fox, Ed Shenk, and Vince Marinaro mentored Baltz, who still fondly recalls his memories of Marinaro. He shared the following with me in correspondence: "I began working at the Yellow Breeches Fly Shop in Boiling Springs, Pennsylvania, in early April 1976, and Vince first came into the shop a few days later. He was a regular in the shop for eight or nine years, and we did a number of fishing outings, mostly to the Yellow Breeches (very seldom to the catch-and-release area), and took him out grouse hunting ('groutches' to him). I don't remember him ever getting a grouse, but he did catch some trout, most all of which went into his creel. That was a bit of a surprise to me at first. One of the funniest things I ever saw was Vince, upstream from me, with a 9-inch brownie dangling from his 'Guppy' rod. What made the scene so hilarious was that Vince had netted the little trout with the huge net he ALWAYS carried after having lost a big Letort brown many years previ-

ously, and it had gone through the net's meshes. Vince was obviously in a quandary about what to do about that, as he kind of had his hands full. Alas for the trout, he stayed stuck onto Vince's little wet fly long enough for Vince to wade to shore and dispatch him. I never said anything to Vince about having seen that episode.

"We had a fly-tying bench in the shop, and Vince loved to tie and watch some others of us tie too. He would occasionally throw out a suggestion of a material or, more often, how to use a certain material. Typical of all of the (to me) old-timers, Vince seldom said too much, just hinted or suggested something here or there. If you 'got it,' more tips/hints might be forthcoming. He mentored the rod builders, notably Bill Harms, the same way. Some of the greatest influence he had on my personal fly tying and fishing was to think more in terms of fly design than fly pattern, something very much confused by many fly tiers/fishers today, and how, not what, to think about materials, to use them in the best way for a given fly design. We had Vince's slant tank in the shop and learned a lot about how flies might appear to a trout from playing with it. Vince enjoyed the thing immensely! Vince did not show us too many of his designs but did show us some of his tying techniques. He showed me and a few other guys how to tie his famous thorax flies, and in my opinion, no one who did not learn to tie these from Vince has ever cracked a couple of the secrets to making them. Vince never gave up all of the tricks in his books!

"He wanted to see what we did as far as bringing our own ideas to life. That went both ways in some cases too. Back then (the late 1970s), I was really tying and fishing a lot of Frank Sawyer's Pheasant Tail Nymphs. Vince took a few of those ideas and incorporated them into some soft-hackled wet flies, nymphs to him. It was, for me, truly the halcyon years. Vince Marinaro was not always the nicest person and dismissed many things he was not interested in with a grunt, but he was absolutely one of the most interesting and important figures in American fly fishing. We tied all kinds of trout and salmon flies (the full-dress types), and all in all, this was maybe one of the most fun and satisfying times of my personal fly-fishing journey."

Vincent C. Marinaro was one of the top-drawer American fly tiers; he influenced many, and he and his concepts have more than a few admirers to this day. It is unlikely that he'll ever be forgotten along the Cumberland Valley limestone streams that so possessed him.

Green Drake with cut and shaped wings, tied by Vince Marinaro. Marinaro believed cut wings should be well matched, as this was critical to the fly's effectiveness in both ease of casting and its behavior on water. *Pennsylvania Fly Fishing Museum Association collection*

Green Drake Spinner (Coffin), tied by Vince Marinaro. Marinaro used porcupine quill bodies for the spinner stage of *Ephemera guttulata*, a very large mayfly. Marinaro typically used hackle fibers as the wings, tied semispent, although this example was tied with hackle tip wings. *Pennsylvania Fly Fishing Museum Association collection*

Sulphur Dun, tied by Vince Marinaro. Marinaro believed that "the imitation of bodies on the dun or subimago of the mayfly is meaningless and superfluous." The thorax was more important, as it often touches the surface of the water. Breast feathers made for good wings, as they held together when wet. *Pennsylvania Fly Fishing Museum Association collection*

Hendrickson Spinner, tied by Vince Marinaro. Marinaro favored hackle barbs for spinner wings. The wide-flaring stiff hackle barbs, tied semispent, condensed light like natural spinner wings. Marinaro believed the same effect could not be achieved with hackle point wings. *Pennsylvania Fly Fishing Museum Association collection*

Thorax-style drake, tied by Vince Marinaro. Prominent wings, dubbing tuft thorax, and cross-wrapped hackle were typical of Marinaro's dry flies. *Pennsylvania Fly Fishing Museum Association collection*

Sulphur, tied by Tom Baltz. Baltz's fly closely adheres to Marinaro's design axioms. Baltz fished with Marinaro and was able to learn thorax style dry-fly tying techniques directly from him. The cut wings are perfectly matched, as required by Marinaro's beliefs. *Mike Valla collection*

Jassid, tied by Charles K. Fox. "I have a fly," Marinaro said to Charlie Fox decades ago. "Show me a jassid-eater and I think I can hook him." *John Capowski collection*

Jassid, tied by Chauncy K. Lively. Charlie Fox wrote that Marinaro's original Jassid was tied with orange thread and ginger hackles. Lively was largely influenced by Vince Marinaro. *Anne Lively collection*

Jassid, tied by Vince Marinaro. Jungle cock eyes proved perfect for a fly designed to imitate tiny leafhoppers. Marinaro used them first for a Japanese Beetle imitation. *Catskill Fly Fishing Center and Museum collection*

CHAPTER 30

Chauncy K. Lively
(1919–2000)

Chauncy K. Lively. Lively's brother-in-law and fishing companion, George Aiken, once said that Chauncy's goal was to "better his flies."

Anne Lively collection

His trout, bass, and panfish flies were considered inventive, creative, and unique—patterns that combined the qualities of realism, practicality, and effectiveness. Yet beyond fly tying, Chauncy K. Lively was also a prolific writer and talented photographer who for decades filled the pages of *Pennsylvania Angler* with instructions that helped other tiers duplicate his creations. He always included interesting history in his articles as background to his step-by-step tying instructions, with anecdotes that provided insights into his new flies, creations designed for hatches or specific fishing conditions on his favorite Pennsylvania and Michigan waters. Many of his articles were later compiled into *Chauncy Lively's Flybox: A Portfolio of Modern Trout Flies* (1980), a slender volume that is still a favorite among many fly anglers today.

The patterns Lively showcased in his *Flybox* were compiled largely from some 40 fly-tying articles that appeared in the *Pennsylvania Angler* from the 1950s through the 1970s. His pieces were enormously popular with fly anglers and tiers alike; many readers looked forward to the series of installments that showcased his wide variety of fly types. Lively's inventiveness

Green Drake, tied by Chauncy K. Lively. Lively frequently used cut and shaped flank feathers for wings on mayflies. He was also fascinated with the possibilities that deer hair offered in fly designs. Extended body deer hair patterns were favorites for the large drake mayflies such as *Ephemera guttulata*, the Green Drake. He used the pattern on Pennsylvania's Young Woman's Creek with great success.

Anne Lively collection

at the vise also was featured in other publications, such as the 1964 *Fisherman's Digest*, where three of his unique trout and bass patterns were featured. Readers who followed Chauncy Lively's writings were no doubt convinced that he lived an interesting life, one that combined his passion for fly tying and fishing with time spent with his family and friends.

Chauncy K. Lively was born May 23, 1919, in Charleroi, Pennsylvania, and later grew up in the borough of Waynesburg, tucked away in the southwest corner of the state. While attending Waynesburg College, Chauncy met his future wife, Marion Aiken, who shared with him a passion for fly fishing throughout their lives together. In fact, it was Marion who led to his involvement in the sport, along with her brother George Aiken. According to daughter Anne Lively who recently corresponded with me, "Mom was the one who introduced Dad to fly fishing. As a youngster, he'd done some fishing with worms and dough balls on the ponds around his aunt and uncle's farm in western Pennsylvania, and he did a little off and on in his early 20s. It wasn't until Mom bought him a few books on fly fishing that he became a convert. I don't know what made her choose fly fishing, but I do know that she thought it would be nice for Dad to have some sort of hobby after he was discharged from the army." After graduating from college in 1941, Lively had served in the U.S. Army, becoming a master sergeant.

Chauncy, George, and Marion fished together extensively by whatever means was necessary. Anne recalled that although her parents did not own a car until 1952, that was no deterrent to getting to the water; they took the bus to streams such as Loyalhanna Creek or Fisherman's Paradise at Bellefonte, Pennsylvania.

Several months after Chauncy's death, George Aiken wrote, in the October 2000 issue of *Riverwatch: The Quarterly Newsletter of the Anglers of the Au Sable*, a moving tribute to his brother-in-law and best friend, recalling the early years of their relationship. He said that he, Chauncy, and Marion all had a strong desire to become accomplished fly fishers. Learning to tie trout flies was an early priority, sending Chauncy to downtown Pittsburgh to take fly-tying lessons. Chauncy, a good student, emerged from the classes with a good understanding of fly tying and in turn helped George become reasonably proficient at the tying vise. "He always wanted to do better," George said.

Doing better with fly patterns seemed to be Chauncy Lively's lifelong passion. It is obvious that he was an intent observer, recognizing that dry flies should be tied to float and behave well on water while at the same time considering what the creation might look like from the fish's perspective. "Dad felt that a key to a successful fly was how it looked from the trout's eye view," Anne Lively explained. "To better understand that, he built several glass tanks with slanted sides. He'd float living insects and artificials on the surface and photograph them from below."

In his early fly-fishing years, Lively took note of Vincent C. Marinaro's *A Modern Dry-Fly Code*, studying the theories of thorax style dry flies. The Livelys, along with Aiken, soon wound up on the Cumberland Valley limestone trout streams—Falling Spring Branch, Big Spring Creek, and the famed Letort Spring Run, where Lively ran into Marinaro squatted on the bank near his fishing hut stretch. There is no doubt that the Letort laboratory inspired Lively to look at fly patterns from a new perspective, with a keen eye, just as the stream had done for Marinaro and Charlie Fox years before.

Lively's own creations are as innovative as any others crafted by inventive fly tiers. He was particularly intrigued with the floating qualities of folded deer hair and used the material for the bodies of many of his terrestrial patterns, such as the Quill Back Beetle, Quill Back Japanese Beetle, Quill Back Cricket, Horse Fly, Robber Fly, and Single-Hank Hopper. Step-by-step tying instructions for these patterns and others appeared over the years in the pages of *Pennsylvania Angler*. Originally tied as a bass pattern, Lively's intriguing folded deer hair Carpenter Ant pattern was first field-tested for trout on the Letort, where it successfully tempted the stream's hypercritical brown trout. Charles K. Fox's *Rising Trout* (1978) explains that Lively's use of folded black deer hair came from John Crowe's *The Book of Trout Lore* (1947) and his Crowe Beetle. The ant also proved successful on Pennsylvania freestone streams such as Young Woman's Creek. I became intrigued with the Carpenter Ant in my teenage years, more than 40 years ago, and it has remained a favorite pattern ever since for late-summer water conditions.

Chauncy K. Lively at his tying bench. Lively's patterns were uniquely his own, flies tied to suit his fishing needs for trout, bass, and panfish. *Anne Lively collection*

Lively became well known to many fly tiers through the large number of articles he wrote for *Pennsylvania Angler* magazine from the late 1950s into the 1980s. *Anne Lively collection*

In an article titled "Chauncy K. Lively" that appeared in the *Eastern Fly Fishing* magazine winter 2012 issue, I described the circumstances that led me to Lively's ant pattern: "It was a Saturday morning in 1969 or 1970, and my cousin Dave and I were on a treasure hunt, wandering around Binghamton, New York, in search of old fishing books and magazines at used bookstores and antique shops. In my teenage years, fly-fishing trade magazines were virtually nonexistent, and there never seemed to be enough fly-fishing stories in other outdoor publications on the magazine racks to satisfy my growing enthusiasm for the sport. The search was always on for anything in print pertaining to fly fishing. Dave spotted a 1964 *Fisherman's Digest* on the shelf at a musty, basement bookstore. As I thumbed through its pages, it seemed like a perfect find." I described my own success with Lively's ant in the July/August 2011 issue of the same magazine in an article titled "Highway 20 Corridor, NY: Beating the Heat in Summer." The Carpenter Ant was and still is my choice pattern on streams such as the Oriskany Creek in central New York state, during low water conditions in summer.

The *Digest* was filled with stories written by angling personalities that I was already aware of—Joe Brooks, A. J. McClane, Lee Wulff, John Alden Knight, and several others—but in the mix were three stories by a fly fisher I'd never heard of: Chauncy K. Lively. Lively's articles covered both bass and trout patterns, but one contribution in particular instantly caught my attention—his folded black deer hair Carpenter Ant.

The story described an August fishing trip on Young Woman's Creek during dismal drought conditions and how Lively's Carpenter Ant saved the trip. The striking macro photography in the article that visually explained his ant-tying techniques blew me away. During the off-season, hundreds of Carpenter Ants emerged from my vise. I ordered black deer hair in bulk from Herter's tying supply house. I was so intrigued by my own success with the ant that I sent a letter to Lively asking if he still found the fly effective on his favorite streams. He sent me a most welcome return letter, and from that point forward, the search was on for anything Chauncy Lively wrote.

The Carpenter Ant remains a great terrestrial pattern. However, Lively liked the floating qualities of hollow deer body hair for many of his patterns, not just terrestrials; mayflies and other aquatic insects were also on his list. The concept of using deer body hair found its way into stonefly and mayfly patterns, and even emerging nymphs. Lively's Green Drake design typifies his keen observations of how a natural insect floats on water and how it might appear to a feeding trout. The fly proved excellent for Lively during a Young Woman's Creek Green Drake hatch, when he caught so many large trout that he hesitated sharing the experience with friends for fear of being accused of tale-telling.

The use of a detached, thread-bound deer hair body solved one issue: a detached hair body enabled the tier to use a small, light wire hook on a fly that imitated the supersize Green Drake dun. Other tiers had used extended deer hair bodies for large drake patterns; Lively combined that practice with alternative hackling techniques and the use of very large feather wings. Clipping some of the hackle into a V-notch on the underside of the body or wrapping the hackle in parachute style beneath the body addressed fly balance for many of his mayfly patterns.

Lively also was particularly interested in creating lifelike wings on his dry flies. He shaped wings from ribbed feathers such as from a pheasant back, hackles, duck quill slips, and even the synthetic, clothlike Micro Web material that Barry Beck introduced him to in the late 1970s. Tying dry flies with clipped wings, often fabricated with the aid of a nail clipper (a Poul Jorgensen technique), was a favorite Lively style. His March Brown, Light Cahill, and other dun patterns have lifelike wings created by the clipped feather technique. Other tiers experimented with clipped wings, but combining his preferred hackling style with handsome clipped wings is what made Lively's dun patterns unique. Not all of his dry flies were crafted with clipped wings; other practical winging techniques emerged from his vise as well. Lively tied the little

Sulphur Dun with a clipped rib feather but also favored a shaped mallard quill slip wing version.

Lively wrote that he tied his Sulphur Dun to imitate the little *Ephemerella dorothea* naturals, which provide a good six weeks of fishing on Pennsylvania streams. Lively believed that such a long emergence gave trout the upper hand against fly anglers, as the fish became well acquainted with the natural mayfly's appearance. His V-clipped underside hackle gave just the right on-water floating posture. Mallard quill slips offered a good wing resemblance, but as every classic fly tier knows, such material lacks durability. Lively's solution was to shape the wings, tie them in and divide them, then add a thin coat of vinyl cement at the base and up through the tips.

Lively provided more detailed information concerning shaped mallard quill wings, along with other types, in what he called "backtrack" articles. He devoted two consecutive *Pennsylvania Angler* articles, in the October and November 1978 issues, to clipped rib feather, shaped quill slip, and synthetic Micro Web wing fabrication techniques. Both articles included interesting background history concerning dry-fly wings, yet there was another wing type that Chauncy Lively used for both mayfly and stonefly patterns—the Wonder Wing.

Lively created his Wonder Wings by stroking the barbs of hackles away from the feather tip toward the hackle stem root. He lashed the barbs down to the hook shank and snipped the tip of the hackle feather off cleanly, forming the wing. Lively tied a Little Black Stonefly (featured in his book) using Wonder Wings. The reversed barbs suggested wing veins. "Best of all," Lively wrote of the Wonder Wing in his book, "it retains its shape and silhouette after repeated use and is far superior to hackle tips, which tend to become mere slivers after repeated wettings."

The Wonder Wing patterns are realistic, impressionistic, yet practical, as was true with all of his creations. Lively's flies were very effective, whether fished on Pennsylvania's Cumberland Valley limestone streams, like the Letort and Falling Spring Branch; freestone waters, such as Young Woman's and Penn's Creeks; or other waters, such as his beloved Au Sable River in Michigan. An experimenter and inventor, Chauncy Lively was always searching for new techniques and materials to "better his flies," as his fishing companion George Aiken aptly stated. To "better his flies" meant thinking outside the box, setting aside tying norms and traditions. That's exactly what Chauncy Lively did when hackling his dry flies.

On a palmer hackled, winged pattern, for instance, Lively would first set the tails at the hook bend, then set wings behind the hook eye. He then attached the hackles in *front* of the wing. With the hackles so positioned and left in place for subsequent winding, dubbing was attached to the thread and wound *back* to the hook bend. The thread rested at the hook bend, waiting for the hackles. The hackles were wound, in-

dividually, to the hook bend, where they were tied down. Lively finished off the fly with a whip-finish applied at the hook bend. The technique is shown in his book and also mentioned in the August 1993 issue of *Pennsylvania Angler*. In the article, he wrote, "This configuration provides maximum support to the rear half of the fly, where it is needed most because of the weight of the hook bend." Other fly tiers, such as the Dettes, wound palmer patterns in a reverse manner, and Lively also wound dubbing in a reverse fashion.

Besides using his own creativity, such as reverse tying his palmered dry flies, Lively sometimes embraced fly-tying theories, techniques, or patterns developed by other tiers. His influences included John Crowe, Charlie Fox, Ed Hewitt, Vince Marinaro, Joe Messinger Sr., Poul Jorgensen, and the iconic cane-rod builder Paul Young.

Paul Young's hackled Redhead and his clipped hair moth-type Gill Bug, dry-fly bass patterns, along with a great trout taker called a Michigan Stone Fly were among his favorite patterns. Paul and Martha Young introduced the Michigan Stone, tied to imitate the Yellow Sally, an insect in the genus *Isoperla*, to Chauncy and Marion while fishing Michigan's famous Au Sable River. The fore-and-aft grizzly hackled pattern, with its fine deer body hair wing, was also effective on Pennsylvania streams. The Livelys also field-tested the Michigan Stone on a rare opportunity when they fished chalkstreams in England, where it proved very effective. It is obvious that Chauncy Lively took great pains to closely imitate the natural insects that floated along the riffles, runs, and pools of his favorite Pennsylvania and Michigan streams. Yet his creativity wasn't limited to dry flies.

While Chauncy Lively is often best remembered for his floating patterns—including everything from midges, such as his Speckled Midge, to bass patterns, such as his clipped hair Marapole tadpole imitation and the Hair-Crawdad—creative nymphs also filled his fly box. For the most part, Lively's nymphs were intricately tied exact imitations, designed and tied after having scrutinized every anatomical component of the natural insect, which were then reflected in his designs. The nymph patterns featured in *Chauncy Lively's Fly Box* and in numerous articles are so realistic that they appear ready to crawl along a streambed. His intricately tied March Brown, Sulphur, Isonychia, and Paraleptophlebia Nymphs feature exacting details imitating those found in naturals. There are jointed legs often formed from wood-duck breast feather fibers, along with unique abdomen and thorax components that are equally lifelike.

Lively also tied damselflies, hellgrammites, and dragonflies in nymph form. His Old Ugly dragonfly nymph, presented in articles in both a 1962 *Pennsylvania Angler* and 1964 *Fisherman's Digest*, led to an improved version that appeared in his book. His dragonfly and hellgrammite nymphs display the same attention to detail found in his mayfly and stonefly nymphs. He created flat underbodies from thin copper sheets, trimmed and shaped to form. Besides giving the flies realistic shape, the copper bodies also added weight, making them quick sinkers. Copper, this time fine wire, was also used for Lively's smaller nymph patterns to get them down deep quickly.

In his later tying years, Chauncy Lively continued to exhibit the same creativity at the tying vise that he had been known for since the 1950s. His Copper-Bodied Pupa, featured in the January 1982 issue of *Pennsylvania Angler*, was a minute pattern designed for use on flat water where microcaddis emergences were common. He wanted a fly that would sink—but not too fast. Using lead wire would create a bulky, fast-sinking pattern; fine-gauge wire (.009-inch, #32) was a better choice. Lively dressed the fly on a short-shank, up-eye hook in sizes 18 to 22. For this simple pattern, he wrapped the hook shank with the fine copper wire. He added peacock herl at the hook eye, with the tips extending under the back to the bend to represent wing stubs. Another copper-bodied pattern that was not Lively's original, but one he promoted in the November 1983 issue of *Pennsylvania Angler*, is the Brassie Nymph. Lively was introduced to the Brassie while fishing the Platte River in Colorado. Lively also employed copper wire bodies on streamers; his Bicolor Leatherneck was created to supplement the traditional streamers designed by Carrie Stevens and Bill Edson.

Chauncy Lively did not cover streamers in his book, but the April 1981 issue of *Pennsylvania Angler* introduced a fur-strip pattern called the Leatherneck. A follow-up story in the January 1983 issue of the same magazine featured the Bicolor, a two-toned version of the pattern. The pattern used rabbit, mink, or muskrat—almost any two-toned contrasting fur shades were acceptable. Lively liked to leave the guard hairs on the fur strips; they gave the fly sheen and made it more attractive. The Bicolor Leatherneck proved a good producer for both bass and trout.

The Bicolor Leatherneck streamer joined the family of Chauncy K. Lively creations developed over a lifetime of enjoyment at the tying vise and study onstream. His creativity never waned until he left our fishing world on February 24, 2000. Creative fly tying along with fly fishing was his life. His love for fly fishing always included family, making his experiences all the more enjoyable. In correspondence with me, his daughter Anne recalled, "Most evenings Dad could be found in his study writing, tying flies, or taking photos for his articles. It was a cozy place with bookshelves filled with his fly-fishing, entomology, and photography books and stacks of fishing magazines and records. Under one window was a heavy old desk at which he tied flies. When Dad wanted to photograph flies for his articles, he set up a card table in the middle of the room. On the walls were fishing prints and photos. Always there was music, played loud. Dad loved the 20th-century composers, and Bartok, Poulenc, Prokofiev, and Schnittke were constant companions while he worked. Mom, Claudi [Anne's sister], and I often made use of a sofa in the room, doing homework or reading, and there always seemed to be cats and a dog around. Sometimes Dad would bring his tying gear down and tie on the dining room table, but mostly I remember him in his study with his feathers and fur and his books and his music, door always open to whoever wanted to drop in."

Hendrickson, tied by Chauncy K. Lively. Lively also achieved dry-fly floating balance by tying the hackle in parachute style beneath the body. *Anne Lively collection*

Sulphur Dun with clipped and shaped wing and parachute hackle. Lively embraced the clipped wing concept for mayfly patterns. *Anne Lively collection*

Clipped and shaped wings were favorites, such as in these March Brown, Hendrickson, and Sulphur dry flies, tied by Chauncy K. Lively. *Anne Lively collection*

March Brown, tied by Chauncy K. Lively. Lively used two mottled ring-necked pheasant feathers or similar plumage for his March Brown. He trimmed a wide V from the hackle underneath the fly to create better flotation and stability. *Anne Lively collection*

Quill Back Beetle, tied by Chauncy K. Lively. By varying the color of the quill, the concept can be applied to many types of beetles. Folded deer hair floated the fly; a section of dyed duck quill forms the top of the fly. *Anne Lively collection*

Brassie Nymph, tied by Mike Valla. The Brassie is not original with Lively, but he promoted it in the early 1980s in *Pennsylvania Angler* magazine.

Robber Fly, tied by Chauncy K. Lively. Lively's fascination with extended deer body hair patterns led to his Robber Fly. *Anne Lively collection*

Carpenter Ant, tied by Mike Valla. This is Lively's original version, with deer hair legs projecting back from the head. A later version put the legs at the middle of the body. Lively originally designed the pattern in larger sizes for bass, but he later fished his black folded deer hair ant for the hypercritical brown trout in Pennsylvania's Letort Spring Run.

Lively's Carpenter Ant performed well for him throughout his home state of Pennsylvania. Hypercritical brown trout were successfully fooled by Lively's pattern.

Young Woman's Creek, Pennsylvania. Lively field-tested and fished many of his fly creations on his beloved Young Woman's Creek in northcentral Pennsylvania. His Carpenter Ant performed well for him on the creek during low water late in the season.

Synthetic Wing Stonefly, tied by Chauncy K. Lively. Lively was introduced to the synthetic, clothlike Micro Web material by Barry Beck in the late 1970s. He saw great potential in synthetics such as Micro Web and similar materials for fabricating wings.

Dragonfly Nymph, tied by Chauncy K. Lively. Lively's nymphs were intricately tied patterns, very lifelike in appearance. He tied several different versions of Dragonfly Nymphs, improving on early examples such as his Old Ugly. The Dragonfly Nymph displays the same attention to detail found in Lively's mayfly and stonefly nymphs. *Anne Lively collection*

Wonder Wing Mayfly, tied by Chauncy K. Lively. Ever the experimenter, Lively developed his Wonder Wings, crafted from hackles. He also used the wings for adult stonefly patterns such as his Little Black Stone. *Anne Lively collection*

Leatherneck Streamer, tied by Mike Valla. Lively introduced this pattern in 1981. It's a simple fly with fur strip wings and a copper wire body. Lively believed it to be a good alternative to marabou, as he said was also true of Zonker Streamers.

Michigan Stone, tied by Chauncy K. Lively. Cane-rod builder Paul Young of Michigan originated the pattern. Lively fished it with Paul and Martha Young on the Au Sable River. He tied it in two versions: one for the *Isoperla* (shown here) and another for the *Alloperla*, featuring yellowish olive hackles. *Anne Lively collection*

CHAPTER 31

Ed Shenk
(1927—)

Ed Shenk holding a beauty netted on a Pennsylvania limestone stream. *Ed Shenk collection*

Nearly 50 years have passed since Ed Shenk finally landed that big Letort Spring Run brown trout. It took 25 years of Letort fishing know-how and 150 angling hours to bring "Old George" to net. But in the end, the 27¼-inch, 8½-pound trout smashed a Silver Garland Marabou streamer, tied to a 10-foot, 2X leader hanging off a 5-foot, 1-ounce glass rod built by the fly angler who took it. Only then did he find out that "Old George Was a Lady," a fitting title for the feature article that Ed Shenk wrote for the February 1966 issue of *Sports Afield*.

Old George, the big bruiser that shook its head "like a punch-drunk fighter" when it slammed the Marabou on May 14, 1964, was not the only large trout Shenk took from the Letort. And that is not surprising. Joe Humphreys' introduction in *Ed Shenk's Fly Rod Trouting* (1989), explained that few fly fishers had Shenk's experience: "He has fished the Letort almost daily from his initial outing at age four, throughout grade school and high school and on to adulthood. There is no finer classroom in which to learn, and none more challenging."

Shenk's Sulphur Cut-Wing, tied by Ed Shenk. Shenk also used wingless Sulphurs but wrote that he favored cut-wing versions for highly fussy trout. *Ed Shenk collection*

Based on his vast experience on his beloved Letort, as well as other nearby trout streams such as Yellow Breeches, Big Spring, Green Spring, and Falling Spring Branch, Shenk designed a variety of interesting and effective patterns that attracted many a fine trout and helped ensure his fishing success. His fly box included everything from spinners to sculpins to terrestrials to "flies that trout like to chew," as Shenk said in *Ed Shenk's Fly Rod Trouting*.

Shenk's Doubles are particularly interesting patterns. There are the tiny Double Trico spinners he fished on the lower Letort and Falling Spring. His Double Ephoron spinners proved effective on the Yellow Breeches at Allenberry. In his Winter 1978 *Fly Fisherman* article, Shenk explained that his original idea was to apply the concept only to the smallest of flies—the Tricos. However, he soon tied the Double Ephoron spinner to better his catch numbers when the natural *Ephorons*, commonly called White Flies, appeared on the Yellow Breeches in August. In his story, he explained the *Ephoron* situation on that well-known stream: "The trout in this fish-for-fun area become more and more selective as the hatch progresses, and the imitations that fooled them the first week show very limited success later on. The trout really look them over for refusal. This is a blanket hatch, and the spinner fall is fantastic, with spent flies floating all over the stream's surface. I tried the double fly last August just to show them something they hadn't seen before. It worked so well, it really wasn't much fun."

Shenk credited Barry Beck with originating the Poly-Winged Spinner, which he considered the best imitation he had found. It worked particularly well for Shenk on his Double Tricos, which allowed for a larger hook size. He used size 18s, a big advantage over the typical smaller hook sizes used to imitate the minute mayfly spinners. In essence, he tied two Tricos on one hook. When fishing the big western rivers, Shenk found the larger hook size an added advantage to help bring a large brown trout to net. However, Shenk added one caveat concerning the Trico in his article: "I feel that in most instances the double fly should not be used as a substitute for the one-fly proper size idea. For the odd occasion when an over size fish is rising and a larger hook is needed to give the fisherman an even chance to land the quarry, it's worth a try."

In addition to Shenk's interest in spinners such as Tricos and *Ephorons*, he also enjoyed fishing the Sulphur hatch, commonly called the *dorothea* hatch, during peak emergences on his home waters in May and June. He recognized that there were many fine Sulphur patterns from which to choose and reported on those fly selections in a couple *Fly Fisherman* stories he wrote in the 1980s. In a June 1987 article titled "Sulphurs," Shenk wrote, "I don't feel I can get along with a single dun imitation, but if I had to pick no more than two, my first would be my general purpose Sulphur dun, a heavy hackled pattern without wings." However, he said, his second pattern of choice, for superselective risers, would be his variation of Vince Marinaro's cut-wing pattern. The wingless version was featured in Eric Leiser's *Book of Fly Patterns* (1987); *Ed Shenk's Fly Rod Trouting* also highlighted this pattern, as well as Marinaro's cut-wing Sulphur dry fly and Shenk's variation.

While Ed Shenk's mayfly patterns are still favorites, he is also well known for his sculpin patterns, the Black Sculpin, White Sculpin, and Tan Sculpin. Some anglers might assume that sculpin flies are restricted to use on western waters, where they were made popular. Dave Whitlock led the charge for sculpin development, yet Pennsylvania fly tiers such as Al Troth and Ed Shenk also added a few to the mix. Shenk liked to incorporate marabou into his sculpins, since it was a marabou pattern that enticed "Old George"—proof enough of its effectiveness.

During his early years, when Shenk killed an occasional big trout, he often found sculpins in their stomachs or even still stuck in their throats. Such findings led him to conclude that a series of sculpin patterns was necessary to increase success on his home Letort and other nearby streams. Shenk designed sculpins that featured muskrat, fox, or rabbit bodies trimmed to a wedge shape, flat on the bottom. He added broad clipped deer hair heads and pectoral fins, with some flies featuring marabou wings. The marabou tails were trout teasers, for sure.

Shenk's sculpins have intrigued many a fly fisher, including Mike Heck, one of Pennsylvania's top guides and author of *Spring Creek Strategies*. In correspondence with me, Heck

Ed Shenk. Fly fisher Joe Humphreys called Shenk "one of the best in the country, one that few can equal and I am proud to call my friend." Ed is a member of the Letort school of fly tiers, which included such luminaries as Vince Marinaro, Charlie Fox, Ross Trimmer, and many others who developed flies for that stream. *Ed Shenk collection*

recalled an experience observing Ed Shenk fishing his sculpins: "I can remember pulling into the Bonnybrook parking lot [on the Letort] in the early 1990s. Two guys just tossed a few streamers under the bridge to no avail. They walked off and drove away. So here comes along Ed, and I stopped and let him fish under the wooden bridge. He didn't walk over the bridge, but flipped in his sculpins and within a few small gentle strips had landed a 13-inch or so brown. I had met Ed several times before this, but we had a chance to speak a bit more in length. I had said something like 'Sculpin always works for me.' Ed said, 'Yes, but I call them Old Ugly and they are chewy flies.' Ed told me they literally will chew on them. He also showed me a little about 'sculpinating.' I pondered on the 'chewy' thing for a long time, until one day on Falling Spring Branch I was working sculpins across a watercress bed. A large brown shot out and gulped down the fly. I'm watching the darn brown chew on this sculpin and

Right: "Old George," the monster brown trout that took Ed Shenk 150 fishing hours and 25 years, to capture on a Silver Garland Marabou streamer. *Ed Shenk collection Below:* Letort Spring Run, just downstream from the Bonnybrook parking area. Shenk spent a lifetime fishing the little creek, running patterns such as his sculpins through its currents and undercut banks. He developed many of his patterns based on his hours of fishing experience on the stream. *Photo by Valerie Valla*

could not set the hook until its mouth was shut. Ed has caught trout on the sculpins all over the country."

In a March 1985 *Fly Fisherman* story titled "Sculpinating Trout," Shenk wrote, "Results with these new patterns were exciting. At times they appeared to drive the fish into a frenzy, and trout that should know better seemed to abandon all caution and shyness." Marabou-enhanced sculpins, or Old Ugly patterns, as he called them, proved effective for Ed Shenk, and he also applied the material to other "chewy" patterns. A fly named the Minnow #1, or Shenk's White Streamer, was another of his creations. Yet another interesting fur-bodied pattern that predated Shenk's soft-bodied "chewy" sculpins and minnows was the Cress Bug. With its trimmed fur body, this fly rounded out Ed Shenk's underwater arsenal.

Ed Shenk's sculpins, minnows, and Cress Bugs, along with his Sulphurs, Double Tricos, and Double Ephoron spinner dry flies were all creative patterns that fished well on his beloved Pennsylvania streams. And he is well known for these patterns. But some of his most famous flies are his terrestrial patterns, including Shenk's Letort Hopper and Letort Cricket, which he also valued. In *Ed Shenk's Fly Rod Trouting*, he wrote, "Dear to my heart are the [Shenk's] Letort Hopper and the Letort Cricket. Although there are numerous hopper and cricket patterns around, I have never felt the necessity of carrying them except on occasion. Call me biased, but they're my babies, and I love 'em." His favorite size for both the Hopper and Cricket is 14, in 2XL.

Shenk prefers his Cricket over all the other terrestrials he has fished—it's easy to tie and floats well. He has fished the Cricket from the East Coast to the West, and others around the globe have done well with it too. He also developed a Sunken Hopper and a Sunken Cricket.

Coincidentally, Ernie Schwiebert also created a pattern called the Letort Hopper, so named by Charlie Fox and Ross Trimmer, which has caused some confusion in Letort country. "Everything in these patterns was a series of coincidences and neither of us knew that our similar patterns had identical names," Shenk wrote in his book. Ed added "Shenk's" to the name of his version to avoid confusion.

There may have been some confusion surrounding Shenk's Letort Hopper, but there's no confusion whatsoever concerning all that Ed Shenk has done to advance new and exciting trout-fly patterns. He brought ingenuity to his fly designs, inspired by decades of experience fishing for highly selective trout.

Shenk's Double Tricos, tied by Ed Shenk. This pattern has two imitations tied on one hook shank. The concept allowed the use of a slightly larger hook. *Ed Shenk collection*

Shenk's Cress Bug, tied by Ed Shenk. A simple pattern, this fly is tied with clipped muskrat, mink, or otter fur. *Ed Shenk collection*

Shenk's Black Sculpin, tied by Ed Shenk. Shenk discovered that sculpin patterns are highly effective on many trout streams, including his home Pennsylvania waters. *John Capowski collection*

Shenk's Beetle, tied by Ed Shenk. Shenk also developed folded deer hair body terrestrials such as this beetle.

Shenk's White Sculpin, tied by Ed Shenk. *Ed Shenk collection*

Shenk's Double Ephoron, tied by Ed Shenk. Double Ephoron spinners proved effective for selective trout on the Yellow Breeches at Allenberry. *Ed Shenk collection*

Shenk's Tan Sculpin, tied by Ed Shenk. Shenk added eyes to this sculpin pattern. *Ed Shenk collection*

Shenk's White Minnow, tied by Ed Shenk. A "chewy" fly, the pattern is composed of trimmed white fur and a marabou tail. *Mike Valla collection*

Shenk's Sunken Cricket, tied by Ed Shenk. *Ed Shenk collection*

Shenk's Banded Minnow, tied by Ed Shenk. This minnow is another of the "chewy" soft-bodied minnows. *Ed Shenk collection*

Shenk's Letort Cricket, tied by Ed Shenk. Shenk called the pattern his favorite among the terrestrials. *Mike Valla collection*

Shenk's Sunken Hopper, tied by Ed Shenk. *Ed Shenk collection*

Shenk's Letort Hopper, tied by Ed Shenk. Ed attached his name to the pattern, sometimes referenced as Shenk's Flatwing Hopper, to avoid confusion with the Letort Hopper developed coincidentally by Ernie Schwiebert. *John Capowski collection*

CHAPTER 32

Franz B. Pott
(1890–1955)

Franz Pott, creator of unique woven trout flies. A German immigrant barber and wig-maker who lived in Missoula, Montana, Pott was an avid fly angler who started tying flies in his barbershop in the early 1920s. *Mike Wilkerson collection*

The most famous of Franz Pott's patterns were known as the Mighty Mites, strange little flies with stiff hackles projecting outward from intricately woven bodies. The flies displayed knitted bright silk strips along the bottom, characteristic of Pott's style. Precursors of the gigantic nymphs crafted by George Grant, Pott's patterns set the foundation for all woven flies that followed.

The majority of East Coast tiers never heard of the 30 woven flies that emerged from Missoula, Montana, yet in western circles, the odd-looking sinking flies were known for their unquestioned effectiveness in bringing trout to the net. Joe Brooks makes a brief mention of the famous Mites in *The Complete Book of Fly Fishing* (1958), where he listed all five: Sandy Mite, Lady Mite, Mr. Mite, Buddy Mite, and Dina Mite. Brooks's book was popular among East Coast fly anglers; his mention of the Mite flies no doubt helped introduce Pott and his patterns beyond western waters. And fly tiers have relied on western fly anglers to keep Pott's work above the radar.

Orange Fibber, tied by the Pott Fly Company. Fibbers have peacock herl heads. The late George Grant, known for his woven nymph flies, said that the Fibbers were so named in response to fly fisher Ed Hewitt's claims concerning nymph designs.
Frank Johnson collection

Frank Johnson of Sheridan, Wyoming, an enthusiastic contemporary woven-fly aficionado who has instructed tiers in Pott's tying techniques, has done fly-fishing history an enormous favor by not allowing the art form to die. Johnson was introduced to the Pott flies early in life, as a kid, when he was living in Sheridan. The local pool hall on Main Street served as the town's fly shop. In correspondence with me, Frank told his story: "The proprietor of the pool hall was a fly tier, and when not racking balls, he was at the vise. Sam Mavrakis was more than a little helpful to me as I fantasized about becoming a fly fisherman. Today I can only thank him so much for his often used expression, 'Hey, you little shit, get out of here and go fishing.' As I hung around the pool hall, I heard talk of Lady Mites and Sandy Mites: 'They were the best flies you could use.' Or 'I caught four on a Sandy last night.' Time passed and I cleaned chicken coops and cut grass and finally bought two or three of the 'Mites.'" He was hooked on the Mites ever since.

It was during the early 1970s, when Johnson moved to Missoula, Montana—he's now living back in Sheridan—that

Franz Pott on a trout stream. Pott's flies were effective trout catchers. *Mike Wilkerson collection*

he became acquainted with Gene Snyder, then owner of the Pott Fly Company. Johnson sold some Pott flies from his shop, mostly to older gents. But gradually Pott's famous woven-hair flies fell out of favor with fly fishers who would rather fish nymphs than antiques such as the Mites. "Over the years, changes of ownership of Pott Fly Company, changes in fishing techniques and pattern styles, and production costs caused the company to more or less fade away. My friends Ray Prill and Mike Wilkerson operated the company for several years, until the mid-1990s, when it became totally inactive. Several years ago I was thinking about Pott flies and how they were tied and what an important part of western American fly-fishing history they were. I thought that if I could at least learn to tie them, I could spread the word so we would not entirely lose this small part of fly-fishing history. It was not totally easy to learn it all, as Franz Pott was a very secretive man and unwilling to have his techniques known. Working with Mike and Ray and others, I have learned to weave the hair hackle and tie the flies. It has proved to be a fun and fascinating project."

Frank Johnson isn't the only Franz Pott fan. In *Fly-Fishing Pioneers & Legends of the Northwest* (2006), historian Jack Berryman told Pott's story and the history of the Pott Fly Company. According to Berryman's research, Pott was a German immigrant who operated a barbershop in Missoula, Montana, sometime around 1918. In addition to haircutting, Pott brought with him to America another talent—wig making. An avid fly angler, Pott soon turned his attention from weaving wigs to weaving trout flies. He was certain that he could improve flies that were available to fly anglers in that era and manufacture them at a lower price. The popularity of Pott's newfangled creations led to his establishing the Pott Fly Company in 1924.

At this time, American fly-tying creativity seemed to be burgeoning everywhere. By the mid to late 1920s, the Catskill school of fly tiers was growing, and they were tweaking Theodore Gordon's creations and shedding old British standards. Over in Michigan, Len Halladay sparked the birth of the Adams, and at Upper Dam, Carrie Stevens was experimenting with her Rangeley streamers. Similarly, Franz Pott did not allow his creativity to be limited by East Coast pattern standards.

Over the decades since, Pott's ardent fans have refused to let his creations fade into obscurity, and flies such as his Sandy Mite are still fished in trout streams everywhere. Individuals such as Frank Johnson, Jack Berryman, and fly-fishing historian Paul Schullery have helped keep Pott's history and craft alive, as did George Grant, who wrote about Pott's flies in *The Art of Weaving Hair Hackles for Trout Flies* (1971). "These hand-woven hair flies are, without doubt, the most consistently successful trout flies for western fishing that have ever been devised," Grant maintained, "and their success is due in large part to the woven hair hackle." George Grant's admiration of Pott is unquestioned; he expressed high regard for him as the "originator of the woven hair hackle."

Grant used strong words concerning the significance of Pott's patterns. He believed that Franz Pott's woven creations were far more effective than the enormously popular Muddler Minnow but did not gain the national recognition that they deserved. He also wrote: "Although it was probably not a conscious effort on his part, I believe that Pott contributed more than anyone else to the establishment of the sport of fly fishing in Montana by creating flies that were especially suitable to the waters in which they were intended to be used and thereby gave an unschooled fishing public the confidence they needed to convince them that trout could be readily taken by a more interesting, imaginative and humane method than using a snelled hook and a worm."

It is not surprising, given Grant's complete endorsement of Pott's patterns and his belief in their significance, that he was a bit miffed at the puny summary of Mite patterns that appeared in a popular early book devoted to fly patterns and their origins. Although Grant didn't name the book's author, Harold Hinsdill Smedley's *Fly Patterns and Their Origins* devoted so few words to the Mites it is a wonder he even included them in his work. Smedley gave the Mr. and Mrs. Mite (the Lady Mite) a lukewarm, one-sentence description: "This congenial pair of flies are the work of Mr. Pott, of Missoula, Montana." Although Smedley's slim volume could not possibly have explored the entire worth of Pott's Mites, he could have written a lot more about them that would have been within the scope of the book's intent. However, the story of Pott's growing operation and his almost compulsive insistence on maintaining fly quality was better left to those closest to him, such as George Grant.

As Grant explained, when the popularity of Pott's flies exceeded his ability to meet the demand, he brought in others to assist him. Female students from the University of Montana constructed the fly bodies, while Pott wove the hackles himself. It has been speculated that he may have done this to keep his hackle crafting techniques a closely guarded secret. However, maintaining quality control could have been the primary reason for his hands-on involvement. Shortly after receiving his trademark from the U.S. Patent Office, Pott leased the business to Finline Tackle Company in Denver. The contract stipulated that "high quality" be maintained in fabrication of the flies. But he was so dissatisfied with the quality of Finline's flies that he broke the lease and moved production back to Missoula.

Despite Pott's insistence on quality, his flies were not without structural imperfections; after taking trout, they could transform into ragged forms yet still maintain effectiveness. They were so effective that fly anglers snatched them up by the thousands, even in the Depression years, at a price of 35 cents each or three for a dollar. In *Montana Trout Flies* (1981), George Grant wrote that one Pott pattern, the Sandy

Mite, "for approximately fifty years was the most successful Montana wet fly." Grant added that in his own retail and wholesale trout-fly business, the Sandy Mite "outsold its closest competitor five to one."

Grant believed that the popular ox hair Sandy Mite, with its yellowish tan or honey blonde appearance, bore little resemblance to colorations found among natural aquatic insects, yet he still attributed its effectiveness to its shade. However, Pennsylvania fly tier and angler Chauncy K. Lively recognized that the Sandy Mite was an excellent selection when he fished the *Epeorus vitreus* emergence on the Penitentiary stretch of Spring Creek. Color aside, its behavior in water proved perfect for fishing the common Sulphur hatch. Sulphurs emerge a bit differently than other mayflies, and Lively believed the Sandy Mite approximated the natural's behavior as it rose from its depths to the water surface.

In his February 1972 *Pennsylvania Angler* story, titled "The Mighty Mites," Lively described the Sulphurs' upward ascent to the water surface, where they seemingly popped out and promptly became airborne. His experience on Spring Creek showed that the mayflies did not take a leisurely ride along the water surface before flight, and thus dry flies were largely ineffective. Fishing a size 16 Sandy Mite dead drift just below the surface produced consistent takes. "It is during the fly's ascent to the surface that it becomes available to trout and a well-fished Sandy Mite is particularly effective at such a time," Lively wrote.

Lively acknowledged that the Mites never gained widespread popularity east of the Mississippi but felt that they deserved more attention. The patterns never fully colonized the East Coast fly box. The idea of stiff hackles on a wet fly would have been difficult to accept, given the more acceptable soft-hackle theories promoted by Pennsylvania greats Jim Leisenring and Pete Hidy. However, Chauncy Lively was the consummate experimenter, always looking for a new angle concerning fly design. It is not surprising that he tried the Pott fly concept, although he didn't adhere to their basic design in his own tying. Lively's Mite bodies were not woven, and the characteristic orange belly stripe was missing; orange thread was wound as ribbing along the body. In constructing the body, he simply tied hair at the hook bend and then wrapped it forward, twisting it as he went. His Sandy Mite was tied with a traditional feather hackle, not a woven-hair hackle, and his Mister Mite had hair hackle that was created by trimming body hair ends that projected forward from the hook eye, then pushed backward and tied in.

Although Chauncy Lively's Mites were not crafted using traditional techniques, his article helped introduce Franz Pott to East Coast fly tiers who were unfamiliar with him and his five Mite patterns. Beyond the Mites, Pott's other woven flies are rarely discussed on East Coast waters and are becoming less and less frequently mentioned along western streams. Aside from his common Coachmans and Ants, the names are as peculiar as the flies themselves. The others never exceeded the Mites in popularity, but they were interesting all the same—the Cliffs and Specials, the Fizzles and Fibbers, the Black Jacks and Badgers, the Rockworms, Maggots, and Ants.

The Fizzles and Fibbers are particularly interesting patterns. The subtle differences between all Pott's flies, beyond shade, seem almost arbitrary, yet Pott attached specific purposes to the odd flies. According to George Grant, the Red, Orange, Yellow, and Peacock Fizzles were Pott's versions of shellback nymphs; brochures printed by the Pott Fly Company's owners simply said that the Fizzle "is a surface fly with a motion of a fly or bug darting across the top of the water." Grant wrote that the Fibber was a pattern attached to Catskill fly angler Ed Hewitt's experimentation with nymph designs. In *Montana Trout Flies*, Grant implied that Pott apparently disagreed with Hewitt, hence the name Fibber. The peacock herl heads set Fibbers apart from the other flies in Pott's series.

All of Pott's patterns are tedious to tie, no doubt dissuading many fly tiers from attempting their construction. However, there was enough demand for the flies to keep the commercial Pott fly operation alive until the 1990s. Franz Pott kept ownership of his operation until the early 1950s. A few years later, Gene Snyder, who operated his Hamilton, Montana, area Angler's Roost shop, took control of the company, and in 1986, Dwain Wright purchased all interests in the business, including Pott's 1934 patent. Wright employed both hackle weavers and fly assemblers, turning out a respectable number of flies until he stopped production in 1990. Jack Berryman wrote that Wright's operation produced some 1,000 dozen flies a year, until Ray Prill, John Satre, and Mike Wilkerson bought the company in 1991 "so that it would be kept alive in Montana."

I think it is safe to say that throughout the West, the Sandy Mite has been fished more and caught more fish than any other fly in history."

From top, left to right: Buddy Mite, Sandy Mite, Mr. Mite, Dina Mite, and Lady Mite, tied by the Pott Fly Company. These Mighty Mites, strange little flies with stiff hackles projecting outward from intricately woven bodies, were Pott's best-known patterns. *Frank Johnson collection*

Red Fizzle and Yellow Fizzle, tied by the Pott Fly Company. The Fizzles are surface patterns that are meant to simulate insects darting across the water surface. *Frank Johnson collection*

Black Ant, tied by the Pott Fly Company. This is one of two Ant patterns developed by Franz Pott; the other is the Sandy Ant. *Frank Johnson collection*

Yellow Badger, tied by the Pott Fly Company. The Badger flies are fished as an ordinary wet fly and were popular on the Yellowstone River. *Frank Johnson collection*

Black Jack, tied by the Pott Fly Company. This fly was originally designed for late-evening fishing. *Frank Johnson collection*

Maggot and Rock Worm, tied by the Pott Fly Company. The Maggot (left) is made from woven badger hair. The Rock Worm was originally fished by allowing it to sink and then gently bringing it up to the surface. *Frank Johnson collection*

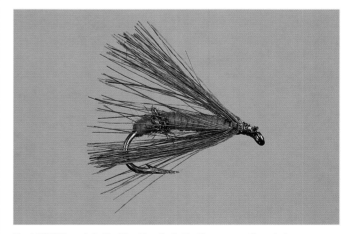

Red Cliff Special, tied by the Pott Fly Company. Specials were among Pott's favorites. *Frank Johnson collection*

CHAPTER 33

George F. Grant
(1906–2008)

George F. Grant, with Gary Borger looking on as Grant does his work at the vise in 1980. Grant brought artistry to his fly-tying bench, creating realistic large nymph patterns. Borger admired George's realistic tying methods. *Photo by Christine Fong*

The prolific angling author Joseph D. Bates Jr. was a great admirer of all things beautiful in fishing flies. If there was something interesting, even stunning, about a fishing fly pattern, Bates made certain readers would know about it. It was no surprise that he recognized George F. Grant as an innovative fly tier, an artesan who intricately crafted nymph imitations that fly anglers everywhere viewed with reverence and awe. Grant tied other fly patterns that were also works of art, but it was his woven creations that elevated him to the rank of fly-tying artist.

Bates could not have said it better when he wrote in the foreword to Grant's book *Montana Trout Flies* (1981), "Any fly tier worthy of the name can make nymphs that will catch fish, but those who treat their dressings as fine art can produce examples so intricately and exactly reproduced that they seem to all but crawl."

The Black Creeper, tied by George Grant. Many consider the Black Creeper Grant's signature flat-bodied woven nymph. Grant maintained that this pattern was responsible for taking more large brown trout from the Big Hole River than any other pattern fished. *Mike Valla collection*

Big Hole River. The Big Hole served as a proving ground for many of Grant's woven patterns, such as his Black Creeper. *Photo by Jay Nichols*

A native of Butte, Montana, Grant started fishing the Big Hole River in the mid-1920s and was devoted to protecting the stream throughout much of his long life. Besides being known for his conservation efforts, the "father of the Big Hole," as he was called, received international recognition for his fly-tying skills. Fly tying was a part of Grant's early life while he held various jobs around Butte. An interview with Grant by Bob Wiltshire was published in the Winter 2003 issue of the Federation of Fly Fishers' publication *Flyfisher*. The article provides interesting insights into Grant, his early tying years, and the origination of his famous flies.

In the interview, Grant told Wiltshire that his earliest association with trout flies began with patterns tied by Franz B. Pott. He took serious note of Pott's Mite flies, patterns that were beginning to gain in popularity throughout the state. "Before I started tying flies," he said, "I would have Saturday afternoons off from work and I would go buy a Lady Mite, a Sandy Mite and a Mr. Mite. These were Pott flies and real fishermen used Pott flies. They were three for a dollar. Of course that was a lot of money to me and I would fish those flies until they were completely destroyed." He tried to figure out Pott's woven-fly technique but then decided to create his own method. The problem was that Pott filed a patent on

woven flies, which was awarded in 1934. In *Montana Trout Flies*, Grant mentioned that Pott first had a 1925 patent dealing with woven Rock Worm bodies, but that it also alluded to woven hackles. Grant figured out another method, leading to his own patent in 1939.

George Grant freely admitted that once he developed his own methods of tying woven trout flies, it led to some competition with Pott, but that did not alter his admiration for the man. As Grant put it in his book, "I know he took great pride in his flies and that he maintained an excellence of uniformity and quality over his many years of tying."

Grant was drafted and served in the army from 1942 to 1945. Upon his discharge, he briefly operated a tackle store in West Yellowstone. A year later, he headed back to Butte and opened Grant's Fly Shop, a store he operated for about four years. He eventually took a job with Treasure State Sporting Goods, where he remained until his retirement in 1967.

After he retired, he was far from settling into a period of inactivity—a calling awaited him to increase his involvement in conservation activism, fly fishing, and writing about fly tying. He soon served the fly-tying world with two significant books: his privately published *The Art of Weaving Hair Hackles for Trout Flies* (1971) and shortly after, a paperback book titled *Montana Trout Flies* (1981). Both of these books were updated and expanded a decade later, resulting in hardcover special editions of his *Master Fly Weaver* (1980) and *Montana Trout Flies* (1981).

The Art of Weaving Hair Hackles was a collection of typed pages, crudely bound together with a spring-lock clip. Yet in the pages of that roughly constructed publication, Grant introduced the fly-tying world to his craft, revealing his methods for tying his unique flies and describing the advantages associated with them. Grant sent one of the first copies printed to Joseph D. Bates Jr. along with a letter stating his appreciation for Bates's writings, which he had enjoyed over the years. He called his own methods "unorthodox" yet effective.

In his *Art of Weaving Hair Hackles* Grant summarized the fivefold advantages of using woven-hair hackle:

1. A woven-hair hackle won't collapse along the fly body when fished and thus will appear more lifelike, especially in swift water. The fibers keep their position—splayed out from the fly—even when wet.

2. A woven-hair hackle adheres more tenaciously to the fly hook. By comparison, if a fly tier simply gathers individual hair hackle fibers into a bunch and then binds them down on the hook, they often won't hold in place after repeated use.

Grant's 1971 *The Art of Weaving Hair Hackles for Trout Flies* described the unique woven-hair flies first conceived by Franz Pott. Grant used his ingenuity to build on Pott's concept, resulting in his own pattern styles and tying techniques.

3. A woven-hair hackle can be created with individual hair fiber lengths sized exactly as desired for a particular fly.

4. A woven-hair hackle creates even distribution of the hair fibers. This results in a space between each fiber and a sparse finished fly. Grant argued that that western fly fishermen recognized that sparse wet flies were a prime requisite for them to be most effective in catching fish.

5. A woven-hair hackle produces a narrow rib. He compared what he called a "rib" to a quill that is found along the center of a rooster hackle feather. Because the rib was narrow, it could be easily wrapped around a hook shank and used to tie any type of dry fly that is traditionally tied with a feather hackle. What Grant was trying to say is that the process of weaving hair created what was essentially an artificial feather hackle quill, enabling the hair fibers to be wrapped around the hook shank just as a feather would be wound for creating dry flies.

All of Grant's arguments are, of course, debatable. However, the most intriguing of the five advantages, and most apparent in Grant's woven-hair flies, is the first. Grant observed that traditional-hackled sinking flies behave in a way that forces the feather barbs back, covering the fly body when fished. Hackle of woven hair or Tynex nylon, which Grant used later, maintains its position regardless of water swiftness or duration of time the fly is fished. Grant explained that even on dead drifts, the hair would protrude out from the fly, giving it more natural qualities. With Grant's woven flies, even if you try, it's next to impossible to force the hair projections close to the hook shank; they want to stay put and hold their position.

The soft-hackle school of fly anglers, following the theories of Jim Leisenring and Pete Hidy, would no doubt take exception to Grant's justification for using woven hackle, yet he firmly believed what he preached. Grant promoted his woven flies with their signature flat, hard bodies throughout his tying career.

Some of Grant's contemporaries, like Polly Rosborough, wanted nothing to do with hard-bodied nymphs, as they appear "dead in the water" to trout. In essence, trout would eject them immediately if intercepted in the water, causing missed strikes. Grant didn't totally discount Polly's fuzzy-bodied nymphs; it would have been difficult for him to do so, given the growing popularity of fuzzy patterns. But Grant's flat, hard-bodied patterns were tied to imitate the large *Pteronarcys* nymphs, and in his mind, close imitation, rather than suggestion, required flies like his. A large nymph, Grant argued, could be scrutinized by trout and easily detected as a fraud. Suggestive flies just wouldn't do; Grant's task was to craft close imitations.

The flat bodies characteristic of Grant's nymphs were formed by adding ½-inch-long brass pins along the sides of a wool or floss core foundation. An advantage of using brass pins was that the added weight allowed the fly to sink. Grant

Originator of:

THE "BLACK CREEPER" TROUT FLY
WOVEN HAIR HACKLE DRY FLIES
WOVEN HAIR BODY NYMPHS
ALL-NYLON NYMPH-BODY WET FLIES
NARROW BASE WOVEN HAIR HACKLES
(Patented)

March 1, 1971

Col. Joseph D. Bates, Jr.,
45 Prynnwood Road,
Longmeadow, Mass. 01106.

Dear Colonel:-

This is one of the first copies ever printed of my book, "The Art of Weaving Hair Hackles for Trout Flies", and it is my pleasure to present it to a man whose writings have provided me with so much interesting reading.

Your article "Upper Dam Pool and Its Two Famous Flies" (68th Issue UFT Roundtable) relative to Carrie J. Stevens and the development of the streamer fly was one of the most interesting and appealing that I have ever read.

I am sure that you will agree that my book, if nothing else, is original and unorthodox, but I can assure you that flies thus tied have long since been proven on our big western rivers. I sincerely hope that you will enjoy reading this little volume.

Best regards,

GEORGE F. GRANT
CREATIVE FLY TYING
2215 NORTH DRIVE
BUTTE, MONTANA 59701

Grant's letter to Joseph D. Bates Jr., sent along with a copy of his 1971 book, expressed his satisfaction with the effectiveness of his creations in taking fish. Ten years later, in 1981, Bates wrote the foreword to Grant's *Montana Trout Flies*. Bates wrote that he looked upon Grant's flies "with admiration approaching awe."
Mike Valla collection

originally used heavy thread for the outer monofilament shell, but he switched to oval monofilament and later semiflat monofilament once it became available.

Grant's famous Black Creeper was the progenitor of many other, similar patterns that followed. The earliest rudimentary pattern had its birth in 1931, but it wasn't until 1937 that it took its final form. In *Montana Trout Flies*, Grant wrote of the Black Creeper, "There is little question but that it was the first successful western commercial pattern to be tied with an outer shell of round nylon monofilament, and it was certainly the forerunner of all subsequent patterns having an underbody shaped and weighted with straight pins." Beyond its monofilament shell and use of straight pins to obtain a flat body, other Black Creeper features, such as its hackle and striped underbody, make it interesting and typical of the beautiful Grant nymphs.

It wasn't until 1933, when he taught himself the technique, that Grant used woven natural hair from black ox or skunk to craft his Black Creeper. He later used boar bristle, before switching to Tynex nylon. The final form of Grant's Black Creeper came in 1937. The Black Creeper's body seg-

mentation is well defined, created by round nylon monofilament, and accented by the orange floss belly stripe interwoven with the monofilament.

The Black Creeper is not only stunning, but also effective. Grant wrote that many accomplished fly anglers on the Big Hole River used the pattern, which resulted in many large fish being taken. He maintained that the Black Creeper was responsible for taking more large brown trout from the Big Hole than any other pattern fished.

While there is little doubt that George Grant is best associated with his unique flat-bodied woven nymphs, his Black Creeper among them, he also experimented with tying a wide variety of trout flies using weaving techniques. Beyond nymphs, Grant's *Art of Weaving Hair Hackles for Trout Flies* explores dry flies, wet flies, and even using his weaving techniques for popular flies that appeared in sporting magazines such as *Field & Stream*.

It was as if he were preparing for a doomsday when all types and styles of trout flies would have to be created with entirely different techniques. Weaving would become the redesign that could ensure quality flies, regardless of style and intended use. Grant lamented the availability of good fly-tying materials and considered the potential situation that over time, natural materials would be difficult to obtain. "We are all aware of the growing shortage of good materials necessary for the construction of trout flies. Even such a commonplace item as a grizzly hackle neck of dry fly quality is becoming scarce at any price." His prophetic tone offered hope for the development of a mechanized weaving machine that would produce hackle by the yard, like chenille. All we needed was the technology to manufacture hackle—his patterns were ready. Sinking flies or floating, his techniques could be used for all types of creations, including sculpin imitations.

Commonly referred to as the bullhead in some regions, the "grotesque little fishes with large heads" as Grant described them, were not without a woven-fly imitation. A. J. McClane's July 1968 *Field & Stream* article in the "Match-the-Minnow Streamer Fly Series" and Dave Whitlock's September 1970 *Field & Stream* article titled "The Sculpin and Its Imitations" introduced a unique fly called the Whitlock Sculpin and brought additional attention to the ugly little minnow. Grant also provided a few interesting woven-fly patterns that he believed better approximated the form and size of the small fish than existing flies such as the Muddler Minnow.

His Badger Bullhead, Miller's Thumb, and Squirlpin were large flies made with woven badger and squirrel hackle, which projected away from both the head area and the tails. The Squirlpin, first conceived in 1938, was unique in that its body was crafted entirely from woven squirrel hackle, head to tail. The sculpin patterns sank well and offered the lifelike form and functionality that Grant strived for in all of his woven flies.

His minnow patterns were far from arbitrary in their design, created after careful consideration of the needs for functionality and durability; his woven hackle dry flies were also designed to meet the needs for their intended use. Grant believed that dry flies should float well, have good visibility, and be durable enough to withstand damage from the big trout inhabiting large western rivers. His woven-hair hackle dry-fly patterns were created based on his belief that large western trout would best be attracted to large flies. Patterns such as his Badger Buck, Gray Buck, and Brown Fox were all tied on size 10 hooks, the Mustad 94840 or 2XL 9671, using woven white-tailed deer or gray squirrel hair hackle.

While Grant made a valiant attempt to justify the use of woven hackle for all types of fishing flies, including experimentation with large dry flies, he is still best remembered for his nymph patterns. Fly anglers such as Ernest Schwiebert took serious note of Grant's large, flat-bodied nymph designs. Schwiebert tied his big *Perla* nymph body with flat nylon over a striped amber underbody. He used brown lacquer along the dorsal and lateral areas of the fly body, suggesting the distinctive tergite markings found in the natural.

Schwiebert accepted Grant's nymph form and coloration theories, although he used soft pheasant feathers instead of woven hackle legs. However, it is noteworthy that Schwiebert was influenced by Grant's concepts and mentioned the flat-foundation technique frequently in his book *Nymphs* (1973).

George F. Grant's woven hackle flies were beautiful, yet tedious and time-consuming to tie. While it is true that such designs were impractical to tie in large commercial quantities, one cannot deny that they were an art form. The flat-bodied nymph design theory is not unique to Grant; other anglers, such as John Alden Knight, proposed flat-bodied designs earlier. But Grant's patterns are unique, and he adhered tenaciously to his fly design theories.

Although Grant was influenced by the creative mind of Franz Pott, he took his own pattern designs in a completely different direction, and they are still admired by many. It is true that the vast majority of fly anglers have never actually fished a George Grant pattern. They are much too beautiful to cast into a tumbling western river like the Big Hole and are best used as a source of inspiration. One thing Grant made clear is that there is always a different way to tie a trout fly.

A trio of woven-hair nymphs, tied by George Grant. Grant stood by his large patterns throughout his entire tying career. While Franz Pott held a patent on several of his woven-fly features, Grant held the patent on the method for weaving hair hackles. *Mike Valla collection*

Black Creeper, tied by George Grant, showing the underside of burnt orange floss interwoven with monofilament. *Mike Valla collection*

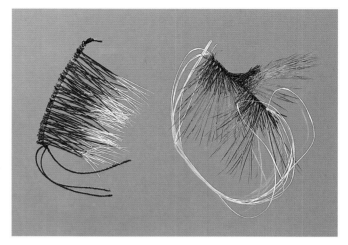

Woven-hair hackles crafted by George Grant. Grant wrote that casual examination of hair hackle does not immediately suggest its superiority over feather hackle. However, he offered several reasons for its effectiveness over traditional chicken hackle.

Banded Featherback Nymphs, tied by George Grant. Grant said that his Banded Nymphs were "highly reminiscent" of Pott's Lady Mite woven fly. He used North Dakota sharp-tailed grouse feathers to create the banding on this large stonefly pattern. He said that a "veteran big-water fly fisherman would not question the possibilities of this pattern." *Catskill Fly Fishing Center and Museum collection*

Integration streamer, tied by George Grant. Grant was also a talented streamer tier. His Integration combined Mylar tubing with polar bear hair wings. *Mike Valla collection*

Jungle Cock Featherback, tied by George Grant, is an example of one of his unique woven hackles. *Mike Valla collection*

Trude, tied by George Grant. Grant suggested that the Trude was created in 1901 after Chicago mayor Carter H. Harrison visited the A. S. Trude Ranch in Idaho. Grant described the fly in *Montana Trout Flies*. *Mike Valla collection*

Murder Orange, tied by George Grant. Grant said that this pattern was used "exclusively during the salmon fly season." He liked the visibility of the fly. Tackle dealer and fishing guide Dave Stratford was the first to show Grant the pattern. *Mike Valla collection*

Badger Royal, tied by George Grant. Grant used badger hair to create this variation of the famous Royal Coachman. *Mike Valla collection*

CHAPTER 34

Don Martinez
(ca. 1903–1955)

Don and Mary Martinez. Martinez brought traditional eastern dry-fly styles to the West. He spent summers in Wyoming and Montana and the off-season in California.

American Museum of Fly Fishing collection

Although his early fly-tying influences came from East Coast Catskill school tiers, Donald Skillman Martinez made his name in the West. George F. Grant, who called Martinez a "western dry fly master," credits him for bringing to West Yellowstone, and possibly the entire state of Montana, "real knowledge of how to tie and fish dry flies." Martinez adapted fly pattern concepts learned in the East to the demands of the western fly angler. Yet regardless of the region, when the name Don Martinez comes up in discussion among fly tiers and anglers, the simple Woolly Worm trout pattern that he promoted is usually mentioned. However, Martinez was responsible for much more than this simple fly made from chenille wrapped up a 3XL hook, palmered with hackle and ribbed with tinsel.

Don Martinez tied a variety of interesting trout patterns, such as the Whitcraft, sometimes referred to as Quill Adams, and his popular Martinez nymph. But he also tied many other patterns to meet fly fishers' needs. He was a versatile tier, a master fly craftsman, and a complicated individual with an interesting personality and background.

Woolly Worms, tied by Mike Valla. Don Martinez is credited with popularizing the Woolly Worm. It's considered his signature pattern, although it is not original with him. Martinez originally tied the hackle palmer with the concave side of the grizzly feather pointed to the hook eye. However, it can also be tied with the concave side toward the hook bend.

Martinez was born in about 1903 in Washington, Connecticut. His father's side of the family was from New Orleans, and his mother was part of an old New England family named Skillman. Correspondence that goes back to 1935 shows that his letterheads carried his full name across the top—Donald Skillman Martinez.

Don Martinez is said to have been well educated on the East Coast, and then eventually moved to Chicago, where he was engaged in the real estate business. During his brief years there, he was able to fish rivers in Michigan such as the Boardman, the birthplace of the famous Adams dry fly, a pattern that became one of his favorites. By the early 1930s, he moved to San Diego, California, but soon relocated to Los Angeles. George F. Grant knew Martinez well. In an article Grant wrote for the Spring 1982 issue of the *American Fly Fisher*, he said that Martinez had opened a tackle shop in West Yellowstone in 1932–1934 but returned home to California every winter.

Recent correspondence with West Yellowstone resident Cal Dunbar, who met Martinez and his family in about 1938, also provided additional background on Martinez's Los Angeles years. Don Martinez's son introduced Cal and a friend to his father when the three boys were teenage classmates at the local junior high school. The Martinez family consisted of Don's wife, Nola; his son, David; and a daughter, Mary,

who became an excellent fly tier herself. The boys were invited into the Martinez home, where they were introduced to fly tying. Cal remembered it this way: "Don usually sat at the card table in the occasional chair and tied. Sometimes he had a book open, and apparently he could sporadically read as he tied. I saw him tie the floss-bodied Pink Lady pattern flies once. The typical floss bodies were tapered, smooth, and seamless. The macaw quill bodies on the quill dry flies were always smooth and regular." The Pink Lady was George M. L. La Branche's signature pattern, embraced by many fellow Catskill region fly anglers when it was introduced in the early 1900s.

Martinez's Catskill connection is also made apparent from his interactions with area fly tiers. We know from letters Martinez sent to Catskill fly tiers Walt and Winnie Dette that in 1935, he was well into fly tying and pattern design while he lived in San Diego. And trout flies were not the only patterns Martinez was tying; bass patterns also emerged from his vise. On December 17, 1935, he wrote a letter to the Dettes about fly-tying materials: "There is also enclosed some neck feathers from California Valley Quail cocks. You may find these useful for wings of dry flies. In use these feathers make a somewhat more durable wing than you might think from looking at them. I have a surplus of this particular feather this year but no skins to spare. Have no way of pricing these quail

Martinez sold flies to eager customers at his shop in West Yellowstone, Montana (which eventually became Bud Lilly's fly shop). He also sold flies during the short time he joined Bob Carmichael's shop in Moose, Wyoming, which is in Jackson Hole country.

Robert Dotson collection

feathers but will be glad to send you some more to be exchanged for any standard item of material of which you have a surplus. In recent years I have been making up large streamer flies, which are used for big-mouth bass in the lakes and reservoirs around this section of the country. You will note that the hackles used are very large. It occurs to me from studying your catalog that you must throw out quite a lot of large hackle that I could use. What I am interested in is the lower portion of hackle skins, from size 4 on up to the largest, particularly white for dying. If you care to save these neck skins for me I will pay $1.50 a dozen for them net, provided that at least six in each dozen are white, or pale cream and ginger that can be dyed red or yellow." Martinez's mention of quail feathers for winging is not surprising; he designed a dry-fly pattern he called the Golden Quail, a fly he provided to Ray Bergman for inclusion in the book *Trout*.

The Dettes apparently were not close friends with Martinez, for their response letter was addressed simply to "Dear Sir." While they did not have in stock great numbers of the large feathers Martinez requested, they offered to send what they had. They also commented that although his samples looked "very nice," they had no real use for the California Valley quail.

Ten days later, the Dettes filled Martinez's fly-tying materials order. The order that he submitted, along with his letter, gives some clue to what he was tying in those early years. Martinez purchased three rooster capes: one brown, one white, and one gray grizzle (the Dettes always referred to grizzly capes as gray grizzles). The white cape might have been dyed for use in his bass flies, as he mentioned in his letter to the Dettes. It is not surprising that he also purchased three packets of "extra select" gray grizzle rooster hackles. He was obviously tying dry flies, which very well could have been Adamses, since that pattern calls for a brown mixed with grizzly hackle collar. He may have used the "extra select" grizzly hackle for the fly collar and selected grizzly hackle point tips off the regular cape for winging.

Two years before his death in 1955, Don Martinez was still praising dry flies that combined brown and grizzly hackle. In a June 1953 *Field & Stream* article titled "The Right Dry Fly," he wrote, "On first thought, I'm of the school that considers fly pattern unimportant, but on first reflection I have to confess that like all other anglers I'm a sucker for some. The Adams and similar flies combining a brown and a Plymouth Rock [grizzly] hackle will get my vote every time."

The Whitcraft, or Quill Adams, another dry fly that used a grizzly and brown hackle mix, is attributed to Martinez. But it is unclear if he cocreated the pattern or was largely responsible for promoting it, or both. Many references give him full credit for the fly, basically an Adams with a quill body. In *Fishing Flies and Fly Tying* (1951), fly tier William F. Blades listed the Whitcraft as a Martinez fly. The pattern used blue and yellow macaw quill for the body, brown hackle tails, a mix of grizzly and brown for the hackle collar, and grizzly hackle points for winging.

Before Martinez left West Yellowstone in the World War II years and relocated to Jackson Hole country in Wyoming, he tied flies for Bob Carmichael's Moose, Wyoming, fly shop. An interesting April 6, 1946, letter that Carmichael sent to author and fly fisher J. Edson Leonard, which appeared in Leonard's classic *Flies* (1960), describes the origin of the Whitcraft and Don Martinez's association with it. "Not being completely satisfied with the bulkiness of either the Adams or Adams (Ray Bergman) [Bergman preferred fully spent wings and grizzly hackle barb tails] and also the golden pheasant tail (not durable or especially attractive) I had Martinez, then in West Yellowstone, tie for me a macaw quill bodied R.I. red, spike tail, and very sparse mixed (Adams hackle) with Plymouth Rock hackle point, upright wings… From the start the pattern was deadly. Many of my customers or 'dudes' we were teaching or guiding used it almost exclusively. Fishermen with no dry-fly experience at all took limits consistently. Wanting a name for the new 'killer-diller,' and already having a 'Carmichael' I decided to call it 'Whitcraft' in honor of my fishing pal, Tom Whitcraft, the famous fishing superintendent of the Grand Teton National Park. It is our belief that Tom Whitcraft will become immortal from the popularity of this grand dry-fly. Incidentally, Martinez, who at that time was tieing [*sic*] flies for me, supplied some of his other customers with the pattern, calling it a 'Quill Adams.'"

Other flies are also associated with Martinez, including the Bradley M dry fly, a pattern similar to the Whitcraft that substituted Rhode Island Red hackle point wings for grizzly to imitate the local Brown Drake mayfly. He also tied a variety of patterns, standard wet flies and steelhead flies among them, but he tied mostly dry flies.

It has been said that an array of boxes could be found on Martinez's tying table, filled with completed orders including Bivisibles, Spiders, Hair-Wing Wulffs, and no doubt his still famous Martinez Black Nymph. His flies had what George Grant called "the unmistakable touch of a master craftsman." Martinez liked his dry flies tied so that they could support themselves, hook off a tabletop, by both stiff-hackle tails and collar.

In remembering Martinez's dry flies, Cal Dunbar said, "Don's flies are easily recognized. He tied according to what is known as the Catskill school (after the tiers of the New York State Catskill rivers area). This means a graceful long tail; a slender, beautifully tapered body; long, stiff hackles to support the fly well off the surface; and dainty, graceful wings. The minimal bodied fly is supported by the tail and the hackles with a buoyancy imitating the natural."

Martinez brought that style to the West, but over time his dry-fly style changed, adapting to the needs of the western fly angler. In his Spring 1982 *American Fly Fisher* article, George Grant cited a letter Martinez wrote in 1939 to iconic

Catskill fly angler Preston Jennings, in which he expressed his initial dismay concerning adapting his dry-fly tying style to western desires: "For my own use, and for a limited number of my customers I prefer a fly with scanty hackle. However, in order to please the majority of the people I work for it is necessary to make a pretty bulky fly."

Martinez's promotion of his Rough Water series of dry flies, brought to the attention of many anglers through the second edition of Ray Bergman's *Trout* (1952), reflected his change of heart in tying to please the western angler. These were not the slender-bodied, delicate dry flies that Martinez cherished and had hoped to colonize the West with; they are fat-bodied, dyed blue, yellow, or natural white clipped caribou dry flies tied on heavy-wire hooks, created for rough-water streams like the lower Madison in Montana or the Snake in Idaho. Martinez called these flies "effective and a downright pleasure to use."

The Rough Water flies were born out of the influences of Joe Messinger Sr.'s Irresistible—Martinez said as much in correspondence he had with A. J. McClane, published in McClane's *Practical Fly Fisherman* (1953). Martinez explained that "these bulky flies not only worked fully as well as the slim-bodied affairs we'd always used in the past; they worked even better." Martinez recognized that the caribou hair bodies tended to soak up water and become waterlogged, and he looked for a solution to seal off the hollow hairs. He tried treating the flies with common Mucilin combined with squeezing and milking out the water. Coating the hair bodies with DuPont auto fabric sealer was equally ineffective—all that did was leave a waxy coating on the fly, gumming up the hackles. Yet the flies did perform, even on surprisingly slow-moving water on the Firehole in Yellowstone National Park and Flat Creek at Jackson, Wyoming.

Don Martinez might have wished to be remembered for his theories concerning dry-fly design, or perhaps for his cleverly crafted long-stemmed, hand-held "pin" tying vise, which enabled him to tie flies at his armchair. However, he is most associated with the common Woolly Worm fly, a pattern that he did not invent but indeed promoted and popularized.

In the second edition of Bergman's *Trout*, Martinez acknowledged that the famous Woolly Worm was "not original with me," but instead came from a Missouri bass fly. According to McClane in *Practical Fly Fisherman*, the fly went all the way back to Izaak Walton and eventually was introduced into Ozark bass waters in the 1920s. In its Ozark form, the fly was tied yellow, but it evolved into a black shade once it hit western trout waters. McClane wrote that Walter Bales from Kansas City, Missouri, took a prizewinning rainbow on the fly in 1935 and passed the pattern on to Martinez at West Yellowstone. "Don nursed it along," McClane said. Soon the fly became a well-known and frequently fished western trout pattern.

McClane described the palmer hackle on the Woolly Worm as being intentionally wound with the barbs directed forward toward the eye, although most tiers today pay little attention to the hackle barb direction. McClane wrote that "this causes the fibers to point forward at rest, resulting in a marked breathing action when the fly is fished stop and go." George Grant, in his 1982 *American Fly Fisher* tribute to Martinez, also mentioned the hackle barbs pointing forward and noted that from observation of actual flies, the hackle was tied in at the bend by the quill butt first, then wound forward, resulting in a gradual taper of hackle barb length from back to front. The Jack Atherton trout-fly illustrations that appeared in John McDonald's classic May 1946 *Fortune* article "Fly Fishing and Trout Flies" featured the Woolly Worm among the western pack, with the hackle wound in this fashion. The caption attributed the example to Don Martinez, West Yellowstone, Montana.

In addition to the Woolly Worm, McClane also mentioned other Martinez patterns, such as the Dunham, a high floater that was intended to be fished blind during nonhatch periods, enticing fish to it from the bottom. An interesting pattern, the Dunham sported a blue and yellow macaw quill body along with red golden pheasant breast feather tailing. The hackle collar consisted of coch-y-bondhu at the rear and dyed blue grizzly up front near the hook eye. Martinez's Dunham inspired Ray Bergman to develop the Hopkins Variant, a dry fly that borrowed some of the Dunham's features. Both the Dunham and the Hopkins Variant are illustrated in Bergman's *With Fly Plug, and Bait* (1947). Of Martinez's Dunham, Bergman wrote, "It was first introduced to me by Don Martinez of West Yellowstone, Montana, and proved so good since that I've kept using it." Bergman continued with a lengthy anecdote concerning an experience with the fly that proved to him "the Dunham was a fly worth considering."

Bergman was on a tributary of the Green River at Pinedale, Wyoming, in mid-September, fishing through snow and sleet squalls. He was so cold and wet, with water slopping over into his waders, that he had to go to shore and build a fire to thaw him out. When the sun finally returned, trout started to rise, but all of his favorite patterns were refused. Then he tied on a Martinez size 12 Dunham. "I hadn't yet used it, but thought this was as good a time as any," Bergman wrote. Another squall came, hitting Bergman square in his face, blocking his vision. He lifted his hand with the rod to shield his face, finding that a fine trout was on the line. Martinez's Dunham performed well that day, fished through the snow squalls, and convinced Ray Bergman that the fly was worthy of his box.

Other Martinez flies that A. J. McClane and Ray Bergman wrote about included the Grovont Shellback Nymph, Ginger Quill Nymph, Red Quill Nymph, and Jungle Variant dry fly. The majority of these flies, favorites of Don Martinez, have vanished from the fly boxes of the American fly angler. However, they have a place in our angling history and serve as a reminder of Don Martinez and his fly-tying art.

Phantom Wooly Worm [*sic*], tied by Mike Valla. Chauncy K. Lively introduced this variation of the famous Woolly pattern, palmered with badger hackle, in an article in the April 1965 issue of *Pennsylvania Angler*. He said that even beginners can tie the pattern, which also holds true for the original pattern.

Golden Quail, tied by Mike Valla. In a later edition of *Trout*, Ray Bergman quoted Martinez as saying that the Golden Quail "has nothing special to recommend it but good looks, but that goes for quite a few things, and people in this world are becoming more philosophical." He tied it in hook #12-14 because the quail feathers he used fit those hooks sizes.

Along the Snake River near Jackson Hole, Wyoming. After leaving West Yellowstone, Montana, Martinez operated a shop during World War II in the picturesque Jackson Hole region in Wyoming. Martinez's patterns were embraced in Jackson Hole, yet the scenery in Teton Mountains region was not enough to hold him there.

Ginger Quill Nymph, tied by Mike Valla. A. J. McClane mentioned this pattern in his 1953 *Practical Fly Fisherman*. The pattern again demonstrates Martinez's liking for macaw quill bodies, on both dry flies and nymphs.

Whitcraft, or Quill Adams, tied by Mike Valla. Martinez did much to promote and popularize this effective pattern, a spin-off of the famous Adams dry fly. Martinez favored macaw quill bodies in many of his patterns.

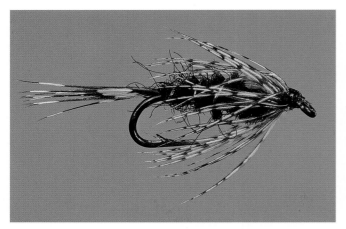

Martinez Black Nymph, tied by Don Lieb. The Martinez Black was a popular fly sold by Buz Buszek out of his shop in Visalia, California. Lieb, now in his 90s, tied the pattern for Buszek's shop back in the mid-1960s, after Buz died.

Rough Water Yellow, tied by Mike Valla. Martinez's promotion of his Rough Water series of dry flies demonstrated his change of heart to please the western angler. These were not the slender-bodied, delicate eastern-style dry flies that Martinez cherished.

Martinez created his Rough Water dry flies for the swift and tumbling waters found on the lower Madison River in Montana. Don Martinez corresponded with author Ray Bergman and provided him with details concerning many of his patterns, including his Rough Water dry flies.

Dunham, tied by Mike Valla. The fly is a high floater that was intended to be fished blind during nonhatch periods, enticing fish to it from the bottom. An interesting pattern, the Dunham sported a blue and yellow macaw quill body along with red golden pheasant breast feather tailing.

Hopkins Variant, tied by Mike Valla. Martinez's Dunham inspired Bergman to develop a dry fly, the Hopkins Variant, which borrowed some of the Dunham's features.

CHAPTER 35

Wayne "Buz" Buszek
(1912–1965)

Wayne "Buz" Buszek of Visalia, California, operated one of the most popular fly shops in the country. He developed patterns such as the Western Coachman, Kings River Caddis, and Buz Hopper. *Rosalie Buszek collection*

It has been said that Wayne "Buz" Buszek had the kind of hands and fingers that a piano player would envy. His daughter, Rosalie Powell, remembered his ability to completely peel an orange in one continuous ribbon, delighting children in his presence. But it was Buszek's dexterity at the vise that launched his reputation as a talented and influential West Coast fly tier. Almost half a century after his death in 1965, the fly patterns he created or popularized are still being discussed among those that were closest to him.

Fly angler David Johnson has taken on the role of a Buz Buszek historian. In the late 1990s, Johnson conducted taped interviews with a circle of Buz's family members and followers—Rosalie Powell and her husband, Mickey Powell; Judy O'Key; Darwin Atkin; Wayne Wolf; Alan Brazill; and Don Lieb. Much of the material in this chapter was obtained from those interviews along with printed materials kindly provided by David Johnson. Don Lieb, in his mid-90s at the time of this writing and an avid fly angler, offered additional recent insights into Buszek, his history, and his flies.

Western Coachman, tied by Wayne "Buz" Buszek. The Western Coachman, Buz's signature pattern, soon colonized the entire country. *Don Lieb collection*

Wayne Buszek was born in Porterville, California, on March 6, 1912. Wayne Wolf, who knew Buz when they were neighborhood boys in Lindsay, California, called him "an entomologist, self-made, from the get-go," which was later expressed in his fly tying. Wolf remembered that the young Buszek was a naturalist who knew the names of practically every wildflower in the mountains. When he was 10 or 12, Buszek began fishing, at first with bait—salmon eggs and crickets. But he soon switched to fly fishing and made the natural progression to tying trout flies.

By the age of 19 or 20, while working as a U.S. mail carrier, Buszek started tying flies for his own use and then started selling them to an eager group of older fly anglers. Wolf explained: "It was apparent to those of us who could see his product that this was something which was exceptional because anything he tied beat anything we could buy in stores. He quickly built up a clientele who were looking for them, ordinarily older fishermen; the younger group in those days almost confined themselves to bait fishing."

Mickey Powell recalled that Buz's fly-tying business evolved; in the beginning he was giving away flies, but soon the numbers of anglers offering to purchase his flies grew, and he eventually decided to leave his job with the Postal Service. Buz's shop, Powell further explained, began in the back bedroom of his home in Visalia, California, where he lived with his wife, Virginia, and then moved to a nook area off the kitchen. Powell described the scene at the Buszek home in the early years: "[Customers] simply knocked on the front door, and when Virginia answered, they walked straight through the living room, across Virginia's carpet and out to the shop out back. It didn't matter if they were wearing waders or field boots."

By the early to mid-1950s, Buz's Fly and Tackle Shop started to mature and eventually expanded into a new home with a large garage necessary to house the growing operation. Buszek now entered the mail-order fly-tying materials business, purchasing the Feather River Trading Company in Rough and Ready, California, which had been his primary source of wholesale materials. He modeled the business after Dan Bailey's operation in Montana and other catalog establishments such as E. Hille in Pennsylvania and Reed's in New Jersey. Virginia was responsible for the growing fly-tying materials part of the operation, and sales of materials contributed substantially to their bottom line, but Buz's flies were always in demand. To keep up with and even ahead of demand, Buz brought wholesale tiers who worked out of their homes into the operation. Wholesale flies were sold to various sport shops throughout the country, but Buz insisted on tying the flies for retail sales himself.

There is no doubt that retail customers were after several popular fly patterns associated with Buszek. Buz helped popularize patterns such as the Prince Nymph, but his own patterns included the Kings River Caddis, Western Coach-

Don Lieb at his tying bench in Visalia. Don, who knew Buz well, tied flies for the Buszek shop after Buz died in 1965. Now in his mid-90s, Lieb is still tying superb examples of Buz's favorite patterns. *Photo by David Johnson*

man, and Buz's Hopper. As is true with many popular fly patterns, some were created as adaptations of others already in existence. The Western Coachman was a spin-off of a fly called the Old Grey Mare. Mickey Powell tells the story: "The Western Coachman is the most notable one [of Buz's flies]. Buz would be the first to say that no contemporary fly tier really invented anything new. Buz always contended that most new patterns were simply variations of something that already existed. And he would be the first to concede that the Western Coachman was no more than that. He was shown a fly called the Old Grey Mare. It was a fly that had a red floss body and a green chenille butt, and no bump of chenille or other material in front of the red floss body. Otherwise it was like a Coachman."

Powell explained that the Western Coachman was most popular in its wet-fly version, although Buz also offered a dry-fly version that didn't sell nearly as well. Changing standard white duck quill wings found on a regular Coachman to coarse hair wings caused the fly to behave differently when fished in water. Powell believed that unlike bucktail or calf tail, which allowed the fly to sink, the utilization of coarse deer body hair allowed it to ride just under the water surface; it didn't fully sink or fully float. The visibility was still there, allowing anglers to detect fish strikes, yet drag on a swing didn't cause a wake on the surface. Don Lieb described the Western Coachman as "not truly a wet fly but rather a 'semi' dry fly."

The Western Coachman had its birth in 1934. But in 1949, the fly flew above the radar when it was used for promotional purposes. Dr. Eugene Mathias, one of Buz's angling and tying companions, told the story in the May 1984 issue of *Fly Tyer* that the Pacific Olive Company sent out more than 2,000 Western Coachman flies as a sales gimmick. Yet it was the fly's effectiveness that contributed to its popularity, its productivity proven on rivers like the Kaweah, Tule, Kern, and Kings in central California. After a dozen years fishing the Western Coachman with great success, beginning on the Tule River, Buz wrote to author Ray Bergman singing the virtues of the new pattern that had colonized the East Coast. The fly soon made appearances in various fly-fishing books and manuals.

In another story that was published in *Kaweah Flyfishers*, Mathias cited fly tier and angler Jack Dennis's remembrances of the Western Coachman. Dennis used the fly in both wet-fly and dry-fly styles, using stiffer hackle when a better float was desired. He reported great results fishing the fly in Idaho, Montana, and Wyoming but added that eastern fly anglers found it productive as well. In his popular *Western Trout Fly Tying Manual* (1974), Dennis wrote of the Western Coachman, "I learned this pattern from my father who once owned a tackle shop in Jackson Hole, Wyoming during the late 40s. In those days it was customary for a tackle shop owner to hire local talent to tie his flies, but Buz's flies were so well tied that my father decided to have this California tyer produce all the

Buz wrote to angling author Ray Bergman, describing the development and success of the Western Coachman. *Jill and Mark Schwarz collection*

flies for his customers. It was the close scrutiny of Buz's fine work that helped me develop some of my own tying methods and I will be eternally grateful to him for this."

Dennis's book also mentioned another fly pattern synonymous with Buz Buszek—the Kings River Caddis. The Rio de los Santos Reyes ("River of the Holy Kings"), as the Kings River was originally named, harbored some large trout that began appearing below the Army Corps of Engineers–constructed Pine Flat Dam in the San Joaquin Valley, near Piedra, California. In the same *Kaweah Flyfishers* story, Mathias had this to say about the fly, quoting Buz's own words: "Several seasons ago a population of large rainbows appeared below the new dam on the Kings River. They were heavily fished and soon begun refusing every offering. Caddis flies were common on the river, hatching in droves late into the evening. I worked out this pattern to match the hatch and it proved, and still is successful."

The Kings River Caddis, which others have said was already in Buz's hands before the dam was built, proved effective on that water, then soon became popular on other western rivers and eventually throughout the country. Other early caddisfly imitations were developed for western waters, like Don Hager's Buck Caddis. Hager's pattern, referenced by J. Edson Leonard in his book *Flies* (1960), was winged with fine deer hair. Leonard, an East Coast tier, described an imitation called the Green Caddis, an olive-hackled creation that used a dyed green raffia grass body. The wings were crafted from dark brown mottled turkey, the material Buszek used in his Kings River creation.

Leonard also described using "reverse quill wings" for caddis and Alderflies by cutting two quill slips and tying them in back and over the body, concave sides together. Buszek's Kings River pattern, however, had one slip of folded turkey wing quill. Mathias said, "The wing on the Kings River Caddis was, again, an innovative step. He used brown mottled turkey wing by folding a strip in half and then tying the thinner tip in first. The wing now centers over the body nicely, and after clipping the tip obliquely it looks exactly like the real caddis wing."

Turkey quill resembles the wing coloration found in certain species of caddisflies. Other, more contemporary fly tiers have also used it in their own creations. Gary LaFontaine, in his book *Caddisflies* (1989), commented that quill-wing caddis imitations usually are modeled after the old British Frederick Halford patterns or Buz Buszek's Kings River Caddis. LaFontaine listed a Turkey Wing Caddis that was sent to him by Ron Zowarsky. This fly appears to have Buszek influences, with a brown fur body, turkey wings cut to shape, and brown hackle collar. While LaFontaine acknowledged the fragile nature of turkey quill, he admitted its effectiveness when superselective trout were keying in on caddis wing coloration. "No other material has worked quite as well as turkey quill for precise imitation," he said.

Buz's shop catalog. Buz's provided thousands of flies for anglers throughout the country. Many obscure patterns, such as the Prince Nymph, Float-N-Fool, and Strawberry Roan became popular through Buszek, who distributed them nationally. Many tiers from that era fondly remember the catalog cover, featuring a bald-necked rooster.

Buz Buszek may have not been the first to recognize the value of using turkey quill for caddisfly winging, but there is no doubt that his Kings River Caddis helped draw attention to the material for that use. Moreover, Buszek's classic pattern was instrumental in drawing attention to caddisfly imitations and their importance on American trout stream waters.

Fly tier and writer Ted Niemeyer, who has been involved with the sport for many decades, offered an interesting observation concerning caddisfly patterns in a 1977 article in *Fly Fisherman* titled "The Caddis Explosion": "The evolution of caddis fly patterns is unusual in that it has not followed the geographic romance of the mayfly. Mayfly patterns devel-

oped in Europe were sent to America, then spread from the East coast to the West coast, changing in style at various stops along the way. What we are now developing in caddis patterns first evolved from a basic foundation of caddis fly imitations produced by Western tiers."

Eastern fly anglers were aware that caddis played an important role in a trout's diet, yet their attitudes remained primarily mayfly-centric. In *Fishing the Dry Fly as a Living Insect* (1972), East Coast caddis aficionado Leonard M. Wright called it "the fly that fishermen forgot." Wright lamented, "American trout fishing was suffering from caddis neglect." There were a few caddis dry flies in use, such as the famous Pennsylvania born Henryville Special, but not many. Wright's observations led him to develop his signature fly, the Fluttering Caddis. In his opening chapter, Wright had everything to say about the iconic East Coast fly anglers who had let the bug down, but nothing about West Coasters like Buszek, who had been tying and selling his Kings River fly by the hundreds.

However, just before the release of Wright's book, some very competent East Coast tiers began experimenting with caddis dry flies and writing about their creations. Some showed morphologic similarities to Buszek's fly. In a January 1969 *Pennsylvania Angler* article titled "A Dry Fly Caddis Pattern," Chauncy K. Lively, one of the most creative fly tiers of his era, reported on a pattern he called the Cinnamon Sedge. As is true with the Kings River Caddis, Lively's fly employed folded turkey quill, but Lively gave it additional floating capability through the use of hackle palmer along the fur body. Later, in a November 1972 *Pennsylvania Angler* article, Lively introduced his Early Black Caddis. This pattern also had folded quill, this time black duck quill, snipped obliquely at the rear just as on Buszek's his Kings River pattern.

It is not known whether Lively actually studied Buszek's fly, but it would have been hard for him not to have been aware of it. The Kings River Caddis had already landed on the East Coast, appearing in mail-order publications such as the Orvis catalog. In *The Book of Fly Patterns* (1987), fly-tying author Eric Leiser devoted an entire chapter to caddis imitations. Many of the patterns he presented here had first emerged in *The Caddis and the Angler* (1977), a title Leiser coauthored with Larry Solomon. Among the 50 creations Leiser described was Buz Buszek's Kings River Caddis. Definite Buszek influence was also seen in the Flat Wing Caddis, Nat's Caddis, and the Vincent Sedge, which is tied with mottled turkey, V-notched at the rear of the quill.

Together with the Western Coachman, Buszek's Kings River Caddis evolved into a classic trout fly, still discussed among caddis aficionados coast to coast.

Strawberry Roan, tied by Don Lieb. This was another popular dry fly sold at the Buszek shop.

Float-N-Fool, tied by Don Lieb. Buz popularized this high-floating dry fly. He favored the qualities of white calftail hair for both the fly tail and hackle post. The pattern was once featured as the fly of the month by *Field & Stream* magazine.

Zug Bug, tied by Don Lieb. Buz did not originate the pattern—he helped popularize its effectiveness through the pages of his catalog.

Buz's
TROUT FLIES
Hand-tied on HIGHEST QUALITY HOOKS
W. Buszek
Visalia, California
Old Grey Mare
8
CPC

Old Grey Mare, mounted on a sales card, from Buszek's fly shop. This pattern was the precursor to Buz's Western Coachman. *David Johnson collection*

Old Grey Mare, the precursor for Buz's Western Coachman, tied by Don Lieb.

Prince Nymph, tied by Don Lieb. Although the Prince Nymph was not original with Buszek, he helped put the fly on the map—and in the fly boxes of thousands of anglers who purchased the fly through his shop. Buszek met the fly's creator, Doug Prince, on the Kings River. Prince called it a Brown Forked-Tail Nymph; Buz dubbed it the Prince Nymph and sold it in large quantities.

Kings River, California, the birthplace of the Kings River Caddis. *Photo by David Johnson*

Buszek's Hopper, tied by Don Lieb. Buz created his Hopper pattern in 1943 in Jackson Hole, Wyoming. Grasshoppers were falling into Flat Creek when Buszek tied the pattern on the spot. He originally named it a Caddis Fly, but it later became known as Buszek's Hopper.

Kings River Caddis, tied by Don Lieb of Visalia, California. The pattern was first field-tested by Buz Buszek on the Kings River in California. It was one of the first really effective caddis imitations tied, and it served as the foundation for many others that followed.

CHAPTER 36

C. Jim Pray
(1885–1952)

C. Jim Pray of Eureka, California. Pray's Optic patterns were recognized by angling authors such as William Sturgis and Joseph D. Bates Jr.

I n "The Wizard of West Coast Flies," an article that appeared in the April 1952 issue of *True: The Man's Magazine*, Thomas Hardin described a fly tier from Eureka, California, who helped end a prevailing fishing myth. "For a hundred years it was common knowledge that western salmon would not take a fly. That piece of misinformation has largely been wiped out now, and to Jim Pray goes most of the credit." Salmon and steelhead were taken on flies in western waters such as Pray's beloved Eel River at Eureka, but not many relative to the large numbers of fly anglers attempting to do so. C. Jim Pray developed flies that helped change the meager performance experienced by these fly anglers. The story behind Pray's signature flies begins in his boyhood.

Jim Pray was born in Ann Arbor, Michigan, in 1885. He tied his first fishing flies at age eight, after observing anglers fishing the Huron River, a stream that edged the city. Pray began reading books on the subject; he was greatly influenced by Mary Orvis Marbury's *Favorite Flies and Their Histories* (1955). Tying without a vise, something Pray practiced his entire career, he soon

Optic steelhead fly, tied by C. Jim Pray. Pray's unique Optic fly series enhanced winter fly-fishing experiences on the Eel River in California. Pray created other steelhead patterns, but many consider the large, bead-head Optic series his signature flies. *Bill Leary collection*

231

filled his box with colorful flies featured in Marbury's book, Parmachene Belle, Lord Baltimore, Reuben Wood, and Colonel Fuller among them.

Pray eventually left the Huron River bass stretches, where he fished those early colorful patterns. When he was 23, Pray settled on the Eel River at Scotia, California, where he worked in a lumbermill. He left the area after a year, moving around California for some time, but eventually returned to the banks of the Eel at Eureka. "He couldn't buy a cup of coffee when he arrived," Hardin wrote in his story. "He camped near the edge of town and traded flies for groceries, laundry and other essentials." He later became involved in real estate, but the Depression destroyed these endeavors, leaving Pray penniless. He then decided to switch his efforts to professional fly tying. Before getting a shop, Pray tied flies on the mezzanine of a bakery. It was from these beginnings that his signature fly patterns were born.

Among his many popular flies, the Optic is one of his most famous. It's an odd-looking fly with a tinsel body on a heavy, often short-shank hook, its big round head crafted from a brass bead painted with piercing pupils. In his *Streamer Fly Tying and Fishing* (1966), Joseph D. Bates Jr. quoted the great Klamath River steelheader Peter J. Schwab, who called the Optic flies "quaint and comical." Jim Pray didn't invent the Optic fly concept, but he brought great attention to that type of pattern. In *Rising Trout* (1978), Charles K. Fox reported that Carry Manning was tying Optic bucktails in the early 1930s. According to Hardin, in 1938, a record brown trout was taken on a big-eyed pattern, but that fly style was crafted from cork and plastic heads and glass eyes, materials that were unsuitable for western waters. Yet even before that record trout was taken, Joseph D. Bates Jr. wrote in *Streamer Fly Tying and Fishing* (1966) that W. H. Hobbs of Derby, Connecticut, painted eyes on flies he called Optic Bucktails, although these were not tied with bead heads.

What was needed on the big salmon and steelhead rivers, such as the Eel, was a pattern designed to quickly sink. To meet that objective, Pray attached a metal bead at the hook eye. He finished the fly head by coating the bead with lacquer and painting a black pupil centered on a white iris. He then attached back bucktail projecting rearward from the bead head.

Field-testing on the Eel the following morning produced a 10-pound steelhead that slammed Jim Pray's Optic. Silver salmon also willingly accepted the big-eyed pattern. The Black Optic was born, the first of what Hardin called Pray's "owl-eyed" Optic fly series. The Optic flies were quickly accepted among steelhead and salmon-fly anglers as effective fish takers. From 1940 to 1947, Pray caught more than 500 steelhead on the Red Optic.

The "owl-eyed" flies also caught the attention of East Coast anglers and writers such as Joseph D. Bates Jr., with whom Pray corresponded, explaining some of the details be-

hind the creation of the Optic patterns. Bates's *Streamer Fly Tying and Fishing* quoted Jim Pray's comments concerning the Optic patterns, particularly the Cock Robin Optic. In November 1940, the first winter silver salmon and steelhead runs entering the Eel River held for a period of time around Cock Robin Island before heading for the pools beyond the tidewater. The Cock Robin Optic was named for that section of the Eel River where anglers found this pattern particularly productive. The highly popular Orange and Red Optics were found to be great fish takers in the upstream sections of the river. The Red Optic received greater attention after it was described in Ted Trueblood's December 1973 *Field & Stream* article "An Outdoor Philosophy" and many steelhead fly-fishing books that followed. At least two versions of the Red Optic appear in print.

Hardin wrote in his article that the Red Optic was tied with painted *black and white eyes*, with a silver tinsel body topped with red bucktail and then yellow polar bear hair. The illustrations provided by artist and fly angler Jack Atherton depict the black and white eyes. However, Bates said in

Peter Schwab (left) and Jim Pray gazing down their favorite river, the Eel. Schwab, a noted outdoor writer and Pray's close fishing friend, was inspired by Pray's patterns and tying techniques. *Winston Rod Company collection*

Streamer Fly Tying and Fishing that the Red Optic should be tied with *yellow and black eyes*, with red and yellow hair topping the tinsel body. An original Pray-tied Red Optic appears in Bates's fly plates, featuring the yellow and black eyes. But in *Steelhead Fly Fishing and Flies* (1976), Trey Combs also described the pattern as having *black and white eyes*. His version called for red bucktail wings, with no mention of yellow polar bear or other yellow hair. Combs wrote of the Red Optic, "Many anglers would seek out the Eel River's fall and winter steelhead with no other fly."

Although Optic flies are considered Jim Pray's signature patterns, he is also remembered for other patterns that have survived many years after they were created. In a thought-provoking story that appeared in the December 1973 issue of *Field & Stream*, titled "An Outdoor Philosophy," Ted Trueblood wrote, "Despite the fact that he died in 1952, I believe Jim Pray originated more good steelhead patterns than anyone else—the Optic series, the Red, Black, Cock Robin and Orange Optics; Thor, Carter, Silver Demon and Black Demon—plus adapted many old wet-fly patterns to steelhead and West Coast salmon fishing." Two original Pray-tied flies Trueblood mentioned, the Black Demon and Thor, appear in Bates's *Streamer Fly Tying and Fishing* color plates. The Demons and Thor have interesting histories.

The Silver Demon and Black Demon were standard steelhead patterns back in Jim Pray's era. Both were born from the Golden Demon pattern, an import from New Zealand in 1933 or 1934. When Fred Burnham and Zane Grey brought the fly from Down Under to the West Coast steelhead rivers, it was immediately embraced and accounted for many fine catches on the Eel River. In its original recipe, the Golden Demon featured a gold body, brown mallard wing, orange hackle, and jungle cock eye shoulders. Jim Pray decided to tweak the pattern, making it brighter by using silver tinsel for the body and teal for wings, and eliminating the jungle cock. Pray's Silver Demon pattern was created in 1935, and it quickly outsold the popular Golden Demon fly. His effective fly accounted for many steelhead, silver salmon, and king salmon. Similar to the Silver Demon, aside from its black hair wing, the Black Demon was created for use on the Klamath River in 1937.

The Demons and Optics aside, it might be argued that Jim Pray's Thor, first tied in 1936, remains his most popular if not his most well-known pattern. Perhaps the most extensive description of the Thor's history appears in Trey Combs's *Steelhead Fly Fishing and Flies*. It was Christmas evening 1936 when the Eel River's waters started rising fast from a rainstorm that lasted overnight. Eureka residents Walter J. Thoresen, Fred Blair, and Frank Toby were on Dungan Pool on the Eel by morning, facing hopeless conditions. The three decided to change plans based on prevailing water conditions and moved upstream to Fernbridge Pool on the same river, where they fished from rented boats. Thoresen was fishing his 9-foot, 7-ounce Leonard equipped with a Hardy reel

South Fork of the Eel River in California, where many an angler won a steelhead or salmon battle while fishing Pray's Optics and other patterns he originated. *Photo by Jeff Bright*

loaded with silk line. His leader tippet was attached to a new size 6 fly that his close friend Jim Pray had created the day before. The fly did not have a name at the time. The new fly performed well for Thoresen, resulting in steelhead ranging from 8 to 10 pounds. But shortly after these fish were boated, a grand steelhead weighing close to 18 pounds was taken on the fly. Soon Thoresen took his final fish, a 10-pounder.

The 18-pound steelhead won first prize in the 1936 *Field & Stream* fishing contest. Jim Pray decided to name the fly Thor, in honor of his friend and that catch, but it could well have been named the Christmas fly. Two years later, the Thor again captured first place in the *Field & Stream* contest when, fishing the Eel, Gene Sapp landed his Christmas Day 1938 17¾-pound steelhead on the fly. It wasn't long before the Thor appeared in other print.

William Bayard Sturgis's *Fly-Tying* (1940) featured 19 Pray-tied colorful steelhead flies on its jacket cover and inside

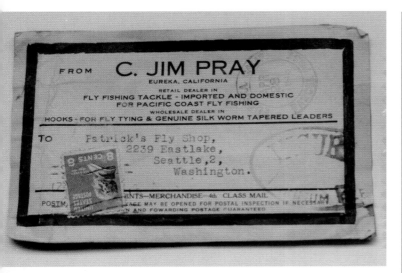

Jim Pray's mailing label. *Pat and Gary Waller collection*

plates. Many of these patterns were Pray's own creations, such as the Thor. In the book, Jim Pray was quoted concerning the Thor, which was tied almost by accident. "At the close of the day of tying, I was about to throw out some left-over material on the table. A piece of red chenille, and orange hackle, some white buck-hair, and a Rhode Island Red saddle hackle were part of what few pieces remained. So I tied these into a fly on a No. 6 hook, and Walter Thoresen of Eureka, later on in the fall took the first prize winning steelhead of the nation on this fly."

Because Sturgis's book was written so close to the time that Pray created the Thor, the dressing given is no doubt original, varying only slightly from Bates's description. Sturgis called for scarlet chenille, while Bates lists dark red chenille—minor points. Other references mention wine or claret shaded chenille. Hackle shade variations also occur: brown, Coachman brown, and furnace are frequently mentioned. However, Sturgis gave the following dressing: deep orange tail, scarlet body, mahogany hackle, and white bucktail wings. It is interesting that many fly tiers fret over their inability to acquire polar bear hair for wings when Pray also recommended bucktail as an option. Beyond material selection, Pray paid particular attention to the hook styles that would enable his patterns to perform best in the waters that they were designed for—steelhead and salmon streams.

Jim Pray preferred heavy-wire, short-shank Limerick bend hooks for his Optic flies. For his regular steelhead patterns,

he used both sproat and Limerick bend hooks, with both long and short shanks. Jim Pray was so particular about hooks that he decided to market his own signature steelhead hooks manufactured by Mustad; the boxes were labeled "Jim Pray's Special Steelhead Hooks." Contemporary tiers have used a variety of hook types and styles when crafting Pray patterns; the models that Pray originally used are largely unavailable.

In *Popular Fly Patterns* (1984), Terry Hellekson favored the Mustad 7079 Limerick bend hook for Pray's Optic series patterns. The heavy-wire 7079 has a slightly longer shank than Pray's original short-shank hook choice. In tying flies such as Pray's Silver Demon, Hellekson used an Eagle Claw 1197-N series nickel-plated hook; nickel-plated steelhead hooks were also recommended by Sturgis for silver-bodied steelhead flies.

Regardless of what model hook they were tied on, Jim Pray's patterns influenced other enthusiastic steelhead fly tiers long before Hellekson admired his creations. In *Fly-Fishing Pioneers & Legends of the Northwest* (2006), Jack Berryman said that noted steelheaders and fly experimenters Pete Schwab and Ralph Wahl created patterns and techniques similar to those originated by Pray. Wahl encouraged winter steelhead angling when few others recognized the potential for good sport during those months; he's considered a pioneer winter steelhead fly angler. Wahl's delightful February 1943 *Field & Stream* story, "Winter Steelhead on Flies," anticipated a growing enthusiasm for winter fly rodding. In his enlightening article, Wahl wrote, "It is freely predicted that fly-fishing will soon become an accepted method of taking winter steelheads in most of the rivers that empty into the ocean." Berryman wrote that Wahl's interest in the sport led to designing his own flies, such as bucktails named Lord Hamilton, Lady Hamilton, and his Painted Lady, created the year Jim Pray died of cancer on March 13, 1952. The three optic-headed patterns crafted by Wahl, based on Pray's influences, took large, prize-winning steelhead featured in the annual *Field & Stream* contest.

C. Jim Pray's steelhead flies served as the foundation for many steelhead and salmon patterns that followed. It might be argued that his "owl-eyed" flies were some of the very first patterns created that incorporated bead heads into fly patterns. His colorful steelhead patterns—Thor, Silver Demon, Carter's Dixie, Railbird, Improved Governor, and others— were among the first steelhead patterns developed, leaving a legacy for other steelhead tiers to admire and follow.

Yellow and White Optic, tying attributed to C. Jim Pray.

Squirrel Tail and Yellow Optic, tied by Pete Schwab. *Pat and Gary Waller collection*

Red and White Optic, tying attributed to C. Jim Pray. *Pat and Gary Waller collection*

Brown and White Optic, tied by Pete Schwab. *Pat and Gary Waller collection*

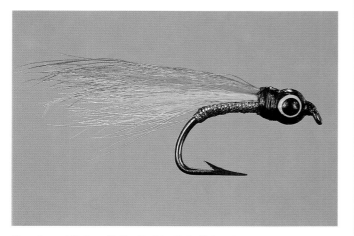

Orange and Yellow Optic, tied by Pete Schwab. *Pat and Gary Waller collection*

Black Demon, tied by Mike Valla. The Black Demon, a standard steelhead pattern in Pray's era, has been tied in different variations. The Black Demon that Pray tied for William Sturgis's book *Fly-Tying* (1940) is tailless; the example Pray tied for Joseph D. Bates Jr., which appears in *Streamer Fly Tying and Fishing* (1966), used barred wood-duck flank for tailing.

Silver Demon, tied by Mike Valla. Like the Black Demon, Pray's Silver Demon was born from the Golden Demon pattern, an import from New Zealand in 1933 or 1934.

Thor, tied by Mike Valla. One of the most popular patterns Jim Pray created, the fly was named in honor of his friend Walter Thoresen, who took an 18-pound steelhead on the pattern. The fish won first place in the 1936 *Field & Stream* fishing contest, and the Thor has been a popular pattern ever since.

CHAPTER 37

Ernest H. "Polly" Rosborough
(1902–1997)

Polly Rosborough at a tying demonstration. Rosborough developed a series of fuzzy nymphs that used blended furs for fly bodies. He is also one of the early fly tiers who promoted the use of synthetic yarns in some of his patterns. *Photo by Christine Fong*

Ernest H. "Polly" Rosborough experimented with a wide range of patterns, including wet flies, dry flies, streamers, steelhead flies, and bucktails. But as a fly tier, he is most remembered for his 25 classic fuzzy nymphs, innovative creations inspired through careful study of immature aquatic insects.

Studying natural nymphs and creating artificial flies that resembled or behaved like them was not new to the fly-angling world when Polly Rosborough presented his patterns in *Tying and Fishing the Fuzzy Nymphs* (1965). British anglers like G. E. M. Skues, Fred Shaw, and Eric Taverner used nymphs on their chalkstreams. Louis Rhead wrote in *American Trout-Stream Insects* (1916) about what he called "creepers" on his Catskill waters. In articles in *Sports Afield* and

Stone Fly Nymphs, tied by Polly Rosborough. From left: Golden Stone Fly Nymph, Little Yellow Stone Fly Nymph; bottom Dark Stone Fly Nymph. Rosborough presented all three of these nymphs in *Tying and Fishing the Fuzzy Nymphs*. While he sang the virtues of blended furs, Polly also promoted the use of synthetic yarns "for greater speed in tying." *Skip Hosfield collection*

Field & Stream, John Alden Knight and Edward Ringwood Hewitt told the interesting stories of their experiences on the Neversink River, where they studied nymphs in the 1930s, leading to their creation of flat-bodied artificials.

Knight and Hewitt brought new attention to nymph fly tying and fishing, but Pennsylvanians James Leisenring and Pete Hidy really got things going when *The Art of Tying the Wet Fly* was published in 1941. In it, Leisenring said, "Angling with the artificial nymph is one of the most interesting and effective methods of catching fish known to man, as well as the least understood in the minds of fly fishermen."

After Leisenring and Hidy, there was occasional exploration of nymph tying and fishing, such as found in the works of John Atherton, Preston Jennings, and Art Flick, and Jim Quick's little *Fishing the Nymph* (1960) also contributed to the topic. Before Quick's book was published, Ray Ovington's *How to Take Trout on Wet Flies and Nymphs* (1952) introduced nymph patterns created by Ed Sens. But then came Polly Rosborough. In *Tying and Fishing the Fuzzy Nymphs*, Rosborough gave explanations concerning the importance of nymphs and the creation of new patterns, all based on his careful observation in the field, not unlike Hewitt's early work.

Rosborough was unaware of Hewitt's work concerning nymphs and felt that fact worked to his advantage; indeed, his starting from scratch without preconceived notions about nymph design led him down a different path. Rosborough studied Hewitt's work in later years and commented that it was fine, but the topic was still in its infancy and in need of

Skip Hosfield at his tying table. Hosfield, who knew Rosborough as a friend for 38 years and considers him his mentor, said of Rosborough's flies, during a conversation with me, "His materials were cemented in with a special brand of lacquer at every stage. No trout could tear them apart." *Skip Hosfield collection*

expansion. Rosborough's book on fuzzy nymphs served that purpose, surpassing most anything else written on the subject. Ernest Schwiebert later wrote in *Nymphs* (1973), "Rosborough and his original research are perhaps the first major contribution to the theory and techniques of American nymph fishing since Leisenring."

Rosborough's book was originally published in 1965, then went out of print in 1968; Orvis published a revised and updated edition in 1969. Even before the book gained national recognition, fly anglers throughout the country were already becoming familiar with Rosborough and his work. In *The Practical Fly Fisherman* (1953), A. J. McClane wrote about Rosborough's Silver Garland Marabou streamer, as did Joseph D. Bates Jr. in *Streamer Fly Tying and Fishing* (1966) and Joe Brooks in *The Complete Book of Fly Fishing* (1958).

Bates's book featured a photo of an orange-feathered Silver Garland Marabou and gave the fly good coverage, mentioning the marabou shade variations, which included a white version. The white version of Rosborough's creation was responsible for Pennsylvanian Ed Shenk's netting of his record Letort Spring Run brown trout. The popular *McClane's Standard Fishing Encyclopedia* (1965) featured 30 Rosborough-tied steelhead flies in its color plates. McClane did the fly-tying world a tremendous service by providing a real look at Rosborough's tying talent. These color plates still serve as a great reference for steelhead anglers and tiers.

When *Field & Stream* fishing editor McClane wrote "Favorite Flies East to West" in the February 1967 issue, readers were further introduced to Rosborough's "top three patterns"—the Salmon Fly, Polar Chub Streamer, and one of his nymphs, the Black Drake. The short article also offered a brief glimpse into Polly Rosborough's background and his first experience with fishing. Fly-fishing historian Jack Berryman provided additional information about his early years in *Fly-Fishing Pioneers & Legends of the Northwest* (2006).

Rosborough was born on September 13, 1902, in Mammoth Springs, Arkansas. He caught his first fish, a 4-inch "punkinseed," when he was three years old, and he loved fishing from that day on. However, he fished little until age 19. While growing up, he lived in Oklahoma, Kansas, and Alberta, Canada, where he graduated from high school. It was during his employment with a box factory in the town of Bray, California, that coworkers nicknamed him "Polly," saying that he talked like "Polly the Parrot."

During his time in Bray, Rosborough fished nearby Butte Creek. At first he used worms, but he soon experimented with flies such as Black Gnats and March Browns. He moved around, working for several different box factories, and eventually in 1926 settled in Klamath Falls, Oregon, and then the nearby Chiloquin, where he lived for most of his life. The Williamson River inspired him, serving as his laboratory for developing fly patterns that he learned to tie with his own hands.

Rosborough's 1971 catalog. *Skip Hosfield collection*

His fly-tying endeavors were briefly interrupted while he served as a gunnery instructor in the army in World War II. After the war, he worked in lumbermills while resuming his studies of trout and their environment. In his 1967 *Field & Stream* article, A. J. McClane wrote that Rosborough took to the fly-tying vise for two reasons. One was that he couldn't purchase flies that closely imitated the natural insects he observed on his home waters. The other was that he got married, and tying was a source of income. Rosborough gave up working in lumbermills and became a professional fly tier, devoting his endeavors exclusively to the sport and pioneering the development of nymph patterns.

Nymphs were still mysterious to many fly anglers during Rosborough's early years. Anglers at that time were reluctant to fish nymphs for a couple good reasons. Outdoor writer Ted Trueblood, a Rosborough contemporary, wrote in his foreword to *Tying and Fishing the Fuzzy Nymphs*, "Year in and year out, cold weather and hot, high water and low, I think they [nymphs] are the most consistent trout catchers of all. Yet, far too many anglers hesitate to fish any nymph because they fear it is too difficult, or else they can't find the types and patterns that catch fish. Both problems are solved in the pages that follow."

In those pages, Rosborough provided readers with information on tying techniques that had evolved from what he called a "revolution" in his own style that began in the mid-1940s, which led to the development of his nymph series. The 1969 reprint of *Tying and Fishing the Fuzzy Nymphs* featured a 20-nymph series, some fuzzier than others. One of the fuzziest was the Casual Dress, an "experimental accident."

The Casual Dress proved its worth on the Deschutes River where it enters Wickiup Reservoir in central Oregon. It was Rosborough's first outing to that water, and in preparation for trip, he decided to tie a few new patterns for field-testing. He tied three of his experimental flies, all thrown together quickly in a "casual manner" on a bare hook. Before all three of the new flies were lost, Rosborough and his fishing partner landed four brown trout from 2 to 4 pounds and hooked up with several other fish.

The Casual Dress was an instant success; from that point forward, it was kept in standard production. Tied on a 3XL hook, the Casual Dress has scraggly muskrat for tail and body, with ostrich herl at the head. Laying a spindle of loose fur into a thread loop and twisting it forward along the hook shank creates the ragged, fuzzy body. Muskrat guard hairs serve as hackle.

The fly was so popular that Eric Leiser gave complete assembly instructions with supporting illustrations in *The Book of Fly Patterns* (1987). Leiser wrote that the fly "shows what can be accomplished by the proper use of both fur and fibers. The result here is an effective pattern that breathes and pulses with life when being fished." The pulsating action gives life to the fly, which is what makes it so attractive to fish. Hewitt's and Knight's hard and lifeless flies with lacquered bodies or those molded plastic imitative patterns lacked effectiveness because trout could more easily detect them as frauds.

It would have been interesting to witness a debate between Hewitt and Rosborough concerning the effectiveness of lacquered, flat, firm-bodied patterns versus fuzzy, pulsating nymphs. Hewitt soaked his nymphs in lacquer and squeezed them flat with the jaws of a pair of small pliers. Ed Hewitt and John Alden Knight were more concerned with the pattern's profile than its action in water. Rosborough gave careful thought to why hard-shell nymph patterns could not compare in effectiveness to his fuzzy nymphs. "It took a while for the light to dawn on me," he wrote, "but when it did, I thought, 'How stupid can one be? As we all know, a fish rejects an artificial immediately on detecting a fraud, so it follows that biting down on a hard body makes the fraud that much more quickly detected and rejected. Conversely, a soft body feels more natural, so it is held in the mouth that fraction of a second longer that allows for secure hooking.'"

The Williamson River served as Polly's laboratory for developing fly patterns that he learned to tie with his own hands. *Photo by Marlon Rampy*

Rosborough featured other soft-bodied yet very ragged fuzzy nymphs in his book that appeared as no more than fur wads on hooks—like the Hare's Ear and the Fledermouse. A 1949 pattern with that name, but slightly different in appearance, was discussed by A. J. McClane in *The Practical Fly Fisherman* and attributed to Jack Schneider, of San Jose, California. In a May 1963 *Field & Stream* story titled "Flies for Sophisticated Trout," Ted Trueblood explained that he was present when Schneider tied the very first Fleder*maus*. (There are two spellings attached to the fly; Trueblood used both in his writings.) Rosborough wrote in *Tying and Fishing the Fuzzy Nymphs*, "With one small exception my way of tying this nymph is modeled after the pattern pictured in Al McClane's old column in *Field & Stream*, 'One for the Book,' some fifteen years ago." McClane spelled the pattern "Fleder*mouse*" and Rosborough followed suit.

Beyond the fuzziest of nymphs, Polly Rosborough is also known for his stonefly patterns, among them the Dark Stone Fly Nymph, Little Yellow Stone Fly Nymph, and Golden Stone Fly Nymph. He also tied two interesting winged stones: the Dark Stone, also known as the Dark Salmon Fly, and the Golden Stone, or Light Salmon Fly.

These last two did not appear in his book, but the Dark Stone was featured in George F. Grant's *Montana Trout Flies* (1981). Grant wrote that Rosborough's Dark Stone was "a copy of what is known in Oregon as the "Dark Salmon Fly"

and was an effective pattern for the Montana "salmon fly." However, he said that Rosborough's Dark Stone *Nymph* was somewhat different in appearance from the Montana natural that eventually hatches into the airborne "salmon fly."

Rosborough's winged stones were as well constructed as his nymphs, known for their ability to withstand a battering from trout. Skip Hosfield, who knew Rosborough as a friend for 38 years and considers him his mentor, attributed the durability to the method used to tie them: "His materials were cemented in with a special brand of lacquer at every stage. No trout could tear them apart," Hosfield said in a recent conversation. Concerning Rosborough's fuzzy nymphs, Hosfield added, "His method of felting fur, rolling it into what he called a noodle, and spinning it into a thread loop to make a tapered segmented body simply astounded me."

Hosfield first met Rosborough on a late-October day in 1960. An eastern transplant from Ohio, Hosfield was already a good tier when he arrived in Oregon. Eager to meet Polly Rosborough, he and his friend George Twining came banging on Polly's door at 10:30 in the morning. They awakened Rosborough, and after some grumbling, he invited them in.

"Watching Polly tie and listening to him explain what he was doing, and why he did it in just that way, was a revelation to us," Hosfield wrote to me. "George and I were fairly competent amateur tiers, but we were from the East, and what we knew had been learned from books written by easterners of the Catskill school. Of course, we tied and fished with nymphs, but we had never seen nymphs like his. And the large wet flies and streamers used on the Williamson were all new to us. He was a great influence in my development as a fly tier."

Rosborough's flies were not works of art; they were fishing flies tied with particular attention to the colors exhibited by the natural insects. "He was a nut on dyeing materials," Hosfield told me in a recent chat. "And he didn't particularly like tying dry flies or streamers, but he did so to meet customer needs. And he didn't like to tie with biots. Biots, in Rosborough's mind, were too stiff, and he believed fish would likely spit out a nymph tied with that material."

Although Rosborough didn't like some materials, such as biots, Skip Hosfield said that he was open-minded about trying new things, including using synthetics in his patterns as far back as the 1960s. He would wander through fabric shops picking out yarns, and as long as the material was soft and fuzzy, he'd try it. Furs were always a favorite, but Rosborough blended in synthetics if the characteristics were just right for his needs.

Blending was accomplished by mixing the fur clippings into detergent water, stirring it up, and then squeezing it out. The result was a matted felt ball of sorts. In preparation for attachment to the hook shank, Rosborough rolled a portion of the matted fur between his hands to create a tapered spindle. He tied in this fur spindle along with a loop of thread the length of the noodle. He secured the fur and thread in his hackle pliers, then spun it all very tight. Once he wrapped it up a cement-covered hook shank, the fly body appeared segmented. Rosborough scored the tightly wrapped body with scissor points, making parallel strokes along the hook shank, which resulted in a frayed, fuzzy body. "Polly's flies were bullet-proof, indestructible," Hosfield said.

Many other fly tiers, such as Dave Whitlock, also took note of Rosborough's fuzzy and frayed pattern designs. In discussing one of his own creations, the Red Fox Squirrel-Hair Nymph, Whitlock wrote, "When I first began tying soft, fur-bodied nymphs I was most influenced by the flies tied and fished by Thom Green, Ted Trueblood and Polly Rosborough."

Polly Rosborough's little book, which explains in detail the techniques described above, is credited with being one of the first classic fly-fishing volumes written by a western author. His patterns led to heightened interest in the renowned waters he once studied and fished. Whether it be his popular Green Damsel nymph, a pattern Rosborough described in his book as being very effective when fished on Davis Lake, where damselfly hatches abound, the Casual Dress drifted through Oregon's Deschutes River riffles, or any one of his creations twitched through the Williamson, Rosborough's flies will catch fish, and the patterns and their creator alike will win the admiration of anglers who tie and use them.

Casual Dress, tied by Polly Rosborough. The Casual Dress, tied primarily with muskrat fur, was an "accidental" fly. Rosborough tied three of the flies, all thrown together quickly in a "casual manner" on a bare hook, for field-testing on the Deschutes River. *Catskill Fly Fishing Center and Museum collection*

Hare's Ear, tied by Polly Rosborough. The fly produced well for Rosborough on Oregon's Diamond Lake. It's tied with blended muskrat, rabbit, and mink furs. *Skip Hosfield collection*

Shrimp, tied by Polly Rosborough. Rosborough liked fishing this fly during the "doldrums," when fish were feeding deep or not at all. *Catskill Fly Fishing Center and Museum collection*

Silver Admiral, tied by Polly Rosborough. Joseph D. Bates Jr. featured this pattern in *Streamer Fly Tying and Fishing*, writing that the fly was useful for winter steelhead in turbid water. *Catskill Fly Fishing Center and Museum collection*

Midge Pupa patterns, tied by Polly Rosborough. Tied in several shades—tan to red. Rosborough found the flies effective for fish feeding on midges just barely submerged. He said, "You can't fish a nymph any shallower than this one without fishing it dry." *Catskill Fly Fishing Center and Museum collection*

Green Rock Worm, tied by Polly Rosborough. The fly represents caddisfly larva. Rosborough first fished it on Elk Creek, a tributary of the Klamath River. He used synthetic yarn to craft the pattern. *Catskill Fly Fishing Center and Museum collection*

Green Damsel Nymph, tied by Polly Rosborough. Rosborough said lake fishing is "truly where the Green Damsel comes into its own." *Catskill Fly Fishing Center and Museum collection*

Muskrat Nymph, tied by Polly Rosborough. Rosborough believed this pattern simulated a black midge larva or a gray crane fly nymph, since both have gray bodies and black heads. In his book, he provided detailed, step-by-step instructions for tying the fly. *Catskill Fly Fishing Center and Museum collection*

Fledermouse, tied by Polly Rosborough. Rosborough's pattern is tied a bit differently than Jack Schneider's 1949 Fleder*maus* pattern, which was featured in A. J. McClane's *Practical Fly Fisherman* and Ted Trueblood's May 1963 *Field & Stream* story, "Flies for Sophisticated Trout." *Skip Hosfield collection*

Dark Caddis Dry Fly, tied by Polly Rosborough. It has been said that Rosborough wasn't crazy about tying dry flies. *Skip Hosfield collection*

Black Drake Nymph, tied by Polly Rosborough. Rosborough wrote of the prolific Black Drake hatches on his local waters. Of the nymph, he humorously suggested that "if your wife has a pale maltese cat," you will have a constant supply of just the right fur shades. However, his suggestion of using muskrat, rabbit, and beaver dubbing blends might be a better choice. *Catskill Fly Fishing Center and Museum collection*

Silver Garland Marabou, tied by Polly Rosborough. Angling writers A. J. McClane, Joseph D. Bates Jr., and Ed Shenk all featured this popular pattern. Pennsylvanian Shenk took his monster Letort Spring Run brown trout called "Old George" on the pattern back in the mid-1960s. *Catskill Fly Fishing Center and Museum collection*

Dark Stone (or Salmon), tied by Polly Rosborough. In *Montana Trout Flies*, George Grant likened this pattern to a popular Oregon pattern called the Dark Salmon Fly. It's also tied in a dry-fly form. *Skip Hosfield collection*

Polar Chub, tied by Polly Rosborough. According to Bates, the pattern was first crafted in 1955. It represents many baitfish species and is fished in both fresh and salt water. It's tied with stainless steel or nickel finished hooks. *Catskill Fly Fishing Center and Museum collection*

Golden Stone Dry Fly, tied by Polly Rosborough. The pattern is a high floater and effective for stonefly hatches. *Catskill Fly Fishing Center and Museum collection*

CHAPTER 38

Ted Trueblood
(1913–1982)

Ted Trueblood in 1968. Trueblood embraced nymphs but recognized that the development of patterns did not involve the careful study and attention given to dry flies.

Ralph Wahl photo collection, Center for Pacific Northwest Studies, Western Washington University

In *Angler's Handbook* (1949), Ted Trueblood wrote, "No nymphs bear romantic names like wet and dry flies and so they are not well known. The average tackle salesman has only a hazy idea of the insect that any particular nymph is supposed to imitate and so he can be of no help to the beginner in this branch of trout fishing." It is interesting that Ted Trueblood's own nymph patterns were empty of anything "romantic," either in name or in style and appearance. Trueblood shunned decorating his creations with prettifying labels.

Peter Barrett, a close friend and fishing companion of Trueblood's, shared thoughts in a May 1986 *Field & Stream* article titled "The Trout Flies of Ted Trueblood": "Unfortunately for posterity, Ted Trueblood was modest about his flies and rarely dignified any with a name. One exception I can think of in our long association was the black and white bucktail that he named the Integration because 'black and white came together in harmony.' Yet a nymph he used mostly in lake fishing for trout he referred to casually as 'my tan nymph.'"

In a follow-up January 1989 *Field & Stream* story called "Tie Your Own Flies," Barrett told an amusing story about Trueblood's habit of assigning undignified names to his flies. "Once I

Otter Shrimp, tied by Mike Valla. Ted Trueblood's signature pattern was once considered a "must-have" in any fly angler's box. The pattern's "insectness"—its shape, color, size, indistinct outline, and translucence contributed by natural fur dubbing—satisfied a trout's "visual requirement." It also performed well in waters where freshwater shrimp were not found.

was fishing with Ted Trueblood in Newfoundland, prowling up a creek. Ted spotted a grilse, climbed atop a huge boulder, and caught the salmon below on a blonde-bodied nymph. 'What's that body material?' I asked. 'I call this nymph The Back of Dan's Head,' he told me with a grin. He gathered hair clippings from his eldest son." Trueblood also treated dry-fly creations with simple nomenclature such as "my blue damselfly pattern," "my coachman pattern," or "my grasshopper pattern."

Such was the way with Ted Trueblood, whose personality Jack Berryman described in *Fly-Fishing Pioneers & Legends of the Northwest* (2006) as "friendly, straightforward, and down to earth."

Ted Trueblood was born on June 26, 1913, near Homedale, Idaho. He was a prolific writer, and his first article was published when he was barely out of high school. From the time this article, titled "A Certain Idaho Trout," appeared in 1931 in *National Sportsman* magazine, readers couldn't get enough of him. His stories, not limited to fishing, appeared in magazines such as *Field & Stream*, where he served as fishing editor; *Rod and Gun*; and *True: The Man's Magazine*. His fishing books were equally well received, among them *Trout Trouble* (1946), *The Angler's Handbook* (1949), and *How to Catch More Fish* (1955). He was in an on-again, off-again situation as fishing editor at *Field & Stream*, hired in 1941, soon laid off, then rehired in 1944. But living on the East Coast—particularly in Pleasantville, New York—was no thrill for Trueblood, and he soon headed back to Idaho, moving to Nampa, where he continued to write for *Field & Stream* and the other magazines as a freelancer.

The consummate outdoorsman, Trueblood wrote about a range of hunting and fishing topics. Yet he was an ardent fly angler, a love that began in his teenage years. According to Jack Berryman, Trueblood recalled that he "had become fairly proficient at tying flies" by the age of 17. During his development as a fly tier, he had witnessed an evolution in dry-fly creations and in his May 1963 *Field & Stream* article titled "Flies for Sophisticated Trout," he commented, "That we have progressed so far with dry flies, guided only by theory and endless experimenting, and lacking any real knowledge of the vision of trout, is actually quite remarkable." Yet Trueblood recognized early that with all the attention directed to dry flies, the lowly nymph had been largely ignored.

During the 1940s, Trueblood relied on wet flies as his trout takers, but at the same time, he took an interest in nymphs. After spending hours onstream, he realized that nymphs were better producers than the classic wet flies the vast majority of fly anglers were fishing. By the time Trueblood's "Flies for Sophisticated Trout" was published, he had all but abandoned the old stand-by sinking patterns in favor of nymphs, writing of the latter, "In fact, they have worked so much better for me that my wet-fly box no longer contains any of the winged patterns on which I depended so heavily twenty years ago."

Trueblood embraced nymphs but recognized that the development of patterns did not involve the careful study and attention given to dry flies. He was also puzzled that nymph patterns had not reached their true potential as trout getters, as most of the food fish obtained was beneath the water surface. Trueblood was aware of the flat-bodied patterns developed in the early 1930s by Ed Hewitt and John Alden Knight on the Neversink River in the Catskills, but he didn't buy into the alleged effectiveness of these fur-bodied creations soaked in lacquer, then squeezed flat with pliers.

In his April 1958 *Field & Stream* article "Nymphs Are Easy," he wrote, "Although my experience may not necessarily parallel that of other anglers, I have had generally poor results with both flat-bodied and hard-bodied nymphs, and with those made of rubber, plastic and like materials in an attempt to achieve exact imitation. Nearly all of my nymphs, both weighted and unweighted, are made with dubbing bodies." One might conclude that the nymphs he eventually developed were as arbitrary as the simple names he attached to them. However, his pragmatic approach that led to what appeared to many as globs of fur on a hook was the result of careful thought and resultant theories: fish don't see things the way a human would. His patterns were empty of the details found in exact imitation patterns, which he shunned. Ted Trueblood embraced impressionism over imitation; he believed that "insectness" in fly pattern design was of paramount importance.

Trueblood studied theories proposed by British fly angler G. E. M. Skues in *The Way of a Trout with a Fly* (1949), where he wrote, "The nature and needs of trout differ greatly from those of man and it need not therefore surprise us if examination should lead us eventually to the conclusion that his perception by eyesight differs materially from that of man." Beyond Skues, Trueblood studied research conducted at MIT that concluded that frogs cannot see their world as we do.

Ted Trueblood cogitated on both Skues's ideas and the MIT studies but was particularly intrigued by Skues's statement that "the balance of probability, I think, leans to the theory that the trout is so obsessed by the pressure of appetite that he sees only what he wants to see—his supposed insect prey." Trueblood accepted Skues's theory citing the fact that no matter how imitative a fly pattern is, not many natural insects have metal hooks hanging off their tails. Trueblood concluded that the trout "doesn't have the visual equipment to see the hook; consequently he *can't* see it."

The bottom line for Trueblood was that trout flies require the quality of *appearing* to be insect prey. As an example, he cited the Adams fly, which doesn't represent anything in particular but has a high quality of "insectness." Ted Trueblood attributed the great effectiveness of his signature fly, the

Otter Shrimp, to "insectness," even though he knew a fresh-water scud is not an insect. Yet his pattern's approximate shape, color, size, indistinct outline, and translucence contributed by natural fur dubbing satisfied a trout's "visual requirement." His famous Otter Shrimp, also known as Trueblood's Shrimp, was effective in waters that did not have freshwater shrimp because, he believed, it satisfied a trout's perception that it was food—its quality of "insectness" enticed a trout to strike.

In a July 1979 *Field & Stream* article titled "The Rewards of Experimenting," Trueblood wrote that he had developed the Otter Shrimp after fishing the Henry's Fork of the Snake River, Henry's Lake, Wood River, Magic Reservoir, and Silver Creek. He observed that these waters were loaded with freshwater shrimp, or scuds, but the fly patterns available to entice trout that were feeding on the naturals were ineffective. "In fact," Trueblood wrote, " some of them were nothing but hippies; they didn't work at all." It was obvious to Trueblood that a new pattern was sorely needed.

At first he tried tying a better shrimp pattern on hooks that he bent, then wrapped fat with cream-colored latex. Although the attempts looked good to his eyes, the trout didn't like them. He bent a lot of hooks to imitate the quarter-moon bend displayed by the naturals when held in his hand, and he experimented with a lot of different materials. Yet Trueblood was still unable to create just the right pattern that would tempt trout. It wasn't until he more closely studied the naturals darting about in the water that he realized that they actually were straight and not bent at all while swimming. He gave up on self-bent hooks, went to straight shanks, and abandoned the idea of creating an exact shrimp-fly imitation. After further experimentation, he finally arrived at his Otter Shrimp.

In creating his new fly, Trueblood mixed pale otter belly fur with a bit of white seal fur for body dubbing. This was spun on Nymo 2042 thread attached to Mustad 7948A hooks in sizes 6, 8, 10, and 12. Otter Shrimp enthusiasts such as Terry Hellekson, Eric Leiser, and Randall Kaufmann have recommended using the Mustad 3906 wet-fly hook. The guard hairs of the mixed fur trapped bubbles that held against the nymph's body, a feature that Trueblood believed added to its effectiveness. Peter Barrett wrote that Trueblood changed his Otter Shrimp slightly from his original creation; the final version was tied with a strip of tying thread along the fly's belly from head to tail.

As is true with many flies, the pattern has slight variations in both its name and materials used, with other materials often substituted for the natural seal. The fly is sometimes called the Trueblood Shrimp (Kaufmann), Trueblood Shrimp Nymph (Hellekson), or Trueblood's Otter Nymph (Leiser). Fly tiers have their favorite versions; John Shewey ties a handsome example on a 1XL hook and ribs the fly with fine copper wire.

The fly's effectiveness encouraged Ted Trueblood to trumpet the pattern in many of his fishing articles, particularly in *Field & Stream*. Barrett wrote that Trueblood didn't have reason to promote the dry flies he fished, since floaters and theories surrounding that type of fly had already received ample attention from many fly-fishing writers. On the other hand, Barrett said, he thought that nymphs "needed publicity from anglers like himself and so he wrote about them in this magazine [*Field & Stream*] and others sometimes including step-by-step tying pictures to demonstrate how simple a nymph is to put together."

The Otter Shrimp received a tremendous amount of publicity and captured the attention of many authors of fly-tying and fly-pattern books. Randall Kaufmann wrote in his *American Nymph Fly Tying Manual* (1975), "This very simple fly has crept into use on nearly every trout water in the country, being especially popular for lake fishing when casting for cruisers over weed beds and drop-offs. It is also very effective when crept across the bottom of lakes or drifted in spring creeks. The buggy translucence of seal and otter has accounted for many trout at the end of a dancing rod." Ted Trueblood embraced other "buggy" fur-bodies nymph patterns that also danced rods; Jack Schneider's Fledermaus was among them.

In his May 1963 *Field & Stream* article "Flies for Sophisticated Trout," Trueblood wrote that he was present when Schneider tied the very first Fledermaus for late-evening fishing when bats start to fly about—hence its name, which is German for bat. After witnessing Schneider take a 5-pound brown trout on the fly, tied on a 5/0 hook, Trueblood decided to try it in smaller hook sizes. It proved effective for daylight fishing when tied with a slight variation: he clipped the squirrel-tail wing. Trueblood wrote, "But since the wing was part of Jack's pattern I tie it and trim it on the stream."

As is true with many trout flies, patterns are sometimes slightly altered just as Ted Trueblood did with Schneider's original creation. Polly Rosborough also altered Schneider's pattern after reading about the fly in an article written by A. J. McClane. Since McClane spelled Schneider's pattern Fleder*mouse*, Rosborough followed suit. In his *Popular Fly Patterns* (1984), Terry Hellekson listed both a Fledermaus and a Fledermouse, reflecting slight variations in the original pattern. His Fledermouse retained Schneider's red fox squirrel hair wing.

In "The Trout Flies of Ted Trueblood," Peter Barrett described Trueblood's final Fledermaus. On April 1, 1968, Ted Trueblood sent his friend Barrett a box labeled "my flies." Barrett said one of the flies he received was "the basic Fledermaus pattern, but the wing has disappeared and, shortened a bit, has now become throat hackling." Barrett felt strongly that Trueblood's final version should be called the Trueblood Fledermaus, not Trueblood's Fledermaus, since it was a variation of Schneider's creation. It was a ragged fly

Wade Lake, Montana. Trueblood's fishing companion, Peter Barrett, had success on the picturesque water casting Ted's patterns such as My Tan Nymph and Trueblood's Stonefly, sometimes called Ted's Stonefly. The success of Trueblood's Stonefly on Wade Lake surprised its creator, since the water is devoid of stonefly naturals. Barrett landed a 3-pound rainbow on the fly during their Wade Lake outing, to Ted's amazement.

dubbed with mixed muskrat and coyote tail spun on a double thread loop.

Ted Trueblood's ragged fur-bodied nymphs, tied with everything from wild furbearer clippings to house cat combings, were not his only creations; he also tied more traditional-looking nymphs as well as streamers. Another nymph that Trueblood tied was a Stonefly pattern labeled as the Trueblood's Stonefly (Hellekson) or Ted's Stonefly (Leiser). It was a spin-off of the Montana Nymph. In his *Book of Fly Patterns* (1987), Eric Leiser noted that the fly was tied in the same basic manner as the Montana Nymph except for the tails; Trueblood used goose quill fibers for tailing. However, Peter Barrett, who

fished the pattern with Trueblood for rainbows at Wade Lake in the high country of southern Montana, wrote that the fly was a lighter brown than most regular Montana Nymphs.

Ted Trueblood's life ended on September 12, 1982, in his home in Nampa, Idaho, from a self-inflicted gunshot injury. Cancer had overtaken his life and he could no longer enjoy his passion for the natural world. His readers remember him and his stories, and many of us continue to carry with us the fly patterns he developed on the rivers and streams that he loved. Flies such as his Otter Shrimp are still discussed whenever Ted Trueblood's name is mentioned in fly shops or on stream.

Integration Bucktail, black and white version, tied by Mike Valla. Trueblood named the fly Integration because in its construction, "black and white came together in harmony." Writer Peter Barrett said this was one of Trueblood's few patterns that were named with any dignity. He typically gave names to his flies that were rather colorless.

Trueblood Fledermaus, tied by Mike Valla. Trueblood altered Jack Schneider's original pattern by eliminating the wing. Both Schneider's and Trueblood's Fleder*maus* differed from the Fleder*mouse* tied by Polly Rosborough.

Integration Bucktail, blue dun and white version, tied by Mike Valla. This is a variation of Trueblood's first version.

Trueblood's Stonefly Nymph, tied by Mike Valla. This fly is a spin-off of the well-known Montana Nymph, with goose quill fibers for tailing. Peter Barrett, who fished the pattern with Trueblood for rainbows on Wade Lake in the high country of southern Montana, wrote that the fly was a lighter brown than most regular Montana Nymphs.

CHAPTER 39

Cal Bird
(1914–1997)

Cal Bird, doing what he loved to do—tie flies. Bird focused on impressionism in his fly designs. The late Mike Fong, a well-known West Coast fly angler, once said he was "an artist with a vise."
Photo by Christine Fong

During the 1960s, there was a dearth of comprehensive fly pattern reference books that could assist tiers with their craft. There were some specialty titles, such as Joseph D. Bates's classic *Streamer Fly Tying and Fishing* (1966), a book that included color plates created from actual photographs of popular bucktails and streamers. Tiers could still refer to Ray Bergman's *Trout* (1938) and the numerous fly illustrations by Dr. Edgar Burke. The slim *Noll Guide to Trout Flies and How to Tie Them* (1965), with its color paintings by G. Don Ray, was a reasonable reference too. However, most fly tiers in that era turned to *McClane's Standard Fishing Encyclopedia* (1965) and its color plates with photographs of the most popular fly patterns—dry flies, wet flies, streamers, salmon flies, and nymphs.

Most of the patterns featured in McClane's book were tied by Harry and Elsie Darbee, but western patterns were tied by icons such as Polly Rosborough from Oregon and Dan Bailey in Montana. Among the numerous classic Catskill patterns tied by Harry Darbee was an interesting long-shank dry fly of western descent, called Bird's Stonefly. Dan Bailey provided two nymphs

Bird's Stonefly, tied by Cal Bird. Cal's fly was one of the first good dry-fly patterns useful during stonefly emergences throughout the country. East Coast anglers fished it on rivers such as the Delaware in New York state. *Keith Barton collection*

for the same color plate named Bird Stonefly Nymphs, No. 1 and No. 2. For many eastern fly tiers, the Bird flies in McClane's book provided a first introduction to the Stonefly patterns that emerged from West Coaster Calvin Bird's vise.

It is not surprising that Bailey had something to do with the inclusion of Cal Bird's work in McClane's volume, since he heavily promoted the patterns through his Livingston, Montana, shop. And Darbee's close proximity to New York's Delaware River and its prolific emergences of big stoneflies no doubt necessitated featuring an effective large dry-fly imitation. While Bird's long-shank Stonefly floater, with protruding antennae, wasn't an exact imitation of the species found on the big water of the Delaware, it was big, floated well, and was attractive to fish. He also had created its companion fly, Bird's Stonefly Nymph, a pattern equally effective on stonefly-inhabited waters in both West and East.

Bird's Stonefly Nymph, as it is shown in many reference books, was traditionally tied with hackle wrapped through the thorax. Later versions used teal flank instead of hackle. Bird was an experimenter and created variations of his patterns that departed from his originals. Californian Keith Barton, a close friend of Bird's, offered his thoughts in recent correspondence with me: "Cal tied a lot of flies and tinkered with hundreds of materials. The dyed teal represents one of his 'phases' where he became so caught up in a material that he altered it to suit all of his patterns—as well as any classics he tied. Hence the teal was on some of the steelhead flies also."

Beyond his famous Stoneflies, Bird focused on impressionism in fly design. The Bird's Nest Nymph, a fly first field-tested by Bird on the Truckee River, a stream that flows off the eastern Sierra Nevada in California, typifies his impressionistic approach to fly design. "It was part of Cal's mantra," Barton remembered. "Outside of his Bird's Stoneflies, he was impressionistic—inventing flies that resembled everything and nothing, relying on their color, sparkle, and movement to provide the real elements of seduction. He possessed an artist's appreciation for color, understanding the color wheel and how to make complementary and associative colors to blend into his dubbing or leap out from it. He was the first person I heard coin the 'spectral' theme."

Cal sometimes commandeered Barton's vise and materials to show his friend something he was fiddling with. Barton described Bird's humble nature and almost apologetic stance concerning his past work, calling him "a shy and bashful fellow who never raised his voice, never mentioned his pedigree, and was ever the gentleman." Barton recalled how Cal would meet him at a shop called Angler's Beat on Sundays with his vise and materials in one hand and a cake in the other. "As a young lad, I worked in all the major fly shops in San Francisco. One of the smaller shops, called Angler's Beat, was out in the Avenues by Golden Gate Park, home to the Golden Gate Angling and Casting Club. Cal lived out in the same area. On weekends, Cal would sneak away from his wife

and responsibilities, grab a handful of cigars, and stop by a Russian bakery between the shop and his house and score a wreath cake. He knew I'd have a pot of coffee going at the shop, so he'd stop by and we'd jawbone and tie flies. As he was a quiet, soft-spoken fellow, most customers had no idea that he was an angler of any import. Cal would chat them up while showing them how to tie something. He passed on to me, as older guys commonly want to do, a lot of his theories on color and dyes and how to create nymph and dry-fly dubbing. Recognizing that I'd lucked into a really talented fellow, whose interest in fishing was multidimensional and at the same time was one of the nicest gentlemen I'd ever met, he had me glued to his every word."

Keith Barton learned much from his humble friend, including some of his favorite techniques. With the stub of an unlit cigar clenched between his teeth, Bird would set to work, crafting his favorites from the barred teal or mallard flank he so liked in his patterns. In tying with teal or mallard flank, Bird attached the dyed feathers to the hook in his own special way, first removing the feather's center for use as a tail, and then collapsed the rest of the feather around the hook shank.

Others, too, admired Cal Bird's patterns, his tying techniques, and how he viewed fly design. Among his many fans were Ralph Cutter and the late Michael Fong, who echoed some of Keith Barton's observations. "Cal was an artist first and a fly tier second," noted California fly-fishing author and angler Ralph Cutter said in recent correspondence with me. "Tying with Cal was like tying with a chemist. His ability to blend colors to attain exactly the creation he was developing was in itself amazing. If he didn't have the right color or dye to match his need, he simply invented a way to get the color. He soaked feathers and fur in witch's brews of gunpowder, picric acid, match heads, coffee grounds, rusted nails, and anything else he might have in the garage. On a subconscious level, he encouraged me look at anything and consider its value in making a fly. When we went looking for materials he'd rather go to Reno's [Nevada] Twin Cities army surplus store or the Mill End Fabrics outlet than any fly shop. One time I was having my jet boat serviced and he 'borrowed' a glob of purple marine grease from the shop just to see what he could do with it. Most tiers consider the shape, size, silhouette, movement, and color of their patterns. Cal dissected each of those values into subvalues such as translucency, sheen, hue, and saturation. His mastery of balance and fine art can be seen in even careless, disheveled looking bugs such as the Bird's Nest."

Michael Fong, who first met Bird in the mid-1960s, was also a great admirer of the Bird's Nest and the pattern's creator—his mentor Cal Bird, who taught him to tie flies. Fong and his wife, Christine, had just returned to California after graduate school in Iowa. They settled in San Francisco and soon discovered Bird's fly shop in the Avenues. In an article titled "Beginnings and Endings" in the March 1998 issue of

Inside Angler, Fong wrote of Cal Bird, "He was kind enough to take me under his wing, a comforting haven for one so ignorant of all things connected to fly fishing." Fong called his mentor "an artist with a fly vise and with brush in hand, on canvas."

Michael Fong became one of the most knowledgeable fly anglers of his era, writing stories for many publications from the late 1960s until his untimely death in 2002. He shared with fly fishers everywhere his fascinating adventures, describing seemingly every nook and cranny that held trout all over his western waters. His forays into the Sierra Nevada could be likened to travelogues.

In his February 1992 *Fly Fisherman* story titled "Fishing a Bird's Nest," Fong shared his thoughts about his mentor's pattern and its effectiveness on waters such as Hat Creek. He wrote that Bird never expected any recognition for his creations, but fly anglers quickly learned of the Bird's Nest's effectiveness. At the time Fong wrote his story, a shop in Northern California expected to sell 20,000 of the pattern in one season. Shops everywhere were after the Bird's Nest even though anglers weren't quite sure what the scraggly thing was intended to imitate.

"It is difficult to describe the Bird's Nest," said Fong; "it does not fit the description of any popular order of insects mimicked by tiers. It looks like a mayfly nymph, but it lacks the clear definition of a top-mounted wingcase, and the head is too bulbous. A trout could mistake it for a caddis pupa, but immature caddis do not have a tail. You could say it will pass for a stonefly nymph, and it does, but the abdomen is not nearly as elongated as the natural's abdomen, and the many protruding fibers do not suggest the hard exoskeleton of that order."

Fong believed it was the fly's *suggestiveness* of some type of insect that made it so effective. Ted Trueblood would have concurred; Fong's observations agreed fully with the theories of "insectness" that Trueblood had proposed many years before. The fly obviously appeared to fish as something highly suggestive of life. The 5-pounder Fong took on lower Hat Creek convinced him that the Bird's Nest could fool wary big browns.

The Bird's Nest has been tweaked in recent years, morphed into a bead-head style. Ralph Cutter felt that Cal Bird "would be aghast at many of the commercial imitations of his patterns on the market today." Matt Grobert, a talented fly tier and angler from Tewksbury, New Jersey, fishes his copper bead-head version with great success. In correspondence with me, he explained the evolution of his fly: "I was introduced to Cal Bird's Bird's Nest Nymph in the late 1970s while fishing the Williamson River in Choliquin, Oregon,

near one of the great tiers, Polly Rosborough. In fact, that was my first introduction to that style of nymph pattern—tied in the round and fuzzy—and I quickly filled my fly boxes with Bird's Nests and Casual Dress Nymphs. Although I fished the flies with success all that summer, after I returned home to the East Coast in September I fished the flies less and less. Not so much because they didn't work, but I had become obsessed with the Catskill style of tying both my nymphs and drys.

"A decade or so later, I fished the Beaverhead River in Montana with a friend that lived there, and he reintroduced me to the Bird's Nest. This time, though, it was a small size 18 and had a pearl glass bead added to the head. Again, this fly was tied 'in the round' and worked quite well. Having long since passed my 'Catskill style only phase,' I started tying them again with and without the glass bead, but not in the round. I tied my Bird's Nests with the wood-duck hackle/legs only on the sides. I did this simply because natural aquatic nymphs only have their legs on each side of their bodies, and so in my mind, imitations should be tied that way as that is how the trout see them. This change gave me more confidence in the fly because it looked to me as it should, and that's the key with any fly—the better a fly looks to the user, the more confidence they have in it, and in turn the fly works better.

"Like many effective flies, the Bird's Nest metamorphosed once again, as I discovered while fishing the trout streams of Northern California, where the fly was invented by Mr. Bird. This time [it changed with my addition of] a copper bead head, and that seemed to really give it fish appeal. Of course, the fly was tied in the round, as many believe it should be due to the fact that the originator tied it that way. With no disrespect for Mr. Bird, I continued to tie the fly with the legs only on the sides for the reasons stated above. And it worked as well as ever; in fact, since that trip it has become one of my few 'go-to' patterns that continually produce for me on every trout stream I visit."

Many would argue that once the characteristics of the original pattern are altered or changed—such as the way the duck flank is tied on the hook or the addition of a bead—the fly is no longer a Bird's Nest. However, out of reverence for Cal Bird and his original pattern, his name has been attached to many Bird's Nest variations.

Although Cal Bird is no longer with us, his legacy lives on with all of those who tie or fish the patterns that bear his name—the Bird's Stonefly and Bird's Nest Nymphs, the attractive Bird's Silver Marabou and Bird's Cutthroat Streamers, and many others. All of Cal Bird's patterns continue to perform well on water across America and around the globe.

Bird's Cutthroat Streamer, tied by Cal Bird. Bird tied a variety of patterns, including this vibrant streamer. *Keith Barton collection*

Bird's Silver Marabou Streamer, tied by Cal Bird. This is another beautiful example of Bird's streamer work. The long, slender head is typical of his streamers. *Keith Barton collection*

The Truckee River, the outlet of Lake Tahoe, flows from the east slope of the Sierra Nevada in California to Nevada. The Truckee is considered the birthplace of the Bird's Nest. *Photo by Doug Ouellette*

Group of Bird's Nest flies, tied by Cal Bird. Bird tied his pattern in several sizes and shades. The pattern doesn't suggest any one type of aquatic insect. *Keith Barton collection*

Bird's Stonefly Nymphs (variation), tied by Cal Bird. Ever the experimenter, here Bird was experimenting with a different version of his original Stonefly Nymph pattern. *Keith Barton collection*

Bird's Nest variation, tied by Cal Bird. The pattern was first field-tested on the Truckee River. *Keith Barton collection*

Bird's Nest version, tied by Cal Bird. Bird experimented with dying teal flank feathers for use on several versions of his pattern. *Keith Barton collection*

Grobert's Beadhead Bird's Nest, tied by Matt Grobert. Although this fly is much different in style from the original Bird's Nest, Grobert named his fly out of reverence for Cal Bird.

CHAPTER 40

André Puyans
(1935–2005)

André M. Puyans. John Randolph described Puyans as "fly fishing's 'Jason of Jason and the Argonauts,' the 'Pied Piper' and 'Johnny Appleseed' of fly fishing." *Jannifer Puyans collection*

Seth Norman's *Meanderings of a Fly Fisherman* (1996) included a speech that was presented at the February 4, 1995, Northern California Council Federation of Fly Fishers Hall of Fame event. At the sold-out gathering, Norman spoke of the difficulty in fully conveying to an audience everything the honoree had done for the sport of fly fishing and all that surrounds it. "Of the many ways by which one might measure a man none of any value will fit him into fifteen minutes," Norman lamented as he "spoke by proxy" to a room packed with friends and admirers of André Michel Puyans, many of whom no doubt were his former fly-tying students. Norman then referenced *Fly Fisherman* magazine editor John Randolph's description of Puyans as "fly fishing's 'Jason of Jason and the Argonauts,' the 'Pied Piper' and 'Johnny Appleseed' of fly fishing."

Puyans's former fly-tying students, the number of whom by the time of his death was estimated at some 6,000, will tell you that he was all those things to the art of fly tying. His students will also tell you stories about how the colorful character that they so admired directed their

Loop Wing Macaw Adams, tied by André Puyans. Puyans is credited with designing the unique wings crafted from duck flank feather fibers, such as teal and mallard. *Jannifer Puyans collection*

fingers though the steps necessary to craft a well-tied fly. It would be hard to find an accomplished former Puyans tying student who has more admiration and reverence for his mentor than Californian Rick Ackel. Ackel and a small group of former Puyans students reconvene in November every year to tie flies using the techniques that their mentor insisted they employ.

Ackel dove into fly fishing around 1980, after visiting Puyans's Creative Sports fly shop. With fly-fishing equipment in hand, he tested the waters on a camping trip with a friend. The friend, who was one of Puyan's students, sat down and tied a fly one morning. Ackel was mesmerized and asked his friend where he had learned his techniques. On returning home from the trip, he immediately signed up for Puyans's tying class. Ackel stayed by his mentor's side and continued to learn from him until André Puyans's death in 2005. Rick and I discussed Puyans and his accomplishments. "As a teacher/tier," Rick wrote in a letter to me, "Andy was a bit of a perfectionist. He could be a bear at times but truly was a teddy bear. He was tough, but like the Jim Croce song, 'he had a thundering velvet hand.' As you were learning, if the fly wasn't up to

standards, he would take a razor blade and cut off the material or take a Bic lighter and burn off the materials and have you do it again—with proper materials and proportions."

Andy Puyans's insistence on perfectionism is easy to understand when one considers his roots in the art, stemming back to his boyhood days on the East Coast, where he was first introduced to crafting fishing flies. It was a family doctor who approached Puyans when he was just a boy and encouraged him to try fly tying. Puyans's newfound interest eventually led him to Jim Deren's famed Angler's Roost, located in the Chrysler Building in New York City.

The Roost—which many still remember as the most disorganized, messy, cramped tackle supply shop that probably ever existed—was a magnet for the "who's who" in fly-fishing personalities. Beyond what influences may have been picked up at the Roost, Puyans also was influenced by other East Coast notables who wandered through the Angler's Roost, New York City stockbrokers included, who introduced the young Puyans to other fly-tying perfectionists such as Jack Atherton. Atherton was an illustrator who prided himself in developing fly patterns incorporating the principles of art-

Henry's Fork of the Snake River. Puyans fly-tying student Jim Pruett said, "I think half if not more of the anglers that frequent Henry's Fork were influenced by him." The Henry's Fork was Puyans's laboratory water during the fishing season. *Photo by Valerie Valla*

based impressionism. Additionally, Puyans witnessed many Catskill school fly tiers insist on fly-tying perfectionism.

The importance of careful attention to detail when tying trout flies was no doubt instilled during André's early years. The foundation well set, in 1958 Puyans headed to Abercrombie and Fitch's San Francisco store location, where he was commissioned to tie trout flies, armed with East Coast influences. Puyans developed his own set of fly-tying standards and techniques that resulted in his own creations or improvements made to patterns created by other fly tiers.

Puyans improved existing patterns such as John Goddard's Caddisfly imitation and Jack Horner's folded deer body hair fly commonly called the Humpy. He also tweaked tying methods used in such patterns as British fly angler Frank Sawyer's Pheasant Tail Nymph and promoted variations of Al Troth's Elk Hair Caddis dry fly. Yet André's own signature flies are some of his most interesting, still discussed by his former students around tying tables and on the water.

Puyans's former students will quickly mention names such as the A.P. Nymph series, Loop Wing dry flies, and a peculiar pattern called the Floor Shrimp. Jannifer Puyans, André's wife, believes the A.P. Nymph concept might have had its birth as far back as the late 1950s. In *Nymph Fishing: A History of the Art and Practice* (2005), Terry Lawton wrote that André Puyans's A.P. series was "perfected" by 1963; Puyans himself put the date at around 1961.

The A.P. Nymphs are effective generic mayfly nymph patterns admired and discussed by fly-fishing authors such as Ernie Schwiebert, Terry Hellekson, and Eric Leiser. In *The Book of Fly Patterns* (1987), Leiser wrote of the A.P. Nymphs, "Puyans has made the job of tying his nymph series relatively simple by designing a basic structure for all of them, adjusting only the size, shape, and color in relation to the natural." Puyans tied the A.P. Nymphs with a variety of natural furs, including dyed and natural beaver, hare's ear, and muskrat. Dyed seal was sometimes blended with the fur. One pattern uses peacock herl for the fly body. Fine copper, gold, or other shade of wire ribbing is typical of the A.P. Nymphs. Nine popular A.P Nymphs are the Hare's Ear, Muskrat #1, Muskrat #2, Claret and Beaver, Olive, Beaver, Hendrickson, Black Beaver, and the Peacock and Pheasant.

In his Fit to Be Tied column in the May/June 1975 *Angler* magazine, titled "Tying the A.P. Nymph Series," Puyans described the rationale behind the series' development: "The reasons I first started tying a different style and series of nymphs were all based on my frustration with the then existing patterns. Either the nymphs were very time consuming to tie or they represented an un-lifelike blob of something on a hook, unknown in nature. Consequently some fourteen years ago the A.P. Nymph Series started."

Puyans was not in favor of shiny, finished thread heads; he preferred to take dubbing clear up to the hook eye, giving the nymph heads a greater resemblance in color to the nat-

urals. André Puyans's ideas concerning artificial nymphs and their design contrast with those of earlier American fly tiers and anglers Ed Hewitt and John Alden Knight, who favored flat-bodied imitations. Rather than concentrate on imitating naturals that cling to the undersides of rocks and thus are less available as trout food, Puyans directed his attention to the more mobile species, paying careful attention to gill movement and body texture. Nymph titan Polly Rosborough and his contemporary Ted Trueblood likely would have embraced Puyans's use of natural furs and blends that offer gill-like movement through water when fished.

"Most mayfly nymphs have substantial texture," Puyans wrote. "This texture is alive and formed by gills along the abdomen, filaments along the abdomen and thorax areas. To represent this texture there is no substitute for natural fur." Lifelike movement provided by the materials selected was important to Puyans; it is thus understandable that André Puyans embraced flies designed by Frank Sawyer, a British nymph pattern enthusiast.

In *Nymphs and the Trout* (1958), Sawyer described his unique Pheasant Tail (PT) Nymph. The PT was tied entirely with pheasant tail fibers wrapped with fine reddish brown copper wire along the hook shank; thread was not used. The wire resulted in a weighted pattern, the copper offered interesting coloration, and the fuzzy pheasant tail body simulated fine gill-like movements in water. There were a few differences in how Puyans tied the pattern: Sawyer recommended four strands of pheasant tail, while Puyans liked six, and Puyans started the wire on the hook shank in a slightly different fashion than Sawyer, but the end product—a slender, effective nymph—was essentially very close in appearance to Sawyer's original.

Besides studying nymphs, André Puyans also focused his attention on creating or modifying patterns that imitated emerging as well as adult stage mayflies. Puyans developed a unique loop wing style that resulted in some of his most creative patterns. In an article in the Spring 1979 issue of *Fly Tyer* titled "The Loop Wing: Its History and Development," Puyans said, "The loop wing style of tie was first used in 1961 to imitate an emerging mayfly . . . it is surprising no one had come up with this tying technique before this time because it is a rather logical extension of the wing case on a nymph." Loop wings were also used for dry flies.

In *Trout* (1978), Ernest Schwiebert wrote enthusiastically about the loop wings, calling the technique "a remarkably simple method of suggesting the crystalline wings of mayfly spinner." A variety of feather fibers are tied in a loop to suggest the outlines of wings on the naturals. In correspondence with me, Rick Ackel described the materials used for loop wings: "The loop wing can be made out of a variety of materials: flank feathers, hackle, goose and duck fibers. Depending on the size of the fly, it has three to four fibers on each side. For mayflies, on loop wings, we tended to use teal/barred

Creative Sports Enterprises in Pacheco, California, was a magnet for Puyans admirers. Many who never met André knew him through his advertisements; this one was a favorite.

mallard on Adams type flies and mallard flank dyed wood duck or actual [natural] wood duck for Cahills, etc."

In correspondence with me, another Puyans student, Randy Roehl, also provided some details on the loop wing materials and technique: "For my Baetis flies, I have some gray goose covert wing feathers that Andy gave me many years ago for loop wings. For my loop wing Adams, I generally trim the barbs on both sides of a grizzly feather to about 1/32 inch and use that instead of teal; it's incredibly durable but a pain to trim."

The loop wings are a generic concept and can be applied to many standard patterns, such as the Adams that Roehl mentioned. One of Puyans's favorites was the Loop Wing Macaw Adams. Don Martinez used macaw tail feather, with its striking blue and gold coloration, extensively since the 1930s for dry-fly and nymph bodies. Martinez was tying flies for Bob Carmichael in Wyoming during those early years. Carmichael instructed Martinez to tie Adams flies with macaw quill bodies, resulting in a fly Carmichael named the Whitcraft. Martinez also supplied this fly to his own customers and dubbed it a Quill Adams. The fly gained in popularity, appearing in William F. Blades's *Fishing Flies and Fly Tying* (1951), where the Whitcraft was called a Martinez fly. In *The Practical Fly Fisherman* (1953), A. J. McClane listed several Martinez flies that had macaw bodies.

Martinez's patterns no doubt helped popularize macaw-bodied dry flies, but it was Jim Quick who first dropped a Macaw Adams into André Puyans's hands. In *Trout Fishing and Trout Flies* (1957), Quick described the Macaw Adams, a variation that used dark blue dun hackle tip wings instead of grizzly hackle tips as called for in a regular Adams dry fly. Jannifer Puyans, an equally talented fly tier, explained in a recent chat how the Loop Wing Macaw Adams was created after Quick introduced his Macaw Adams to her husband when the two were together on the water. Fishing was slow, and Quick suggested that Puyans try the Macaw Adams. The fly produced well and Puyans added the pattern to his arsenal but later replaced dun hackle tip wings with his loop wings. While macaw had been used for dry-fly bodies, such as for Adams dry-fly variations, the laurel for adding loop wings to such patterns goes to André Puyans.

Typical of the creativity that Puyans applied to the Macaw Adams, he frequently scrutinized other existing patterns or concepts and suggested improvements. The Goddard Caddis was developed after Puyans, while in England, took a close look at a popular British pattern created by Cliff Henry and John Goddard, called the G&H Sedge. According to Jannifer Puyans, "Andy examined their pattern and offered suggestions [to Henry and Goddard] on possible improvements to the somewhat crude-looking fly. Andy gave the fly its new name, the Goddard Caddis." Puyans's talents with spinning and clipping a well-formed hair body were applied to the fly, and a prototype was born.

Just as André Puyans's keen eye recognized the potential for improvements to the G&H Sedge, an important western pattern called the Horner Deer Hair also received his attention. As was his habit, he scrutinized a good pattern and was determined to improve it. One can almost imagine Puyans, pipe in mouth, turning and examining Jack Horner's creation, known also as the Humpy or Goofus Bug. Puyans instilled in his students the belief that careful attention to material selection was a must to craft a well-tied fly. Not all deer hair is the same, he said. The correct type and texture of hair had to be selected and matched to the goal at hand. In an article titled "The Horner Deer Hair," which appeared in the September/October 1975 issue of *Angler*, Puyans wrote, "The right color, texture and length of hair must be selected for the size of the fly to be tied. As an example, the hair one would choose for a size 8 or 10 fly should be totally different than that used on a size 16 or 18 fly."

"The Humpy was his specialty," said Jannifer. "He loved the Horner Deer Hair. What Andy did in modification to the fly was to improve its tying steps and increase the two folds [of hair] to three layers for better flotation." André believed that proportions were critical. He thought that the Humpy would fish better with a shorter tail and recommended a length of one and a half times the hook gap. He also believed that tying on the wing first, rather than the tail, resulted in more consistent overall proportions.

Puyans also embraced other deer hair patterns, such as Al Troth's Elk Hair Caddis, but again he sought to improve

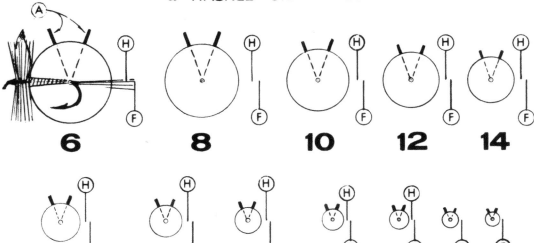

DRY FLY PROPORTION CHART
& HACKLE SIZE CHECK

6 **8** **10** **12** **14**

16 **18** **20** **22** **24** **26** **28**

(H) Hairwing Tail Length (F) Featherwing Tail Length – Measure from top of hook bend.
(A) Wing Angle. To check Hackle size, Wing length and angle, place the eye of the hook on the center circle. Center can **be punched** out so the hook eye can be inserted.

Creative Sports

1924 C OAK PARK BOULEVARD   PLEASANT HILL, CALIFORNIA 94523   510-938-2255

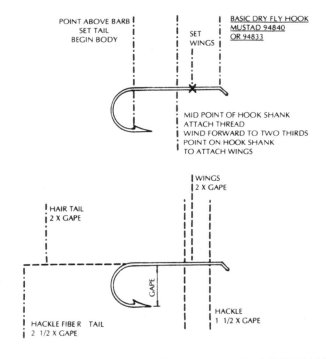

POINT ABOVE BARB
SET TAIL
BEGIN BODY

SET
WINGS

BASIC DRY FLY HOOK
MUSTAD 94840
OR 94833

MID POINT OF HOOK SHANK
ATTACH THREAD
WIND FORWARD TO TWO THIRDS
POINT ON HOOK SHANK
TO ATTACH WINGS

WINGS
2 X GAPE

HAIR TAIL
2 X GAPE

GAPE

HACKLE FIBER TAIL
2 1/2 X GAPE

HACKLE
1 1/2 X GAPE

BASIC DRY FLY PROPORTIONS BY ANDRE PUYANS©

Puyans's Dry Fly Proportions Chart. Puyans was a hard-core "proportions are everything" tier, something he instilled in his students.

the pattern, deciding that creating a bullet head on Troth's fly when tying in the wing would be a better choice. According to Rick Ackel, "Andy felt this led to a much more durable fly (since this fly gets eaten so much!) and therefore referred to the fly as the 'Bullet *Proof* Caddis.' Also, due to the way he tied it, it had a bit more flotation, as there is slightly more deer hair in the fly (in tying in the bullet head) than a regular Elk Hair Caddis. In addition, the tying process is a bit faster and therefore more efficient. Again, Andy was always looking to take a good fly and make it better by adding simplicity and efficiency to the tying process. Durability was also of importance."

While Puyans obviously followed new fly creations, ever mindful that they might be improved, he also delved into experimenting with materials that were unknown during his early tying years. Jumping on the cul de canard (CDC) bandwagon, he developed the CDC Pontoon Dun. (Rick Ackel pointed out that Puyans's good friend, the accomplished fly tier and angler René Harrop, developed a similar fly.)

Experimentation and careful thought concerning how tying materials behave and ultimately fish on the water were of paramount importance to André Puyans. However, he came up with one popular pattern that made onlookers smile when tied at shows or in public. The fly was a peculiarity that demonstrated you could use almost anything to tie a fly that could catch fish, even leftover clippings and scraps. "The Floor Shrimp basically was tied with discards that ended up on the floor from other tiers," Jannifer Puyans said. "It was a way Andy showed that you can dub with anything as long as you understand the technique."

Whether using scraps on a tying floor or discarded feathers left over from another fly, Puyans was a dabbler, relishing the sheer enjoyment of trying different things at the vise. Jannifer fondly recalled the creation of one fly, still unnamed, that Puyans cobbled together from feathers she had rejected while tying Matuka patterns. "I wanted something more mottled. Andy kept the rejected feathers in his wallet, which he often practiced, and finally found the right tying class to use them in a demonstration. The lessons were probably on how to properly prepare and install the wings and fold hackle so that the barbs would project backwards without forcing them that direction by wrapping tying thread to force them back into position." The fly, shown here on page 263 for the first time, remained stuck in a wine cork and enclosed in a display case for nearly a decade. It's a lovely pattern worthy of a name. Puyans also tied beautiful steelhead flies equally deserving of a shadow box.

Some of André's steelhead flies also are variations of popular patterns. "He had enjoyed fishing for steelhead since his move to California in 1958," Jannifer explained. "He loved to tie this style of fly and I think it is probably due to his Atlantic salmon background. His activity just went wild here. In his collection are variations of everything. It's hard to tell if he had a favorite, but the styles and colors of the Van Luven are very repeated. He was incorporating the color purple, and he used to replace some chenille bodies with peacock. He tied a good number of General Practitioner flies." The General Practitioner is a fairly complicated British shrimp pattern originated in 1953 by Col. Esmond Drury for salmon fishing.

Jim Pruett, another fly-tying student, sent me a nice correspondence reflecting on the seven or eight years he knew Puyans: "I remember taking a fly-tying class from him in Idaho; he put a hook in his vise and talked about the history of hooks for at least an hour. It felt like he was never going to tie a fly. Later that week we were at his cabin and I admired one of his Goddard Caddises. He told me if I could tell him what hook it was tied on, I could have it. I didn't correctly identify the hook, and he gave me a lecture on how important it was to look at a fly and know the hook it was tied on; he was not gentle with me but did give me the fly. Last year I fished with a guide in Idaho that had guided Andy and Jannifer more than once; he told me Andy taught him how to think outside the box. We had a great day fishing ants during a Blue-Winged Olive hatch. I think half if not more of the anglers that frequent Henry's Fork were influenced by him."

Bob Lay of Helena, Montana, one of Puyans's fly-tying students during 2002–2003 when he lived in Concord, California, reflected on the enormous influence Andy Puyans had on the thousands of youth he instructed. A note that he sent to me provided additional understanding of the scope of Puyans's influence on other fly tiers. "Today you hear talk of 'Andy's Kids.' To those who knew him, it is a reference to younger people he had taught fly tying and fly fishing. This was over a period of many, many years. Today some of his students are in their 40s and 50s, but they started out with Andy as youngsters. As a result of Andy's instruction, many are still involved in fly tying and fly fishing. To some it became a vocation and they are employed in the fly-fishing industry."

From his simple drab nymphs to his simple yet colorful steelhead flies to his complex salmon patterns, such as the Durham Ranger, André Puyans's flies were works of art. Yet he was not one to boast about his talents at the tying vise. "What is tricky about Andy," said Jim Pruett, "is that he contributed much to both fly fishing and fly tying but was hesitant to take credit for his contributions. This characteristic along with his knowledge made him one of the best teachers of any sort I have ever encountered; my guess is that he would like to be remembered more for his teaching than anything else."

Renegade variation, tied by André Puyans. Renegades have been tied in many variations, some with white front hackle, but others in a variety of hackle shades. *Randy Roehl collection*

A.P. Black Beaver Nymph, tied by André Puyans. *Jannifer Puyans collection*

C&H Mutant Midge variation, tied by André Puyans. Rick Ackel believed that this pattern was a spin-off from a fly developed by Curt Collins and Hale Harris, a former Bighorn River guide. André used to tie the fly with an undersize hackle thorax, but not clipped. *Jannifer Puyans collection*

A.P. Muskrat #2, tied by André Puyans. *Jannifer Puyans collection*

Stonefly, tied by André Puyans. Puyans experimented with many kinds of flies, including large dry-fly patterns such as this one. *Jannifer Puyans collection*

A.P. Natural Beaver, tied by André Puyans. *Jannifer Puyans collection*

P.T. Sawyer Nymphs, tied by André Puyans. Puyans tweaked the tying method used in such patterns as this one created by British fly angler Frank Sawyer. *Randy Roehl collection*

A.P. Peacock and Pheasant, tied by André Puyans. *Jannifer Puyans collection*

Black Goddard Caddis, tied by André Puyans. This is a black version of the popular pattern. *Jannifer Puyans collection*

Goddard Caddis, tied by André Puyans. While in England, Puyans took a close look at a popular British pattern called the G&H Sedge, created by John Goddard and Cliff Henry. Puyans scrutinized the fly, then offered Henry and Goddard suggestions on how the fly might be improved, resulting in what he called the Goddard Caddis. *Randy Roehl collection*

Humpy, tied by André Puyans. Andy believed the Humpy fished better with a shorter tail and recommended a length of one and a half times the hook gap. He also thought that tying on the wing first, rather than the tail, resulted in more consistent overall proportions. *Jannifer Puyans collection*

Bullet Proof Caddis, tied by André Puyans. Student Rick Ackel said that Puyans felt that using a bullet head style "led to a much more durable fly," hence its name. *Jannifer Puyans collection*

Durham Ranger, tied by André Puyans. Puyans was capable of tying everything from tiny nymphs to large salmon flies such as this Durham Ranger. *Jannifer Puyans collection*

Floor Shrimp, tied by André Puyans. Puyans often tied this pattern at tying shows with discarded materials he found on the floor. Jannifer Puyans said that it was a way he hammered home the idea that a tier could dub with anything. *Randy Roehl collection*

General Practitioner, tied by André Puyans. Puyans also tied many of the old classic patterns, such as this fairly complicated British shrimp pattern originated in 1953 by Col. Esmond Drury for salmon fishing. *Jannifer Puyans collection*

The Experiment, tied by André Puyans. The fly, shown here for the first time, remained stuck in a wine cork and enclosed in a display case for nearly a decade. It's a lovely pattern worthy of a name, but right now it doesn't have one. Jannifer Puyans had asked Andy to tied something with mottled wings; he came up with this as an experimental fly. *Jannifer Puyans collection*

Selected Dressings

John Atherton

Atherton Number One

Hook: #12-16 Mustad 94840
Thread: Tan
Tail: Light dun hackle barbs
Wing: Light, glassy dun hackle points
Body: Pale cream fox-belly fur
Rib: Narrow oval gold tinsel
Hackle: Light cree or pale ginger and light grizzly mixed

Atherton Number Two

Hook: #12-16 Mustad 94840
Thread: Tan
Tail: Light brassy or rusty dun hackle barbs or light ginger and light dun mixed
Wing: Wood-duck flank
Body: Buff or pale tan fox-belly fur mixed with natural seal fur and a little hare's ear
Rib: Narrow oval gold tinsel
Hackle: Light cree and medium dun mixed

Atherton Number Three

Hook: #12-16 Mustad 94840
Thread: Tan
Tail: Medium cree hackle barbs or ginger and grizzly mixed
Wing: Wood duck or medium dun hackle points
Body: Seal fur blended with bright yellow seal fur, fox-belly fur dyed yellow, or dyed mohair
Hackle: Rusty dun or medium dun and ginger mixed

Atherton Number Four

Hook: #12-16 Mustad 94840
Thread: Tan
Tail: Cree hackle barbs or ginger and grizzly hackle barbs mixed
Wing: Wood duck
Body: Natural seal fur mixed with dyed red seal, small amount each of hare's ear and muskrat fur
Rib: Narrow oval gold tinsel
Hackle: Medium dun and cree mixed

Atherton Number Five

Hook: #10-18 Mustad 94840
Thread: Tan
Tail: Dark cree or red brown and grizzly hackles mixed
Wing: Wood duck
Body: Hare's ear (use both short speckled hairs and pinkish hair at base of ears)
Rib: Narrow oval gold ribbing
Hackle: Dark cree or red-brown and grizzly mixed

Atherton Number Six

Hook: #12-18 Mustad 94840
Thread: Tan
Tail: Dark rusty dun hackle barbs
Wing: Bronze mallard flank
Body: Dark muskrat mixed with red-brown fur, such as dyed seal fur
Rib: Narrow oval gold ribbing
Hackle: Rusty dun or dark natural dun and red-brown mixed

Note: Materials do not necessarily appear in the order in which they are tied.

Atherton Number One Nymph

Hook:	#10-14 Mustad 9671
Thread:	Tan
Tail:	Wood-duck flank, three strands
Wing Cases:	Jungle cock eyes, two small
Body:	Natural seal fur
Rib:	Oval gold tinsel
Hackle:	Partridge

Atherton Number Two Nymph

Hook:	#8-14 Mustad 9671
Thread:	Tan
Tail:	Ring-necked pheasant tail feathers, three fibers
Wing Cases:	Bright blue kingfisher or floss
Body:	Hair's ear tied rough and picked out
Rib:	Oval gold tinsel
Hackle:	Partridge

Atherton Number Three Nymph

Hook:	#8-14 Mustad 9671
Thread:	Tan
Tail:	Dark furnace hackle barbs
Wing Cases:	Bright blue kingfisher or floss
Body:	Natural seal fur blended with bright yellow seal fur, fox-belly fur dyed yellow or dyed mohair
Rib:	Oval gold tinsel
Hackle:	Dark furnace

Ray Bergman

Black Angel

Hook:	#12-16 Mustad 94840 or equivalent
Thread:	Black 8/0
Tail:	Black hackle barbs
Wing:	Black hackle points
Body:	Black floss or dubbing
Hackle:	Black

Coch-y Variant

Hook:	#14-16 Mustad 94840 or equivalent
Thread:	Black 6/0
Tail:	Coch-y-bondhu hackle barbs, long
Wings:	Dun clipped and shaped hackle tips, short
Body:	Narrow fold tinsel
Hackle:	Light coch-y-bondhu, long

Dark Coty

Hook:	#12-16 Mustad 94840 or equivalent
Tail:	Dun
Wing:	Dun hackle tips
Body:	Muskrat blended with small amount of scarlet wool
Hackle:	Dark dun

Early Brown Stone

Hook:	#16 Mustad 94840 or equivalent
Thread:	Rusty brown 8/0
Tail:	Two pheasant tail fibers
Wing:	Bunch of dun hackle fibers
Body:	Two pheasant tail fibers twisted together, then wrapped
Hackle:	Light furnace

Ginger Quill Wet

Hook:	#6-14 Mustad 3906 or 3906B
Thread:	Black 8/0
Tip:	Gold tinsel
Tail:	Ginger hackle barbs
Wing:	Mallard wing quill slips
Body:	Stripped peacock eye quill
Hackle:	Ginger

Golden Badger Variant

Hook:	#14-18 Mustad 94837 or equivalent
Thread:	Black 8/0
Tail:	Badger hackle barbs
Body:	Narrow gold tinsel
Hackle:	Golden badger or ginger

Gray Squirrel Silver Streamer

Hook:	#6-10 Mustad 3665A or equivalent limerick-bend
Thread:	Black 6/0
Wing:	Gray squirrel tail, two gray grizzly hackles
Body:	Embossed silver tinsel
Throat:	Golden pheasant crest dyed red
Cheeks:	Jungle cock eyes

Green Body Cut-Wing

Hook:	#12-18 Mustad 94837 or equivalent
Thread:	Tan 8/0
Tail:	Light dun hackle barbs
Wing:	Cut and shaped hackle tips
Body:	Insect green dubbing
Hackle:	Light dun

Strawman Nymph

Hook:	#12-16 Mustad 3906B or equivalent
Thread:	Tan
Tail:	Teal or mallard flank fibers
Body:	Sparsely tied deer body hair, clipped
Rib:	Yellow floss

Stripped Quill Variant

Hook:	#16 Mustad 94837 or equivalent
Thread:	Black 8/0
Tail:	Dun hackle fibers, long
Body:	Stripped Rhode Island Red hackle quill tied on shank, then varnished
Hackle:	Golden badger, long

White Marabou Streamer

Hook:	#6-8 Daiichi D7131 (modern)
Thread:	Black
Wing:	White marabou; peacock herl top
Body:	Oval silver tinsel
Shoulder:	Jungle cock eyes
Throat:	Red hackle barbs

Yellow Spinner

Hook:	#12 Bergman Red Label or equivalent long-shank dry-fly
Thread:	Tan or black 8/0
Tail:	Yellow hackle barbs
Wing:	Mallard flank, dyed yellow
Body:	Yellow floss
Rib:	Black thread
Hackle:	Badger

Fran Betters

Ausable Wulff

Hook:	#8-16 Mustad 94840 or 9671
Thread:	Hot orange
Tail:	Guard hair from woodchuck
Wing:	White calf tail
Body:	Australian possum dyed rusty orange
Hackle:	Grizzly and brown

Ausable Bomber

Hook:	#8-14 Mustad 9671 or other long-shank
Thread:	Hot orange
Tail:	Guard hair from woodchuck
Wing:	White calf tail
Body:	Palmer with brown and grizzly hackle
Hackle:	Grizzly and brown

Light Haystack

Hook:	#10-18 Mustad 9671
Thread:	Hot orange 4/0 or 5/0
Tail:	Small bunch of bleached-out cream deer hair
Wing:	Larger bunch of same color deer hair
Body:	Cream Australian possum

Dark Haystack

Hook:	#10-18 Mustad 9671
Thread:	Hot orange 4/0 or 5/0
Tail:	Dark brownish deer hair
Body:	Dark brown muskrat or beaver
Hackle:	Larger bunch of same color deer hair

Standard Mini-Muddler

Hook:	#8-10 Mustad 9671 or 9672
Thread:	Black or hot orange 5/0
Tail:	Mottled turkey quill or hen pheasant
Wing:	Mottled turkey or hen pheasant
Body:	Gold or silver Mylar tinsel
Collar:	Fine deer hair

Brook Mini-Muddler

Hook:	#8-10 Mustad 9671 or 9672
Thread:	Hot orange 5/0
Tail:	Mottled turkey quill or hen pheasant
Wing:	Yellow duck quill
Body:	Gold Mylar tinsel
Collar:	Fine deer hair

Note: This pattern is for rainbows and brookies.

The Usual

Hook:	#14-22 Mustad 94840 or 94842
Thread:	Hot orange 6/0
Tail:	Small bunch of hair from rabbit's pad
Wing:	Larger bunch of hair from rabbit's pad
Body:	Underfur from rabbit's foot dubbed on thread; use a blend of gray next to skin and very fine light tan guard hairs mixed in to make it float better

Cal Bird

Bird's Black Marabou Streamer

Hook:	#4-10 Mustad 3665A limerick-bend
Thread:	Black (long and tapered at head)
Wing:	Sparse orange bucktail; black marabou
Body:	White floss, tapered

Bird's Cutthroat Streamer

Hook:	#4-10 Mustad 3665A limerick-bend
Thread:	Black 6/0 (long and tapered at head)
Wing:	Dun bucktail top, white bucktail over body
Body:	White floss back two-thirds, red floss front one-third
Rib:	Narrow flat silver tinsel
Throat:	Three to four peacock herls and teal flank
Head:	Tapered red lacquer eye with yellow pupil

Bird's Nest (Mike Fong's version)

Hook:	#8-16 Mustad 7957BX, Mustad 9671, or Tiemco 3761
Thread:	Tan 6/0
Tail:	Mallard or teal flank feathers, tied short, dyed bronze
Body:	Grayish tan Australian opossum two-thirds the hook length
Rib:	Medium copper wire
Thorax:	Same color and material as body, although fuller and one-third the body length
Hackle:	Mallard or teal flank feathers, same color as tail

Bird's Stonefly (original brown)

Hook:	#8-12 Mustad 38941 or equivalent
Thread:	Orange
Tail:	Brown stripped goose tied in a V
Wing case:	Turkey quill
Body:	Beaver fur
Thorax:	Peacock herl palmered with brown hackle
Rib:	Orange thread

Bird's Stonefly (George Grant's version)

Hook:	#4-6, 2XLS Mustad 9671
Thread:	Orange 6/0
Tail:	Two strands coarse dark brown hair, divided
Wing:	Tan bucktail from northern white-tailed deer
Body:	Dark orange floss
Rib:	Furnace or dark brown saddle, clipped short, close turns
Antennae:	Same as tail, but longer
Hackle:	Furnace or dark brown, tied full, dry-fly style

Bird's Stonefly Nymph (experimental)

Hook:	#8-10 Mustad 38941 or equivalent
Thread:	Orange
Tail:	Two brown stripped goose, orange thread tag
Body:	Beaver fur abdomen, peacock herl thorax
Rib:	Orange thread
Throat:	Teal flank dyed brown

Copper Beadhead Bird's Nest (modern Matt Grobert fly)

Hook:	#12-18 Dai-Riki 285
Thread:	Olive 6/0 Danville
Tail:	Wood-duck flank fibers
Abdomen:	Medium Australian opossum
Thorax:	Medium Australian opossum fairly heavy and picked out to make it fuzzy
Rib:	Copper wire
Legs:	Wood-duck flank fibers
Head:	Copper bead to match hook size

Joe Brooks

Argentine Blonde

Hook:	#1/0-2/0 Mustad 34007 or equivalent
Thread:	Black 4/0 UNI-Thread
Tail:	White bucktail fibers
Wing:	Medium blue bucktail
Body:	Flat gold tinsel

Black Blonde

Hook:	#1/0-2/0 Mustad 34007 or equivalent
Thread:	Black 4/0 UNI-Thread
Tail:	Black bucktail fibers
Wing:	Black bucktail
Body:	Flat gold tinsel

Honey Blonde

Hook:	#1/0-2/0 Mustad 34007 or equivalent
Thread:	Black 4/0 UNI-Thread
Tail:	Yellow bucktail fibers
Wing:	Yellow bucktail
Body:	Flat gold tinsel

Pink Blonde

Hook: #1/0-2/0 Mustad 34007 or equivalent
Thread: Black 4/0 UNI-Thread
Tail: Pink bucktail fibers
Wing: Pink bucktail
Body: Flat gold tinsel

Platinum Blonde

Hook: #1/0-2/0 Mustad 34007 or equivalent
Thread: Black 4/0 UNI-Thread
Tail: White bucktail fibers
Wing: White bucktail
Body: Flat gold tinsel

Strawberry Blonde

Hook: #1/0-2/0 Mustad 34007 or equivalent
Thread: Black 4/0 UNI-Thread
Tail: Orange bucktail fibers
Wing: Red bucktail
Body: Flat gold tinsel

Wayne "Buz" Buszek

Buszek Hopper

Hook: #10-12 Mustad 94840
Thread: Black
Tail: Golden tippet fibers
Wing: Mule deer body hair bunch tied on so it flares out
Body: Dark straw or tan colored chenille
Hackle: Fiery brown

Note: Dressing from Herter's, tied by Don Lieb

Float-N-Fool Multi-Color

Hook: #12-16 Mustad 94838
Thread: Black 6/0
Tail: White calf
Body: Peacock herl
Rib: Reverse-wrapped fine gold wire
Winding post: White calf
Hackle: Brown and grizzly wrapped around white calftail post parachute style

Note: Dressing per Don Lieb

Kings River Caddis

Hook: #10-16 Mustad 94840
Thread: Brown or black 6/0
Wing: Mottled brown turkey quill section tied in at tip end
Body: Dubbed raccoon fur
Hackle: Brown

Note: Dressing per Don Lieb

McGinty

Hook: #8-14 Mustad 94840
Thread: Black 6/0
Tail: Red hackle fibers
Wing: White-tipped mallard duck secondary quill sections tied in on edge back over the body
Body: Yellow and black chenille; there are two bands of each color starting with black at the rear of the fly, and each band has two wraps of chenille
Hackle: Brown (wet)

Note: Dressing per Don Lieb

Old Grey Mare

Hook: #8-14 Mustad 94940
Thread: Brown or black
Tail: Scarlet red hackle fibers
Body: Red floss
Butt: Small green chenille
Hackle: Brown tied on as a collar

Note: Dressing per Don Lieb

Prince Nymph (Forked Tail Nymph)

Hook: #8-14 Mustad 7957BX
Thread: Black 6/0
Tail: Two brown goose biots
Wing: Two white goose biots (short side of the first flight feather)
Body: Peacock herl
Rib: Fine flat gold tinsel, counter-wrapped
Hackle: Two turns of furnace hackle (wet)

Note: Dressing per Don Lieb

Rio Grande King

Hook: #10-18 Mustad 94840
Thread: Brown or black 6/0
Tip: Fine gold tinsel
Tail: Golden pheasant tippets
Wing: White duck quill sections
Body: Fine black chenille
Hackle: Brown

Note: Dressing per Don Lieb

Western Coachman

Hook:	#6-14 Mustad 7957BX or standard wet-fly
Thread:	Buck Nymo A (original) or black 3/0-6/0
Tail:	Golden pheasant tippets
Wing:	White deer hair from flank of northern white-tailed deer
Body:	Peacock herl
Rib:	Fine gold wire, counter-wrapped through body
Hackle:	Coachman brown (wet)

Note: Dressing per Don Lieb

Zug Bug

Hook:	#8-14 Mustad 9671
Thread:	Black 6/0
Tail:	Peacock herl fibers two-thirds the length of body
Wing:	Lemon wood duck
Body:	Peacock herl
Rib:	Small oval silver tinsel
Hackle:	Soft furnace hackle

Note: Dressing per Don Lieb

Rube Cross

Cross Special

Hook:	#12-18 Mustad 94840 or equivalent
Thread:	Tan
Tail:	Light blue dun hackle fibers
Wing:	From flank feathers of drake wood duck or mandarin
Body:	Grayish white fox fur dubbing
Hackle:	Light blue dun cock hackle

Ray Arden

Hook:	#6-10 Mustad 3665A
Thread:	Black
Wing:	Brown bucktail over black bucktail
Body:	Red wool
Rib:	Flat gold tinsel
Underbelly:	White bucktail

Jack Schwinn

Hook:	#6-10 Mustad 3665A
Thread:	Black
Wing:	Brown bucktail
Body:	Orange wool
Rib:	Flat gold tinsel
Underbelly:	Yellow bucktail

Beaverkill

Hook:	#6-10 Mustad 3665A
Thread:	Black
Wing:	black bucktail
Body:	White wool
Rib:	Flat silver tinsel
Underbelly:	White bucktail

Brown Mallard

Hook:	#10-16 Mustad 94840
Thread:	Tan
Tail:	Bronze mallard with a couple ginger hackle fibers
Wing:	Bronze mallard
Body:	Tan fox fur
Hackle:	Dark to medium ginger

Art Neu

Hook:	#4-10 Mustad 79580
Thread:	Black
Tail:	Yellow hackle point tip and red hackle point tip
Wing:	White bucktail
Body:	White chenille
Rib:	Heavy red thread on rear third of body
Hackle:	Red and yellow mixed
Cheek:	Two long jungle cock eyes along wing

Harry and Elsie Darbee

Black Gnat

Hook:	#12-18 Mustad 94840 or equivalent
Thread:	Black
Tail:	Black cock hackle fibers
Wing:	Tied double, divided from slips of medium gray duck quill
Body:	Black chenille
Hackle:	Black

Coffin Fly

Hook:	#10-12 3XL or 4XL Mustad 94840 or equivalent
Thread:	White
Tail:	Black bear hair or black cock hackle fibers
Wing:	Black hackle tips
Body:	Clipped white deer hair
Hackle:	Badger

Dark Cahill

Hook: #10-18 Mustad 94840 or equivalent
Thread: Black
Tail: Red-brown cock's hackle fibers
Wing: From flank feather of drake wood duck or mandarin
Body: Gray muskrat fur dubbing
Hackle: Natural red-brown

Dun Variant

Hook: #10-12 Mustad 94837 or equivalent
Thread: Black
Tail: Natural dun cock hackle fibers
Body: Stripped quill from dark brown cock hackle, well lacquered
Hackle: Extralong stiff natural dun

Fanwing Royal Coachman

Hook: #10-12 Mustad 94840 or equivalent
Thread: Black
Tail: Golden pheasant tippet strands
Wing: Two matched white feathers from breast of drake wood duck, mandarin, or other wild duck
Body: Three equal parts: First third, peacock herl; center third, scarlet silk floss; last third, peacock herl
Hackle: Natural red-brown

Female Beaverkill

Hook: #12-16 Mustad 94840 or equivalent
Thread: Black
Tail: Ginger cock hackle fibers; egg sac, yellow wool or fine chenille
Wing: Tied double, divided slips from gray duck quill
Body: Gray muskrat fur dubbing
Hackle: Ginger

Ginger Quill

Hook: #12-16 Mustad 94840 or equivalent
Thread: White
Tail: Fibers from ginger hackle
Wing: Tied double, divided slips from mallard duck quill
Body: Stripped peacock quill; may be reinforced with fine gold wire
Hackle: Ginger

Gold-Ribbed Hare's Ear

Hook: #12-14 Mustad 94840 or equivalent
Thread: White
Tail: Furnace hackle fibers
Wing: Tied double, divided from sections of light gray mallard duck quill
Body: Hare's ear fur dubbing
Rib: Flat gold tinsel
Hackle: Furnace or coch-y-bondhu

Irresistible

Hook: #10-14 Mustad 94840 or equivalent
Thread: White or black
Tail: Dark deer hair from body of white-tailed deer
Wing: Body hair of white-tailed deer, same color as tail
Body: Dark gray clipped deer hair
Hackle: Dark rusty dun

Light Cahill

Hook: #10-18 Mustad 94840 or equivalent
Thread: White
Tail: Pale ginger cock hackle fibers
Wing: Flank of wood duck or mandarin drake
Body: Cream-colored fox fur dubbing
Hackle: Pale ginger

Pale Evening Dun

Hook: #12-18 Mustad 94840 or equivalent
Thread: White
Tail: Pale blue dun
Wing: Tied double, divided from slips of light gray duck quill
Body: Primrose yellow ribbed with fine flat gold tinsel
Hackle: Pale blue dun

Quill Gordon

Hook: #12-18 Mustad 94840 or equivalent
Thread: Black
Tail: Medium blue dun cock hackle fibers
Wing: From flank feather of drake wood duck or mandarin
Body: Stripped peacock quill; may be reinforced with fine silver wire
Hackle: Medium blue dun

Rat-Faced McDougall (Original)

Hook: #10-14 Mustad 94840 or equivalent
Thread: White
Tail: Ginger cock hackle fibers
Wing: Cream grizzly hackle tips
Body: Clipped tannish gray deer hair
Hackle: Ginger

Rat-Faced McDougall (White Wing)

Hook: #10-14 Mustad 94840 or equivalent
Thread: White
Tail: Ginger hackle fibers
Wing: White calftail hair
Body: Clipped tannish gray deer hair
Hackle: Ginger

Red Quill

Hook: #12-14 Mustad 94840 or equivalent
Thread: Black
Tail: Dark dun cock hackle fibers
Wing: From flank of wood duck or mandarin
Body: Stripped quill from dark brown cock hackle, well lacquered
Hackle: Dark dun

Spate Fly

Hook: #1/0 regular salmon-fly
Thread: Red
Tag: Oval gold tinsel
Tail: Golden pheasant crest feather
Wing: Bunch of brown bucktail, reaching to point of tail
Body: Dark brown seal fur or polar bear fur, spun on and slightly picked out
Rib: Medium-size oval gold tinsel
Throat: Several turns of black hackle, tied on as a collar and pulled down, the longest fibers reaching nearly to point of hook
Shoulders: Fairly wide strips of black and white wood duck, set on both sides of the bucktail and two-thirds as long

Note: From Bates's *Atlantic Salmon Flies & Fishing*

Wickham's Fancy

Hook: #12-14 Mustad 94840 or equivalent
Thread: Black
Tail: Ginger
Wing: Medium light gray tied double, divided from slips of duck quill
Body: Flat gold tinsel palmered with ginger hackle
Hackle: Ginger

Woodruff

Hook: #12-16 Mustad 94840 or equivalent
Thread: Black
Tail: Medium ginger cock hackle fibers
Wing: Tied spent of grizzly hackle tips
Body: Chartreuse green wool dubbing
Hackle: Medium ginger

Walt and Winnie Dette

Blue Quill

Hook: #10-16 Mustad 94840 or equivalent
Thread: White 6/0 UNI-Thread waxed to beige
Tail: Medium dun
Wing: Double-slipped mallard quill
Body: Stripped peacock eye quill
Hackle: Medium dun

Bradley Special

Hook: #10-16 Mustad 94840 or equivalent
Thread: White 6/0 UNI-Thread waxed to beige
Tail: Red cock
Wing: Mallard flank wings, slightly flared
Body: Back fur of red squirrel spun between two strands of red silk
Hackle: Red cock

Brown Bivisible

Hook: #10-16 Mustad 94840 or equivalent
Thread: White 6/0 UNI-Thread waxed to beige
Tail: Brown
Body: Palmered brown hackle
Front hackle: White

Dark Cahill

Hook: #10-18 Mustad 94840 or equivalent
Thread: White 6/0 UNI-Thread waxed to beige
Tail: Brown hackle fibers
Wing: Wood-duck flank
Body: Muskrat dubbing
Hackle: Brown

Light Cahill

Hook: #10-18 Mustad 94840 or equivalent
Thread: White 6/0 UNI-Thread waxed to beige
Tail: Light ginger
Wing: Wood-duck flank
Body: Dark cream fox fur
Hackle: Light ginger

Late Era Coffin Fly

Hook: #12-14 Mustad 79580
Thread: White 6/0 UNI-Thread waxed to beige
Tail: Three peccary fibers tied forked
Wing: Teal flank upright divided
Body: Trimmed white saddle hackle over white poly yarn
Rib: White 3/0 thread
Hackle: Golden badger, black centered and black edged

Conover

Hook: #12-18 Mustad 94840 or equivalent
Thread: White 6/0 UNI-Thread waxed to beige
Tail: Cream (straw shade)
Body: Muskrat and red wool blended to heathery claret gray
Hackle: Golden badger, no black edge

Corey Ford Variation

Hook: #12-16 Mustad 94840 or equivalent
Thread: White 6/0 UNI-Thread waxed to beige
Tail: Cream
Wing: Light dun hackle tips
Body: Creamy yellowish green fur dubbing
Hackle: Cream

Dark Hendrickson

Hook: #10-18 Mustad 94840 or equivalent
Thread: White 6/0 UNI-Thread waxed to beige
Tail: Medium dark dun hackle fibers
Wing: Wood-duck flank
Body: Muskrat dubbing
Hackle: Medium dark dun

Gordon

Hook: #12-16 Mustad 94840 or equivalent
Thread: White 6/0 UNI-Thread waxed to beige
Tail: Badger
Wing: Wood-duck flank
Body: Orange silk
Hackle: Badger

Fanwing Lady Beaverkill

Hook: #12-16 Mustad 94840 or equivalent
Thread: White 6/0 UNI-Thread waxed to beige
Tail: Ginger hackle barbs
Wing: Wood-duck breast feathers ("dirty" shade)
Body: Yellow chenille egg sac; muskrat fur
Hackle: Medium ginger

Fanwing Queen of Water

Hook: #10-12 Mustad 94840 or equivalent
Thread: White 6/0 UNI-Thread waxed to beige
Tail: Light ginger
Wing: Wood-duck breast feathers
Body: Orange silk
Hackle: Medium ginger

Isonychia Nymph

Hook: #10-12 Mustad 9672
Thread: White 6/0 UNI-Thread waxed to beige
Tail: Three or four cock ring-necked pheasant tail fibers
Wing case: Light shad mallard wing quill section, shiny side showing on top after section is pulled forward
Body: Abdomen of natural gray ostrich herl over a dubbing blend of two-thirds muskrat and one-third red wool
Underbody: Lead wire
Thorax: Muskrat dubbing fur
Rib: Brown thread, counter-wound to thorax for reinforcement
Legs: Brown partridge
Head: Brown lacquer

March Brown Nymph

Hook: #10-12 Mustad 9671
Thread: White 6/0 UNI-Thread waxed to beige
Tail: Fibers from center tail of cock ring-necked pheasant
Wing case: Hen pheasant
Abdomen: Brown fox fur
Thorax: Brown fox fur, humped
Rib: Medium gold oval tinsel
Legs: Brown partridge

The Quack

Hook: #10-16 Mustad 94840 or equivalent
Thread: White 6/0 UNI-Thread waxed to beige
Tail: Brown hackle fibers
Wing: White calftail fibers
Body: Peacock herl divided by band of red floss
Hackle: Brown

Quill Gordon

Hook:	#12-16 Mustad 94840 or equivalent
Thread:	White 6/0 UNI-Thread waxed to beige
Tail:	Medium to dark dun
Wing:	Wood-duck flank
Body:	Stripped peacock eye quill, counter-wound with beige thread
Hackle:	Medium to dark dun

Woodruff

Hook:	#12-16 Mustad 94840 or equivalent
Thread:	White 6/0 UNI-Thread waxed to beige
Tail:	Grizzly
Wing:	Grizzly hackle tips, tied spent
Body:	Dark chartreuse
Hackle:	Brown

Yellow Stonefly Nymph

Hook:	#10-14 Mustad 9672
Thread:	White 6/0 UNI-Thread waxed to beige
Tail:	Fibers from center tail of ring-necked pheasant
Wing case:	Barred lemon wood-duck section pulled forward
Abdomen:	Pale yellow wool
Thorax:	Same as abdomen but fuller
Underbody:	Fine lead wire
Rib:	Brown nymph thread
Legs:	Brown partridge hackle
Head:	Brown lacquer

Note: Materials have been slightly altered over time; the Dettes treated their thread fly heads with marine spar varnish, which darkened the heads; some nymphs were also coated with brown lacquer.

Art Flick

Black-Nose Dace

Hook:	Short-shank wet-fly
Thread:	Black
Tag:	Red yarn, very short
Wing:	Top of brown bucktail; middle of black bear or black skunk tail; bottom of white bucktail or natural polar bear
Body:	Flat silver tinsel

Blue-Winged Olive

Hook:	#16-18 Mustad 94837 or equivalent
Thread:	Olive (original) or black (optional)
Tail:	Dark dun, extralong
Body:	Olive yarn and muskrat fur blended
Hackle:	Dark dun, extra long

Dun Variant

Hook:	#10-12 Mustad 94840 or equivalent
Thread:	Olive
Tail:	Dark dun, long
Body:	Rhode Island Red rooster hackle, stripped and soaked
Hackle:	Dark dun

Dun Variant Nymph

Hook:	#10-12 Mustad 3906
Thread:	Olive
Tail:	Three very short pieces of peacock herl
Body:	Dark claret seal fur mixed with black wool
Hackle:	Grouse

Cream Variant

Hook:	#10-12 Mustad 94840 or equivalent
Thread:	Yellow
Tail:	Cream hackle barbs, long
Body:	Cream or white stripped rooster quill, well soaked
Hackle:	Cream, extra large

Early Brown Stone

Hook:	#14 Mustad 3906B
Thread:	Black
Wing:	Two small dun hackle points tied flat over body
Body:	Rhode Island Red rooster quill, stripped and well soaked
Hackle:	Soft dun hen

Grey Fox

Hook:	#12-14 Mustad 94840 or equivalent
Thread:	Primrose
Tail:	Ginger hackle barbs
Wing:	Mallard drake flank feathers
Body:	Light fawn-colored fur from red fox
Hackle:	Grizzly and light to medium ginger mixed

Grey Fox Variant

Hook: #10-14 Mustad 94840 or equivalent
Thread: Primrose
Tail: Ginger hackle barbs
Body: Light ginger or cream stripped rooster quill
Hackle: Mixed light ginger, dark ginger, and grizzly

Hendrickson

Hook: #12-14 Mustad 94840 or equivalent
Thread: Primrose
Tail: Light to medium dun
Wing: Wood-duck flank
Body: Pinkish gray fur from red fox
Hackle: Light to medium dun

Hendrickson Nymph

Hook: #12 Mustad 3906
Thread: Olive
Tail: Wood-duck flank feather
Wing case: Light gray wing quill
Body: Blended gray fox, beaver, and claret seal
Hackle: Partridge

March Brown

Hook: #10-12 Mustad 94840 or equivalent
Thread: Orange
Tail: Ginger hackle barbs
Wing: Wood-duck flank feather with heavy bars
Body: Light fawn-colored red fox fur
Hackle: Mixed grizzly and dark ginger

March Brown Nymph

Hook: #10-12 Mustad 3906
Thread: Orange
Tail: Three strands of pheasant tail fibers
Wing case: Ring-necked pheasant tail fibers
Body: Seal fur dyed amber blended with fawn red fox fur
Rib: Brown embroidery thread
Hackle: Partridge

Quill Gordon

Hook: #12-14 Mustad 94840 or equivalent
Thread: Primrose
Tail: Medium dun hackle barbs
Wing: Wood-duck flank
Body: Stripped peacock eye quill, counter-wrapped with fine gold wire
Hackle: Medium dun

Red Quill

Hook: #12-14 Mustad 94840 or equivalent
Thread: Black or very dark rust
Tail: Medium dun hackle barbs
Wing: Wood-duck flank
Body: Rhode Island Red rooster quill stripped and soaked
Hackle: Medium dun

Keith Fulsher

Thunder Creek Series Flies

Marabou Shiner Thunder Creek

Hook: #2-10, 4XL or 6XL straight-eye streamer
Thread: White 3/0 and 6/0
Flanks: Silver Krystal Flash
Back: Black marabou
Belly: White marabou
Head: Epoxy
Gills: Red enamel
Eyes: White and black enamel

Silver Shiner Thunder Creek with a Tail

Hook: #2-10, 4XL or 6XL straight-eye streamer
Thread: White 3/0 and 6/0
Tail: Two lesser covert feathers from hen pheasant wing
Flanks: Medium-width silver Mylar tinsel
Back: Brown bucktail
Belly: White bucktail
Head: Epoxy
Gills: Red enamel
Eyes: White and black enamel

Brook Trout

Hook: #2-10, 4XL or 6XL straight-eye streamer
Thread: White 3/0 and 6/0
Flanks: Pearl red Krystal Flash under grizzly hackles dyed olive on top of hook; bright orange bucktail under hook
Back: Brown part of a bucktail dyed blue
Belly: White bucktail
Gills: Red enamel
Eyes: White enamel with a dot of black enamel

Golden Shiner

Hook:	#2-10, 4XL or 6XL straight-eye streamer
Thread:	White 3/0 and 6/0
Flanks:	Yellow Krystal Flash under yellow bucktail
Back:	Brown part of a bucktail dyed green
Belly:	White bucktail
Gills:	Red enamel
Eyes:	White enamel with a dot of black enamel

Largemouth Bass

Hook:	#2-10, 4XL or 6XL straight-eye streamer
Thread:	White 3/0 and 6/0
Flanks:	Black floss ribbed with silver tinsel
Back:	Brown part of a bucktail dyed green
Belly:	White bucktail
Gills:	Red enamel
Eyes:	White enamel with a dot of black enamel

Smallmouth Bass

Hook:	#2-10, 4XL or 6XL straight-eye streamer
Thread:	White 3/0 and 6/0
Flanks:	Root beer Krystal Flash under barred ginger hackles
Back:	Brown part of a bucktail dyed green
Belly:	White bucktail
Gills:	Red enamel
Eyes:	Red enamel with a dot of black enamel

Rainbow Trout

Hook:	#2-10, 4XL or 6XL straight-eye streamer
Thread:	White 3/0 and 6/0
Flanks:	Pink Krystal Flash under pink bucktail
Back:	Brown part of a bucktail dyed green
Belly:	White bucktail
Gills:	Red enamel
Eyes:	White enamel with a dot of black enamel

Redfin Shiner (Spawning Male)

Hook:	#2-10, 4XL or 6XL straight-eye streamer
Thread:	White 3/0 and 6/0
Flanks:	Silver Krystal Flash on top of the hook shank; red bucktail under the shank
Back:	Brown bucktail
Belly:	White bucktail
Gills:	Red enamel
Eyes:	White enamel with a dot of black enamel

Redlip Shiner

Hook:	#2-10, 4XL or 6XL straight-eye streamer
Thread:	White 3/0 and 6/0
Flanks:	Pale yellow bucktail
Back:	Black bucktail
Belly:	Pale yellow bucktail
Tails:	Black floss
Body:	Black floss
Fins:	Short sections of orange floss tied to top and bottom of hook while wrapping body
Rib:	Embossed gold tinsel
Gills:	Red enamel
Eyes:	White enamel with a dot of black enamel
Lips:	Red enamel

Silver Shiner (Female and Immature)

Hook:	#2-10, 4XL or 6XL straight-eye streamer
Thread:	White 3/0 and 6/0
Flanks:	Silver Krystal Flash
Back:	Brown bucktail
Belly:	White bucktail
Gills:	Red enamel
Eyes:	White enamel with a dot of black enamel

Spottail Shiner

Hook:	#2-10, 4XL or 6XL straight-eye streamer
Thread:	White 3/0 and 6/0
Flanks:	Embossed gold tinsel
Back:	Brown part of bucktail dyed green
Belly:	White bucktail
Gills:	Red enamel
Eyes:	White enamel with a dot of black enamel
Caudal spot:	Black floss

Steelcolor Shiner

Hook:	#2-10, 4XL or 6XL straight-eye streamer
Thread:	White 3/0 and 6/0
Flanks:	Silver Krystal Flash under medium blue bucktail
Back:	Brown part of bucktail dyed blue
Belly:	Pale yellow bucktail
Gills:	Red enamel
Eyes:	White enamel with a dot of black enamel

Striped Jumprock

Hook:	#2-10, 4XL or 6XL straight-eye streamer
Thread:	White 3/0 and 6/0
Flanks:	Root beer Krystal Flash under pale orange bucktail
Back:	Dark brown bucktail
Belly:	Pale orange bucktail
Gills:	Red enamel
Eyes:	White enamel with a dot of black enamel

Wedgepot Shiner

Hook:	#2-10, 4XL or 6XL straight-eye streamer
Thread:	White 3/0 and 6/0
Flanks:	Black floss ribbed with embossed silver tinsel, with a strand of brown floss
Body:	Black floss
Back:	Brown bucktail
Belly:	White bucktail
Gills:	Red enamel
Eyes:	White enamel with a dot of black enamel

Atlantic Salmon Flies

Green Reynard

Hook:	#4 Gaelic
Thread:	White and black 6/0
Tag:	Oval gold tinsel
Tip:	Fluorescent green floss
Tail:	Guinea hen hackle fibers
Wing:	Red fox guard hair
Body:	Flat gold tinsel
Rib:	Oval silver tinsel
Head:	Black
Hackle:	Green hen, collar style

Rusty Rat

Hook:	#4 Gaelic
Thread:	Fluorescent red 6/0
Tag:	Fine oval gold tinsel
Tail:	Peacock sword tinsel
Wing:	Gray fox hair
Body:	Back half, fluorescent orange floss veiled over the top with a strand of orange floss; front half, peacock herl
Rib:	Fine oval gold tinsel
Head:	Fluorescent red
Hackle:	Grizzly hen, collar style

Squimp

Hook:	#6 Gaelic
Thread:	White 6/0
Tag:	Flat silver tinsel
Tail:	Long white bucktail, topped with several strands of pink Krystal Flash
Body:	Rear one-third, medium-width white chenille with Amherst pheasant tippets tied on as a veil; front two-thirds, fine white chenille ribbed with oval silver tinsel
Head:	White
Hackle:	Light dun hen, collar style

Don Gapen

Kennebago Muddler

Hook:	#6-12 Mustad 9674
Thread:	GSP 100 or similar strength, color to match deer hair
Tail:	Mallard flank
Underwing:	Gray squirrel tail
Overwing:	Mallard flank
Body:	Gold tinsel
Collar and head:	Spun deer hair in natural, yellow, or olive colors

Original Muddler Minnow

Hook:	#1-12, 3XL
Thread:	Black
Tail:	Natural turkey wing quill
Wing:	Moderately large bunch of gray squirrel tail hair with a fairly large section of mottled turkey wing feather tied on each side nearly as long as the bucktail
Body:	Wound with flat gold tinsel
Shoulders:	Natural deer body hair spun on to surround hook, flattened and clipped short at front and tapering longer backward, leaving a small part as long as possible
Head:	Black (red for weighted flies)

Missoulian Spook

Hook:	#6-12 Mustad 9674
Thread:	Black
Tail:	Mottled turkey wing quill fibers
Tag:	Red [chenille]
Wing:	Light turkey wing quill, almost white; white calf hair and teal underwing
Body:	White wool
Rib:	Silver tinsel

Note: Based on Joe Brooks's recipe in his October 1963 *Outdoor Life* article

Theodore Gordon

Bumblepuppy
(based on McDonald's description)

Hook:	#2-10 Mustad 79580
Thread:	Black
Tag:	Silver tinsel and red silk floss
Tail:	Red mallard quill wing slips
Wing:	White hair from deer over which are strips of goose quill
Body:	White silk chenille
Rib:	Medium flat silver tinsel
Throat:	Badger hackle
Shoulder:	Teal flank
Butt:	Red
Cheeks:	Jungle cock

Bumblepuppy
(Chauncy K. Lively version)

Hook:	#2-10 Mustad 79580
Thread:	Black
Tag:	Silver tinsel and red silk floss
Tail:	Red mallard quill wing slips
Wing:	White hair from deer over which are strips of goose quill
Body:	White silk chenille
Rib:	Badger hackle palmer
Throat:	Badger hackle
Shoulder:	Teal flank
Butt:	Yellow chenille
Cheeks:	Jungle cock

Bumblepuppy
(based on Herm Christian version)

Hook:	#2-10 Mustad 79580
Thread:	Black
Tail:	Red hackle fibers
Wing:	White bucktail; lower half of bucktail bunch is clipped off at about half its length after being tied in, over which is a wing of two sections of brown turkey quill
Body:	White chenille
Rib:	Single strand of red wool yarn
Throat:	Mixed red and white neck hackle

Ginger Quill

Hook:	#12-16 Mustad 94840
Thread:	Brown
Tail:	Ginger hackle barbs
Wings:	Mallard quill slips
Body:	Stripped peacock quill
Hackle:	Ginger

Gordon

Hook:	#12-16 Mustad 94840 or equivalent
Thread:	Beige
Tail:	Cream badger hackle fibers
Wing:	Wood-duck flank
Body:	Old gold silk floss ribbed with fine gold oval tinsel
Hackle:	Cream badger

Quill Gordon

Hook:	#12-16 Mustad 94840
Thread:	Black
Tail:	Dun
Wing:	Wood-duck flank
Body:	Stripped peacock eye quill
Hackle:	Dun

George Grant

Black Creeper

Hook:	#8, 3XLS Mustad 9672
Thread:	Black
Floss core:	Any color, built up to form taper
Underbody:	Formed by binding ½-inch-long straight brass pins on each side of core
Outer shell:	.018-inch-diameter round nylon monofilament, dyed black
Belly stripe:	Burnt orange floss
Hackle:	Woven elk hair or black Tynex nylon fiber, ½ inch lateral length

Murder Orange

Hook:	#4-8, 3XLS Mustad 9672 or Wilson salmon
Tip:	Fine flat gold tinsel (optional)
Tail:	Orange polar bear
Wing:	White bucktail (original) or polar bear
Body:	Deep orange chenille, thick
Rib:	Fine gold oval (optional)
Hackle:	Dark brown (original) or deep orange

Trude

Hook:	#4 salmon fly
Thread:	Orange
Wing:	Red squirrel tail tied long to show dark band
Body:	Red yarn
Rib:	Silver tinsel
Hackle:	Brown

Liz Greig

Campeona

Hook:	1/0-3/0 black salmon, upturned and tapered loop eye
Thread:	Red
Tag:	Four or five turns of narrow silver tinsel
Tail:	Two long sections of red duck quill
Wing:	Fairly large bunch of peacock herls of equal length, extending beyond tail
Body:	Bright medium green wool, applied as dubbing, pulled out loosely, especially on underside of body, after ribbing has been applied
Rib:	Medium flat silver tinsel
Throat:	Three or four turns of dark red hackle, rather long and gathered downward; the body's wool dubbing should nearly reach tip of throat toward front of body
Shoulder:	Tip of a teal body feather, covering the peacock and one-third as long as wing
Butt:	Three turns of fine white chenille

Lizzie

Hook:	1/0 Mustad 340B O'Shaughnessy
Thread:	Red
Wing:	Red bucktail, two times length of hook shank
Body:	Pink floss
Rib:	Oval silver tinsel
Hackle:	Red and white collar

George Griffith

Griffith's Gnat

Hook:	#14-24 Mustad 94840 or equivalent
Thread:	Black
Body:	Peacock herl
Hackle:	Grizzly palmered to head

Hi-Viz Griffith's Gnat

Hook:	#14-24 Mustad 94840 or equivalent
Thread:	Black
Post:	Fluorescent orange, pink, or chartreuse McFlylon
Body:	Peacock herl
Hackle:	Grizzly palmered to head

Len Halladay

Adams

Hook:	#10-20 Mustad 94840 or equivalent
Thread:	Black 8/0
Tail:	Golden pheasant tippets (original) or mixed grizzly and brown hackle barbs (modern)
Wing:	Grizzly hackle tips tied semispent (original) or upright (modern)
Body:	Gray wool (original) or muskrat fur (modern)
Hackle:	Mixed grizzly and brown

Adams Female

Hook:	#12-18 Mustad 94840 or equivalent
Thread:	Black 6/0
Tail:	Brown and grizzly hackle fibers
Wing:	Grizzly hackle tips
Body:	Muskrat
Butt:	Yellow chenille
Hackle:	Mixed brown and grizzly (dry)

George Harvey

Harvey's Night Fly

Hook:	2/0-8/0 extra long shank
Thread:	Black
Tail:	Small kickers made of stiff stems (optional)
Wing:	Pheasant body feathers
Body:	Black dubbing or chenille
Hackle:	Black or dark blue dun, palmered

Harvey Sulphur

Hook:	#14-16 Mustad 94840 or equivalent
Thread:	Pale yellow
Tail:	Light ginger or dyed sulphur rooster hackle fibers
Wing:	White hen hackle tips
Body:	Pale yellow, orange, or light pink dubbing
Hackle:	Light ginger or dyed sulphur rooster

Spruce Creek Dry Fly

Hook:	#12-20 Mustad 94840 or equivalent
Thread:	Black
Tail:	Dark dun rooster hackle fibers
Wing:	Wood-duck flank or dun hen hackle tips
Body:	Black quill from peacock sword
Hackle:	Dark dun, nearly black

Ed Hewitt

Badger Bivisible

Hook:	#10-#14 Mustad 94840, Mustad 94831, or equivalent
Thread:	Black or beige
Tail:	Two badger hackle tips
Hackle:	White tied in near head; badger behind to bend of hook

Black Bivisible

Hook:	#10-14 Mustad 94840, Mustad 94840, Mustad 94831, or equivalent
Thread:	Black or beige
Tail:	Two black hackle tips
Hackle:	White tied in near head; black behind to bend of hook

Brown Bivisible

Hook:	#10-14 Mustad 94840, Mustad 94831, or equivalent
Thread:	Black or beige
Tail:	Two brown hackle tips
Hackle:	White tied in near head; brown behind to bend of hook

Dun Bivisible

Hook:	Mustad 94840, Mustad 94831, or equivalent
Thread:	Black or beige
Tail:	Two dun hackle tips
Hackle:	White tied in near head; dun behind to bend of hook

Light Cahill Bivisible

Hook:	Mustad 94840, Mustad 94831, or equivalent
Thread:	Black or beige
Tail:	Cream hackle barbs
Body:	Light fox fur
Hackle:	White tied in near head; cream halfway down hook shank behind white

Olive Bivisible

Hook:	Mustad 94840, Mustad 94831, or equivalent
Thread:	Black or beige
Tail:	Two olive hackle tips
Hackle:	White tied in near head; olive behind to bend of hook

Royal Coachman Bivisible

Hook:	Mustad 94840, Mustad 94831, or equivalent
Thread:	Black or beige
Tail:	Golden pheasant tippet
Body:	Rear, peacock herl; middle, red silk; front, peacock herl
Hackle:	White hackle tied in near head; brown hackle behind

John Alden Knight

Cochy Knight

Hook:	#12-14 Mustad 94840 or equivalent
Thread:	Tan
Tail:	Coch-y bondhu or furnace hackle barbs
Body:	Cream shade fox fur
Hackle:	Coch-y bondhu or furnace palmer

Flat-Bodied Nymph

Hook:	#10-16 Mustad 3906 or equivalent
Thread:	Brown, tan, or black
Tail:	Brown hackle barbs
Body:	Red fox fur, top darkened with marker, pressed flat with pliers
Rib:	Dark brown heavy thread
Hackle:	Sparse brown, trimmed top and bottom

Knight's Brown Bomber

Hook:	#3/0 Orvis 13KE, black-finish, straight-eye
Thread:	Black 6/0
Tail:	Yellow bucktail
Wing:	Two to four brown saddle hackles; underbody yellow bucktail
Body:	Light brown wool
Rib:	Narrow oval gold tinsel
Shoulder:	Yellow duck or goose quill slips
Hackle:	Yellow

Knight's Delaware

Hook: #3/0 Orvis 13KE, black-finish, straight-eye
Thread: Black 6/0
Tail: Red goose quill
Wing: Two to four white saddle hackles; underbody white bucktail
Body: Yellow chenille
Rib: Narrow oval silver tinsel
Tag: Red chenille
Shoulder: Red duck or goose quill slips
Hackle: Red

Mickey Finn

Hook: #4-12 Mustad 79580
Thread: Black 6/0
Wing: Three layers of dyed bucktail: Top, yellow; middle, red; bottom, yellow
Body: Flat silver tinsel
Rib: Oval silver tinsel

Mickey Finn, Bass Version

Hook: #3/0 Orvis 13KE, black-finish, straight-eye
Thread: Black 6/0
Wing: Three layers of dyed bucktail: Top, yellow; middle, red; bottom, yellow
Body: White wool
Rib: Narrow oval silver tinsel

Sunshine Fly

Hook: #12-18 Mustad 94840 or equivalent
Tail: Light badger hackle barbs
Body: Olive floss or dyed dubbing
Hackle: Light badger palmer

Jim Leisenring and V. S. "Pete" Hidy

Hare's Ear

Hook: #13-14
Thread: Primrose yellow
Tail: Two or three fibers of fine mottled feather of wood duck or mandarin duck
Wing: English woodcock secondaries with buff tip
Body: Fur from lobe or base of hare's ear spun on primrose yellow thread
Rib: Narrow flat gold tinsel
Legs: A few fibers of dubbing picked out for legs

Note: See photo of hook models on page 172

Iron Blue Wingless

Hook: #14-15
Thread: Crimson or claret
Tail: Two short dark honey dun cock fibers
Body: Dark mole fur spun on crimson thread, very thin at tail to expose thread
Rib: Fine gold wire (optional)
Hackle: Honey dun hen with red points or a very dark honey dun

Note: See photo of hook models on page 172

Old Blue Dun

Hook: #12-14
Thread: Primrose yellow
Tail: Two or three glassy fibers from rusty blue dun cock's hackle
Wing: Starling (optional)
Body: Muskrat underfur spun on primrose yellow thread, a little thread showing through dubbing at tail
Rib: One strand yellow buttonhole twist
Hackle: Blue dun hen

Note: See photo of hook models on page 172

Stewart's Red Spider

Hook: #14-15
Thread: Primrose yellow
Body: Waxed tail thread
Hackle: Landrail

Note: See photo of hook models on page 172

Tup's Nymph

Hook: #13-14
Thread: Primrose yellow
Body: Rear half of primrose yellow buttonhole twist; thorax or shoulder of mixed yellow and claret seal fur dubbing spun on primrose thread
Hackle: Very small light blue hen or medium dark honey dun hen

Note: See photo of hook models on page 172

Eric Leiser

Black Angus

Hook: #2-4 Mustad 79580
Thread: Black
Tail: Four black neck hackles flaring away from each other
Body: Heavy lead wire underbody covered with black floss
Overbody: Black marabou feathers wound around hook shank
Head: Black deer hair spun and trimmed to a wedge shape

Chuck Caddis

Hook: #10-18 Mustad 94840
Thread: Orange, gray, or brown
Wing: Woodchuck guard hairs
Body: Dirty orange dubbing
Hackle: Brown and grizzly mixed

Note: Gray, olive, black, and yellow dubbing can also be used

Llama

Hook: #6-12 Mustad 3665A
Thread: Black
Tail: Grizzly hackle fibers
Wing: Woodchuck guard hair fibers; all colored bands on guard hairs should show
Body: Red floss
Rib: Flat gold tinsel
Hackle: Grizzly hen
Head: Black and white painted eye on head

Chauncy K. Lively

Brassie Nymph

Hook: #12-20 Mustad 7957BX in larger sizes, 94840 in smaller sizes
Thread: Black 8/0
Body: Wire in various gauges, depending on hook size
Thorax: Muskrat fur including guard hairs

Carpenter Ant (Original)

Hook: #12-16 Mustad 94840 or equivalent
Thread: Black 6/0 to 8/0
Body: Three folds of black deer body hair, segmented
Legs: Four or five clipped deer hair fibers on each side of head

Note: Later tied with legs extending from waist area

Green Drake Dun

Hook: #12 Mustad 94804 or equivalent
Thread: Beige 6/0
Tail: Three ring-necked pheasant tail feather fibers
Wing: Two mottled ring-necked pheasant back feathers, cut and shaped
Body: Rear, buff shade deer or elk body hair tied as extended body from just short of hook bend; main, yellow dyed fur palmered with grizzly or grizzly and brown hackle; palmered hackle trimmed from underside, leaving an inverted V
Hackle: Grizzly and brown

Note: Front of main body is sometimes tied with just brown hackle

Hendrickson's Dun

Hook: #12-14 Mustad 94840 or up-eye dry-fly
Thread: Beige
Tail: Medium dun hackle barbs
Wing: Cut and shaped flank feather
Body: Tannish-yellowish natural fur blend (body extends in front of wings)
Thorax: Tannish-yellowish natural fur blend
Hackle: Medium dun tied as parachute underneath body

Leatherneck Streamer

Hook:	#4-6 Mustad 7957BX, Mustad 3906B, or equivalent
Thread:	Black 6/0
Tail:	Stiff red hackle barbs
Wing:	Short section of muskrat, mink, or rabbit fur Zonker Strip folded over body
Body:	Copper wire in various gauges, depending on hook size
Throat:	Red hackle barbs

Note: The wing is secured both at the hook bend and after it is folded forward over the body.

March Brown Dun

Hook:	#12 Mustad 94840 or equivalent
Thread:	Brown to beige 6/0
Tail:	Two fibers from wood-duck flank feather (original) or other two-fiber tail
Wing:	Two small mottled ring-necked pheasant back feathers, cut and shaped
Body:	Fawn shade fox fur; brown and grizzly hackle, palmered
Hackle:	Grizzly and brown with barb length two times hook gap

March Brown, Wonder Wing Style

Hook:	#12 Mustad 94840 or equivalent
Thread:	Beige 8/0
Tail:	Two fibers from very light brown deer or elk hair
Wing:	Inverted light brown hackle tips, preferably mottled
Body:	Rear, light brown deer or elk body hair tied from just short of hook bend as extended body, secured with wraps of heavy brown thread; main, fawn shade fox fur, brown and grizzly hackle mixed and palmered, extending to just short of hook eye; palmered hackle trimmed from underside, leaving an inverted V
Hackle:	Brown and grizzly, palmered

Note: Tied in thorax style

Michigan Stone Dry Fly

Hook:	#16 Mustad 94840 or equivalent or up-eye dry-fly
Thread:	Light yellow 8/0
Wing:	Fine-textured deer body hair
Body:	Yellow dyed rabbit fur
Hackle:	Tied fore and aft, grizzly at hook bend and in front of wing

Robber Fly

Hook:	#12-14 Mustad 94840 or equivalent
Thread:	Black 8/0
Wing:	Natural elk or deer hair
Body:	Rear: Light deer or elk body tied from just short of hook bend as extended body, secured with wraps of heavy beige thread; main: Peacock herl
Hackle:	Mixed brown and grizzly

Sulphur Dun

Hook:	Mustad 94840 or equivalent or up-eye dry-fly
Thread:	Cream or light yellow 8/0
Tail:	Light dun hackle barbs
Body:	Dyed yellow natural fur or material of choice
Hackle:	Medium dun tied as parachute underneath body

Note: Tied in thorax style; Lively tied this pattern in different variations, sometimes with mallard quill slip wings and palmered hackle.

Yellow Stonefly

Hook:	#10-12, 2XL Mustad or up-eye dry-fly
Thread:	Light yellow 6/0-8/0
Tail:	Two light goose biots, separated
Wing:	Micro Web or similar synthetic material of choice, cut and shaped
Body:	Yellow foam
Hackle:	Light dun, palmered, extending to just short of hook eye; palmered, trimmed from underside, leaving an inverted V

Mary Orvis Marbury

Grasshopper

Hook:	#8-12 Mustad 3899
Thread:	Black
Tip:	Gold
Tag:	Green floss
Tail:	Yellow goose and barred wood duck
Wing:	Jungle cock eyes and strips of yellow and red goose over
Body:	Orange cotton embroidery thread, doubled
Head:	Peacock herl
Hackle:	Red

Imperial

Hook:	#2/0 Mustad 3899 Sproat
Tag:	Flat silver tinsel
Tail:	White and scarlet married goose; slate capercaillie
Wing:	Mallard black-tipped wing feather; scarlet goose splits
Body:	Pink floss
Rib:	Silver round tinsel (vintage eight-ply with black markings)
Head:	Red Berlin wool
Hackle:	White and black

McCloud

Hook:	#3/0 Allcock 1906m Sproat
Tag:	Oval gold tinsel, light yellow floss
Tail:	Lemon mallard or unbarred wood duck red/scarlet goose
Wing:	Mottled turkey, red splits
Body:	Light green floss
Rib:	Oval gold tinsel
Head:	Red Berlin wool
Butt:	Scarlet floss
Hackle:	Yellow

Notion

Hook:	#3/0 Allcock 1906 Sproat
Tag:	Oval silver tinsel (vintage)
Tail:	Golden pheasant crest, blue macaw
Wing:	Golden pheasant tippet feather, yellow turkey, brown mottled turkey, and blue turkey
Body:	Aft, gold embossed tinsel (vintage); fore, brown seal fur
Rib:	Brown schlappen
Throat:	Brown schlappen
Cheek:	Chatterer
Sides:	Teal
Head:	Black ostrich herl
Hackle:	Dark green schlappen

Parm Belle

Hook:	#4-12 Mustad 3899
Thread:	Red
Tip:	Gold
Tag:	Peacock herl
Tail:	Red and white goose
Wing:	White goose with red strip over
Body:	Yellow wool
Rib:	Silver
Hackle:	Red and white mixed

Royal Coachman (Antique Version)

Hook:	#4-8 Mustad 3899
Thread:	Red
Tip:	Fine gold tinsel
Tag:	Red silk
Tail:	Barred wood duck
Wing:	White goose quill slips
Body:	Rear, peacock herl; middle, red silk; front, peacock herl
Hackle:	Brown

Williams

Hook:	#9 Allcock 5907 Kensey
Thread:	Red
Tag:	Flat silver tinsel
Tail:	Red and yellow goose, peacock swords
Wing:	Yellow-dyed gray mallard
Body:	Yellow floss
Rib:	Oval silver tinsel and dark green hackle, palmered from midbody
Hackle:	Dark green schlappen
Cheek:	Scarlet ibis or red spoon feather

Vince Marinaro

Fanwing Sulphur Dun

Hook:	#14-16 Mustad 94840 or equivalent
Thread:	Dark yellow or tan
Tail:	Dun hackle spread out
Wing:	Grayish duck breast feathers or equivalent
Body:	Yellowish dubbing at thorax position and at head area
Hackle:	Badger tied crisscross around wings

Green Drake Spinner (Coffin Fly)

Hook:	#8-12 wide-gap, short-shank, up-eye
Thread:	Black
Tail:	Three long rabbit whiskers or long chocolate hackle fibers, if available
Wing:	Dun hackle wrapped as hackle, clipped top and bottom, or wide hackle-tip wings
Body:	Porcupine quill

Green Drake Thorax Dun

Hook: #10-12 Mustad 94840 or equivalent
Thread: Dark yellow or amber
Tail: Three long mottled stripped hackle quills or equivalent
Wing: Wood-duck flank feathers, cut and shaped, tied in thorax position
Body: Creamy yellow fur dubbing
Hackle: Badger tied in crisscross

Hendrickson Spinner

Hook: #12, 2XL dry-fly
Thread: Black
Tail: Three dun hackle fibers, long and widely separated
Wing: Bronze dun hackle, clipped top and bottom
Body: Rusty dubbing

Jassid

Hook: #18-28 Mustad 94837 or equivalent
Thread: Orange (original)
Wing: Jungle cock eye
Body: Palmered ginger hackle, clipped top and bottom

Pontoon Hopper

Hook: #8 Mustad 94840 or equivalent
Thread: Brown
Body: Turkey tail feather quill tip
Legs: Small quills from duck flight feathers
Antennae: Moose mane (optional)

Don Martinez

Dunham

Hook: #12-18 Mustad 94840 or equivalent
Thread: Beige
Tail: Brown tied very long
Body: Yellow and blue macaw quill
Hackle: Rear, furnace; front, grizzly dyed blue

Ginger Quill Nymph

Hook: #10-14 Mustad 3906B or equivalent
Thread: Beige
Tail: Two fibers, quite long
Wing case: Peacock sword
Abdomen: Natural and yellow macaw quill
Thorax: Yellow chenille with peacock sword (wing cases)
Hackle: Sparsely tied ginger

Golden Quail

Hook: #12-14 Mustad 94840 or equivalent
Thread: Beige
Tail: Golden pheasant crest
Wing: Grayish white quail breast feathers or equivalent
Body: Rear, gold tinsel; front, one wrap orange chenille
Hackle: Grizzly

Hopkins Variant

Hook: #12-16 Mustad 94840 or equivalent
Thread: Beige
Tail: Brown
Wing: Jungle cock eye, short
Body: Yellow and blue macaw quill
Hackle: Furnace sized very long

Martinez Black Nymph

Hook: #8-12 Mustad 9671
Thread: Black 6/0
Tail: Speckled guinea body feathers
Wing case: Green raffia
Body: Black seal fur or lamb's wool
Rib: Small oval gold tinsel
Thorax: Black chenille
Hackle: Gray Hungarian partridge

Phantom Wooly Worm

Hook: #2-12 Mustad 79580 or equivalent
Thread: Beige
Tail: Peacock sword bottom; red wool piece top
Body: Black chenille
Hackle: Golden badger, palmered

Note: This is Don Martinez's spelling of the traditional Woolly Worm.

Rough Water Yellow

Hook:	#10-12 Mustad 94840 or equivalent
Thread:	Beige
Tail:	Grizzly hackle barbs
Body:	Dyed yellow deer hair, clipped
Hackle:	Grizzly

Whitcraft or Quill Adams

Hook:	#12-16 Mustad 94840 or equivalent
Thread:	Beige
Tail:	Mixed brown and grizzly hackle barbs
Wing:	Grizzly hackle tips (rooster)
Body:	Yellow and blue macaw quill
Hackle:	Mixed grizzly and brown

Woolly Worm

Hook:	#2-12 Mustad 79580 or equivalent
Thread:	Black
Tail:	Red hackle barbs
Body:	Black chenille
Hackle:	Grizzly palmered

Note: Original had concaved hackle toward eye but can be tied either direction

Joe Messinger Sr.

Irresistible

Hook:	#10-16 Mustad 94840 or equivalent
Thread:	Black
Tail:	Brown deer body hair
Wing:	Brown bucktail
Body:	Dun or brown top, white belly
Hackle:	Claret or dun

Messinger Meadow Frog

Hook:	#1/0-1 Mustad 3366 or #6-10 Tiemco 8089
Thread:	Black
Legs:	Golden brown bucktail top, yellow bucktail bottom; plated brass pins, with heads removed, embedded in hair; black lacquer applied to thread at knees
Body:	Clipped golden brown deer body hair top, white bottom
Eyes:	Flexible plastic: Cover with acetone in small jar and let stand overnight; then roll small pieces into balls; put small amount Duco cement on head where eyes will be positioned; press jelly-like plastic balls into head, then flatten; paint gold after eyes harden

Thaddeus Norris

Alder

Hook:	#8-12 Kirby eyeless hook, snelled
Thread:	Black
Wing:	Brown hen wing quill
Body:	Black mohair, front picked out downward to represent legs

Note: A modern hook option for all the Norris flies is Mustad 94840 with the eye clipped off, then snelled.

Black Palmer Hackle Fly

Hook:	#4-12 Kirby eyeless hook, snelled
Thread:	Black
Body:	Black floss
Hackle:	Black, palmered, front one-third of fly body

Dotterel

Hook:	#8-12 Kirby eyeless hook, snelled
Thread:	Black
Body:	Yellow floss
Hackle:	Gray partridge

Ginger Hackle

Hook:	#8-12 Kirby eyeless hook, snelled
Thread:	Black
Body:	Ginger shade fur body
Rib:	Fine oval silver tinsel
Hackle:	Ginger

Grouse Hackle

Hook:	#8-12 Kirby eyeless hook, snelled
Thread:	Black
Tip:	Gold tinsel
Body:	Peacock herl
Hackle:	Partridge, snipe, or woodcock

Palmer

Hook:	#4-12 Kirby eyeless hook, snelled
Thread:	Black
Body:	Peacock herl
Rib:	Fine oval gold tinsel
Hackle:	Brown palmer

Red Spinner

Hook:	#8-12 Kirby eyeless hook, snelled
Thread:	Black
Tail:	Long brown hackle barbs
Wing:	Starling wing or mallard quill slips
Body:	Hog's wool dyed red-brown
Hackle:	Amber stained hackle barbs

Lew Oatman

Brook Trout

Hook:	#6-10 Mustad 3665A or equivalent or streamer
Thread:	Olive green on top and sides, white underneath
Tail:	A bunch of fibers from rich orange hackle, a bunch from black hackle, and a bunch from white hackle; the orange is on top, the black below, and the white below the black, forming the color scheme of a trout's fin
Wing:	Two olive green saddle hackles outside of two grizzly hackles; the olive green hackles are stained along the quill with yellow and scarlet dots
Body:	Rear three-quarters, white floss; front one-quarter, salmon pink floss tapered quite full and ribbed with medium flat gold tinsel
Throat:	Same as tail
Cheeks:	Jungle cock eyes

Cut Lips

Hook:	#6-10 Mustad 3665A or equivalent or streamer hook of choice
Thread:	Black
Tail:	Bunch of fibers from blue dun hackle feather
Wing:	Pair of dark blue dun saddle hackles outside of two olive green saddle hackles
Body:	Lavender floss or wool ribbed with medium narrow flat silver tinsel
Throat:	Same as tail
Cheeks:	Jungle cock eyes

Ghost Shiner

Hook:	#6-10 Mustad 3665A or equivalent or streamer
Thread:	Same as wing color
Tail:	Few fibers from light green hackle
Wing:	Sparse bunch of very light brown or tan summer sable tail
Body:	White floss, tapered, ribbed with medium flat silver tinsel
Throat:	Fibers from white hackle
Cheeks:	Jungle cock eyes

Golden Darter

Hook:	#6-10 Mustad 3665A or equivalent or streamer
Thread:	Black
Tail:	Mottled turkey wing quill
Wing:	Two golden-edged badger saddle hackles
Body:	Clear yellow floss, slightly tapered, ribbed with medium narrow flat gold tinsel
Throat:	Tip of jungle cock body feather
Cheeks:	Jungle cock eyes

Golden Shiner

Hook:	#6-10 Mustad 3665A or equivalent or streamer
Thread:	Black
Tail:	Orange fibers from base of an orange hackle or goose or swan nashua feather
Wing:	Bunch of clear yellow bucktail topped with four peacock herl and flanked on either side with gray blue dun saddle hackles
Body:	White floss, tapered, ribbed with medium flat gold tinsel
Throat:	Bunch of white bucktail and below that a wisp like the tail
Cheeks:	Jungle cock eyes

Gray Smelt

Hook:	#2-12 Mustad 3665A or equivalent or streamer
Thread:	Gray
Tail:	Golden pheasant crest feather
Wing:	Two blue dun saddle hackles outside of two light green saddle hackles
Body:	White floss, tapered, ribbed with medium flat silver tinsel
Cheeks:	Jungle cock eyes

Little Brown Trout (a Sam Slaymaker II fly)

Hook:	#4-12 Mustad 3665A or equivalent or streamer
Thread:	Black
Tail:	Very small breast feather from ring-necked pheasant
Wing:	Top to bottom: Medium dark squirrel tail, very small bunch reddish orange bucktail, very small bunch yellow bucktail
Body:	White spun wool
Rib:	Flat gold tinsel or copper wire
Cheek:	Jungle cock eyes

Mad Tom

Hook:	#2-4 standard-shank
Thread:	Black
Tag:	Several turns of medium flat silver tinsel down to bend of hook
Tail:	Two bunches of marabou fibers: Small short bunch of white above longer bunch of tobacco brown extending about 1½ inches from bend of hook
Body:	Wrap hook shank with white floss; just ahead of tail, tie on a bunch of black marabou fibers that top the full length of tail, then tie in the end of a thick black chenille rope and wind back and forth, tying off at head
Hackle:	Coarse hackle with fibers about 1 inch long wound on as a collar

Male Dace

Hook:	#4-12 Mustad 3665A or equivalent or streamer
Thread:	Black
Wing:	Two golden-edged badger saddle hackles outside of two olive green saddle hackles, all same length and all slender
Body:	Very pale cream floss, tapered, ribbed with medium narrow gold tinsel
Throat:	Few fibers from rich orange hackle
Cheeks:	Jungle cock eyes

Red Horse

Hook:	#8-6 Mustad 3665A or equivalent or streamer
Thread:	Black
Tail:	Tips of orange dyed hackle outside of two yellow dyed
Wing:	Two gray blue dun saddle hackles outside of two olive green saddle hackles, same length and extending well beyond the tail
Body:	White wool ribbed with oval silver tinsel
Throat:	Same as tail
Cheeks:	Jungle cock eyes

Shushan Postmaster

Hook:	#4-12 Mustad 3665A or equivalent or streamer
Thread:	Black
Tail:	Turkey quill slip
Wing:	Red squirrel tail
Body:	Yellow floss, tapered
Throat:	Red duck or goose quill fibers
Cheeks:	Jungle cock eyes

Silver Darter

Hook:	#4-12 Mustad 3665A or equivalent or streamer
Thread:	Black
Tail:	Silver pheasant wing quill
Wing:	Two white-edged badger saddle hackles
Body:	White floss, slightly tapered, ribbed with medium narrow flat silver tinsel
Throat:	Fibers from peacock sword feather
Cheeks:	Jungle cock eyes

Trout Perch

Hook:	#2-10 Mustad 3665A or equivalent or streamer
Thread:	Gray tan to match upper body
Tail:	Fibers from a blue dun hackle
Wing:	Small bunch of fine straw-colored summer sable tail hair
Body:	White floss, tapered, ribbed with medium flat silver tinsel
Throat:	Same as tail
Cheeks:	Jungle cock eyes

Yellow Perch

Hook:	#2-6 Mustad 3665A or equivalent or streamer
Thread:	Black
Tail:	Fibers from a yellow dyed hackle
Wing:	Two yellow saddle hackles outside of two yellow dyed grizzly hackles with wide dark bands
Body:	Pale cream or amber floss ribbed with medium flat gold tinsel
Throat:	A few yellow hackle fibers edged with four or five orange hackle fibers
Cheeks:	Jungle cock eyes (not too large)
Topping:	Several peacock herl

Franz Pott

Black Ant

Hook:	#10-12 Mustad 3960
Thread:	Black
Body:	Rear half, dyed black badger hair; front half, size A yellow thread; underbody stripe, size A yellow thread
Hackle:	Dyed black badger hair

Note: Eurasian badger is much different from North American badger, which is not appropriate for Pott-style flies. Yarn is cotton embroidery material.

Black Jack

Hook: #10-12 Mustad 3960
Thread: Black
Body: Rear quarter, natural barred badger hair; front three-quarters, white hair; underbody stripe, size A orange thread
Hackle: Dyed black badger

Buddy Mite

Hook: #10-12 Mustad 3960
Thread: Black
Body: White badger hair with size A orange thread underbody stripe
Hackle: Natural white badger with black bars and white tips

Dina Mite

Hook: #10-12 Mustad 3960
Thread: Black
Body: Black dyed badger with size A yellow thread underbody stripe
Hackle: Black dyed badger

Lady Mite

Hook: #10-12 Mustad 3960
Thread: Black
Body: Natural sandy ox ear hair with two turns of black hair at rear and size A orange thread underbody stripe
Hackle: Natural white badger with black bars with white tips

Maggot

Hook: #10-12 Mustad 3960
Thread: Black
Body: White badger hair with size A orange thread underbody stripe
Hackle: Dyed black badger

Mr. Mite

Hook: #10-12 Mustad 3960
Thread: Black
Body: White badger hair with size A orange thread underbody stripe
Hackle: Dark brown dyed badger

Orange Fibber

Hook: #10-12 Mustad 3960
Thread: Black
Body: Orange yarn twisted
Hackle: Natural sandy ox ear hair

Red Cliff Special

Hook: #10-12 Mustad 3960
Thread: Black
Body: Red yarn, peacock herl wrap at rear
Hackle: Dark brown dyed badger

Red Fizzle

Hook: #10-12 Mustad 3960
Thread: Black
Body: Red yarn with dark brown badger over top
Hackle: Dark brown dyed badger

Rockworm

Hook: #10-12 Mustad 3960
Thread: Black
Body: Cream and white yarn with silver tinsel twisted together
Hackle: Natural Eurasian badger hair with black bars and white tips

Sandy Mite

Hook: #10-12 Mustad 3960
Thread: Black
Body: Natural sandy ox ear hair with size A orange thread underbody stripe
Hackle: Natural sandy ox ear hair

Yellow Badger

Hook: #10-12 Mustad 3960
Thread: Black
Body: Orange and yellow yarn twisted
Hackle: Natural badger hair with black bars and white tips

Yellow Fizzle

Hook: #10-12 Mustad 3960
Thread: Black
Body: Yellow yarn twisted with dyed black badger hair over top
Hackle: Natural badger hair with black bars and white tips

C. Jim Pray

Black Demon

Hook:	#2-4 Mustad 7970
Thread:	Black
Wing:	Black bucktail or dyed black polar bear
Body:	Flat gold tinsel
Hackle:	Orange

Silver Demon

Hook:	#2-8 Eagle Claw 1197N
Thread:	Black
Wing:	Teal flank feather
Tail:	Orange hackle barbs
Body:	Oval silver tinsel
Hackle:	Orange

Note: Pattern based on Sturgis's *Fly Tying*, from actual flies tied by Jim Pray that appear in the color plate; hook based on Hellekson's pattern

Black Optic

Hook:	#2-4 Mustad 7970
Thread:	Black
Wing:	Black bucktail
Body:	Gold oval tinsel
Throat:	Black hackle
Head:	Black bead with yellow iris and black pupil

Brown and White Optic

Hook:	#2-4 Mustad 7970
Thread:	Black
Wing:	White bucktail bottom; brown bucktail top
Body:	Oval silver tinsel
Head:	Black bead with yellow iris and black pupil

Cock Robin Optic

Hook:	#2-4 Mustad 7970
Thread:	Black
Wing:	Squirrel or badger hair
Body:	Silver oval tinsel
Throat:	Orange hackle
Head:	Black bead with yellow iris and black pupil

Orange Optic

Hook:	#2-4 Mustad 7970
Thread:	Black
Wing:	Orange bucktail
Body:	Silver oval tinsel
Throat:	Red hackle (sometimes tied without a throat)
Head:	Black bead with white iris and red pupil

Red Optic

Hook:	#2-4 Mustad 7970
Thread:	Black
Wing:	Red bucktail bottom; yellow bucktail top
Body:	Silver oval tinsel
Head:	Black bead with yellow or red iris and black pupil

Red and White Optic

Hook:	#2-4 Mustad 7970
Thread:	Black
Tail:	Red polar bear
Wing:	White polar bear bottom; red polar bear top
Body:	Embossed silver tinsel
Head:	Red bead with white iris and black pupil

Yellow Optic

Hook:	#2-4 Mustad 7970
Thread:	Black
Tail:	Yellow bucktail
Wing:	White bucktail bottom; yellow bucktail top
Body:	Oval gold tinsel
Head:	Yellow bead with white iris and black pupil

Thor

Hook:	#2-4 Mustad 7970
Thread:	Black
Tail:	Orange hackle barbs
Wing:	White bucktail or polar bear
Body:	Scarlet red chenille
Hackle:	Brown

André Puyans

Loop Wing McCaw Adams

Hook:	#12-18 Mustad 39803, 94840, or 94845
Thread:	6/0 Danville Flymaster prewaxed in proper color
Tail:	Hackle fibers
Wing:	Teal fibers tied in loop fashion
Body:	Natural or synthetic dubbing
Head:	Dubbing
Hackle:	Brown and grizzly mixed

A.P. Beaver Nymph

Hook:	#10-18 Mustad 3906B
Thread:	Black
Tail:	Dark moose hair
Wing case:	Dark moose hair
Body:	Dark beaver dubbed
Rib:	.006-inch copper wire (abdomen only)
Head:	Dark beaver, same color as body
Legs:	Dark moose hair

A.P. Black Beaver Nymph

Hook:	#10-18 Mustad 3906B
Thread:	Black
Tail:	Dark moose hair
Wing case:	Dark moose hair
Body:	Dyed black beaver
Rib:	.006-inch copper wire (abdomen only)
Head:	Thread or dubbed black beaver
Legs:	Dark moose hair

A.P. Claret and Beaver Nymph

Hook:	#10-18 Mustad 3906B
Thread:	Black
Tail:	Dark moose hair
Wing case:	Dark moose hair
Body:	Blend dubbing: Two-fifths medium beaver, one-fifth claret seal fur, one-fifth fiery seal fur, one-fifth hare's ear
Rib:	.006-inch gold or copper wire (abdomen only)
Head:	Thread, varnished or dubbed with body mix
Legs:	Dark moose hair

A.P. Hare's Ear/Beaver Nymph

Hook:	#10-18 Mustad 3906B
Thread:	Tan prewaxed (varnished) or brown 1523 Nymo (lacquered)
Tail:	Bronze mallard
Wing case:	Bronze mallard
Body:	Blend half hare's ear, half medium color beaver dubbing
Rib:	.006-inch gold wire (abdomen only)
Legs:	Bronze mallard

A.P. Hendrickson Nymph

Hook:	#10-18 Mustad 3906B
Thread:	Tan 6/0 prewaxed
Tail:	Bronze mallard or dark elk hair
Wing case:	Bronze mallard or dark elk hair
Body:	Reddish brown dyed beaver
Rib:	.006-inch copper wire (abdomen only)
Head:	Tan 6/0 prewaxed (varnished) or dubbed with body color
Legs:	Bronze mallard or dark elk hair

A.P. Muskrat Nymph #1

Hook:	#10-18 Mustad 3906B
Thread:	Gray 6/0 prewaxed
Tail:	Blue dun hackle fibers
Wing case:	Bronze mallard (not too dark)
Body:	Dark muskrat (from back of muskrat)
Rib:	.006-inch gold wire (abdomen only)
Head:	Gray 6/0 prewaxed (varnished) or dubbed muskrat
Legs:	Bronze mallard (not too dark)

A.P. Muskrat Nymph #2

Hook:	#10-18 Mustad 3906B
Thread:	Gray 6/0 prewaxed
Tail:	Dark moose hair
Wing case:	Dark moose hair
Body:	Dark muskrat (from back)
Rib:	.006-inch gold wire (abdomen only)
Head:	Gray 6/0 prewaxed (varnished) or dubbed muskrat
Legs:	Dark moose hair

A.P. Olive Nymph

Hook: #10-18 Mustad 3906B

Thread: Olive 6/0 prewaxed

Tail: Finely marked dyed olive mallard flank

Wing case: Finely marked dyed olive mallard flank

Body: Beaver dyed medium olive

Rib: .006-inch gold wire (abdomen only)

Head: Olive 6/0 prewaxed or dubbed with same olive beaver

Legs: Finely marked dyed olive mallard flank

Note: Wing case can be darkened with a black felt pen

A.P. Peacock and Pheasant

Hook: #10-18 Mustad 3906B or 9671

Thread: Black

Tail: Pheasant center tail section

Wing: Pheasant center tail section

Body: Bronze peacock herl

Rib: .006-inch copper wire (abdomen only)

Head: Black thread (varnished)

Legs: Pheasant center tail section

Note: Select pheasant center tail sections so dark center portion covers wing case

C&H Mutant Midge

Hook: #18-22 TMC 102Y

Thread: Black

Tail: Wood-duck flank, clipped

Wing: Black poly looped to head

Body: Stripped peacock eye quill, segmented; thorax of grizzly hackle, clipped

E. H. "Polly" Rosborough

Black Drake Nymph

Hook: #10-12 Mustad 38941 or equivalent

Thread: Gray 6/0

Tail: Very finely barred guinea hen body feather fibers

Wing case: Six natural grayish black ostrich flues, clipped off square

Body: Muskrat, beaver, and rabbit blend

Hackle: Sparse guinea hen body feather fibers

Black Midge Pupa

Hook: #12-18 Mustad 3906

Thread: Gray 6/0

Body: Black ostrich flues tag; muskrat or similar shade synthetic yarn tapered forward

Hackle: Grizzly at rear tag

Casual Dress

Hook: #4-10 Mustad 38941 or equivalent

Thread: Black 6/0

Tail: Muskrat with guard hairs

Head: Black ostrich

Body: Muskrat with guard hairs, picked out to very rough texture

Collar: Muskrat with guard hairs, flared back

Dark Caddis

Hook: #6-10 Mustad 94840

Thread: Black 6/0

Tail: Brown hackle barbs projecting from body material at hook bend

Wing: Brown bucktail

Body: Tangerine dubbing of choice

Rib: Palmer furnace or brown hackle

Hackle: Furnace

Dark Salmon (or stone) or equivalent

Hook: #4 Mustad 38941 sproat bend

Thread: Black 6/0

Tail: Two turkey quill slips, short

Wing: Brown bucktail

Body: Tangerine wool or dubbing of choice

Rib: Heavy nickel-shade thread

Hackle: Brown

Dark Stonefly Nymph

Hook: #2-4 Mustad 38941 or equivalent

Thread: Pale tan

Tail: Four or five dark mottled turkey fibers or equivalent

Wing case: Dark brown mottled turkey, clipped short

Body: Dirty or off-white fox fur or badger underfur; top side mottled turkey or equivalent

Rib: Heavy tan thread

Hackle: Dark brown mottled turkey fibers, sparse

Fledermouse

Hook: #2-16 Mustad 3906B

Thread: Tan 6/0

Wing: Gray mallard mixed with brown wigeon (original) or equivalent

Body: Blend of muskrat and natural brown mink with a small amount of rabbit fur, tied very rough and ragged

Green Rock Worm

Hook: #8 Mustad 3906B

Thread: Black 6/0

Head: Black ostrich flues

Body: Light green synthetic yarn

Hackle: Guinea hen fibers or dark teal flank fibers dyed slightly green

Golden Stone Dry Fly

Hook: #4-6 Mustad 38941 or or equivalent

Thread: Golden yellow or dark yellow 8/0

Wing: Golden dyed deer hair

Body: Golden yellow chenille, palmered with golden yellow dyed hackle

Hackle: Golden yellow

Golden Stonefly Nymph

Hook: #4-6 Mustad 38941 or equivalent

Thread: Antique gold or dark yellow substitute

Tail: Teal dyed rich gold, well barred

Body: Teal dyed rich gold top; white fox underfur dyed rich gold

Rib: Heavy antique gold thread

Hackle: Teal dyed rich gold

Green Damsel Nymph

Hook: #10 Mustad 38941 or equivalent

Thread: Olive 6/0

Tail: Olive marabou

Wing: Olive marabou tuft

Body: Olive rabbit or yarn

Rib: Heavy dark olive thread

Hackle: Teal dyed olive

Hare's Ear

Hook: #6-14 Mustad 3906B

Thread: Black 6/0

Wing: Speckled black and brown leghorn hen wing feather slips

Head: Three twisted ostrich flues

Body: Blend of muskrat belly, rabbit back, and medium brown mink

Little Yellow Stonefly Nymph

Hook: #10-12 Mustad 38941 or equivalent

Thread: Pale chartreuse or dark yellow 6/0

Tail: Mallard flank feathers, dyed chartreuse

Wing case: Mallard flank dyed gold (chartreuse original)

Body: Rabbit fur dyed chartreuse

Rib: Heavy chartreuse thread

Meadow Grasshopper

Hook: #10 Mustad 38941 or equivalent

Thread: Pale yellow or white 6/0

Wing: Turkey quill slips dyed pale yellow

Body: Creamy yellow dubbing

Hackle: Body palmered with light yellow hackle; light dun in front of wing

Muskrat Nymph

Hook: #6-10 Mustad 38941 or equivalent

Thread: Black 6/0

Head: Ostrich

Body: Muskrat, beaver belly, and rabbit blended

Hackle: Guinea hen fibers

Polar Chub

Hook: #2-6 Mustad 38941

Thread: Olive 6/0

Wing: Bottom, white polar bear; middle, golden olive polar bear; top, olive brown polar bear

Head: Painted yellow eye with black pupil

Body: Underbody floss; oval silver tinsel

Shrimp

Hook: #6-10 Mustad 3906

Thread: Tan 8/0

Tail: Medium to light ginger hackle tip

Body: Tan synthetic yarn or natural fur blend of same shade; ginger hackle palmer, trim top side of hackle

Silver Admiral

Hook:	#1-6 Eagle Claw 1197N
Thread:	Black 6/0
Tail:	Hot pink hackle barbs
Wing:	White polar bear or bucktail
Body:	Hot pink yarn
Rib:	Medium silver tinsel
Hackle:	Hot pink

Silver Garland Marabou

Hook:	#2-8 Mustad 79580
Thread:	Black 6/0
Wing:	White marabou; ostrich flues top
Body:	Silver tinsel chenille
Head:	Painted yellow eye with black pupil

Helen Shaw

Bubble Pup

Hook:	#2-6 Mustad 79580
Thread:	Yellow
Wing:	Two black saddle hackles
Head:	Yellow deer body hair clipped in front at angle; flared deer body hair projecting rear from back of head

Female Beaverkill Variation

Hook:	#10-16 up-eye dry-fly
Thread:	Brown
Tail:	Teal flank fibers tied very short
Wing:	Dark mallard quill slips
Body:	Gray floss
Butt:	One wrap yellow chenille
Hackle:	Brown

Golden Furnace Streamer

Hook:	#4-8 Mustad 3665A
Thread:	Black
Tip:	Gold flat tinsel
Tail:	Golden pheasant tail feather or dark mottled turkey
Wing:	Two pairs of red-gold furnace hackle
Body:	Bright orange floss
Rib:	Flat gold tinsel
Throat:	Light golden brown furnace hackle

Hopper

Hook:	#10 up-eye dry-fly
Thread:	Black
Tail:	Dyed red duck quill slip
Wing:	Turkey quill slips
Body:	Yellow dubbing
Rib:	Palmered badger hackle
Hackle:	Very long badger

Red Shiner

Hook:	#2/0, 2XL Jamison barbless ringed
Thread:	Pearl gray
Tail:	Red and orange bucktail mixed
Wing:	Polar hair above hook; white bucktail next; topped with natural brown bucktail hair dyed slate blue
Body:	Flat silver tinsel
Rib:	Fine oval silver tinsel or silver wire
Throat:	Orange and red bucktail mixed
Underbody:	Three cones of red and orange bucktail hair mixed long enough to cover hook point
Cheeks:	Silver pheasant; jungle cock eyes

Ed Shenk

Black Sculpin

Hook:	#8-10 Tiemco 300 or equivalent
Thread:	Black
Tail:	Black marabou plume
Wing:	Black marabou (optional)
Body:	Black fur, tied as fur chenille and trimmed to a wedge shape
Fins:	Untrimmed tips of black deer hair from head, extending flared on either side of body
Head:	Black deer hair, trimmed broad and flat

Ed Shenk Cress Bug

Hook:	#12-20 Mustad 3906B
Thread:	Gray or olive, prewaxed
Body:	Muskrat, mink, or otter fur, straight colors or blended; form a fur of dubbing, loop, wrap solidly to head of fly, tie off, and trim fur flat on bottom, shallow oval on top, broad oval on sides

Double Ephoron

Hook:	#14, 3XL Mustad 9672
Thread:	White
Tail:	White deer hair spread into V shape
Wing:	White polypropylene, tied spent
Body:	Chalky white fur head, thorax, and abdomen

Double Trico (Male)

Hook:	#18, 3XF Mustad 94840 or 94833
Thread:	Black
Tail:	Three strands bucktail dyed palest blue dun, spread into a wide V
Wing:	Palest blue dun polypropylene tied spent for each body
Body:	Rear body: Black fur with enlarged thorax tied to center of hook; front body: Black fur, enlarged thorax tied to eye of hook

Double Trico (Female)

Hook:	#18, 3XF Mustad 94840 or 94833
Thread:	Black
Tail:	Three strands bucktail dyed palest blue dun, spread into a wide V
Wing:	Palest blue dun polypropylene tied spent for each body
Body:	Rear body: Cream abdomen, black fur body and thorax; front body: Black fur head, thorax, and abdomen

Double Trico Spinner

Hook:	#18 Mustad 94840
Thread:	Black
Tail:	Three white hairs from a deer tail, spread wide
Wing:	White polypropylene tied spent
Body:	Abdomen, white for female, black for male; thorax, black fur behind and in front of spent wings

Note: Make the completed fly on rear half of hook, then repeat another fly on forward half of hook. Front fly does not require a tail.

Shenk's Letort Hopper

Hook:	#6-18 Mustad 9671 or 9672
Thread:	Black
Wing:	Section of mottled tan turkey feather, folded and tied flat, with tip trimmed
Body:	Yellow, cream, tan, or orange spun fur or Fly Rite
Head:	Spun tan deer hair, trimmed to shape
Hackle:	Swept-back tips of tan deer hair from head, trimmed on underside

Shenk Minnow Series

Hook:	#8-10, 3X-4XL Tiemco 300 or equivalent
Thread:	White
Tail:	White marabou plume not quite as long as hook shank
Body:	Cream or white fox fur tied as fur chenille, trim to minnow shape
Head:	Black or gray nylon thread; painted eyes optional

Sulphur Dun

Hook:	#16 Mustad 94840 or equivalent
Thread:	Yellow
Tail:	Stiff cream hackle fibers
Body:	Cream for abdomen, orange for thorax
Hackle:	One each of buff, light ginger, and cream

Sulphur Dun, Cut-Wing

Hook:	#14-16 Mustad 94840 or equivalent
Thread:	Yellow
Tail:	Brown bucktail or light dun hackle barbs, split into V shape
Wing:	Pale blue dun body feathers shaped with wing cutter
Body:	Abdomen, yellowish dubbing; thorax, orange dubbing; head region, fine yellowish dubbing
Hackle:	Buff or cream tied behind and in front of wing, trimmed on underside

Carrie Stevens

Colonel Bates

Thread:	Black
Hook:	#2-6 Allcock 1810
Tail:	Dyed red duck quill slip
Wing:	Two yellow saddle hackles, with a slightly shorter white saddle hackle on each side
Body:	Flat silver tinsel
Throat:	Soft brown hackle barbs
Shoulder:	Teal breast feathers
Cheeks:	Jungle cock eyes

Note: Modern hook options for all the Carrie Stevens streamers include the Gaelic Supreme Mike Martinek's Carrie Stevens Streamer Hook, made in Redditch, England, or other streamer hook of choice. Carrie's signature mark was to tie the head with a red band, which is not listed in the patterns.

Don's Delight

Hook:	#2-6 Allcock 1810
Thread:	Black
Tail:	Red hackle fibers
Wing:	Four white saddle hackles
Body:	Medium flat gold tinsel
Throat:	White hackle fibers
Shoulder:	Golden pheasant tippet feather
Cheeks:	Jungle cock eyes

Embden Fancy Streamer

Hook:	#2-6 Allcock 1810
Thread:	Black
Wing:	Several strands of peacock herl; two blue saddle hackles surrounded by an orange saddle hackle on each side, then those surrounded on each side by a grizzly saddle hackle dyed dark or golden yellow
Body:	Flat silver tinsel
Underbody:	Small bunch of white bucktail that extends beyond hook bend
Throat:	Gray mallard fibers
Cheeks:	Jungle cock eyes

F.R.S. Fancy

Hook:	#2-6 Allcock 1810
Thread:	Black
Wing:	Bottom, white bucktail; top, orange bucktail topped by brown bucktail
Body:	Flat silver tinsel

General MacArthur

Hook:	#2-6 Allcock 1810
Thread:	Red, white, and blue
Tail:	Red hackle barbs
Wing:	Two white saddle or neck hackles, on each side of which is a light blue saddle hackle; on each side of these is a grizzly saddle hackle
Body:	Medium flat silver tinsel
Throat:	Beginning underneath the head, dark blue hackle barbs, followed by white hackle barbs, followed by red hackle barbs
Cheeks:	Jungle cock eyes

Gray Ghost

Hook:	#2-6 Allcock 1810
Thread:	Black
Tag:	Narrow flat silver tinsel
Wing:	Four olive gray saddle hackles tied over a golden pheasant crest feather curving downward
Body:	Orange floss
Rib:	Flat silver tinsel
Underbody:	Small bunch of white bucktail that extends beyond hook bend
Throat:	Peacock herl strands
Shoulder:	Silver pheasant body feather
Cheeks:	Jungle cock eyes

Gray Lady

Hook:	#2-6 Allcock 1810
Thread:	Black
Wing:	Several peacock herl, with four dun saddle hackles
Body:	Flat silver tinsel
Underbody:	Small bunch of white bucktail that extends beyond hook bend
Throat:	White soft hackle barbs
Shoulder:	Light blue feather
Cheeks:	Jungle cock eyes

Indian Rock

Hook:	#2-6 Allcock 1810
Thread:	Red
Wing:	Several peacock herls, with two dyed red saddle hackles surrounded by two dyed olive saddle hackles
Body:	Flat silver tinsel
Underbody:	Small bunch of white bucktail that extends beyond hook bend
Throat:	Soft white hackle barbs
Cheeks:	Jungle cock eyes

The Judge

Hook:	#2-6 Allcock 1810
Thread:	Red
Wing:	Several peacock herls, over which are tied dyed red grizzly hackles; white bucktail projects from bottom of fly head past hook bend
Body:	Flat silver tinsel
Underbody:	Small bunch of white bucktail that extends beyond hook bend
Throat:	White hackle barbs

Note: The book on Stevens by Hilyard and Hilyard also reports dyed red grizzly hackle barbs and white hackle barbs on the throat

Morning Glory

Hook: #2-6 Allcock 1810
Thread: Red
Wing: Black silver pheasant crest, over which are tied four yellow saddle hackles
Body: Red floss
Rib: Flat silver tinsel
Underbody: Small bunch of white bucktail that extends beyond hook bend
Throat: Small bunch of blue hackle barbs
Shoulder: Red macaw body feather
Cheeks: Jungle cock eyes

Note: The Hilyard and Hilyard book also describes black hackle barbs along with the blue for the throat.

Pink Lady

Hook: #2-6 Allcock 1810
Thread: Black
Wing: Several peacock herls tied in with four grizzly saddle or neck hackles
Body: Pink floss
Rib: Flat silver tinsel
Throat: Soft pink hackle barbs
Shoulder: Finely barred mallard flank feathers
Cheeks: Jungle cock eyes

Rapid River

Hook: #2-6 Allcock 1810
Thread: Black
Wing: Two light green hackles, with dun saddle or neck hackles on each side
Body: Orange floss
Rib: Flat silver tinsel
Throat: Green and pink hackle barbs; golden pheasant crest below
Shoulder: Finely barred mallard flank feather extending halfway down hook shank
Cheeks: Jungle cock eyes

Shang's Favorite

Hook: #2-6 Allcock 1810
Thread: Black
Wing: Four grizzly saddle or neck hackles
Body: Red floss
Rib: Flat silver tinsel
Shoulder: Dyed red breast feather from duck or goose
Cheeks: Jungle cock eyes

Ted Trueblood

Integration
(Black and White Version)

Hook: #10 Mustad 79580
Thread: Black
Wing: Black bucktail top; white bucktail bottom
Body: Oval silver tinsel

Integration
(Dun and White Version)

Hook: #10 Mustad 79580
Thread: Black
Wing: Dyed blue dun bucktail top; white bucktail bottom
Body: Oval silver tinsel

Montana Nymph

Hook: #8-10 Mustad 38941 or equivalent
Thread: Black 6/0 to 8/0
Tail: Two goose quill
Body: Brown chenille abdomen; orange chenille thorax; top of thorax brown chenille
Hackle: Black

Trueblood Fledermaus

Hook: #8-16 Mustad 7957BX
Thread: Black
Body: Mixed muskrat and coyote tail fur
Throat: Red squirrel tail hair tips

Trueblood Shrimp

Hook: #8-16 Mustad 7957BX
Thread: Brown
Tail: Brown partridge fibers
Body: Mixture of otter and natural cream seal
Hackle: Brown partridge fibers

Trueblood's Stone Fly

Hook: #6-12 Mustad 38941
Thread: Black
Tail: Natural gray goose quill fibers taken from back of flight quill and tied in a V
Body: Dark brown chenille

Dave Whitlock

Dave's Hopper

Hook:	#6-12 Tiemco 5263
Thread:	Hopper yellow 170 Wapsi UTC Ultra Thread
Tail:	Natural dyed red deer hair, short and stiff
Wing:	Speckled oak secondary wing quill of turkey or peacock
Underwing:	Pale yellow deer hair
Body:	Yellow, tan, or olive polypropylene yarn
Rib:	Brown or cree neck or saddle hackle
Kicker legs:	Cock golden or ring-necked pheasant center tail feathers
Collar and head:	Natural dark deer hair from northern white-tailed or roe deer
Weed guard:	Mason hard nylon, three-quarters diameter of hook
Cements:	Dave's Flexament, Zap-A-Gap, and spray fixative, clear

Matuka Sculpin

Hook:	#2-10 Tiemco 9395
Thread:	Yellow 170 Wapsi UTC Ultra Thread
Tail and back:	Red cree and olive variant neck hackles
Body:	Foundation: Mason hard nylon, diameter of hook wire; weight: Lead or lead-free wire, diameter of hook wire
Rib:	Medium brass wire
Throat:	Minnow gills, red Whitlock originals plus #24 SLF dubbing
Belly:	Minnow belly, pale yellow Whitlock originals plus #22 SLF dubbing
Collar and head:	Pale yellow, natural gray-brown, black, golden brown, and olive deer hair
Pectoral fins:	Cock ring-necked pheasant back feathers
Eyes:	Yellow and black solid plastic doll eyes
Snag guard:	Mason hard nylon, three-quarters diameter of hook
Cements:	Dave's Flexament, Zap-A-Gap, and Goop

NearNuff Crayfish (Brown)

Hook:	#4-10 Tiemco 5263
Thread:	Orange 6/0 Danville Flymaster
Tail and nose:	Natural brown rabbit fur
Body:	Foundation: 0.018- to 0.028-inch Mason hard nylon; dubbing: NearNuff Crayfish natural brown Whitlock plus #19 SLF dubbing
Weighting:	Small, medium, or large lead dumbbell eyes with brown epoxy paint
Eyes:	0.025-inch Mason hard nylon with black enamel paint
Antennae:	Black Spanflex, gold Krystal Flash, and pumpkin seed Sili Legs
Legs:	Golden grizzly hen
Claws:	Dark ginger hen saddle with fluorescent red acrylic enamel
Cements:	Dave's Flexament and Zap-A-Gap

NearNuff Sculpin (Olive)

Hook:	#4-10 Tiemco 5263
Thread:	Orange 6/0 Danville Flymaster
Body:	Olive dubbing
Tail:	Grizzly hen hackles dyed olive
Eyes:	Painted lead eyes
Thorax:	Black dubbing
Head:	Olive dubbing
Hackle:	Soft hackle grizzly dyed olive, palmered
Accent:	Olive Krystal Flash

Whit Hopper

Hook:	#6-12 Tiemco 5263
Thread:	Hopper yellow 170 Wapsi UTC Ultra Thread
Tail:	Natural dyed red deer hair, short and stiff
Wing:	Speckled oak secondary wing quill of turkey or peacock
Underwing:	Pale yellow deer hair
Body:	Yellow, tan, or olive coarse deer or elk rump hair; foundation: Mason hard nylon, diameter of hook wire
Rib:	Tying thread or medium gold wire
Kicker legs:	Dyed yellow cock golden pheasant center tail feather or grizzly neck hackle
Collar and head:	Natural gray-brown and pale yellow deer hair from white-tailed or roe deer
Antennae:	Brown neck hackle stems
Weed guard:	Mason hard nylon, three-quarters diameter of hook
Cements:	Dave's Flexament, Zap-A-Gap, and spray fixative, clear

Whitlock Sculpin

Hook: #1/0-8, 3XL, 2X stout TDE; Mustad 9672 or 38941; or Buz's special 2X stout
Thread: Light orange 1560 Nymo or equivalent
Wing: Two dark well-marked soft webby cree neck hackles, tinted golden brown or golden olive
Underwing: Red fox squirrel tail
Body: Dubbing blend of light amber seal, tan fox, yellow seal, and white rabbit; tint should be rich yellowish cream
Rib: Gold oval tinsel
Weight: Lead wire
Gill: Red wool dubbing
Pectoral fins: Two fanlike breast feathers from body of hen mallard, prairie chicken, or hen pheasant
Collar: Natural light dun-brown deer hair tinted yellow, golden brown, or golden olive. combined with black or very dark brown deer hair, clipped and shaped
Head: Same as collar

Note: From *Art Flick's Master Fly Tying Guide*

Art Winnie

Michigan Caddis

Hook: #8 Mustad 94831 or equivalent long shank
Thread: Gray or black
Tail: Three bucktail hairs
Wing: Mallard wing quill slips
Body: Yellow floss
Hackle: Dark ginger hackle tied fore and aft

Michigan Hopper

Hook: #8-10 Mustad 94831 or equivalent
Thread: Black
Tail: Long dyed red duck or goose quill fibers
Wing: Turkey feather slips
Body: Yellow chenille
Hackle: Ginger

Lee Wulff

Gray Wulff

Hook: #10-12 Mustad 94840 or longer-shank, heavier-wire Mustad 9671
Thread: Black 6/0
Tail: Brown bucktail
Wing: Brown bucktail
Body: Gray angora or rabbit fur
Hackle: Dun

Royal Wulff

Hook: #10-12 Mustad 94840 or longer-shank, heavier-wire Mustad 9671
Thread: Black 6/0
Tail: Brown bucktail
Wing: White bucktail or calf tail
Body: Peacock herl back, red floss center, peacock herl front
Hackle: Brown

White Wulff

Hook: #10-12 Mustad 94840 or longer-shank, heavier-wire Mustad 9671 or Daiichi salmon hook 2421
Thread: Black
Tail: White bucktail
Wing: White bucktail
Body: White angora fur
Hackle: White badger

BIBLIOGRAPHY

Aiken, George. "Fishing with Chauncy." *The Riverwatch* 34 (January 2000): 10–13.

Atherton, John. *The Fly and the Fish*. Mineola, NY: Dover Publications, 1951.

Barrett, Peter. "Tie Your Own Flies." *Field & Stream* 93, no. 8 (January 1989): 46–49.

———. "The Trout Flies of Ted Trueblood." *Field & Stream* 91, no. 1 (May 1986): 129–30, 134.

Barry, Ann. "An Angling Classic Returns to Print." *New York Times*, October 30, 1988, 8, S1.

Bashline, Jim. *The Final Frontier: Night Fishing for Trout*. Wautoma, WI: Willow Creek Press, 1987.

Bates, Joseph D., Jr. *Atlantic Salmon Flies & Fishing*. Harrisburg, PA: Stackpole Co., 1970.

———. "Stories of Famous Streamer Flies." *Pennsylvania Angler* 21, no. 10 (October 1952): 20, 27.

———. *Streamer Fly Fishing in Fresh and Salt Water*. New York: D. Van Nostrand, 1950.

———. *Streamer Fly Tying and Fishing*. Harrisburg, PA: Stackpole Co., 1966.

Bergman, Ray. "Flies for Odd Situations." *Outdoor Life* 79, no. 5 (May 1937): 60, 62.

———. "Fly Tying Made Easy." *Popular Science* 140, no. 3 (March 1942): 156–160.

———. *Just Fishing*. New York: Outdoor Life, 1932.

———. *Trout*. 1938; reprint, New York: Alfred A. Knopf, 1945, 1952.

———. *With Fly, Plug, and Bait*. New York: William Morrow & Co., 1947.

Berryman, Jack W. *Fly-Fishing Pioneers & Legends of the Northwest*. Seattle, WA: Northwest Fly Fishing, LLC, 2006.

Betters, Fran. *Fran Betters' Fly Fishing, Fly Tying and Pattern Guide*. 2nd ed. Wilmington, NY: Ausable Wulff Products, 1986.

Betters, Fran, Eric Leiser, and Warner Wales. "How Many Flies Can a Woodchuck . . ." *Fly Fisherman* 10, no. 6 (June 1978): 77, 87–88.

Blades, William F. *Fishing Flies and Fly Tying*. Harrisburg, PA: Stackpole and Heck, 1951.

Borger, Gary A. *Naturals: A Guide to Food Organisms of the Trout*. Harrisburg, PA: Stackpole Books, 1980.

Brasseur, Ed. "Experimenting with Artificials for Trout." *Pennsylvania Angler* 12, no. 6 (June 1943): 4, 15.

Brooks, Joe. "Best All-Round Trout Fly." *Outdoor Life*, 132, no. 4 (October 1963): 64–65; 149; 151–157.

———. *The Complete Book of Fly Fishing*. New York: Outdoor Life, 1958.

———. "Those Deadly Blondes." *Outdoor Life*, 132, no. 6 (December 1963): 24–27; 71–73.

———. *Trout Fishing*. New York: Harper & Row Publishers, 1972.

Bryant, Nelson. "Wood, Field and Stream: Old Mickey Finn Slipped into Action Earns a Quick Catch on Salmon Trip." *New York Times*, August 23, 1973, 46.

———. "Wood, Field and Stream: Mickey Finn, the Lord of Flies, Proves Key to Fishing Success in Quebec." *New York Times*, September 16, 1971, 59.

———. "Wood, Field and Stream: Ouananiche Get Hit with a Mickey Finn in Unnamed Lake of Eastern Quebec." *New York Times*, September 14, 1971, 53.

Calabi, Silvio. "Flies of the Future." *Fly Rod & Reel* (July/October 1986), 27–29.

Camp, Raymond R. "Wood, Field and Stream." *New York Times*, June 6, 1941, 34.

———. "Wood, Field and Stream." *New York Times*, March 14, 1941, 26.

———. "Wood, Field and Stream." *New York Times*, February 26, 1942, 25.

———. "Wood, Field and Stream." *New York Times*, June 6, 1946, 34.

———. "Wood, Field and Stream: Anecdotes Add to Interest Hunting Licenses for Boys." *New York Times*, October 1, 1940, 37.

———. "Wood, Field and Stream: Gyro Fly Popular against Netting of Bass Title Skeet Shoot Loantaka Team . . ." *New York Times*, February 23, 1939, 33.

———. "Wood, Field and Stream: Natural Brown Bucktail Exercises Self-Control." *New York Times*, February 14, 1940, 32.

———. "Wood, Field and Stream: Some Favored Fly Patterns Successful with Brown Trout Prospects for Black Salmon." *New York Times*, April 19, 1940, 33.

Carmichael, Hoagy B. "Chauncy Lively: An Innovative Fly Tier and a Consummate Fly Fisherman." *American Fly Fisher* 35, no. 2 (Spring 2009): 10–16.

Combs, Trey. *Steelhead Fly Fishing and Flies*. Portland: Frank Amato Publications, 1976.

Cross, Rube. *The Complete Fly Tier*. New York: Dodd, Mead & Co., 1950.

———. *Furs, Feathers and Steel*. New York: Dodd, Mead & Co., 1940.

———. *Tying American Trout Lures*. New York: Dodd, Mead & Co., 1936.

Darbee, Harry, with Mac Francis. *Catskill Flytier*. New York: J. B. Lippincott Co., 1977.

Dennis, Jack H. *Western Trout Fly Tying Manual*. Jackson Hole, WY: Snake River Books, 1974.

Dorsey, Pat. *Tying and Fishing Tailwater Flies*. Mechanicsburg, PA: Stackpole Books, 2010.

Dunham, Judith. *The Atlantic Salmon Fly: The Tyers and Their Art*. San Francisco: Chronicle Books, 1991.

Ellis, Jack. *Bassin' with a Fly Rod*. Guilford, CT: Lyons Press, 2003.

Ferdon, Winifred. Diary, 1928. Private collection, Mary Dette Clark.

Flick, Art. *Art Flick's Master Fly-Tying Guide*. Piscataway, NJ: Winchester Press, 1972.

———. "Dry Fly Deception." *Pennsylvania Angler* 21, no. 5 (May 1952): 14–15.

———. *New Streamside Guide to Naturals and Their Imitations*. New York: Crown Publishers, 1969.

———. *Streamside Guide to Naturals and Their Imitations*. New York: G. P. Putnam's Sons, 1947.

Fong, Michael. "Beginnings and Endings." *Inside Angler* 7, no. 2 (March 15, 1998): 2.

———. "Fishing a Bird's Nest." *Fly Fisherman* 23, no. 2 (February 1992): 70–71.

Ford, Corey. "The Best-Loved Trout Stream of Them All." *True: The Man's Magazine* 30, no. 179 (April 1952): 30–31, 82–87.

Fox, Charles K. "Coffee Bean Jap Beetles." *Pennsylvania Angler* 13, no. 3 (February 1944): 21.

———. "A New Kind of Fly." *Fisherman* (March 1958): 24–25, 54–55.

———. *Rising Trout*. 2nd ed. New York: Hawthorn Books, 1978.

———. "Skater Dry Fly Fishing." *Pennsylvania Angler* 12, no. 5 (May 1943): 9, 20.

———. "Some Dry Flies Up Close." *Pennsylvania Angler* 11, no. 3 (March 1942): 8–9, 22–23.

———. *This Wonderful World of Trout*. Rev. ed. Rockville Centre, NY: Freshet Press, 1971.

———. "Tobacco Juice 'Hopper." *Pennsylvania Angler* 25, no. 8 (August 1956): 15–17.

Francis, Austin M. *Catskill Rivers: Birthplace of American Fly Fishing*. New York: Winchester Press, 1983.

Francis, Francis. *A Book on Angling*. London: Longmans, Green and Company, 1876.

Fulsher, Keith. *Atlantic Fly Tyer: A Memoir*. New Milford, CT: Flyfishing University Press, 2008.

———. *Thunder Creek Flies: Tying and Fishing the Classic Baitfish Imitations*. Mechanicsburg, PA: Stackpole Books, 2006.

———. *Tying and Fishing the Thunder Creek Series*. Rockville Center, NY: Freshet Press, 1973.

Gill, Emlyn M. *Practical Dry Fly Fishing*. New York: C. Scribner's Sons, 1912.

Gingerich, Scott. "The Steelhead Flies of Edward Livingston Haas, Part I: A Study of Simple Elegance." *Art of Angling Journal* 1, no. 1 (Winter 2001): 90–111.

Girard, Jerry. "Thaddeus Norris, Jr.: America's Greatest Fly-Fisherman." *Art of Angling Journal* 2, no. 1 (2003): 8–19.

Gordon, Theodore. "American Notes." *Fishing Gazette* (July 6, 1907).

———. "American Notes." *Fishing Gazette* (May 26, 1906).

———. "American Notes on the Bumblepuppy, Etc." *Fishing Gazette* (April 25, 1903).

———. "American Notes: Fowls, Hackles, Insects, Etc." *Fishing Gazette* (May 10, 1913).

———. "Dry Fly Fishing in America Before 1865." *Fishing Gazette* (February 27, 1892).

———. "Letters from a Recluse." *Forest and Stream* 67, no. 17 (April 28, 1906): 675–677.

———. "Little Talks about Fly Fishing." *Forest and Stream* 74, no. 12 (March 19, 1910): 459–460.

Grant, George. *The Art of Weaving Hair Hackles for Trout Flies*. Self-published manual, 1971.

———. "Don Martinez." *American Fly Fisher*, 9, no. 2 (spring 1982): 8–14.

———. *Montana Trout Flies*. Portland, OR: Champoeg Press, 1981.

Greenfield, George. "Wood, Field and Stream." *New York Times* April 12, 1936, S6.

Griffith, George A. *For the Love of Trout*. Grayling, MI: George Griffith Foundation, 1993.

Halford, Frederic M. *Dry Fly Man's Handbook: A Complete Manual Including the Fisherman's Entomology and the Making and Management of a Fishery*. London: George Routledge & Sons, 1913.

Hardin, Thomas. "The Wizard of West Coast Flies." *True: The Man's Magazine* 30, no. 179 (April 1952): 54–56, 65–70.

Harms, Bill, and Tom Whittle. *Split & Glued by Vincent C. Marinaro*. Harrisburg, PA: Stony Creek Rods, 2007.

Harrop, René. *Learning from the Water*. Mechanicsburg, PA: Stackpole Books, 2010.

Harvey, George. "The Frustrating Trico." *Fly Fisherman* 19, no. 6 (September 1988): 26–29, 59.

———. *George Harvey: Memories, Patterns and Tactics*. Edited and compiled by Daniel L. Shields. Lemont, PA: DLS Enterprises, 1998.

———. "Just a Dry Fly Nut." *Pennsylvania Angler* 6, no. 8 (August 1937): 8–9, 17.

———. "New Dry-Fly Wings." *Fly Fisherman* 22, no. 1 (December 1990): 58–59, 73–74.

Heacox, Cecil E. "The Catskill Flytyers." *Outdoor Life* 149, no. 5 (May 1972): 64–67, 158,160.

———. "The Charmed Circle of the Catskills." *Outdoor Life* 143, no. 3 (March 1969): 50–55, 88, 90, 94.

———. "The Charmed Circle Completed." *Outdoor Life* 143, no. 4 (April 1969): 80–81, 177–80.

Hellekson, Terry. *Popular Fly Patterns*. Layton, UT: Peregrine Smith Books, 1984.

Hewitt, Edward Ringwood. *Telling on the Trout*. New York: Charles Scribner's Sons, 1930.

———. *A Trout and Salmon Fisherman for Seventy-Five Years*. 1948; reprint, New York: Arno Press, 1966.

Hidy, Lance. "In Tune with Trout: Vernon S. 'Pete' Hidy." *Freshwater* 4, no.1 (Spring Issue): 2012.

Hidy, V. S. "The Origins of Flymph Fishing." *Anglers' Club Bulletin* 53, no. 3 (Autumn 1974).

Hills, John Waller. *A History of Fly Fishing for Trout*. London: Philip Alan & Co., 1921.

Hilyard, Graydon R., and Leslie K. Hilyard. *Carrie Stevens: Maker of Rangeley Favorite Trout and Salmon Flies*. Mechanicsburg, PA: Stackpole Books, 2000.

Hofland, Thomas C. *The British Angler's Manual*. London: H. G. Bohn, 1848.

Holden, George Parker. *The Idyl of the Split-Bamboo*. Cincinnati: Stewart & Kidd Company, 1915, 1920.

———. *Streamcraft*. New York: D. Appleton and Co., 1927.

Hughes, Dave. *Wet Flies: Tying and Fishing Soft-Hackles, Winged and Wingless Wets, and Fuzzy Nymphs*. Mechanicsburg, PA: Stackpole Books, 1995.

Humphreys, Joe B. *Joe Humphreys's Trout Tactics*. Harrisburg, PA: Stackpole Books, 1981.

———. *On the Trout Stream with Joe Humphreys*. Harrisburg, PA: Stackpole Books, 1989.

Jennings, Preston J. *A Book of Trout Flies*. New York: Derrydale Press, 1935; reprint, New York: Crown Publishers, 1970.

Johnston, Eldy. "I'll Take the Adams." *Pennsylvania Angler* 27, no. 6 (1958): 17.

Kaufmann, Randall. *American Nymph Fly Tying Manual*. Portland, OR: Frank Amato Publications, 1975.

Knight, John Alden. "Bass-Bug Fishing." *Pennsylvania Angler* 21, no. 8 (August 1952): 14–15, 27–28.

———. "Birth of a Nymph." *Fishermen's Digest* edited by Tom McNally. Chicago, IL: The Gun Digest Company, 1964: 59–63.

———. *Black Bass*. New York: G. P. Putnam's Sons, 1949.

———. *Fishing for Trout and Bass*. New York: Ziff-Davis Publishing Co., 1949.

———. *The Modern Angler*. New York: Charles Scribner's Sons, 1936.

Knight, John Alden, and Richard Alden Knight. *The Complete Book of Fly Casting*. New York: G. P. Putnam's Sons, 1963.

Koller, Larry. *The Treasury of Angling*. New York: Ridge Press, 1963.

Kreh, Lefty. "Joe Brooks." Recorded interview (July 26, 1974), Ralph E. Wahl collection, Center for Pacific Northwest Studies.

———. *Saltwater Fly Patterns*. Gilford, CT: Lyons Press, 1995.

La Branche, George M. L. *The Dry Fly & Fast Water and The Salmon & the Dry Fly*. New York: Arno Press, 1967.

LaFontaine, Gary. *Caddisflies*. New York: Lyons Press, 1989.

Lawson, Mike. *Spring Creeks*. Mechanicsburg, PA: Stackpole Books, 2003.

Lawton, Terry. *Nymph Fishing: A History of the Art and Practice*. Mechanicsburg, PA: Stackpole Books, 2005.

Leisenring, James E. *The Art of Tying the Wet Fly*. New York: Dodd, Mead & Company, 1941.

Leisenring, James E., and Vernon S. Hidy. *The Art of Tying the Wet Fly & Fishing the Flymph*. New York: Crown Publishers, 1971.

Leiser, Eric. *The Book of Fly Patterns*. New York: Alfred A. Knopf, 1987.

———. *The Complete Book of Fly Tying*. New York: Alfred A. Knopf, 1977.

———. *The Dettes: A Catskill Legend*. Fishkill, NY: Willowkill Press, 1992.

———. *Fly Tying Materials*. New York: Crown Publishers, 1973.

———. "Steelhead Flies of Edward Livingston Haas. Conclusion: Paying the Price." *Art of Angling Journal* 1, no. 2 (Spring 2002): 40–53.

———. "Tying the Llama Fly and Why." *Fly Fisherman* 4, no. 6 (June/July 1973): 56–62.

Leonard, J. Edson. *Flies*. New York: A. S. Barnes & Co., 1960.

Lively, Chauncy. "The Bicolor Leatherneck." *Pennsylvania Angler* 52, no.1 (January 1983): 12–13.

———. "The Brassie Nymph." *Pennsylvania Angler* 52, no. 11 (November 1983): 18–19.

———. "Carolina Palmer." *Pennsylvania Angler* 62, no.8 (August 1993): 20–21.

———. "The Carpenter Ant." *Fishermen's Digest* edited by Tom McNally. Chicago, IL: The Gun Digest Company, 1964: 138.

———. *Chauncy Lively's Flybox: A Portfolio of Modern Trout Flies*. Harrisburg, PA: Stackpole Co., 1980.

———. "A Dry Fly Caddis Pattern." *Pennsylvania Angler* 38, no.1 (January 1969): 14–14.

———. "The Early Black Caddis." *Pennsylvania Angler* 41, no. 11 (November 1972): 22–23.

———. "Early Season Trout and the Phantom Wooly Worm." *Pennsylvania Angler* 34, no. 4 (April 1965): 18–19.

———. "Emerging Nymphs." *Pennsylvania Angler* 39, no. 5 (May 1970): 30–31.

———. "A Fly for the 'Special Box.'" *Pennsylvania Angler* 39, no. 2 (February 1970): 22–23.

———. "Fly Tying." *Pennsylvania Angler* 47, no. 10 (October 1978): 26–27.

———. "Fur-Bodied Spent Ants." *Pennsylvania Angler* 47, no. 12 (December 1978): 26–27.

———. "Green Drake. Part One: The Dun." *Pennsylvania Angler* 40, no. 4 (April 1971): 36–37.

———. "The Hair Crawdad." *Pennsylvania Angler* 37, no. 12 (December 1968): 18–19.

———. "Hewitt's Venerable Skater." *Pennsylvania Angler* 47, no. 1 (January 1978): 26–27.

———. "The Leatherneck Streamer Fly." *Pennsylvania Angler* 50, no. 4 (April 1981): 28–29.

———. "Lightweight Bug for Heavyweight Fish." *Pennsylvania Angler* 39, no. 3 (March 1970): 20–21.

———. "The Mighty Mites." *Pennsylvania Angler* 42, no.2 (February 1972): 24–25.

———. "Nymph Fishing Notes and Notions." *Pennsylvania Angler* 22, no. 15 (May 1953): 14–15, 26–28.

———. "Paul Young's 'REDHEAD' Premier Bass Fly." *Pennsylvania Angler* 44, no. 10 (October 1975): 26–27.

———. "Special Techniques in Fly Dressing." *Pennsylvania Angler* 47, no. 11 (November 1978): 26–27.

———. "The Spent Midge." *Pennsylvania Angler* 39, no. 4 (April 1970): 22–23.

———. "Theodore Gordon's Favorite Streamer Fly." *Pennsylvania Angler* 41, no. 3 (March 1972): 22–23.

———. "Tying a Simplified Hair Frog." *Pennsylvania Angler* 38, no. 11 (November 1969): 24–25.

Marbury, Mary Orvis. *Favorite Flies and Their Histories*. 1892; reprint, Boston: Charles T. Branford Co., 1955.

Marinaro, Vincent C. "The Hidden Hatch." *Outdoor Life* 144, no. 7 (July 1969): 48–51.

———. *In the Ring of the Rise*. New York: Crown Publishers, 1976.

———. *A Modern Dry-Fly Code*. New York: Crown Publishers, 1950.

———. "Secret of the Neversink Skater." *Outdoor Life* 157, no. 6 (June 1976): 75–77, 134, 143–45.

———. "The Thorax Dry Fly." *Fly Fisherman* 19, no.1 (December 1987): 34–37.

Martinez, Don. "The Right Dry Fly." *Field & Stream* 58, no. 2 (June 1953): 68–72.

Mathias, Eugene. "Buz Buszek and the Western Coachman." *Kaweah Flyfishers* (June 2002): 4–6.

———. "Buz Buszek's Western Coachman and Kings River Caddis." *Fly Tyer* (May 1984): 57–58.

McCafferty, R. W. "Trout Tackle Suggestion." *Pennsylvania Angler* 7, no. 4 (April 1938): 2–3.

McClane, A. J. "Favorite Flies East to West," *Field & Stream* 71, no. 10 (February 1967): 58–59.

———. "Match-the-Minnow Streamer Fly Series." *Field & Stream* 73, no. 3 (July 1968): 31–37, 72–78.

———. *McClane's Angling World*. New York: Truman Talley Books, 1986.

———, ed. *McClane's Standard Fishing Encyclopedia*. New York: Holt, Rinehart and Winston, 1965.

———. *The Practical Fly Fisherman*. New York: Prentice-Hall, 1953.

———. "Presenting the Muddler Minnow." *Field & Stream* 59, no.6 (October 1954): 104–107.

McClelland, H. G. *The Trout Fly Dresser's Cabinet of Devices; or, How to Tie Flies for Trout and Grayling Fishing*. 5th ed. London: Offices of the Fishing Gazette, 1898.

McDonald, John. "Atlantic Salmon." *Fortune* 37, no. 6 (June 1948): 103–5.

———, ed. *The Complete Fly Fisherman: The Notes and Letters of Theodore Gordon*. Norwalk, CT: Easton Press, 1947.

———. "Fly Fishing and Trout Flies." *Fortune* 33, no. 6 (May 1946): 126–33, 150–62.

———. "The Leaper." *Fortune* 37, no. 6 (June 1948): 107–111, 150–158.

Miller, Gary L. "The Winnies: Traverse City's First Family of Fishing." *NFLCC [National Fishing Lure Collectors Club] Magazine* 16, no. 2 (December 2006): 20–33.

Niemeyer, Ted. "The Caddis Explosion." *Fly Fisherman* 8, no. 4 (April 1977): 56.

Norman, Seth. *Meanderings of a Fly Fisherman*. Guilford, CT: Lyons Press, 1996.

———. "Puyans." *Fly Fisherman* 27, no. 3 (March 1996): 113–18.

Norris, Thaddeus. *The American Angler's Book*. Philadelphia: Porter & Coates, 1864.

———. *American Fish Culture*. Philadelphia: Porter & Coates, 1868.

Oatman, Lew. "The Shushan Postmaster." *Esquire* 45, no. 3 (March 1956).

———. "Streamer Flies from Nature's Patterns." *Esquire* 46, no. 2 (August 1956).

Ovington, Ray. *How to Take Trout on Wet Flies and Nymphs*. Boston: Little, Brown & Co., 1952.

Peper, Eric. "The Thorax Dry." *Fly Fisherman* 19, no.1 (December 1987): 34–37.

Peterson, Kenneth L. "The Adams Family." *Michigan Out-of-Doors* (March 1992): 34–36.

Puyans, André M. "The Horner Deer Hair." *Angler* (September–October 1975): 16–18.

———. "The Loop Wing: Its History and Development." *Fly Tyer* 2 (Spring 1979): 22–23, 37.

———. "Tying the A. P. Nymph Series." *Angler* (May–June 1975): 21–26.

Quick, Jim. *Fishing the Nymph*. New York: Ronald, 1960.

———. *Trout Fishing and Trout Flies*. New York: A. S. Barnes and Company, 1957.

Randolph, John W. "Trout Expert Claims He Can Fish All Summer with Only Six Flies." *New York Times*, May 18, 1958, S11.

Rhead, Louis. *American Trout-Stream Insects*. New York: Frederick A. Stokes Co., 1916.

Ronalds, Alfred. *The Fly Fishers Entomology*. London: Longman, Orme, Brown, Green and Longmans, 1839.

Rosborough, E. H. "Polly." *Tying and Fishing the Fuzzy Nymphs*. 1965; reprint, Manchester, VT: Orvis Company, 1969.

Sawyer, Frank. *Nymphs and the Trout*. London: Stanley Paul, 1958.

Schwiebert, Ernest. *Nymphs*. New York: Winchester Press, 1973.

———. *Remembrances of Rivers Past*. New York: Macmillan Co., 1972.

———. *Trout*. New York: E. P. Dutton, 1978.

Sedgwick, Don, ed. *Joe Brooks on Fishing*. Gilford, CT: Lyons Press, 2004.

Shaw, Helen. *Flies for Fish and Fishermen: The Wet Flies*. Harrisburg, PA: Stackpole Books, 1989.

———. *Fly-Tying: Materials, Tools, Technique*. New York: Ronald Press Company, 1963.

Shenk, Ed. "Doubles." *Fly Fisherman* 10, no. 1 (Winter 1978): 54–55.

———. *Ed Shenk's Fly Rod Trouting*. Harrisburg, PA: Stackpole Books, 1989.

———. "'Hot' Bass, Trout Fly." *Pennsylvania Angler* 36, no. 9 (September 1967): 14–15.

———. "Old George Was a Lady." *Sports Afield* 155, no. 2 (February 1966): 50–51, 102–106.

———. "Sculpinating Trout." *Fly Fisherman* 16, no. 2 (March 1985): 34–37, 78–79.

———. "The Skater Spider." *Fly Fisherman* 19, no. 2 (March 1988): 53–56.

———. "Sublime to the Ridiculous: The Miniature Jassids." *Field & Stream* 73, no.2 (June 1968): 52, 133–136.

———. "Sulphurs." *Fly Fisherman* 18, no. 4 (June 1987): 32–35, 85–87.

Shires, Norm, and Jim Gilford, comp. *Limestone Legends: Papers and Recollections of the Fly Fishers' Club of Harrisburg, 1947–1997*. Mechanicsburg, PA: Stackpole Books, 1997.

Shoemaker, Myron E. "Fishing Surface Lures for Bass." *Pennsylvania Angler* 4, no. 10 (October 1935): 2–3.

———. "Picking Your Fly Rod Lures for Bass." *Pennsylvania Angler* 7, no. 7 (July 1938): 4–5, 19.

Sisty, Ed. "Nymphing for the Postponed Hatch." *Fly Fisherman* 4, no. 2 (October–November 1972): 40–43.

Skues, G. E. M. *The Way of a Trout with a Fly*. 4th ed., London: A & C, Black, 1949.

Slaymaker, S. R., II. *Simplified Fly Fishing*. New York: Harper & Row Publishers, 1969.

Smedley, Harold Hinsdill. *Fly Patterns and Their Origins*. 2nd ed. North Muskegon, MI: Forsyth Press, 1944. 4th ed. 1950.

Solomon, Larry, and Eric Leiser. *The Caddis and the Angler*. Harrisburg, PA: Stackpole Books, 1977.

Sparse Grey Hackle [Alfred Miller]. *Fishless Days, Angling Nights*. New York: Crown Publishers, 1971.

Stewart, W. C. *The Practical Angler*. Edinburgh: Adam and Charles Black, 1857.

Stinson, R. E. "The Adams Fly (Continued): Letter to the Editor." *Michigan Out-of-Doors* (August 1993).

Sturgis, William Bayard. *Fly-Tying*. New York: Charles Scribner's Sons, 1940.

Talleur, Dick. "The Adams Family." *Fly Fisherman* 17, no.7 (December 1986): 28–31.

Tapply, William G. *Bass Bug Fishing*. New York: Lyons Press, 1999.

Teale, Edwin. "Reuben R. Cross: Dry Flies from a Kitchen Workshop." *Outdoor Life* 74, no. 6 (December 1934): 34–35, 63.

Trueblood, Ted. *The Angler's Handbook*. New York: Crowell, 1949.

———. "Flies for Sophisticated Trout." *Field & Stream* 68, no. 1 (May 1963): 43–45, 147–53.

———. "Nymphs Are Easy." *Field & Stream* 62, no. 12 (April 1958): 16–17, 60, 136.

———. "An Outdoor Philosophy." *Field & Stream* 78, no. 8 (December 1973): 14–16.

———. "The Rewards of Experimenting." *Field & Stream* 86, no. 3 (July 1979): 8–9.

———. "The Rough and Ready Feather Merchants." *Field & Stream* 68, no. 1 (May 1963): 43–45, 147–53.

Valla, Mike. "Chauncy K. Lively (1919-2000)." *Eastern Fly Fishing* 8, no. 6 (Winter 2012): 76–79.

———. "Highway 20 Corridor, NY: Beating the Heat in Summer." *Eastern Fly Fishing* 7, no. 4 (July/August 2011): 36–41.

———. *Tying Catskill-Style Dry Flies*. New Cumberland, PA: Headwater Books, 2009.

———. "Winifred Ferdon Dette, Diary of a Catskill Fly Tier." *American Fly Fisher* 33, no. 4: 8–15.

Van Put, Ed. *Trout Fishing in the Catskills*. New York: Skyhorse Publishing, 2007.

Veverka, Bob. *Innovative Saltwater Flies*. Mechanicsburg, PA: Stackpole Books, 1999.

Wahl, Ralph. "Winter Steelhead on Flies." *Field & Stream* 48, no.10 (February, 1943): 34–36.

Wells, George. "An Albino Caddis Newest 'Sure Killer'; It's Good." *Grand Rapids Press*, 1951.

Wentink, Frank. *Saltwater Fly Tying*. New York: Lyons & Burford, 1991.

Wetzel, Charles M. "American Progress in Fly Fishing." *Pennsylvania Angler* 13, no. 6 (June 1944): 5, 16–19.

Whitlock, Dave. "Fishing Sculpins." *Fly Fisherman* 25, no. 5 (July 1994): 36–39, 73–75.

———. "The Four Seasons River." *Field & Stream* 73, no. 1 (May 1968): 70–71, 100, 102–104.

———. "The Sculpin and Its Imitations." *Field & Stream* 75, no. 1 (September 1970): 114–16.

———. *Tying and Fishing the Dave Whitlock Originals*. 5 vols. DVD or VHS.

Wiltshire, Bob. "An Interview with George Grant." *Flyfisher* 36, no. 1 (Winter 2003): 46, 44.

Wright, Leonard M. *Fishing the Dry Fly as a Living Insect*. New York: E. P. Dutton & Co., 1972.

Wulff, Lee. *The Compleat Lee Wulff: A Treasury of Lee Wulff's Greatest Angling Adventures*. Edited and with an introduction by John Merwin. New York: Truman Talley Books, 1989.

———. "The Essential Fly Box." *Fly Fisherman* 9, no.1 (October 1977): 36–38.

———. *Lee Wulff on Flies*. Harrisburg, PA: Stackpole Books, 1980.

INDEX